D1349581

Also by Lady Colin Campbell:

Lady Colin Campbell's Guide to Being a Modern Lady
Diana in Private
The Royal Marriages
A Life Worth Living
Empress Bianca

About the Author:

LADY COLIN CAMPBELL was born in St. Andrew, Jamaica,
and now lives in London with her two sons.
Her books include the international bestseller *Diana in Private*.

This book is dedicated to my sons,
Dima and Misha,
my mother, Gloria Smedmore Ziadie,
and to all those who appreciate
the value of sterling family life.

Lady Colin Campbell

The Real Diana

A

Arcadia Books Ltd
15-16 Nassau Street
London W1W 7AB

www.arcadiabooks.co.uk

ISBN 1-900850-95-8

Typeset in Bembo by Basement Press, London
Printed in the United Kingdom by ???

Arcadia Books distributors are as follows:

in the UK and elsewhere in Europe:
Turnaround Publishers Services
Unit 3, Olympia Trading Estate
Coburg Road
London N22 6TZ

in Australia:
Tower Books
PO Box 213
Brookvale, NSW 2100

in New Zealand:
Addenda
Box 78224
Grey Lynn
Auckland

in South Africa:
Quartet Sales and Marketing
PO Box 1218
Northcliffe
Johannesburg 2115

Arcadia Books: *Sunday Times* Small Publisher of the Year 2002/03

Acknowledgements

This book would not have been possible without the help and assistance of many people, some of whom I have known for over thirty years, others of whom I have known more recently, and some of whom I have only spoken to, or who have spoken to my researchers.

Some of the information in it was obtained in the ordinary course of my life, while other information was more specifically garnered, either for *The Real Diana* or one of my previous books on the Princess of Wales or the Royal Family.

An especial thanks must go to two longstanding friends of mine whose contributions were invaluable: Lady Sarah Spencer-Churchill, a sister of the present Duke of Marlborough and a distant cousin of Diana's, and Joseph Sanders, who was a close friend of Diana's as well as her financial advisor. The fact that I had known the former since the early 1970s in Jamaica, and the latter since the mid 1970s, when I met him at the South Kensington residence of the present Duke of St Albans and his late wife Cynthia, meant that we had decades of trust between us. This was an important consideration when it came to writing this book, for a responsible biographer needs to consider the source of any information, and knowing them as well as I did meant that I could place an appropriate degree of confidence in their knowledge. I would also like to thank Joseph's wife Anita, for she too is a repository of knowledge that is, so far, unknown to the general public.

I am also grateful to the following people, without whom this book could not have been written:

The author and journalist Catherine Olsen (Lady Mancham in private life), a generous friend of decades standing, who handed over a notebook full of research material from the early days of Diana's marriage, when she had done a series on her, and generously introduced me to her press connections at a time when I was firmly on the other side of the fence, written about instead of writing;

John Kennedy, Prince Michael of Kent's former Private Secretary, who was forthcoming in a welcome way;

Lord Charteris of Amisfield, a former Private Secretary to The Queen and a neighbour of mine at the Cundy Street Flats;

H.H. Prince George of Denmark; HRH Princess Margaret of Hesse and the Rhine; Richard Adeney; Margaret, Duchess of Argyll; Dame Barbara Cartland; Baroness Issy van Randwyck; John Welsh; Tristan Millington-Drake; the Duke of Carcaci; Inga Crane; Anton Kristensen; Simon Blow; Margaret Holder; Angela Shand Kydd; Janet Shand Kydd; Adam Shand Kydd; Ruth Rudge; Elizabeth Ridsdale; Heidi Yersin; Sophie Kimball; Eizabeth Russell; Charlotte Pike; Michael Thornton; Lady Edith Foxwell; Katharine Viscountess Macmillan of Ovenden; Lady Elizabeth Hornsby; Dale Lady Tryon; Lady Bowker; Dr Lady Brocklebank; Dr Basil Panzer; Brodrick Haldane; James Hewitt; Lady Diana Cooper; Dr Michael Davies; James Buchanan-Jardine; Tim Willcox; Robert Jobson; Oliver Everett; Judy McGuire; Penny Thornton; Mrs Henry Ford II; Peter Bowring and John Mayo of Help the Aged; John Coblenz; Eva O'Neill; Anthony Taylor; Liz Brewer; Pida Ripley; Jamie Jeeves; Sally Jeeves; Kristi Prenn; Philippa Gitlin; John Rendall; Rita Rogers; Alison Demuth; Jane Hartley; Major Ronald Ferguson; Gordon Birdwood; Charles Pasternak; Alan Frame; Richard Kay; Burnett Pavitt;

Baroness Chalker; Vanessa Hoare; Alan Sievewright; Lady Freyberg; Lady Theresa Manners; Luke, Lord Annaly; Hugh Davies; Sir David English; Nicky Haslam; Paul Sidey; Riccardo Mazzuchelli; Michael Cole; Debbie Gribble; Martin Stenning; Mike Whitlam and Neil Thoms of the Red Cross; Martine Monteil; Barbara Bennett; Vimla Lalvani; Christopher Lambert; Jonathan Dawson; Soraya Khashoggi; Bushra Fakhouri; Princess Martha Arslan; Lorraine Dillon Vidal; Pauline Ryan; Sarah-Jane Gaselee; Robert Jobson; Chrisanthy Lemos; Gregorio Martin; Alice Valentin; Donald Spoto; Chloe Papazahariakis; Eric Petel; Antoine Deguines; Annabel Barrington; Brendan Beirne; Professor Benny Mei; Dr Hua Ya; Paul Burrell; Barbara Broccoli; Dr Frederic Mailliez; Bernard Kouchner; Laurent Sola; Dr Kenneth Azan; Dr Laura Jackson; Liz Tilberis; Roberto Devorik; Richard Szpiro; the Hon George Plumptre; Adam Russell; Simon Berry; James Boughey; Kinty Waite-Walker; Charles Palmer-Tompkinson; Carolyn Bartholomew; Betty Vacani; Jan Govett; Pendry; Lily Snipp; Sonia Palmer; Mohamed Medjahdi; Souad Moufakkir; Cindy Maffre; Robert Lund; Lady Victoria Waymouth; the French Gendarmerie; and the Press Offices of Buckingham Palace, the Prince of Wales's Office at St James's Palace as well as 10 Downing Street.

I would also like to thank Frank Coombs, who is not only expert with computers but kind and patient with technical ignoramuses. Thanks for the many occasions upon which you rescued my work, magically talking me through the intricacies of the computer. In that capacity, my two sons Dima and Misha also deserve special thanks, for they also came to my rescue on several occasions, saving work that their distraught mother would otherwise have lost.

I would like to thank Diana, Princess of Wales, for the information which she conveyed, or caused to be conveyed, to me over the years. I would like to acknowledge how truly exceptional a personality she was, and to regret the circumstances which have allowed The Real Diana to come about.

On the editorial side, this book would not have been possible without the assistance and co-operation of my agent, Joni Evans, and those who worked to make the first, American, edition possible: editor Hope Dellon, publisher Sally Richardson, and publicity director John Murphy, whom I wish to thank for their civility and support. Nor would it now be possible, in its updated edition, without the assistance and co-operation of my British publishers, Gary Pulsifer and Daniela de Groote, to whom I say thanks.

Last and by no means least, I wish to commend my two sons, Dima and Misha, for waiting on innumerable occasions with patience and understanding beyond their eleven years of age, until I was able to release myself from the demands the word processor made upon my, and as a result their, time. No mother was ever more richly blessed than I am with them, and I acknowledge the debt I owe Diana where they are concerned, for without her, I would not have them in my life today.

Preface

Who was the real Diana? What was it about this woman that made her so fascinating to so many people? How is it that she became so popular that her death eclipsed the funeral of the contemporary world's greatest saint, Mother Teresa?

Diana, Princess of Wales, was undoubtedly beloved by millions of people. Few of them, of course, had ever met her. Of those who had, even fewer knew her.

The real Diana, the Diana I knew and liked – and sometimes didn't – was a woman of contradictions. On the one hand, she was sweet and loving. On the other, by her own admission she could be bitter and vengeful. She was intelligent without being intellectual, wily and naïve, vulnerable and tough. She was not shy, as she and several friends such as Sophie Kimball took pains to say over the years, yet she lived the whole of her adult life with people believing – and reacting to – the press-imposed tag of shyness.

From the moment Diana burst upon the world stage in 1980, she possessed one of the most likeable and sympathetic public images of all time. This image, while responsible for much of the adulation Diana received, became a trap. Diana herself tried to break out from its restrictive mould, "to kill the fairy tale," as she put it to me in 1990 when trying to convince me to write the book which Andrew Morton subsequently produced.

The pre-fairy-tale Diana is worth recalling. I distinctly remember meeting her at a party when she was about seventeen. She was totally unmemorable, despite being tall and sweet. She did not yet possess the aura of beauty she later had in such measure. There were no indications of the sense of style she would subsequently develop, and which other teenagers with an interest in art or fashion have by that age. She was utterly traditional, a typical Sloane Ranger, and I would never have remembered her but for the fact that she was introduced to me as her unforgettable (and hated) stepmother Raine Spencer's stepdaughter, and it is as a result of Raine that I have any recollection of the young Diana.

The butterfly who burst out of such a dull chrysalis in the early days of her marriage was more memorable. Once Diana became the Princess of Wales, our paths started crossing with greater regularity as she was launched upon the social and charity worlds. By then, of course, she was immensely famous, but she had not yet grown into the role of Princess of Wales in the way that she later did. Although no longer dull in style, she was still utterly traditional, with nothing individual about her. Moreover, there was an elusiveness to her personality, a "not there" quality that was both intriguing and disturbing.

Throughout the 1980s, I observed Diana growing into her public role with ever-increasing strength. Although I admired the way she conducted herself publicly, I cannot say I enjoyed every encounter with her. While I liked her, and thought her charming, I also sensed an underlying discomfort within herself which did not make one wish to prolong conversations with her. Only later, while we were working on *Diana in Private* together, did I discover that the feeling of discomfort was one which Diana carried around with her at all times. She did not live easily in her skin.

To my chagrin, considering the bitter regrets Diana later had about the Morton book, responsibility for planting the idea of a book in her head lies, in part, with me. Towards the end of the last decade, Britain was in the grips of a profound recession. I was desperately casting about for a means of raising funds for some of my charities when I hit upon the idea of writing an authorized biography of the Princess of Wales focusing on her charity work, with the proceeds to go to three of the charities we had in common. At first Diana was amenable, but by the time I went to Buckingham Palace in August 1990 for an appointment to discuss it with her Press Secretary, she had changed her mind. In a nutshell, she wanted me to write the book that Andrew Morton later published.

Had Diana told me she wanted me to produce a panegyric, I would have turned her down cold. However, she did not. She led me to believe she wanted me to "write the truth of my life," to quote her. "The fairy tale is killing me," she said. "If I don't escape from it, I'll die." I agreed to write what became *Diana in Private* on those conditions, thinking that I would have the liberty of producing a balanced account of her life. Only later, after contracts were signed and the book was well underway, did Diana and I appreciate that we had misunderstood one another's positions. She did not want a truthful account of her life, but a heavily slanted version with which she could gain a separation from Prince Charles, whereas I told her, "I'm not about to trash your husband when he doesn't deserve it."

Although this difference led to three years of "non-speaks," to use the vernacular which Diana's circle employed, we did "kiss and make up," literally and publicly, at a reception at the Russian Ambassador's residence in July 1995. Thereafter, we became what the English call "chummy." We cleared up many of the misunderstandings which had arisen during the War of the Waleses, and grew to be on such cordial terms that I cried on the day of her death.

Much of what I know about the Princess of Wales is not public knowledge – the Diana I knew and liked is a far more complicated, conflicted, intriguing and fascinating person than the wildly disparate saint or lunatic she is frequently portrayed to be. I hope that I have done her greater justice in the forthcoming pages than she often receives, and that I reconcile for the readers what onlookers have so far viewed as puzzling contradictions. I also hope that the picture I paint captures her essence as well as her spirit. Diana had both a great sense of fun and a great burden of pain. I hope I make intelligible for the reader what it was like to be so privileged yet so anguished, so beloved yet so self-loathing, so spoiled yet so deprived, so hopeful by nature and yet so often despairing. To the world, Diana, Princess of Wales, was a living myth, but to herself, she was just a human being trying to make some sense, and to gain some satisfaction, out of a life of extremes. It is the circumstances of that life, and the motives that drove her, which the succeeding pages will lay bare.

One

Diana, Princess of Wales, lived her life as she was born on 1 July 1961: amid intrigue, ambition, privilege, passion, pain and pleasure. Throughout it all, she would be pulled in many different directions, some of them diametrically opposed. She believed that this conflict started before her birth. "I was a disappointment. My parents were hoping for a boy. They were so sure I'd be a boy they hadn't even thought of a girl's name for me." She was finally registered as the Honourable Diana Frances Spencer, named after the eighteenth-century Lady Diana Spencer, who nearly married Frederick, Prince of Wales, and after her own mother, Frances.

In yet another show of what she took to be her diminished status as a girl, Diana, who later developed a heightened interest in status as a result, was the only one of her siblings to be christened without a royal godparent. On 30 August 1961, unlike her eldest sister, Sarah, whose godmother was Queen Elizabeth the Queen Mother, or her elder sister, Jane, whose godfather was the Duke of Kent, or her younger brother, who would boast the Queen as his godmother, Diana had to content herself with the Lord Lieutenant of Norfolk's wife, Lady Mary Colman; her cousin Alexander (Sandy) Gilmour, younger brother of Tory baronet and life peer Ian Gilmour; Christie's chairman, John Floyd; and two neighbours, Sarah Pratt and Carol Fox.

If her parents stamped her with the mentality of a victim, Viscount and Viscountess Althorp had no intention of doing so. They were merely hoping for the heir to the Spencer earldom held by Johnnie Althorp's father, Jack, the 7th Earl Spencer. Along with the earldom came a fortune of some £100,000,000 in present-day terms. This consisted of a portfolio

1

of stocks and shares and Althorp House, which is one of the most beautiful stately homes in England. Built in 1508, it was modernised by Henry Holland, the Prince Regent's architect, who added the white brick façade which gives the house its shimmering lightness. Set in its own 600-acre park and surrounded by a 13,000-acre estate, Althorp House was even more beautiful inside than out. It had vast rooms with magnificent mouldings and high ceilings. Blindingly large chandeliers gave light to two of the finest collections in private hands: a houseful of eighteenth-century furniture made by the finest craftsmen of the day, and wall after wall of portraits and landscapes painted by such masters as Van Dyck, Rubens, Gainsborough, Kneller and Reynolds.

Under the English rule of primogeniture, titles pass from father to son, with the estates entailed upon (legally restricted to) the title. If Frances did not provide a son and heir, after Johnnie's death the earldom and all the wealth accompanying it would therefore pass to his cousin Bobby Spencer. Johnnie's daughters would not even have a right to stay in Althorp House any more, and their inheritance from him would be limited to the savings from the earldom's income that their father had managed to accumulate in his lifetime. To Johnnie Spencer, it was unthinkable that he would leave his daughters in relative penury, especially as the ignominy of this state had been only too familiar to him until his marriage to the wealthy Frances Burke Roche, whose money kept him afloat. He had a 'tiny allowance' from his father, who despised him, and Frances had even had to buy him land in Norfolk so that he could occupy himself being a gentleman farmer until such time as his father died and he came into his inheritance.

For that most sensible of pragmatic reasons, Johnnie Althorp was preoccupied with having a son. Although he loved the seven-pound eleven-ounce baby Diana, and she would always remain his favourite child, he steered Frances to Harley Street as soon as she was on her feet. "He wanted to find out what was wrong with her," Diana later said, while her brother, Charles, maintains that the stress of this quest for a son was what ruined his parents' marriage.

Like most of the Spencers, Johnnie took great pride in his heritage. The Spencers were originally businessmen who made a fortune out of the quick transportation of sheep to the cities in the fifteenth century. Sheep farmers were the computer billionaires of their day, and by 1508 the ambitious John

Spencer had managed to acquire the title Sir and to build Althorp House. Thereafter, there was no stopping the Spencers. They remained rich, married well, and gradually climbed up the peerage. One became Earl of Sunderland, another the Duke of Marlborough when his uncle, only son and heir to John Churchill, the first Duke of Marlborough, died. The result was that the Churchills are not really Churchills at all, but Spencers who added the surname Churchill to their own.

There was another, less fortunate, result of the marriage of the Churchill heiress to the Earl of Sunderland. The Churchills were so much more famous and eminent that the Spencers became the secondary branch of their own family, and even lost their earldom, which was absorbed in the dukedom of Marlborough and has subsequently been used by the eldest son of the duke's heir, the Marquis of Blandford.

That loss notwithstanding, the Spencers flourished throughout the eighteenth century. Sarah, Duchess of Marlborough, the great duke's widow, had for many years been regarded as Queen Anne's closest friend and lover. She was therefore used to wielding power, not only as a result of her husband's position as the most famous general in the world, but also because of her own political influence. One of the richest women in England, she offered the cash-strapped King George II £100,000 (several million pounds today) for the hand of his son and heir Frederick, Prince of Wales, for her favourite granddaughter Diana Spencer. Although the Prime Minister forbade the marriage, thereafter the Spencers remained close to the throne, enabled in no small measure by the vast fortune Sarah, Duchess of Marlborough, left to her favourite grandson, the second Spencer grandson who lost out on the titles of Sunderland and Marlborough.

Thereafter, generation after generation of Spencers were appointed equerries and ladies-in-waiting to royalty, culminating with Diana, Princess of Wales's father being an equerry to King George VI and, later, to Queen Elizabeth II, and her grandmother Cynthia, Countess Spencer, being a Lady of Queen Elizabeth the Queen Mother's Bedchamber as well as the love of the then Prince of Wales's life before she accepted Diana's grandfather Jack Spencer's proposal of marriage in 1919.

When Diana's brother, Charles, the present Earl Spencer, made his funeral oration lambasting the Royal Family and stating that his sister needed "no royal title" to weave her particular brand of magic, commentators decreed that his contempt for the throne was a Spencer tradition, in keeping with the indifference to royalty which the great Whig aristocrats had traditionally displayed. The evidence does not support that contention. For the two hundred and fifty years that separated the abortive and the successful Diana Spencers' possible assumption of the position of Princess of Wales, the Spencers were assiduous in cultivating any link that brought them closer to the throne. They understood that the fount of all honour and privilege was the Crown. And they did their utmost to garner as much of its prestige for themselves as possible. Nor did they fuss whether the connection was legitimate or illegitimate. They therefore took pride in the fact that Lady Georgiana Spencer, who became the most glamorous female of her day as the celebrated Duchess of Devonshire, had a long affair with the Prince Regent, later King George IV, and gave birth to his child. They took greater pride in being descended five times from King Charles II, even though four of those lines of descent were illegitimate, and when the second Diana Spencer married Charles, Prince of Wales, in 1981, they were thrilled that it was through them that Stuart blood was being reintroduced into the royal line.

Yet it was not the Spencers at all who actually ensured that Lady Diana Spencer was placed upon the road to royalty. Credit for that rests with Frances's parents, Lord and Lady Fermoy, whose proximity to the throne was based on personal, not courtly, relationships. And they were altogether a more interesting and accomplished couple than any of the Spencers.

Maurice Burke Roche, the 4th Baron Fermoy, was the son of an American heiress named Fanny (Frances) Work and the Hon. James Roche, later the 3rd Baron. The Roches were an exceedingly good-looking family, with two of the most beautiful ancestral homes in Ireland – Cahirguillamore and Kilshanning – but, through high-living and gambling, they had dissipated their fortune and would have been completely broke had the 2nd Baron's heir not married Frank Work's daughter in the late nineteenth century.

Frank Work was one of New York's most successful stockbrokers of the day, with clients such as the Vanderbilts and Astors. Unfortunately for the Roches, he loathed foreigners and cut Fanny out of his will when she married one, reinstating her only after she left her husband in 1891 and returned home with her two young sons in tow. His proviso while doing so was that she cease using her titled married name and agree not to return to Europe for the remainder of her life. He then carried this interdict further, and left her twin sons, Maurice (the Princess of Wales's grandfather, the 4th Baron Fermoy) and Francis, portions of his fortune only if they became American citizens and remained in the United States for the remainder of their lives.

When Frank Work died, however, his Harvard-educated grandsons overturned his will through the courts. Maurice, who became the 4th Lord Fermoy in 1921, then returned to live in England with the $3,000,000 which he had inherited from his indomitable but controlling grandfather. He avoided Ireland, which was on its way to full independence from Britain, settling in England, which was then at the pinnacle of its power and prestige. Only too soon, he struck up a friendship with King George V's second son, Bertie, the Duke of York, who became King George VI in 1936. So close did they become that the King leased Maurice Park House, a ten-bedroomed-house on the Sandringham Estate which his father, King Edward VII, had built to accommodate the overflow of guests on shoots. Maurice was now literally living on royal property as a friend and neighbour of the King and his son. With his money and international panache, he fitted well into the upper echelons of British society, especially after becoming Conservative Member of Parliament for King's Lynn, something that was possible because he was an Irish peer with no rights to sit in the House of Lords.

Maurice's wife, Ruth, was the perfect foil for him. Although the product of a middle-class background – her father was a colonel from Bieldside in bleak Aberdeen in the north of Scotland – the former Miss Gill was bright and beautiful. The famous flautist Richard Adeney knew her well and remembered "her perfectly symmetrical face and huge eyes. She was awfully nice. Very, very nice." She was also a gifted musician. According to the Scots photographer and socialite Brodrick Haldane, "I knew her before her marriage. In those days, she was far more free-wheeling than she later became. She was wonderfully talented, both as a singer and a pianist. She was at the Paris Conservatoire, and was very highly rated."

It was while Ruth was a student at the Paris Conservatoire of Music that she met Maurice Fermoy. She was more than twenty-five years his junior, but that did not prevent her from encouraging this rich and urbane nobleman with royal friends. In a day and age when women were reared to marry well, this ambitious young woman understood that marriage to Lord Fermoy would be a definite step up in the world. And so, at twenty, she married him and went on to have a wonderful life in the lap of luxury. She produced three children and had something no Spencer had managed for hundreds of years: a happy marriage. She also made a useful contribution to the world of music, founding the King's Lynn Festival after the Second World War and importing musical friends such as Benjamin Britten, Peter Pears and Richard Adeney to perform. She continued living beside the Sovereign until she was widowed, at which point she turned over the lease of Park House to her son-in-law, Johnnie Althorp, so that he and Frances and their children could enjoy the advantage of genuine proximity to the Royal Family.

Ruth, Lady Fermoy, was more than just Diana's grandmother. She played a pivotal role in raising Diana to royal status, and in sowing the seeds that would ultimately destroy this granddaughter who accomplished all the dreams and ambitions her Spencer forebears had held for themselves. "She always had a strong character," Brodrick Haldane told me. "She was never grand, but she became frightfully correct. She knew the rules and played by them." Richard Adeney remembered an instance which highlights that. "She knew what was appropriate. She could be very relaxed, but she also knew when to stand on her dignity. I remember once I was in King's Lynn eating an ice cream on the street. She came by with some royals. We agreed through eye contact that it would be more suitable for her to pass by without us acknowledging each other. To me, that summarized how impeccably mannered she was. It would just have been awkward for her, for the royals, and for me if she'd acknowledged me. She really did have the most exquisite manners."

Appointed a Woman of the Bedchamber to Queen Elizabeth the Queen Mother in 1956, Ruth functioned in a world where breeding and good behaviour were all-important. While she could adopt the latter, there was no way she could invent the former. Her family was neither grand nor impressive. In fact, the only thing that put them beyond the ordinary was the secret they kept hidden. This was that her great-great-grandmother Eliza Kewark was a dark-skinned native of Bombay who had lived, without benefit of matrimony, with her great-great-grandfather Theodore Forbes while he worked for the East India Company. Unsavoury as the taint of illegitimacy was, even at that distance in time, it was nothing compared with the stigma of what was then known as "coloured blood." Had it been generally known that Ruth and her children were part-Indian, they might never have made good marriages. Eliza's true race was therefore expunged from the family tree and she re-emerged as an Armenian. This fiction was maintained even when Diana married the Prince of Wales.

Of all Diana's grandparents, Ruth was the strongest and most resourceful. A good friend of the Queen Mother's since her days as the Duchess of York, Diana's grandmother was as status-conscious as her granddaughter would become. She appreciated that there was no better position to occupy in British society than that of an adjunct to the Royal Family. She and her socialite husband worked to maintain the royal link, never putting a foot wrong in their conduct. While Maurice was alive and their children young enough to be living at home, the Fermoys were rewarded with invitations from the King and Queen on a regular basis-- especially during the shooting season, between the Glorious Twelfth of August and the end of February, when King George VI and Queen Elizabeth were in residence at Sandringham House. Then, invitations flowed from the "Big House" for shooting parties and to tea and dinner, for the children as well as Ruth and Maurice, who was such an integral member of the King's circle that he was present on the shoot the day before George VI died in his sleep in February 1952. Although the Spencers were undoubtedly a grander family in terms of lineage and wealth, in terms of a close royal connection they were easily outstripped by the Fermoys: It was one thing to attend upon the Royal Family in an official capacity as an equerry or lady-in-waiting, but quite another to take part in their everyday lives as personal friends, and the combination of the two was an even more potent brew.

No one lives in an environment without absorbing its written and unwritten rules, and this was especially true of people in Court circles. It was heady stuff being around the royals. Whilst you were in their actual presence, you were waited on hand and foot and treated as if you were an extension of royalty yourself. And when you were away from them, everyone who knew of your connection courted you in the hope that some of the reflected glory of royalty would run off on them. This was, and is, the way of life in royal courts, and both Johnnie and Frances, who were reared in this atmosphere, knew the score. They understood that there was a lot more to the royal way than wearing formal morning wear for memorial services, silk dresses for tea, and white tie and tiaras at state balls. Both before they were married and afterwards, they had to live lives that seemed to be above criticism. They must be invariably polite. They must never gossip about the Royal Family. Any problems they had, must be kept hidden away. Life in royal circles had to seem to be perfect.

Of course, both Johnnie and Frances grew up seeing what happens when even the mighty fall out of favour. They witnessed at first hand how ruthlessly the Royal Family and their courtiers closed ranks to cast Edward VIII out of the hallowed circle when he dared to try to swap the top job for the secondary one of royal duke upon abdication. They could not have remained ignorant of how quickly the disgraced King's nemesis (and Private Secretary) Alex Hardinge followed him into the abyss when he managed to work his way onto the wrong side of Queen Elizabeth. The royal way was one of absolutes. You were absolutely in or absolutely out. You were absolutely spotless or absolutely sullied. There were no half-measures, and while people frequently failed to measure up to the standard in their private lives, fallibility was fine as long as no one saw any evidence of it in public.

Johnnie Spencer and Ruth Fermoy showed the extent of their ambition, and their courtiers' mentalities, when the Prince of Wales displayed a romantic interest in Diana's older sister Sarah in 1977. "When Lady Sarah Spencer started going out with the Prince of Wales, you could see how elated her whole family was," said Ivry, Lady Freyberg, who attended a dinner at Althorp House with her husband Lord Freyberg when Charles went there for a shooting weekend while courting Sarah. This was their chance finally to acquire a legitimate royal connection. Sarah, however, was in the midst of fighting a battle with anorexia nervosa, which left her without the emotional resources to cope with a prince who blew hot one day and cold the next. In an attempt to jerk his chain, she made the mistake of speaking to the press about her feelings, ending up by declaring that she would marry only a man she loved, whether he was a "prince or a dustman." Charles, who had an abiding loathing of the tabloids and one inflexible rule – you're out on your ear if you speak to the papers – promptly dumped her. Neither her father nor her grandmother let their loyalty to their flesh and blood get in the way of their relationship with the future King of England. Sarah must pay the price for her indiscretion.

Although Sarah blew her chance of an alliance with a royal, her twenty-one-year-old sister Jane – "so plain even a mouse would look like Joan Collins beside her," according to Diana - did the family proud the following year, in April 1978, when she married thirty-six-year-old Robert Fellowes. The son of the Queen's Land Agent at Sandringham, Sir William Fellowes, he was Her Majesty's Assistant Private Secretary. Although the most junior of the three Private Secretaries, he was nevertheless well placed in Court circles. The family was exultant. "The marriage meant that invitations would be coming through two separate conduits: Ruth Fermoy in Queen Elizabeth the Queen Mother's household and Robert Fellowes in the Queen's," John Kennedy, Prince Michael of Kent's former private secretary said. "It was no secret that Robert Fellowes was ambitious." Time has shown that assessment to be accurate. In 1986 he was appointed Deputy Private Secretary to the Queen, and in 1990 Private Secretary. Now retired, he has been ennobled and sits in the House of Lords.

Robert Fellowes and Jane Spencer were married in splendour at the Guards Chapel opposite Buckingham Palace. Their wedding reception was held at St. James's Palace. After the honeymoon, the newlyweds returned home to Kensington Palace, where they still live at the time of this writing. Diana was as happy as the rest of the family for Jane's coup. Thanks to Jane's new position as the wife of one of the most influential courtiers at Buckingham Palace, her – and their – ambitions were that much nearer being realized.

Up to that point, all of them harboured ambitions that Diana might one day marry Prince Andrew, whose photograph she had kept beside her bed throughout her years at West Heath School. The prospect of a union between Andrew and Diana was more than mere idle fantasy, though there was no certainty that it would ever materialize. Marriages between the Royal Family and aristocrats were never arranged. They were simply encouraged. That meant that the courtiers had somehow to ignite the particular royal's interest for matrimony to follow. The Spencer family was so convinced that Diana would end up as the consort of the Duke of York (the title customarily bestowed upon the Sovereign's second son) that they nicknamed her Duchess, or Duch for short. For the rest of her life, Diana's sisters and her closest friends, including Sarah, Duchess of York, called her Duch.

Diana and Andrew had a history which the Spencers found hopeful. Andrew, who was a year older than Diana, and his younger brother, Edward, had been friendly with Diana and her younger brother, Charles, when they were children and she was living at Park House, first with both her parents and, after their separation in 1967, with her father. Although the family vacated Park House upon Johnnie's accession to the Spencer earldom in 1975, three years was not so large a gap that Andrew would have forgotten Diana. Yet it was big enough to lend a spark of excitement. They hoped that all she needed to do was visit her sister and be visible before her rangy attractiveness caught the eye of the girl-crazy second son of the Queen. Then she just might become the Duchess of York.

In the interim, Diana's family issued invitations which put her in the royal line of vision and "talked her up," as the Queen's then Private Secretary, Sir Martin (later Lord) Charteris of Amisfield told me, "so that the Royal Family, Queen Elizabeth the Queen Mother especially, would push her into Prince Andrew's path when the time for marriage came."

The best-laid plans come a cropper, but seldom with such unexpected improvement. In July 1980, the Prince of Wales, who barely knew Diana when she was a little girl, became reacquainted with her at the Sussex house of a distant cousin of mine. Commander Robert de Pass was a member of the Royal Household and his wife, Philippa, one of the Queen's ladies-in-waiting. Diana was a friend of his son, Philip, whom she had met via that most exclusive of circles, the courtiers' network. Diana, reared from birth to captivate any royal who might fly into her patch, acquitted herself in exemplary fashion. "She moved me," Charles later said.

Could it really be that Diana might be able to pull off the unimaginable and become the Princess of Wales? "Like a well-trained army, Diana's family closed ranks," according to Lord Charteris. "The Queen and the Prince of Wales still cannot believe that not one member of Diana's family tipped them off about how unsuited she was to the life ahead of her." Ruth, Lady Fermoy, later said, "I had reservations about how Diana would cope. To my lasting regret, I kept them to myself."

This was not surprising. Had the Royal Family understood how ambitious both the Spencers and Ruth Fermoy were, they might well have listened less as Ruth encouraged Queen Elizabeth the Queen Mother to push the young lovers ever closer, and Diana's own family talked Ruth out of the misgivings she had. "The Prince feels that they let him fall into a trap," one of his cousins, Prince George of Denmark, told me.

The trap, however, was not Charles's alone, but Diana's as well. And he at least has survived it, while Diana lies in isolation on a tiny island called The Oval near Althorp House.

Two

The popular myth is that Diana was born into an unhappy family and that her childhood was a misery from day one. That is untrue. Johnnie and Frances Althorp's marriage started happily in 1954. "There was a tremendous physical attraction between them, as there later was between him and Raine," according to Lady Sarah Spencer-Churchill.

The circumstances of Johnnie's meeting with Frances certainly confirm that assessment. He was unofficially engaged to Lady Anne Coke, who subsequently married Princess Margaret's old beau the Hon. Colin Tennant (now Lord Glenconner). He took one look at the tall, striking, statuesque blonde who was making her debut and promptly forgot about the equally statuesque and striking-looking but considerably less passionate Anne. Three weeks later he proposed, and Frances, who always had a tendency to run where her passions led, agreed to follow him for life, although she later came to the view that her money had possibly been an incentive she did not then realize.

The marriage began well. Held at the Guards Chapel, followed by a reception at St. James's Palace, with the Queen and Queen Elizabeth the Queen Mother in attendance, it was everything Ruth Fermoy wanted for her daughter. Viscount Althorp was titled, moneyed and well-connected. He had been an equerry to King George VI and Queen Elizabeth II. Gratifying though it was for Frances to please her mother, she was also pleasing herself. Johnnie was tall, strapping and handsome, with a powerful sex drive. Twelve years older than his eighteen-year-old bride, he seemed worldly and interesting.

If Frances was a source of pride to her mother, Johnnie was the antithesis to his father. According to Lady Sarah Spencer-Churchill, Jack Spencer was an intellectual who despised Johnnie as a "dolt" whose mindless interests went no further than hunting, fishing, shooting and socializing. For the newlyweds, who under normal aristocratic practice would have been expected to live in a large farmhouse on the Althorp Estate until Johnnie succeeded to his father's title, living in close proximity to Earl Spencer was undesirable after a trial period proved disastrous. So Ruth turned over the lease on Park House to the newlyweds for Johnnie and Frances to use as their marital home.

A year after the wedding, Frances gave birth to a daughter, Sarah, followed two years later by another, Jane. Although two daughters in a row were mildly disappointing, the lack of a son was not yet a problem. In 1960, however, Frances gave birth to a deformed son, John, who died the same day. Hope began wearing thin when the replacement turned out to be yet another girl, but the seven-pound, twelve-ounce baby was pretty, with huge blue eyes and a captivating smile. Disappointed though her father was that she was not the cherished heir, Diana, who grew into an endearing little girl, became his lifelong favourite. Then on 20 May 1964 Frances gave birth to the long-awaited boy, Charles, at the London Clinic. The Althorps' world now seemed perfect, even to those who were living as a part of it.

"Lord and Lady Althorp were still very much in love, very affectionate with each other," Inga Crane, a nursery maid who arrived at Park House shortly after Charles's birth, confirmed.

Still living on the Sandringham Estate when I spoke to her, she remembered, "The family were not at all snooty. In fact, they seemed quite ordinary. Just happier than most." Diana would later say that her father taught her to treat all people as equals, but her mother is the parent whom everyone adored. "Lady Althorp was a wonderful woman," Mrs Crane said. "Always laughing. She treated me and the others (there were six servants) like friends rather than staff and she spent a lot of time in the nursery." Unlike most upper-class households of the day, "it wasn't a case of children upstairs and adults downstairs at all. She would always be there in the evening for cuddles and bedtime stories and then she and Lord Althorp would have their dinner at 8 o'clock. They did a lot of entertaining and the house was always full of lights and warmth and people in the evenings. In the daytime it was full of noises the children made because of the little school there." Gertrude Allen, Frances's former governess, came in from the village every morning to conduct classes for each of the Spencer children, who began their education along with a dozen or so other children from the surrounding farms, at the age of four. The doctor's son was also a classmate of Diana's.

Friends of the Althorps confirm that they seemed happy together even after Charles Spencer's birth – despite the claim Diana's brother has made that his parents' marriage disintegrated under the strain of the search for a solution to Frances's inability to produce a son, and despite her confirmation that she was carrying around a cumulative amount of resentment as a result of the way her husband blamed her "faulty genes" for her inability to produce a healthy son. One thing everyone ought to bear in mind when listening to the immediate family is that the Spencers' version of the truth, and their ability to mask it from the world, did not invariably accord with the visible facts. This was a trait that Diana herself would later also display to a stupendous degree, with the result that many people who considered themselves close to her and 'in the know' would discover, too late down the line, that they were as clueless as the most distant stranger in the street about what was really going on in her life and in her head. Whatever the Spencer family's take, or that of their household staff, on the state of the Althorp marriage, it did start to disintegrate after Charles's birth. "Once she produced that son, Johnnie took Frances for granted something rotten," Lady Sarah Spencer-Churchill told me. "She'd served her purpose. He really couldn't be bothered with her any more, except when he was in the mood, which became less and less frequent as time passed." Johnnie had "always been duller than ditchwater, but she didn't notice at first. She was young herself and really caught up in the excitement of being Viscountess Althorp with her own glamorous social life and a young family. And, of course, there was the problem of not producing an heir to distract her. But once that problem was solved, and he started to treat her in an offhand manner, the scales gradually fell from her eyes."

Boredom followed disillusionment for the young viscountess, now approaching thirty. Always scintillating and interesting, "with a brilliance of personality that assured her of being noticed wherever she went," as Lady Sarah Spencer Churchill said. Frances had been raised in an intellectually stimulating environment. Once she faced the personal poverty within her marriage, she wanted to be surrounded by interesting people." To give her her due, she did try to carry him along, but he wasn't interested. He didn't ever want to come up to town (London). To go to the theatre. To see concerts. To mix with interesting people who might be of no social consequence but would have something of intellectual worth to offer."

Faced with the choice of being ignored and bored by Johnnie at Park House on the Sandringham Estate or of experiencing the stimulation of being on her own in London without him, Frances juggled, hoping to satisfy both sides of her personality. Johnnie's response was to become "surly and demanding, without in any way treating her better," which only had the effect of pushing Frances further away from him.

Johnnie Althorp's family background was troubled, and he was behaving in keeping with its tradition. His father, Jack, was "a monster who did everything within his power to make my sister's life a misery, and he succeeded," the late Duke of Hamilton told his friend Hugh Davies. "Cynthia never had a day's happiness with Jack. He was mean and nasty and cruel to her. It was beyond him to be nice or kind or thoughtful or considerate." Cynthia, on the other hand, was well-liked. Stoical too. She endured a lifetime of battery, remaining with her wife-beater because marriage was for life and divorce meant a loss of social position and banishment from Court. Divorcees were not deemed fit to be in the presence of the King or Queen, and Cynthia would have had to resign as a lady-in-waiting and lose her social position.

Johnnie had always been something of a mother's boy, which had the effect of making him love women and treat them better than his father did, as long as things were going his way and he had a use for them. However, once Frances began slipping from his grasp, the role model of Jack took over. Johnnie started beating Frances.

Like many women before her, and doubtless like many more to come, Frances resorted to the battered wives' defence of concealment. Diana would later confirm to me that her mother did indeed have a tradition of hiding away what was really happening in her life. "I'm like Mummy," Diana said. "I can be utterly miserable inside, but outside I'm happy and smiling and no one will ever have a clue as to how I feel."

Frances, however, was no masochist. She wanted happiness. In keeping with her upper-class upbringing, she sought it from the same source as countless other well-born women of her time: through marriage to a well-heeled gentleman. Knowing the rules of the royal game as well as she did, she understood that divorce would mean banishment from the hallowed circle surrounding Their Majesties Queen Elizabeth II and Queen Elizabeth the Queen Mother. As she did not suffer from her mother's fixation with royalty, however, Frances was prepared to pay that price as and when she met the man who would be her passport to a more fulfilling life.

In 1966, Frances and her fate were introduced at a friend's dinner party. Peter Shand Kydd was a former naval officer and heir to a mercantile fortune. He was everything Johnnie was not: scintillating, bohemian, open-minded, adventurous, kindly. Three years before, he had left his half-brother Bill (married to the Countess of Lucan's sister Christina) to run the family firm and moved his family to a thousand-acre sheep farm in Australia. Peter, his wife, Janet, and their three children, Adam, Angela and John, had recently returned to live in Britain, and the two families struck up a friendship "fuelled by the attraction between Peter and Frances," as Janet subsequently observed ruefully. There were various foursomes, culminating in a skiing trip in 1967 which left "no doubt" in Janet's mind that her husband was having an affair with Frances. For his part, Johnnie had "so little interest in the heifer who had produced the prize calf," as Frances put it, that he noticed nothing.

Peter "only ever intended his affair with Frances to remain an affair," Adam Shand Kydd, his son, told me. "He loved" Janet and had no intention of ever leaving her, but he found himself "trapped by his essential decency." This observation has been confirmed by Janet herself, who told a friend, "I still find it hard to believe that we ended up divorced."

The affair started to spiral out of control within days of the two elder Spencer girls, Sarah and Jane, going away to board at West Heath School in September 1967. "There was a party at Park House. Johnnie became abusive towards Frances in front of their guests," Lady Sarah Spencer-Churchill told me. "She was so outraged and humiliated she stormed off swearing she'd had enough." She had. She packed her bags after another episode of violence and left Park House the following day. Diana and baby Charles followed her to London the day after, as did Violet Collinson, a housemaid from Park House who remained in her employ until her retirement.

Frances rented a flat in Cadogan Place, near Sloane Square, in Belgravia. She enrolled Diana in day school and Charles in kindergarten. She had not abandoned her children, nor had she "legged it" without them, as Diana would later unfairly accuse her of doing. Johnnie "appeared not to be devastated by her departure," Lady Sarah Spencer-Churchill said. "If the truth be known, he seemed indifferent to it. He continued his old life at Park House, plodding here and there. Nor did the children seem affected by the disruption in their lives. Diana was a delightful and mischievous little girl. Very self-confident. Always laughing, like her mother. Charles was very young, of course, but he too was a well-adjusted and happy little boy."

Free at last of the bully she had come to despise, Frances set about enticing Peter Shand Kydd away from the wife he still loved. Respectable women in 1967 simply did not remain mistresses to married men; they had to marry them or become fallen women.

Frances encountered no success in her marital objective, however, until Johnnie unwittingly gave her ambitions a helping hand in January 1968. She had taken the children back to Park House, her family home, where he was still ensconced, for Christmas. When the time came to depart with them, he refused to let her take them back with her to London. "I did not leave my children," Frances said repeatedly and emphatically. "I left thinking I'd get them back." She consulted her lawyers, who advised her to issue proceedings for divorce on the grounds of cruelty (i.e., physical violence), and seek custody of the children. Meanwhile, Johnnie enrolled Diana and Charles at Silfield School in nearby King's Lynn, where Ruth, Lady Fermoy, held her annual musical festival.

Feeling that his mistress had lost custody of her children because of their affair, Peter Shand Kydd responded the way he thought a decent man ought to: he left his wife for Frances. Janet Shand Kydd then sued him for divorce on 10 April 1968 on the grounds of his adultery with Frances. The newspapers eagerly seized upon this latest society scandal. This infuriated Johnnie, a proud man, who felt humiliated now that the world knew not only of his rejection but also of Frances's adultery.

If Johnnie was incensed, his fury was nothing compared to Ruth Fermoy's. In true courtier fashion, she had spent three-quarters of a lifetime aping the royals and regarded divorce as one of the greatest forms of disgrace known to humanity. "Ruth disapproved violently," her friend

Brodrick Haldane told me. "In her scale of things, you had to be either mad or bad or both to leave a viscount with palace connections for a wallpaper merchant with none. She felt Frances had let the side down badly and brought shame upon the family. If she'd left Johnnie for the Duke of Rutland that would have been all right, but to leave him for Mr Shand Kydd was more than she could endure." Ruth then did something which would destroy any love that remained between her and her daughter for all time. She threw her lot in with her violent son-in-law and agreed to testify that her daughter was unfit to have custody of the children. "She did that to ensure her grandchildren remained in the palace orbit," Brodrick said. "She didn't want them drifting off to Australia, coming back with 'Strine accents and not fitting in with Palace circles."

"Frances was a devoted and passionate mother," Lady Sarah Spencer-Churchill said. "She was beside herself. She was inconsolable. She cried and cried and cried. She continued crying for years." Diana corroborated this, saying, "Mummy spent all my childhood crying. Every time she couldn't see us, she cried. Every time we had to leave, she cried." The wilfulness of a husband who did not want the children for himself, but simply wanted to deprive his wife of them, was bad enough for any woman to have to swallow. But Frances also had to square away her own mother's treachery, born, as it was, of nothing more profound than snobbery and ambition.

On 12 December 1968, the Althorp v. Althorp divorce was heard. Johnnie produced witness after witness, all with mighty positions and grand names, including Queen Elizabeth the Queen Mother's Woman of the Bedchamber Ruth, Lady Fermoy, his own mother-in-law, to attest to the fact that he had a sterling character and they had never seen him beating his wife. He was therefore, by implication, a wonderful husband, in refutation of Frances's claims of physical violence. Of course, Frances had no witnesses to the brutalization she had endured, but then, how many battered wives do? Such evidence as she did have was discounted by the judge. He was impressed by the roll call of eminent aristocrats who had closed ranks for one of their own against an errant wife, and also influenced by the fact that Frances had played the part of happy wife too well, and had therefore given little inkling to their friends of the monster behind Johnnie's courtly face. Moreover, Frances could hardly deny Johnnie's charge of adultery, when Peter Shand Kydd had admitted as much by default in failing to defend Janet's petition earlier that year, which had named Frances as corespondent. The result was that Johnnie was granted a divorce as well as permanent custody of the four children.

The extraordinary bitterness unleashed during this period marked the lives of all the participants in the drama. By Diana's own admission, "My parents' divorce caused us tremendous misery. Sarah and Jane weren't affected the way Charles and I were. They were away at boarding school. We took the brunt." She stated that "we were happy before the problems started," and this assessment is borne out Inga Crane, who remained on the Sandringham Estate even after the family had left it. She said, "Diana was a cheerful child with a good sense of humour and lots of confidence. She had the habit of putting her head on one side even then. It is nothing to do with shyness. Then the troubles started between her parents. Things got bad."

According to Diana, "Charles wailed himself to sleep every night. It was just awful. I could hear him sobbing for Mummy from my room. I mothered him as best I could, but I was only six and he was three. I was afraid of the dark. Couldn't leave my room to comfort him. When parents lay that sort of emotional burden on children they have a heavy responsibility to bear."

The adult Diana clearly had not yet recovered from what she interpreted as her mother's abandonment. She continued to blame her mother for "legging" it even after she knew that Frances had not actually intended to do any such thing. "I'd never leave my children. Never," she stated passionately, refusing to extend the pity she rightly had for her brother, Charles, and herself to her mother, who had also been a victim.

Mary Clarke, the children's nanny, also reminisced about how seriously Diana was affected. She went from being a "happy child who was always willing to please" to someone who displayed symptoms of obstinacy and uncooperativeness. She locked maids in the bathroom. She put pins in their chairs. She threw their clothes out of the window. She was, in short, in open rebellion, as Diana would admit in her last years.

It is therefore useful to examine what the practical, as opposed to the emotional, outcome of the divorce was. Although Johnnie had official custody, once he got it he saw the children no more frequently than he would otherwise have done, even if Frances had had their custody. This was especially true after Frances married Peter Shand Kydd on 2 May 1969 and settled down to a happy married life in rural Sussex.

Diana's stepsister Angela Shand Kydd recalled a happy upbringing for her brothers and step-siblings. "My father and Frances originally lived in Sussex for four or five years before going up to Scotland," where they farmed. "Diana and I grew up together with all the others." Both lots of children were in boarding school. "We spent our holidays together until we were in our late teens. Both lots of children spent equal time with both lots of parents, except that I think Diana and the Spencer children spent marginally more time with their mother. Perhaps more like 60/40. Anyway they were all enormously close to her and we all got along very well."

In practical terms, therefore, the bitter custody fight had all been for nothing. But in emotional terms, it was an act of vengefulness which certainly warped the lives of the two youngest Spencer children, and Frances's as well. By such follies do the arrogant live.

Three

Upper-class children in Britain are inevitably relegated to boarding school. The Spencers were not an exception. In September 1970, therefore, a year and a half after her parents' divorce, Diana was sent by her father to Riddlesworth Hall in Norfolk.

Nearly two hours' drive from Park House on the Sandringham Estate, Riddlesworth Hall was situated in the depths of the country in a large and well-proportioned neoclassical house. With its high ceilings, intricate mouldings, and fine panelling, it was reminiscent of home to many of the aristocrats who were students there. This similarity extended to the expectations: You were supposed to have good manners, to think of others, to have the veneer of polish that is typically aristocratic. Because Diana had been reared with exquisite manners by both parents, who were well-mannered in the "must write your bread-and-butter thank-you-letters mould" and both also had the classless touch of genuine aristocrats, Diana was not out of place there.

According to Miss Elizabeth Ridsdale, Diana's then headmistress, "She settled in after a period of homesickness." Once Diana made the adjustment to her new environment, she displayed a brilliance in the field of human relations which was a forerunner of her future popularity on the world stage. "She was very self-confident, loads of fun. She laughed a lot and got along with all sorts of people." "Always one to please," as Mary Clarke, a former nanny, described her, Diana was given the Legatt Cup for helpfulness at the end of her first year.

Riddlesworth Hall had a fine academic tradition. It became apparent within weeks, however, that the Hon. Diana Spencer was not earmarked to shine on the fields of academe. She had limited powers of concentration and no real interest in any form of expression save the physical. A born athlete, she was good at tennis and netball, and excellent at dancing and swimming. Moreover, her character complemented her natural gifts. She was fiercely competitive. "Whenever she wanted something, she was unbelievably determined," a schoolfriend remembered, corroborating a comment by Diana's father: "She is fiercely determined and never takes no for an answer." She was not afraid of hard work and would practice endlessly to hone her dancing and swimming to perfection. Her diligence paid off in her final year at Riddlesworth, when she and the other members of the swimming team won the Parker Cup.

Aside from athletic expertise, Diana was exceptional in only one other way at Riddlesworth: The scandal of her parents' divorce set her apart. In all other respects she was typical. Other girls were from equally grand families. Many had equally good names and at least as much money. It was comforting to fit in, after being worried that her parents' "antics" would follow her and mark her out as special in an unacceptable way. However, Frances Shand Kydd and Johnnie Althorp now took care to keep their squabbling private. They visited Diana on alternate weekends and shared her holiday times according to the percentages described by Angela Shand Kydd.

In 1973, Diana switched schools and followed her sisters, Sarah and Jane, to West Heath in Kent. A small school of about 120 pupils, it was located in a large Georgian house in far more beautiful surroundings than Riddlesworth or Park House could boast. Queen Mary was its most famous old-girl, as Princess May of Teck, but Diana had competition from her own family's track record as alumnae. Frances Burke Roche had been captain of everything. Sarah and Jane Spencer also had fine academic records. Before her expulsion for drinking "anything I could get my hands on: whiskey, cointreau, sherry, or, best of all, vodka, which you couldn't smell on my breath," Diana's eldest sister had also proven herself to be a good equestrienne and pianist, while sister Jane, who was a senior and prefect when Diana arrived, was about to whiz through with eleven O Levels.

In many ways, Ruth Rudge was the ideal headmistress for a girl like Diana. Her aim was to instill confidence and character, and she set about it with the no-nonsense spirit typical of her Australian heritage. Writing thank-you notes and saying please and thank you were not enough. All

West Heath girls were made to do community work. Later on, when Diana gained a reputation for humanitarianism through her work for the aged and the infirm, for children and outcasts, few people were aware that the kernel was sown at West Heath. While a student there, once a week Diana had to visit an old lady in the nearest town, Sevenoaks, doing chores such as light cleaning and helping with the shopping. She also had to visit handicapped children at a nearby home.

Miss Rudge remembered Diana as having a mixed standard of behaviour. During her first term, she was disruptive during lessons and noisy in and out of class. She settled down only after coming close to expulsion for sneaking out of her dormitory after the lights were out, the purpose of her excursion being to meet another girl in the school drive who was giving her sweets to replenish her dwindling supply of tuck. Thereafter, she became reasonably well behaved, though she was by no means a Goody-Two-Shoes.

If Diana's behaviour rose to an average standard, the first signs of her eating disorders were less typical. Each morning at eight sharp, when the girls ate breakfast, Diana would take three or four helpings of All-Bran. "I have a huge appetite," she used to admit, and soon her ability to gorge herself became a standing joke at the school. "We had no idea this was an early sign of her eating disorder," the singer Issy van Randwyck, who was a schoolmate though three years younger, remembered. "We thought it was a hoot. We used to dare her to eat a dozen slices of bread at a time. Or three plates full of shepherd's pie. Or four and five kippers and half a loaf of bread. She could eat more baked beans than anyone I've ever heard of before or since. Plates full. Several plates literally. We used to crease ourselves with laughter, amazed at where she put it all." Matron was rather less amused, for Diana was often at the infirmary, complaining of stomach pains caused from her practice of overeating, which she indulged in whether she was dared by her peers or not.

Not surprisingly, Diana was podgy. Despite being two inches short of six feet, and having the long limbs which would later lend her frame such elegance, she was anything but slender. This did not bother her. She had no desire to be model-slim. But she was not fat either. Still intensely athletic, she kept her weight in check with rigorous exercise. "At night I used to sneak out and dance for hours and hours," she said, explaining how she would go down to the new school hall and put music on her portable record player.

Displaying the tenacity and dedication which would later catapult her to great and unsustainable heights, Diana was intent on fulfilling her ambition to become a dancer. "I knew I was destined for something special. I didn't know what it was, but I knew it instinctively. I thought I might become a famous dancer." Or the wife of her neighbour's son, Prince Andrew, whom Diana still saw on a regular, though not frequent, basis when she returned home to Park House on the Sandringham Estate for the holidays, and about whom she used to joke with Pendry, the former Spencer butler, saying, "I'm saving myself for him.". "We (Diana and her brother, Charles) hated going up to the Big House. It (the atmosphere) was always so stuffy," she said, acknowledging only half the picture, for the truth was that Diana already shared her grandmother Ruth Fermoy's fixation with royalty.

Certainly the level of discipline maintained at Sandringham House was destined to have no appeal for a child reared at Park House. At the Queen's house, children were expected to be as well behaved as adults, to exercise the restraint which children who are not spoiled acquire as an essential characteristic. At Johnnie Althorp's, they could do exactly as they pleased. He allowed it, as did the two grandmothers: Ruth Fermoy and Cynthia Spencer, who often came to stay with the children until her death from a brain tumour in 1972. Not surprisingly, the children ran wild. Sarah once brought her horse into the drawing room for tea. Diana and Charles threw out the clothes of any member of the staff they wished to hound into leaving. The children could swim and play tennis whenever they wished, and were none too particular about the messes they left behind. At Christmas they were given the catalogue to the most expensive toy store in Britain, Hamley's, and told to pick whatever they wanted. No matter how excessive their requests, these were always granted. Both Charles and Diana later conceded that this practice helped to make them "materialistic."

Discipline at the Shand Kydd house in Sussex, to which Peter and Frances moved in 1972, was marginally better, though Frances took care not to seem so strict by comparison that the children would prefer being with their father. To a lesser degree even Frances had fallen into the trap to which divided families are prone. The children were indulged excessively, with results that would later be devastating to three of them.

In 1975, the scope for indulgence widened considerably, when the old earl died. Johnnie became the 8th Earl Spencer. He now had access to all the money that came along with Althorp House and the 13,000-acre estate. Diana, Sarah and Jane were no longer mere Honourables. They were now Ladies. Charles, who had started life as an Honourable also, now succeeded to his father's courtesy title and became Viscount Althorp. The family moved out of Park House into Althorp House. The glory days had begun.

The first major change was that the standard of behaviour of the children fell to new depths of laxity. "They were definitely out of control," Lady Sarah Spencer-Churchill said, and Dame Barbara Cartland, whose daughter would subsequently marry their father, corroborated this to me. Sarah hit the bottle and ordered the staff around as if she were a middle-aged chatelaine. Jane would not even abide by the most minimal courtesies unless she was in the mood to do so. Charles was even more surly, displaying the first signs of the careless and arrogant petulance which would eventually earn him condemnation during his divorce proceedings. And Diana, who was the best behaved at home, treated the rules at school with contempt. She was not allowed to wash her hair more than once a week, but nevertheless did so every day. She was not allowed to bathe every day, but nevertheless contrived to do so. By her own admission, instead of sleeping at night she either snuck out of her room and practised her dancing, or stayed up until the early hours reading the romantic novels written by her favourite author, the self-same Barbara Cartland, who would soon become her step-grandmother-in-law. Not surprisingly, Diana's academic accomplishments were nonexistent and she remained firmly at the bottom of her class.

Into this mêlée of confusion came the crisp Raine, Countess of Dartmouth. A former London County Councillor with a reputation, as the Duke of Edinburgh said, "for getting things done," Raine was Barbara Cartland's daughter and the ex-wife of the Earl of Dartmouth. Tall and striking, Raine's appearance spoke volumes about her. The description "perfectly groomed" could have been invented for her. Her hair was always styled so immaculately that she made Nancy Reagan's look windblown. Her maquillage was always so perfect you wanted to send Madonna to her for cosmetic lessons. She never went into the sun, so the porcelain-like attraction of her unblemished complexion had not diminished with time, and indeed, still has not, at the time of writing, though she is now well into her seventies.

Raine had never been popular. My late stepmother-in-law, Margaret, Duchess of Argyll, was one of Barbara Cartland's closest friends from 1930 on and had therefore known Raine since she was a little girl. She said, "Raine has an off-putting manner. People have never been able to abide her, but she has a lot more going for her than she's given credit for."

Raine had been married to Lord Dartmouth for more than twenty years, and was the mother of four children, when she began a torrid romance with Johnnie in the early 1970s after working with him on a book entitled *What Is Our Heritage?* for the London County Council. Many people told me that Raine had "set her cap at Johnnie." Several repeated a variation on this theme: "We wonder just how attractive to her he'd have been, had Althorp House not come along as part of the package." To them, this was not a criticism, simply a statement of the fact that in the 1970s the values of the aristocracy were such that high-powered women sought an outlet for their energy as chatelaines of stately homes. While Johnnie did not yet have Althorp House and the great fortune that came along with the Spencer earldom, he was still the heir, whereas Lord Dartmouth only had an ordinary manor house and a modest amount of money.

Whatever the various strands that converged to make for a great passion, Raine's feelings towards Johnnie certainly were passionate, as her mother confirmed to me. At first, the romance was secret. Their cover, however, was blown when "Johnnie had the first of his strokes while on the job with Raine at the Dorchester Hotel," according to a mutual friend. "They had to call an ambulance and take him to the hospital, with Raine standing by, looking bedraggled and forlorn. It was obvious what they'd been up to. After that, the divorce was inevitable."

Lord Dartmouth divorced Raine for adultery and, in a replay of the Althorp v. Althorp case, also won custody of their four children, though Barbara Cartland was a more loyal mother than Ruth Fermoy, and took her daughter's side. Aristocratic women, it seemed, could not commit adultery without judges in Britain penalizing them in a way that they would never have dared to do with middle-or working-class women.

Once divorced, Raine was astonished to discover that Johnnie was curiously reluctant to marry her. This was largely due to his children, who "loathed Raine," as they all confirmed. Barbara Cartland recounted to me how they used to tell him, "You can marry anybody except Lady

Dartmouth." Whenever anyone telephoned to speak to her father and Raine was in residence, Sarah's favourite trick was to say, "He can't speak right now. He's in bed with Lady Dartmouth." Jane used the silent treatment on her prospective stepmother, sidestepping her without a word, her aquiline nose crinkled to indicate that she was enduring a huge stench. Charles was his customary surly self when he was not writing her venomous letters stressing how much he hated her. Only Diana would sometimes break out of her aloofness into an approximation of normality, though Raine could never rely upon the face presented to her, as Diana used to get her friends to write Raine poison-pen letters and once wrote one herself.

After trying everything to encourage Johnnie to do the decent thing and marry her, Raine turned in desperation to her eldest son, William, presently the Earl of Dartmouth but then Viscount Lewisham. William recounted to some mutual friends and me over dinner one evening how he suggested to his mother, "Get yourself asked on someone's yacht and go cruising for two weeks."

"But, William, I can't do that," Raine said in those pre-mobile phone days, when the only form of communication between land and sea was the ship-to-shore radio. "It won't do any good unless he can speak to me."

"It won't do any good if he can," William cannily counselled.

Faced with the prospect of losing the passionate Raine, Johnnie overrode his children's objections and married her in July 1976 at London's Caxton Hall. None of the four Spencer children was in attendance, nor were Raine's four, William, Rupert, Charlotte and Henry.

"Those children made my life hell on earth," Raine recounted without a lot of exaggeration. "Their capacity for hatred was frightening," a friend of Johnnie and Raine's said. Sarah, always witty and dramatic, summarized their attitude by announcing, "I would sooner take up residence in Lenin's Tomb, cuddling his corpse for warmth, than have Raine Dartmouth (as they continued to refer to her even after the marriage) for my stepmother." Confronted by such naked hatred, Raine resolved to keep her children unpolluted. "They never saw the Spencer children," a mutual friend explained. "Raine kept them apart. They didn't know the Spencer kids at all. William only ever met Diana maybe twice." Barbara Cartland corroborated this to me: "It was always arranged that they (her grandchildren) would come at different times to Johnnie's children and therefore they were never particularly good friends."

When Raine and Johnnie were on their own, or the four Legge children were with them, they had a harmonious family life. Although "Raine is not your typical mother, and is very much the you–fetch–this, fetch–that type," as Margaret Duchess of Argyll, my stepmother-in-law, told me, she was a capable housewife and ran Althorp House "magnificently," as the Spencers' family friend Lady Freyberg confirmed to me.

All this changed when Sarah, Jane, Diana and Charles came for their dreaded visits. "Their venomousness was beyond imagination," Barbara Cartland said. "They never missed an opportunity to be nasty, to belittle Raine, to repel her efforts at being pleasant to them and to everyone else." "Diana was the only one who was nice to me some of the time," Raine has said to friends of ours, another fact her mother corroborated to me. Sarah gave orders to the staff over Raine's head, acting as if Raine did not exist. Jane pointedly refused to address one word to her hated stepmother. And Charles gave vent both orally and in writing to the rage which the world got a glimpse of when his wife Victoria sued him for divorce in South Africa in 1997.

If Raine thought things could only get better, she was wrong. Johnnie Spencer owed more than £2 million in death duties when she married him. She turned the organizational expertise acquired as a London County Councillor to good use, hosting dinners for paying guests; opening up a gift shop to sell souvenirs to visitors to Althorp House; even undertaking futile schemes to raise the number of visitors from a paltry few thousand per annum. Those numbers would never rise beyond 10,000, even after Diana became the Princess of Wales. After she was buried there, of course there was an increase in the number of visitors. This went some way towards meeting the running costs of Althorp House, which are estimated at £300,000 per annum and were a relative amount when Raine was its chatelaine, for the Diana museum was structured in such a way that the estate recouped its expenses, i.e. running costs. However, at the time of writing, the museum is expected to close owing to declining numbers, and once that happens, Lord Spencer will once again face the problem Raine had: of finding an attraction so that the public will pay to see his house.

"Of course the Spencer children should be grateful to Raine because she saved them millions of pounds," Barbara Cartland claimed. She was referring to the financial reorganization and the refurbishment of the house which Raine undertook, selling antiques quietly in an attempt to maintain the veneer of unlimited wealth for which the Spencers were unwarrantedly known, while trying to generate income from Althorp House.

The children, however, were anything but grateful, even after Johnnie had a massive stroke in September 1978 and nearly died. Johnnie was smitten in the courtyard at Althorp and was taken to the local hospital in Northampton. Raine insisted that he be moved to London immediately, and he was driven by private ambulance to the National Hospital for Nervous Diseases in London. In November Raine insisted upon his being transferred to the Brompton Hospital in Chelsea. John Welsh, one of the doctors who subsequently treated him, told me, "As much as people kick at Raine... she probably was responsible for saving his life." Bringing the full power of her efficiency to bear, Raine immediately researched the possible courses of treatment and discovered that an experimental drug gave the comatose Johnnie the best chance of survival. According to John Welsh, "The Duke of Portland himself told me that she asked him to arrange for Aslocillin to be used on him. They were having trials in Surrey, I believe, otherwise it wouldn't have been allowed in the country. He said that Johnnie Spencer would almost certainly have died without the drug."

While Johnnie was lying in a coma, "I willed my life force into him," Raine recounted to Margaret, Duchess of Argyll at her mother's house. "I used to sit by his bed and talk to him for hours, telling him how much I loved him and how he had to get better. I also used to play his favourite arias to him." Knowing how much his children had upset her husband by their hostility towards her, and fearing that the sight of them might loosen his already-weakened hold on life, Raine banned them from visiting.

"The fights were terrible," John Welsh told me. "I overheard several." Sarah in particular felt she had a right to voice her opinion, but all four of them felt that Raine had no right to prevent them from seeing their father. "They used to visit when Raine wasn't around. They didn't get that much opportunity, as she was usually around."

Till his dying day, Johnnie Spencer claimed, "Raine saved my life. If it hadn't been for her, I wouldn't be here." For her part, Raine had no doubt that her course of action was the only one. "I boned up on the subject. I knew what I was doing. And I did it. The fact, that he lived when every doctor said he wouldn't, speaks for itself."

A much-changed Johnnie Spencer came out of the hospital in January 1979. Gone was the robust brute with the easy charm. In its place was a shambling, tetchy but more kindly person. It was apparent to all who met him that he was ill. As there was never much of an improvement until he died in March 1992, he became extremely dependent upon Raine.

Despite this, the Johnnie of old who used to abuse Frances still had kick in his spirit. The American widow of an extremely rich friend of the Spencers, Kristi Prenn, recounted, "He could be mean. We were at dinner one evening and the peas had arrived cold from the kitchen. He ranted and raved at Raine for a good ten minutes, as if it were her fault. He accused her of being no good, of not running the house properly, of not being able to control the staff. And the language he used. Talk about turning the air blue. He was completely out of control. In a real rage. We were stunned. As for the rest of the food, by the time he had finished it was all cold."

"Raine was marvelous with Johnnie," their friend Lady Freyberg told me, giving vent to an opinion consistently shared by their friends and acquaintances. She displayed commendable patience in dealing with a man who had become slow but remained as demanding as ever. While it is true that he was touchingly in love with her and never ceased to say, "I owe my life to Raine," dealing with him "cannot have been easy," according to their friends.

"Not only did she have to cope with the man Johnnie had become," Lady Freyberg said, "but she also had to run the whole show at Althorp. He still had massive debts. Large running expenses. She tried to get the house to pay for itself. She tried to attract visitors, especially after Diana married the Prince of Wales, by brightening up the place to make it more appealing." She called in Partridge (Fine Arts) Limited of Bond Street to do the job. According to their then chief executive, "We were responsible for the entire restoration, in other words all the furniture, ormolu, picture frames, porcelain, that sort of thing. It took eight years."

"Raine is very easy to deal with. She is highly professional. What the press has never said is that she was guided by Peter Thornton, who was the head of the decorative arts section of the Victoria and Albert Museum and by David Laws of Colefax & Fowler. The criticism has been most unfair. The press doesn't know what it's talking about," the then chief executive of Partridge continued.

Raine "is a very shrewd businesswoman," Tristan Millington-Drake, whose first cousin the Duke of Carcaci is married to Raine's daughter Charlotte Legge, told me. "If it hadn't been for her, the house would now be falling down around his (Charles, Earl Spencer's) ears." The house had to have structural repairs, something which is prohibitively expensive for Grade One listed historic houses, because everything has to be vetted and passed by various governmental bodies.

To finance the restoration, Raine sold chattels through either Partridge or Anton Kristensen, a Danish aristocrat whose clients include most of the European royal families. To the Spencer children, Raine deserved condemnation for her efforts, not credit. "She's selling off my inheritance," Charles complained repeatedly. This sentiment was shared by his sisters, each of whom was vociferous in condemning their stepmother for "stripping Althorp bare," to use Diana's phrase.

The Spencers were not a family to suffer in silence, as the world discovered after Diana married the Prince of Wales and they became of rather more interest to the public than they had been previously. Diana and her brother, Charles, who became a journalist until he discovered that you can't run with the hares and hunt with the hounds without getting savaged, were especially critical, using the media to blacken Raine's name, accusing her via leaks to sympathetic journalists such as the aristocratic Simon Blow of destroying Althorp House by selling off the treasures at knockdown prices, and tarting it up so that it looked like a bordello instead of a stately home. "Raine felt she was under siege," Margaret, Duchess of Argyll told me, and "Johnnie was outraged."

Shortly before he died, Johnnie Spencer did wade into the slanging match, accusing his two younger children of being "ingrates" who were carping unfairly and speaking from the vantage point of ignorance. In that, he was proven right. Within a year of his death, his hypercritical heir was also selling off treasures, explaining, as Raine had done before him, that the running costs were forcing him to take a course of action he would otherwise have avoided. Raine, naturally, was exultant to be vindicated, especially as Diana and Charles Spencer had treated her even more abominably at the time of their father's death than they had treated her before. But one must not anticipate the story.

All this was in marked contrast to the way the Spencer children behaved with their mother's new husband, Peter Shand Kydd. "They all got along with my father," Angela Shand Kydd confirmed. "They liked him and he liked them. There were never any problems."

No problems, at any rate, with Peter. With Frances, it was another story, as Diana would later recount to Andrew Morton and myself, and Charles Spencer would indicate during his funeral address, when he bitterly alluded to the "lonely train journeys" they had to endure – train journeys which would have been inevitable no matter which parent had initiated the split or had ended up with custody. Diana never forgave her mother for leaving her, even though she knew it was not her mother's intention to lose custody. In Diana's opinion, "she should have stayed. I'd never leave my boys."

"Close though they were to their mother, Diana and Charles never had the sympathy for Frances that they should have," Lady Sarah Spencer-Churchill said. "Especially when you stop to consider that she was an abused wife. They were astonishingly self-centred, only ever thinking of themselves." This was especially true when they were growing up. "Every time we were leaving she started blubbing," Diana complained to a variety of people over the years. "It struck me that she didn't want the emotional burden of a distressed mother. Diana could be very hard-hearted when her own feelings were at stake. Very self-protective. In that respect, the woman remained very much the sort of person the little girl had been," Lady Sarah Spencer-Churchill said.

Four

Diana took her first meaningful steps towards becoming the Princess of Wales in November 1977, when she was let out from West Heath school to join a shooting party at Althorp which her father was hosting for her sister Sarah's boyfriend, the Prince of Wales. Diana had failed her O Levels that June and was resitting them in December, but that did not stop her headmistress, Miss Rudge, nor her father from keeping their priorities aristocratic: royalty came before examinations, especially when the pupil was as inflexibly unacademic as Diana.

Diana acquitted herself well. "She was absolutely sweet," Lady Freyberg, who was present for the dinner following the shoot, says. "Lord Spencer was very proud of her. He said it was her first grown-up do."

Sarah presented Diana to Charles in the middle of Nobottle Field during the shoot. At the time of their engagement, Charles would say he had noticed how "jolly" she was, but this prince whose taste always ran in the direction of sophisticated women really had only a polite interest in his girlfriend's baby sister. This is borne out by Lady Freyberg's observation, "I was not aware of Prince Charles noticing her in any special way," and by Diana herself, who said, "He barely noticed me."

The following month, Diana sat and failed her O Level examinations yet again. The results came in just before she was due to return for the January 1978 term. She now had to leave school, all hope of her moving up a class having evaporated.

Diana's parents quickly organized for her to be sent to the Institut Alpin Vidamanette near Gstaad in Switzerland. This was where they had sent Sarah after her expulsion from West Heath, before she went on to

Vienna to study music at the conservatoire. Diana had never been abroad before, nor on an airplane.

While Diana was alive, there were many rumours about her days at this finishing school. She was supposed to have been miserable, and to have cut her stay short, to have caused problems with boys. There were other, equally groundless suppositions, but her headmistress, Madame Heidi Yersin, put the record straight. "People say she was homesick and that is why she left early but that is not so. Diana was only ever booked in for one term. She had a good time and wasn't homesick at all. Her humour made her very popular and she made lots of friends. She wasn't shy at all. More modest. Although modest, she could always cope well with everybody."

Diana had no interest in meeting boys outside her own social circle. According to Madame Yersin, "Diana only ever went out to the cinema with all the other girls. They were allowed to go into Gstaad and meet up with the boys from a boys' school but Diana never went. We know this because we have checked the records."

Sophie Kimball, a Conservative MP's daughter who was a classmate of Diana's and became a close friend, corroborated this. "There was no social life in Rougemont. It wasn't a large village. We could go into Gstaad, but that just meant sailing around in one of the large *après-ski* places." To girls who had been reared never to socialize with people to whom they had not been properly introduced, such fraternization was unthinkable. The prospect of becoming involved with anyone common or unsuitable, i.e. not well-born was to be avoided at all costs. Or, as Diana herself said, "I was never one for downtown guys."

Diana's sister Sarah provided the term's excitement by arriving at nearby Klosters for a skiing holiday with the Prince of Wales and his cousins the Duke and Duchess of Gloucester. Sarah had become reacquainted with Charles at Royal Ascot the year before. According to Diana, "Sarah was in a state at that time. She'd just broken up with Gerald (Duke of) Westminster." Sarah hoped to marry Britain's richest aristocrat, who owned most of London's chic Belgravia and Mayfair districts and had the looks of a matinée idol. "It was after this that she developed anorexia nervosa," Diana explained. Although in and out of a St. John's Wood nursing home, where she was under the care of eating-disorder expert Dr Maurice Lipsedge, who would later treat Diana as well, Sarah nevertheless managed to captivate Charles. This was not hard to do. She was bright, witty, sparky and pretty, with the Spencer arrogance and the Fermoy charm. They quickly started a romance and, unusually for a young man, Charles was most sympathetic and supportive of Sarah's struggle against her eating disorder.

It was while Sarah was a member of the royal party at Klosters that she made her disastrous comment to the press about Kings and dustmen. According to Lady Sarah Spencer-Churchill, "Prince Charles, of course, was supposed to rally to Sarah's side, to show the world that he could conquer this pure-hearted girl whose only interest was in love – just in case he was wondering if ambition was responsible for her responsiveness. Sarah misread him totally. She simply didn't understand that he wasn't like the Spencers. He isn't aggressive or domineering. Faced with a personal challenge, he withdraws. The Spencers all rise to challenges like bulls to red flags. Challenges goad them to unthinkable heights." Once Sarah's comments were published, their romance was over, though Charles did remain on friendly terms with her and even asked her to his thirtieth birthday party.

Diana, meanwhile, was packing up to return to England. In those days, Britain had stringent foreign-exchange controls and Sophie Kimball has provided an explanation for why Diana's stay at finishing school was so short. "Most of the English girls only stayed a few months because the exchange rate was dreadful and it was really very expensive."

Not yet seventeen, Diana returned to her mother's home at Cadogan Square. There she based herself until she bought a flat of her own the following year. "I was at a loose end," she told me. "I didn't know what to do."

Diana's family stepped into the breach. "She was never an independent sort," John Kennedy, Prince Michael of Kent's one-time Private Secretary who knew Diana well, told me. But even if she had been independent, there would not have been anything unusual about a girl approaching seventeen getting help from her family. They arranged for her to work as a mother's help to six-year-old Alexandra Whitaker, daughter of Major Jeremy Whitaker, a photographer, and his wife, Philippa, whose brother Willy von Straubenzee became a lifelong friend of Diana's and attended her funeral.

After working with the Whitakers for three months, Diana took time off for a summer holiday. Still trying to find something that she wanted to do, she enrolled for a cookery course in September 1978, shortly before her father was felled by his cerebral haemorrhage. According to Elizabeth Russell, who taught the course from her home in Wimbledon, "We loved her. She was a very good pupil." The course was ten weeks and was "designed so that anybody doing it can earn her living from it afterwards."

Diana, however, had no interest in joining the growing legion of upper-class girls who worked part-time as cooks for company directors and socialites without full-time chefs. Her ambition was still to become a dancer. "They said I was too tall. But I tried to get in through the back door," she said. With that in mind, she approached Madame Betty Vacani, niece of the founder of the famous Vacani Dance School, who had taught everyone from Queen Elizabeth II, Princess Margaret and Elizabeth Taylor downwards. Diana had met Madame Vacani once, when she was judging a dance contest at West Heath which Diana had won. Notwithstanding that the Vacani School had never produced any great ballerinas, merely society figures who could wheel themselves around a dance floor without breaking the ankles of neighbouring dancers, Diana took the initiative in a way that is sorely at odds with the received wisdom about her character, but which shows how resourceful, canny and go-getting she truly was, even as a teenager. "Diana wrote to me and said she had been at West Heath and wanted to train as a dancing teacher," Madame Vacani said.

Hoping that Madame Vacani would recognize how gifted she was, and would find a way to circumvent the problem of her height, Diana started her circuitous climb onstage. "I was full of hope," she said.

Madame Vacani, however, was of the opinion that "at her height, she could never have become a dancer." As Madame recounted the saga, "She was about seventeen at the time, a shy, quiet, nice girl. However, she only stayed a month. She went off skiing and never came back. I think that she felt the training – three years and until 6:30 in the evening – would be too all-embracing. She never gave a reason for not returning. I imagine she felt teaching at the kindergarten would not be so demanding."

In fact, Diana would have happily sacrificed to become a dancer. One of her great virtues was an ability to work hard if her heart was in a project. Not only had she spent many a night at West Heath dancing, but the staff at Althorp House remember her dancing "for hours on end in Wootton Hall after the visitors had left," as Diana put it. But she had no real interest in becoming a dance teacher, so did indeed look around for something easier to do.

There were few options open to a seventeen-year-old without educational qualifications or real interests, so Diana started working three days a week as a cleaning lady for her sister Sarah and Sarah's flatmate Lucinda Craig-Harvey, a Hampshire landowner's daughter who later became a theatrical producer. Her wages were £1 an hour. She had to vacuum, dust, straighten up the flat, wash up dirty dishes, scour out the bath and basins and clean the lavatory. "Sarah made no concessions. That was fine by me," Diana said. "I adored her and I've always loved cleaning."

This job was not sufficient to occupy her, so sister Jane came to the rescue and found Diana more part-time work through a West Heath school friend of hers, Kay Seth-Smith, who ran the Young England Kindergarten in a church hall in Pimlico. "Miss Diana" was employed for three afternoons a week to assist with a new group of younger children. Her duties involved teaching the children basic dancing; helping them to paint pictures, to play with bricks and other games; changing their diapers when necessary; and cuddling them when they cried. Later, she added two mornings to her roster.

Diana still had gaps which needed filling. Never lazy, she signed up with various temporary agencies, including Solve Your Problems, Universal Aunts, and Occasional Nannies. "She came to us with references from the Whitakers and Young England," Jan Govett, formerly of Occasional Nannies, said. "Both were very good. She came to us in October 1979. She said she would look after children aged between one and ten because, of course, she had no formal training and that made it difficult to care for young babies. One of her references said she would be prepared to help with anything – washing up in particular. As she had no training, she was after being more of a mother's help than a nanny.

"She asked for £1 an hour. The first job we gave her was in November 1979 with the Jarmans at Prince of Wales Drive. Then in January 1980 she got her second job, with Mrs Patrick Robinson at Belgrave Square, the American wife of an oil executive. She had to give their child lunch, walk it in the park, and give it a nap in the afternoon. She only wanted to work two days a week.

"One of the girls in the office remembers the first time she came in. She was wearing a bright red jersey, a white shirt and jeans. She blushed very easily and smiled too much."

Diana would stay in two of those jobs until her engagement: as a mother's help to the Robinsons, and an assistant at Young England Kindergarten.

Set up in jobs that "I could do blindfolded," as Diana put it, she bought a flat in 1979 for £50,000 at Coleherne Court. This three-bedroom property was located in a smart, block-sized complex built around a large and beautiful garden between the Little Boltons and Radcliffe Road near Earl's Court in the fashionable southwestern area of London. The money to purchase it came from her American great-grandmother, Fanny Work, on her eighteenth birthday.

Diana spent the next few months doing up the flat with her mother's help. "The flat was pretty. Tastefully furnished, and charming," Anne Bolton said.

To keep her company and help with the expenses, Diana had two flatmates: Sophie Kimball, whom she had met at the Institut Alpin Videmanette, and Laura Greig, whose grandfather had been a doctor to King George VI when he was the Duke of York. Within a year they would be replaced by three other girls from "nice" families: Carolyn Pride, a student at the Royal College of Music who went on to marry party-planner William Bartholomew and who later had a starring role in the Morton saga; Virginia Pitman, an Asprey's shopgirl; and Anne Bolton, of Savills real estate agents.

With home and work both sorted out, Diana was free to focus on her social life and her romantic interests. She had a wide circle of friends, because she had been reared in a world where social life is of consuming importance and networking is the accepted means by which aristocrats expand their circle. She was friendly with such "nobs" as Lady Cleone Crichton, whose father, the Earl of Erne, was the Queen's Lord-Lieutenant for Belfast; Lord Suffield's daughter Caroline Harbord-Hammond; Alexandra Loyd, whose father was the Queen's Land Agent at Sandringham; and the Hay brothers. Her life was one long round of dinner parties, dances, balls, evenings out at the cinema, and weekends in the country. She seldom went to the theater, concerts or museums, though she did occasionally attend the ballet.

It is useful to remember what goals privileged eighteen-year-olds had in the late seventies. Young ladies no longer had any pressure put upon them to marry young. Their late teens and early twenties were a time for testing the waters, for enjoying themselves before settling down. AIDS and the other sexually transmittable diseases, which would so modify behaviour in the eighties and nineties, had not yet been heard of, and unwanted pregnancies could be easily prevented. No one was surprised if boys and girls experimented sexually. The idea of any healthy young woman walking up the altar as a virgin was a thing of the past.

Only when girls were approaching their mid-twenties were they expected to turn their minds to finding a "suitable" husband. At that age, they could even then give themselves two or three good years before anyone raised eyebrows because they were still single.

In aristocratic circles, the criteria for what constituted a good catch had not changed in centuries. To be minimally suitable, a man had to have background and breeding. If he had money as well, he became desirable, and if he possessed a title, he was a catch. The more money and grander the title, the greater the catch. Ironically, looks did not play an important part in the equation of marital suitability. There was a general understanding in the aristocracy that sexual satisfaction could wait until after a couple had provided the heir and the spare. At that point, they could sleep with whomever they pleased, as long as they were discreet about it and didn't seek a divorce. Though no longer a cause for ostracism, divorce was still to be avoided, largely because of the expense, disruption and inconvenience it caused.

Diana was a typical product of her time and environment. This would create conflict for her, as it did for many other well-bred girls who expected to combine "suitable" marriages with romantic satisfaction. Whereas earlier generations understood that marriage was often a choice between ambition and fulfilment, Diana's generation had been reared to believe that personal satisfaction was an essential ingredient of marriage. Without it, marriage was pointless. To someone as status conscious as Diana, however, "the idea of making a match with a man who did not fulfill her family's, and her own, regal ambitions, bore thinking about only as a last resort," Lady Sarah Spencer-Churchill said.

"Diana's dilemma was that she didn't want to do anything except get married. But she and Prince Andrew were too young," Lady Sarah

Spencer-Churchill continued. Of course, she also had no guarantee Andrew would even want her. She therefore hedged her bets, a trait she would develop into an art form in the years to come. On the one hand, she kept herself available for the brilliant match she and her family wished for. On the other hand, she had a series of boyfriends, all of whom were marriage material.

Diana's start in the romantic stakes was as shaky as her start at school or her beginnings in royal life. She was a young seventeen when she met the fourteen-year-old Daniel Wiggin. The son of baronet Sir John Wiggin, Daniel Wiggin was a friend of her brother Charles and would later become his flatmate and the godfather of his eldest daughter, Kitty. He was described by the heir to an Australian fortune: "He's very attractive, dark, sturdy, not tall but not too short, and sexy."

Although her junior, Daniel Wiggin looked and acted older than she did. "He was her first lover," Jonathan Dawson told me, information he received from the Horse's Mouth itself. Diana, of course, always implied that the Prince of Wales deflowered her. While no one can say with certainty that Daniel Wiggin was indeed the first, what can be asserted with confidence is that Prince Charles did not introduce her to the pleasures of the flesh. And Daniel Wiggin, being younger than Diana and a friend of her brother's, remained a peripheral personality in her life, though he never went on to fill the role of boyfriend.

Shortly afterwards, Diana met James Colthurst, a younger son of the baronet who owns Ireland's Blarney Castle, with its famous Blarney stone. Tall, dark, hirsute and handsome, the strapping medical student was staying with Simon Berry, the son of an established London wine merchant, when Diana joined their house party. She had gone on a skiing holiday with Mary-Anne Stewart-Richardson at her family's chalet in Val Claret. The atmosphere, Diana later told me, was not as "jolly" as she had hoped for, however, because the Stewart-Richardson family were getting over a tragedy, so Diana engineered an invitation from Simon Berry. Notwithstanding that she twisted her ankle and was thereafter not able to ski, Diana "had a whale of a time." The future Dr Colthurst, who was very much the physical type Diana went for time and again – "I like them hunky and chunky," she confessed to me – made a lasting impression on Diana. They continued to see one another after the holiday came to an end, and, even after banking the romantic embers, remained friends until he was ill-advised enough to become Diana's "go between" with Andrew Morton. "I won't have my friends making money out of me," was one of Diana's guiding precepts, and as soon as she discovered that he had been rewarded by the publisher, Michael O'Mara, for his efforts, she dumped him as a friend.

Adam Russell, another member of that house party, also became a boyfriend of Diana's. He observed that Diana seemed to be a happy person on the surface, but concluded, with commendable insight, that she had been traumatized by her parents' divorce. Although she had a good sense of humour and was always ready for a laugh, she had a deep-seated sadness. Their relationship developed sufficiently that, when he left England in 1979 after coming down from Oxford University with a degree in languages, he did so with the view of returning to a more committed relationship with Diana.

Yet another boyfriend was James Boughey, a Coldstream Guardsman. "I love a man in a uniform," Diana used to say, and this was true of the well-built lieutenant. Nothing came of this relationship, though she did remain on good terms with yet another of her handsome and brawny romantic interests.

A rather more substantial relationship was Diana's romance with Rory Scott, a well-known lieutenant in the Scots Guards who looked great in and out of a uniform. Diana spent many weekends with Rory at his parents' farm near Petworth in West Sussex and he has admitted, "I found her incredibly sexually appealing." He has also confirmed that their relationship was "not platonic," though he is too much of a gentleman to enter into further discussion on such a personal subject, and if pushed would naturally resort to a gentlemanly protection of an ex-girlfriend's reputation with a decorous denial. Nevertheless, so close were they that Diana used to launder his clothes, a practice she continued even after she was seeing Prince Charles. Only when she "had Charles in the bag," as one friend put it, did she put a stop to her deliveries of ironing to St. James's Palace, where the handsome Scott was stationed.

Another man whose washing Diana did was Willy van Straubenzee, a former boyfriend of her sister Sarah's. Diana tried to entice him with a display of devotion, hoping to ensnare her adored sister's cast-off. "I adored Sarah. I thought the world of her. I wished I was like her. She was so fabulous," Diana told me. An older woman who knew both Spencer girls from childhood says, "They had an interesting relationship. Diana hero-worshipped Sarah before she married the Prince of Wales. But there was a competitive element. Both of them were amazingly competitive. Diana had a history of trying to step into Sarah's shoes. She tried with Willy van Straubenzee. She succeeded with the Prince." Willy van Straubenzee also remained a friend of Diana's long after her romantic compass had shifted elsewhere.

One who did not remain a friend when their romance soured was James Gilbey. Like Carolyn Pride Bartholomew, he would later feature heavily in the saga of the Morton book, but there was a gap of some ten years between Diana's first and second romances with the gin heir. Like all of her other boyfriends, both pre-and post-marital, James Gilbey was a male-model type, with a handsome face and a masculine body. He, however, was rather more cavalier than most of the others. "She was keener on him than he was on her," a friend from that period told me. "One evening he stood her up on a date." Diana retaliated for this slight by mixing a flour-and-egg paste, taking it in the dead of night to Gilbey's home, and pouring it over the paintwork of the car-mad heartbreaker's Alfa Romeo. Overnight, the mixture set solid, with the result that when Gilbey saw the car the following morning, the paintwork had been ruined.

"Diana could be a real bitch. If you crossed her – which didn't necessarily mean doing anything awful, simply not giving her her own way – she turned very, very nasty indeed," Lady Sarah Spencer-Churchill said. This is an opinion shared by many. Diana's close friend Rosa Monckton, at the time of Diana's death the managing director of Tiffany's London, concurred when she publicly stated, "Diana could be vengeful." Richard Kay, the *Daily Mail* and *Mail On Sunday* columnist who was a personal friend of Diana's at the time of her death, is on record acknowledging Diana's "vengefulness," and Diana herself told me, "I can't help it. I've got a vengeful streak." There were some specific examples from this period of her life which show clearly that the Prince of Wales did not distort Diana's identity, as she later wished the world to believe, but that the Spencer venomousness was already a pronounced characteristic. On one occasion, when a friend refused to lend her a car, she glued its locks solid. On another occasion, when someone in a house party slighted her, she got out of her bed in the middle of the night, unscrewed the top of his car's gas tank, and poured water down it, nearly ruining the engine.

Having wreaked her revenge upon James Gilbey's treasured Alfa Romeo, "as far as he was concerned, that was the end of Diana," one of his friends said. "At least, until he saw her at Julia Samuel's in 1989." By then she was no longer just another earl's daughter on the prowl for the best husband she could find, but the celebrated Princess of Wales, who was casting about for a new lover to distract her while her main lover, James Hewitt, was abroad.

"People should think about what Diana was really like," a friend of both Diana and the Prince of Wales said. "She was no saint and certainly no angel. She could be sweet and generous, but she also had a vicious streak in her nature. She could be tremendously and irresponsibly destructive. Malicious really. What she did to James Gilbey's car constituted criminal damage. It was no joke. People have gone to jail for less."

The Hon. Harry Herbert, yet another of Diana's Old Etonian boyfriends, fared rather better, as did his car. The second son of the Queen's close friend and racing manager, the late Earl of Carnarvon, Harry personified the type of man Diana went for. He was tall, dark-haired, handsome, with a good physique and an even better lineage. They remained friends for the remainder of her days, and she even attended his wedding.

Like many of her contemporaries, Diana saw nothing wrong with dating two or three men at the same time. "She frequently drove more than one car at a time," said Joseph Sanders, her close friend, financial (and personal) advisor, delicately referring to her habit, once her marriage was over in all but name, of having two or more lovers on the go at the same time.

While Diana was seeing the Prince of Wales, she also saw a long-standing boyfriend, the Hon. George Plumptre. The third son of Lord Fitzwalter, George Plumptre was eight years older than Diana and very much a man of the world. Although not as good-looking as many of her other boyfriends had been, he still cut a fine-enough figure. Moreover, he had a good sense of humour, the absolute discretion of a true gentleman, and the *élan* which the teenaged Diana found so captivating in older men. As with Rory Scott, she often went away for weekends with George Plumptre.

One of Diana's premarital lovers, whose status of gentleman disallows him from commenting publicly, told me, "Yes. We were lovers. We did have a sexual relationship. I was not the first. She was not a virgin. She was not inexperienced, but I wouldn't say she was an accomplished lover. She was too young. She liked sex and had a strong appetite. She was what I'd call eager. She liked to please and liked being pleased. She was especially affectionate. She liked cuddles, lots of after-lovemaking hugs and kisses and cuddles. She could keep you going with those for hours."

Another man, who enjoyed a passing fling with Diana, said, "She was terribly discreet. About her flings and about her romances (i.e., one-night stands and more substantial relationships)." And Joseph Sanders, with whom she discussed her romantic adventures, said, "She only went out with gents. She was careful about that. She liked men who had the bodies of builders but the manners of nobs."

Lady Sarah Spencer-Churchill said, "She needed the attentions of men. She was clever about protecting her interests. She felt she was earmarked for marriage into the Royal Family so was careful to make sure that the only boys she had flings with were ones who'd keep their mouths shut." At the time, there was a popular misconception that royal males could only marry virgins. While people who were closer to the Royal Family, Diana included, knew that this was not a requirement, they were only too aware that a reputation for purity was an advantage.

Although Diana and Prince Andrew were too young for marriage, she was nevertheless old enough for her family to dangle her before the Royal Family. Prince Andrew was already well known within Court circles to be sexually advanced for his years. His predilections therefore made him an ideal candidate for early marriage, and, as British law forbade royals from marrying without the Queen's approval, that meant that he would have to make his choice from the restrictive pool of suitable maidens. Any girl who had the eye and ear of Andrew's parents already had a tremendous advantage over a girl who did not.

Sister Jane's marriage to the Queen's Assistant Private Secretary now became useful. The first of the family's shots across the royal bow came in November 1978, when Robert Fellowes engineered an invitation for his young sister-in-law to attend the Prince of Wales's thirtieth birthday party at Buckingham Palace. Charles was at the time romancing the actress Susan George, his partner for the evening, and he did not even notice Diana. Diana, however, was not there to catch the heir to the throne's eye, but that of his brother and the rest of the family. As Lady Sarah Spencer-

Churchill said, "All their lives the girls had been told that Diana," whom they called Duch in anticipation of the day she became the Duchess of York, "was reserved for Prince Andrew."

Now that Jane had a toehold – literally – at the Palace, the family set about doing all they could to keep Diana in the royal line of vision. Their next foray took place a mere two months later. It was the very weekend, in January 1979, that Diana's father was released from the hospital following his stroke. She was staying at Sandringham House for a shoot, courtesy of her brother-in-law Robert Fellowes.

In *Diana in Private*, I quoted a friend of Diana's saying, "She was thrilled to go up to Sandringham that first time. It was like being asked to heaven." Jonathan Dimbleby said as much in his acclaimed, authorized biography of the Prince of Wales, when he recounted how Diana endeared herself to her elders by openly stating, "This is the life for me."

The world that the adolescent Diana Spencer was speaking about was enchanted indeed. Most people, including blasé figures such as presidents, first ladies, and royalty, find staying with the Queen of England one of the most thrilling experiences of their already exciting lives. Sandringham, of course, evoked special memories for Diana, who had been living on the estate until four years previously. But she was no longer seeing the royal way of life from the vantage point of a young neighbour. "That first stay at Sandringham showed Diana just how heady and agreeable life in the royal circle can be," a friend of hers said. "She was impressed. It's fair to say she regarded the experience as even better than she expected."

The Queen was a warm and easygoing hostess. "The Queen is always very relaxed when she's there at Sandringham," Prince George of Denmark said. "She has a wonderful sense of humour and loves a good laugh. Nor is she averse to sophisticated humour. You can talk about anything you want. As long as it's done tastefully, there are no forbidden areas of conversation, which is just as well, for we all know how salty the Duke of Edinburgh and the Duke of York can be."

Although Prince Charles was a member of the house party, there was no question of his having any interest in Diana. He was in the process of courting his cousin Amanda Knatchbull. The daughter of film producer Lord Brabourne and the former Lady Patricia Mountbatten, now Countess Mountbatten of Burma, Amanda was also the granddaughter of Charles's "honorary grandfather" Earl Mountbatten of Burma. "Prince

Charles was hoping she'd marry him. They were inordinately fond of each other. He felt love would grow from the bond of affection between them. And she was perfect for the role. Well bred. Good-looking. Elegant. Sweet. Charming. Bright. Fun. And she knew how to behave," Prince George of Denmark said. "Shortly afterwards, he proposed. She turned him down. She didn't want the royal way of life."

The girl who did want the royal role left Sandringham full of ideas. Although Prince Charles did not have the face of a male model, from the neck downwards, he was very much Diana's type: well-built, athletic body, sexy. As many a woman who has met him can attest to, Charles is a far more appealing specimen of masculinity in person than he appears to be in photographs or on television. He exudes sexuality. "His skin was kissable," Diana once said about him in the early days. Added to his streak of genuine kindness, which had ensured that he paid due attention to Diana and the other houseguests during their stay at Sandringham House, Charles's sexuality triggered off something within her. Or, as Lady Theresa Manners, one of the most desirable women of her (and Diana's) generation, and daughter of Charles, Duke of Rutland and Margaret, Duchess of Argyll's daughter Frances Sweeny, said to me, "I can understand why any girl would fall in love with him. He is the nicest, kindest, most delightful man. He is an artist, a poet, a philosopher, a thinker."

"At Sandringham," Diana told me, "my intuition kept telling me what the future might hold, but I discounted it." So should we. Although everyone who knew Diana concedes that she did possess heightened intuitive powers, and that these increased with the passage of time, these were not as unfailingly accurate as she liked to believe. A case in point is her choice of her favourite photograph. This is the famous image of Diana, clad in an exotic shalwar kameez, tenderly clutching to her bosom a little boy at Imran Khan's Shaukat Khanum Memorial Cancer Hospital in Pakistan, her expression suffused with beatific concentration. "My instinct told me he was about to die. He died the following day," she stated. Only after her death did it emerge that nine-year-old Ashraf Mohamed was still alive.

Intuition or none, what is undoubtedly accurate is that Diana returned from Sandringham to London that January of 1979 to knuckle down to her course as a dance teacher at Madame Vacani's. She had stars in her eyes and the first stirrings of a shift in romantic focus. Although she still believed that she was destined for Prince Andrew, she began wondering whether Charles might not be a better marital prospect. The older brother was not only at an age when his father and the British tabloids were putting pressure upon him to find a wife, but he was also in line for "the top job," as Diana put it. To someone as competitive and as transfixed with royalty as she was, this was no small point, and explains why she said to Simon Berry on that skiing trip a few weeks later, how wonderful it would be "to become a dancer or the Princess of Wales." What she really wanted was to be a star, to have the attention she had always craved but never known how to achieve.

In July 1979, Diana received yet another invitation to stay at yet another royal palace through her well-placed brother-in-law. This time she was destined for Balmoral. "Having her around was a way of keeping the flame alight, of keeping her under the Royal Family's eyes, so that when he (Prince Andrew) was ready for marriage, he'd need look no further than her," Lady Sarah Spencer-Churchill said. "It was a speculative and long-term thing rather than short-term and calculating – the way it sounds when I'm telling it. It was deliberate but not cold-blooded."

Once more, Diana acquitted herself favourably. Ruth, Lady Fermoy, was especially pleased. "She was priming Queen Elizabeth (the Queen Mother), who always had an eye open for a suitable bride for her grandsons. Her Majesty was quite taken with Diana. She thought she was a lovely girl. Warm and kind and sweet and such fun. Ideal, really, especially if you consider that both her grandmothers had been lifelong friends of Queen Elizabeth, and her great aunt (the Dowager Duchess of Abercorn) too. It was almost keeping it all in the family," Lord Charteris said.

It was at this point that Diana's interest in Prince Charles heightened. Although still only attentive in a platonic manner, he was sufficiently friendly to the eighteen-year-old Diana for her to start telling her friends, "He's wonderful."

On the other hand, Diana was the last thing on Charles's mind. He perceived his relationship with Amanda Knatchbull as still being salvageable, and they were planning a trip to India together with Lord Mountbatten. Within weeks of Diana's visit to Scotland, however, Lord Mountbatten was assassinated by IRA terrorists in Ireland. By his own admission, Prince Charles went into free fall. He was devastated. He had adored his honorary grandfather.

Even though Amanda Knatchbull had turned down his proposal of marriage, the great-nephew and granddaughter of the last Viceroy of India huddled together to console each other. For Amanda, the loss was even greater than for Charles. Her paternal grandmother, the Dowager Lady Brabourne, and youngest brother Nichoas had also been killed, and both her parents seriously injured, her mother feared blind. In the event, Lady Brabourne, who now succeeded to her father's title as Countess Mountbatten of Burma, eventually recovered.

As the Prince of Wales lapsed into a deep depression, Diana resumed her active life in London. She had her friends, boyfriends, dinner parties and weekends away with friends. She wanted more, however, and she got her chance when Philip de Pass asked her to the family house near Petworth for a weekend. That Sunday they were going to watch Prince Charles play polo, after which he was coming back for a barbecue. Like all great graspers of opportunity, Diana seized the moment when she saw Charles sitting by himself on a bale of hay. "I went up to him, sat beside him and asked him how he was feeling without Lord Mountbatten," she told me. "I said I hoped he wasn't still too sad. I told him he needed someone to take care of him. He practically jumped on me."

Although Diana was taking poetic licence with Charles's reaction, she had indeed triggered something within him. "I found her enormously sympathetic. Really sweet." He also remembered, from previous occasions, how jolly she could be. To a man whose quest was to find a soulmate with whom he could share a life that had frequently been lonely and isolating, Diana held out great promise. The die, while not yet cast, was about to be.

Five

Jonathan Dimbleby made the point in his biography of the Prince of Wales that Charles has always been prone to self-pity. This is information he must have received from practically everyone he spoke to, for even Charles's staunchest admirers admit that self-pity is one of his greatest weaknesses. Although it is a character trait he shared with Diana, his tendency has seldom been treated with the tolerance displayed towards her, doubtless because the eminence of his position as heir to the throne has always blinded people to the fact that there is a human being, and a sensitive one, lurking beneath the panoply of royalty. The one positive aspect to it is that he has usually been as sympathetic to the plight of others as he has been to his own sufferings.

This has had some strange but positive effects. While still in his twenties, Charles formed The Prince's Trust, a charity geared towards helping the disadvantaged and underprivileged in society. To the horror of the more conservative courtiers, who believed that the monarchy should steer clear of activities which could be interpreted as political, Charles dug his heels in. He established schemes such as Business in the Community, where businesses employed inner-city youths, or the Youth Business Initiative, whereby his trust gave small loans and grants to embryonic entrepreneurs. "People need hope," he said. "I have to help. I can and I will." So successful did this scheme become, that he was subsequently approached by the Labour Government to link up with them in a similar Government scheme.

Even Charles's detractors concede that he is a kind and sensitive man, loyal to his friends and dutiful to a fault. Like all Princes of Wales, he was born into a position which is a peculiar mixture of great privilege and hardship. "His life has been warped by prejudice," Prince George of Denmark said. "All his life he's had people sucking up to him or kicking at him simply because he's the heir to the throne. It's given him a unique perspective. On the one hand, he's spoilt. Used to getting his way. Having things revolve around him so that his wishes are the only wishes—only since he's grown up, though. On the other hand, he's had a hard time all his life. He was mercilessly abused at school by the other boys. The tabloids have trivialised him relentlessly since his marriage, speaking rubbish about how he should get a proper job when the role of Prince of Wales is a full-time job in itself, on a par in terms of demands with being the CEO of a multinational company or a head of government. Even as a little boy, he had no escape."

That last statement is particularly true. As a child, the Duke of Cornwall, as Prince Charles was then known, was perceived as a "wimp," especially by his macho father. "The Duke of Edinburgh used to nag him mercilessly," another royal cousin says. "He was a sweet little boy, far nicer and kinder than Anne. She was abrasive and tough. Prince Philip in skirts really. He made no bones about preferring her. Charles's sensitivity irritated him. He used to say he had to toughen the boy up because he was going to have to be tough to cope with his responsibilities. The poor little boy would literally quiver with fear or humiliation after his father laced into him, often over nothing. It was obvious even then that it was going to affect Prince Charles badly. It has, I fear."

The irony, as this royal cousin states, is that "Charles hero-worshiped his father when he was a little boy. Prince Philip was awe-inspiringly dashing and accomplished. He was startlingly masculine, good at everything he did. He was quite the raconteur, great company and a superb athlete. Prince Charles was always trying to emulate him, and being bawled out for his efforts."

Just as Diana was affected by what she saw as the deprivations wrought by her parents' divorce, so, too, was Charles by this gritty father-son relationship. "On the one hand, he was never comfortable with Prince Philip. On the other hand, he grew into a man whose interests were similar to his father's," their cousin says. Whether on the polo field or in areas such as the environment and farming, the adult Prince of Wales simply pushed the boundaries established by his father, who was a great innovator and is the father of the British ecological movement.

Charles's personality has also been shaped by his father's. They are frighteningly similar in their attitude towards women. Both are dyed-in-the-wool male chauvinists though both like and need the company of women. Unusually for a man of his generation, Philip has many female friends with whom he was not romantically involved, despite the rumours to the contrary. An example is Princess Margaret of Hesse and the Rhine, who was often to be found at Buckingham Palace. Charles also has female friends, such as Patty Palmer-Tompkinson and Emilie van Cutsem, who were never romantic interests.

Both father and son had distant relationships with mothers whom they loved. The Queen was always too busy with affairs of state to spare more than the odd half hour with her two elder children, though she did rectify that omission with the younger ones. When she was with any of the four of them, she was not particularly affectionate. "The Queen is not one for cuddles," a friend of Charles says. "She's spent her whole life fighting against her natural inclination, which is that of a reserved countrywoman who prefers horses to people. Yet the demands of royalty have meant that she's spent her life surrounded by politicians and socialites in urban settings. No wonder she's emotionally detached. She's never been allowed to be herself."

Alienated from his parents, Charles had two sources of love within the family. Queen Elizabeth the Queen Mother "has been a source of infinite joy and unfailing support ever since I can remember," Charles claimed prior to her death. Lord Mountbatten's involvement began later, during Charles's teenage years, after which he, too, became a reliable source of "encouragement and wisdom." Charles could speak to his grandmother and great-uncle in a way he found impossible with either parent. Even there, though, he had to be careful to keep separate his relationships with the dowager queen and the former prince. "Queen Elizabeth the Queen Mother never could stand Dickie Mountbatten. She disliked him personally and was deeply suspicious of everything he stood for," Prince George of Denmark said.. "People think he and Prince Philip were close. They weren't. Prince Philip always gave him a wide berth. He was worried too close an association would cause him problems. The Queen is the one who was close to Uncle Dickie. She was responsible for allowing him a say in everything. They usually met at least once a week and he was included in every family conference, much to Prince Philip's and Queen Elizabeth the Queen Mother's annoyance."

When Lord Mountbatten was assassinated, Charles felt he no longer had a sympathetic older man who could guide him through the vicissitudes that came with being the Prince of Wales, who would give him the affection and support that the older generation of a family gives to the younger. Lord Mountbatten had been his sounding board for everything from his love life to the rigours of royal life, something which this worldly and wealthy Admiral of the Fleet and last Viceroy of India knew only too well, having been born a Prince of Battenberg before his family was stripped of its princely rank during the First World War. Lord Louis Mountbatten, as he then became, had had to fight against prejudice and trivialization to achieve the heights which he did. Like Prince Charles, he had experienced the paradox of privilege and prejudice. He, too, had been isolated, cut off from what, in other circumstances, would have been his peers. Intensely proud, he had never succumbed to self-pity, but to an overweening belief in his abilities, with the result that he was frequently accused of vanity. "He felt he had precious little to be modest about, but whatever there was, should be kept well hidden away. He believed in burnishing the carapace of success," Prince George said. This ploy certainly helped him achieve unprecedented success despite the antagonism his royal blood caused in the Navy and Government. He was "very, very wise," Prince Charles has said, and while his detractors might disagree, his outstanding record speaks for itself.

Diana's much-vaunted instincts served her well when she joined Prince Charles, sitting on his own on that bale of hay at the de Pass barbecue. "I knew the way to reach him was to bring up Lord Mountbatten," she told me. Notwithstanding that eleven months had elapsed since the funeral, Diana raised the subject and ended up by saying he needed someone to take care of him. To a man who has always needed sympathy, and whose women have been called upon to play both vamp and nanny, Diana's words were assured of striking the desired chord.

Diana, of course, also knew that there was another reason why Charles was feeling down at that moment. The month before, his romance with Anna Wallace had come to an abrupt and, from his point of view, unwelcome end. Charles had met this beautiful, blonde daughter of a Scottish landowner while hunting with the Belvoir the previous November. He was immediately smitten. She was fiery, provocative and, like Charles, conventional with a maverick quality. A noted equestrienne, her nickname was Whiplash, not because of what she did with the whip while hunting, but what she did with her tongue while talking. They quickly struck up a passionate romance. "She used to come to the Palace constantly," Sonia Palmer, a female clerk in the Prince of Wales's office at the time, told me. "She knew her way around – his office, his apartments, how to get to them from the side door which everyone uses. She was often there, out of view of the press and public.

"He was deeply in love with her. He proposed to her. She didn't turn him down. They had agreed that she would think about it. It was while she was doing so that they broke up."

The first hint of trouble came at Queen Elizabeth the Queen Mother's eightieth birthday party at Windsor Castle. Mindful of his duties as a prince, Charles mingled with a variety of the guests, leaving Anna to her own devices. At first she was understanding, but as time passed and Charles remained scarce, she became increasingly annoyed. Finally she hunted him down and, prior to walking out, snapped, "Don't ever ignore me like that again. I've never been treated so badly in my life. No one treats me like that. Not even you."

Although Charles and Anna made up after that row, she was growing weary of a man who blew hot and cold. "One day he'd be all over the latest girlfriend like a rash," Sonia Palmer said. "Then she wouldn't hear from him for three days, sometimes even a week. He was totally selfish. It wasn't that he intended to be hurtful. Ever since he was a little boy, life had revolved around him. He'd never had to think of anyone but himself. It wasn't a question of people letting him get away with it. This was the way life had always been for him, and all his other girlfriends had complied with the way things were. But not Anna. She wasn't putting up with any nonsense from anyone, not even the Prince of Wales."

The final straw came at a polo ball at Stowell Park, meat-baron Lord Vestey's Gloucestershire estate. "Charles spent the whole evening dancing with Camilla Parker Bowles. He was also romantically involved with her at that time," a guest who was there, and does not wish to be identified, said. Anna was so furious she borrowed Lady Vestey's car and drove away in a huff. Without further reference to Charles, she married the Hon. Johnny Hesketh, Lord Hesketh's younger brother, three weeks later.

"Prince Charles was distressed by the way his affair with Anna Wallace ended," Sonia Palmer said. "He'd been hoping they'd get married. It's true he was still involved with Camilla, but it's equally true he was looking for a way out. She was nothing more than an *amitié-amoureuse*. A friend he was bonking, to be crude, until an all-encompassing relationship, a marriage, presented itself. His ambition was to find a soulmate whom he could share his life with and be faithful to. He certainly hoped that that girl was Anna Wallace."

The Prince of Wales's relationship with Camilla Parker Bowles deserves examination. He had first met Camilla Shand in 1972 when she was a single girl living at Number 1 Stack House in the Cundy Street Flats in Belgravia, the smartest area in London and one which her Cubbit ancestors had developed in conjunction with the exclusive Grosvenor Estate. Although Camilla was not out of Britain's absolute top drawer, her ancestry was redolent with royal connection, her great-grandmother Alice Keppel having been Charles's great-great-grandfather King Edward VII's mistress. Moreover, she had the perfect personality for someone who was as traditionally maverick as the Prince of Wales. Like him, she cared little about the effect she was creating, preferring to concern herself with her motivation for the deed itself. She was gloriously oblivious to style or fashion in a way that only someone whose parameters were the aristocratic world could be. Like him, she had a goonish sense of humour, finding silly accents and goofy behaviour funny. She was natural and above all loving, and it was this latter quality which would ultimately result in her gaining the ascendancy she did.

Lucia Santa Cruz, Charles's first romantic interest from his Cambridge University days, was the person responsible for bringing her two friends together. "I've found just the girl for you," she said to Charles, and set about making arrangements for the introduction, which quickly resulted in Charles and Camilla having an affair. Charles, however, was too young to contemplate marriage while Camilla, more than a year older than Charles, was ready for it. So while he was on board the HMS *Minerva* fulfilling his naval duty, she accepted the proposal of her other boyfriend, Andrew Parker Bowles.

At first, the Parker Bowles marriage followed the conventional path. It produced a godson for the Prince of Wales in the form of Tom, and a daughter, Laura. By the late seventies, Andrew and Camilla Parker Bowles had an "open" marriage. The Catholic Andrew was deeply involved with Nicholas Soames's sister Charlotte Hambro (now Countess Peel), while

Camilla returned to the Prince of Wales for the second stage of their relationship. They did not yet have the overwhelming love they would eventually grow to possess for one another. The affair, as their friend has stated, was still more a friendship with sexual overtones than the great passion it was to become. Both Charles and Camilla accepted it for what it was, and knew it would end as soon as he found the girl who would become the Princess of Wales. "Uncle David's example was held up as a fate worse than death," Michael Thornton, author of an acclaimed book about the Queen Mother and the Duchess of Windsor, said. Charles was therefore strongly motivated to accept the status quo, and the inevitable price it demanded. Both he and Camilla made sure that they never allowed their feelings to cloud their judgement, with the result that they accepted the fact that there was no point in being carried away with a relationship that had to end when Charles found a wife.

Once Anna Wallace was out of the picture, Diana sensed that her chance had come. As she took that chance, Camilla gradually adjusted to the change she would have to make from friendly lover to loving friend.

"It's important to speak to people on their level," was one of Diana's guiding mottoes. "Choose a topic that interests them." With this in mind, and knowing that Charles shared her grandmother Ruth Fermoy's love of music, Diana raised the subject and let him know how much she loved classical music, too.

Charles took the bait. He was due to attend Verdi's Requiem at the Royal Albert Hall with Lady Fermoy. "He liked Diana. She was fun and easygoing," a friend of his told me. "It was the most natural thing in the world to ask her along. He still wasn't interested in her in a romantic way. That came later, after she seduced him. You must convey what an intensely seductive personality she was."

Stephen Barry, Charles's valet at the time, was one of the many people on the scene who confirmed this account of how the romance developed. He said, "Diana pursued him with single-minded determination." Kinty Wake-Walker, Diana's cousin and a fellow teacher from the Young England Kindergarten, also provided corroboration. In the early days of the Waleses' marriage, when people close to Diana still spoke without the reserve they now employ, she stated, "Diana made the running. She used to come to school and admit it. Of course she was in love, and just set out to get her man." In a roundabout way, Diana herself verified this account.

Although she claimed that Charles "jumped on" her at the de Pass house, she also admitted to me, "I was completely besotted with him. I gave him all the right signals. I made it very easy for him. I was very, very accommodating. I suppose it's fair to say things would never have taken off the way they did if I hadn't been so accommodating." In other words, she did seduce him, chasing him subtly until he caught her.

By now Diana, who had a vast romantic streak in her nature, was head over heels in love with Prince Charles. To Diana, the sportif Charles exuded sex appeal, or, as she herself told me, she liked men "hunky and chunky". She, however, needed help to further her cause, for Charles, who was dilatory at the best of times, still had no personal interest in her. Once more she turned to her sister Jane and brother-in-law Robert Fellowes, whose position in the Royal Household proved to be as useful as it had been in the past. "Jane had recently had a baby," Lord Charteris said. "What could be more natural than to have your sister come up to Balmoral to stay while you're in residence with the Court?"

In July 1980, Diana packed her bags and headed north of the border to Scotland. To her credit, Diana seized her opportunity with a brilliance that bedazzled those who saw her in operation. "She had wonderful instincts," Lord Charteris said. "She played the prince perfectly. She kept herself in his line of vision as much as possible. Always looking pretty and being decorous. Always being jolly. She was canny by nature and understood that few men can resist a pretty girl who openly adores them, especially one who has a ready laugh and a witty retort. Everyone in the house party could see for themselves what was going on. She made herself utterly available and sent out very clear messages of worship. The Prince was flattered and enchanted. He's always been drawn to vulnerability. But he didn't take her seriously. To him, she was just an adolescent, even if she made him realize that she was a charming and attractive one."

Nevertheless, Diana went for broke in garnering praise from all onlookers. A friend who was there told Lady Edith Foxwell, "She had a genius for knowing just what to say or do at any given moment to make people form the opinion of her she wished them to have. Even though she was only nineteen, she was a past mistress at the art. It was a gift she must have been born with. It's fair to say she captivated everyone with her natural grace, her sense of humour, her sheer easiness on the ear and eye. She was a pure delight to be with."

Although the big romance had not yet begun, Diana had now sufficiently incorporated herself into the royal scene to receive further invitations. Charles still viewed Diana as the sweet baby sister of his former fling Sarah Spencer, and Diana's next foray with Prince Charles was as a family friend. She joined the *Britannia* for a weekend during Cowes Week with Princess Margaret's daughter, Lady Sarah Armstrong-Jones, whom she had known since childhood. Prince Philip, who presided over the Cowes Regatta each year, was the official host for what was Britain's premier sailing event and a fixture on the social calendar. Surrounded by some of the grandest sailing vessels and richest people in the world, Diana suddenly saw her old circle of friends as adolescent, unexciting, parochial by comparison. "I was mesmerized," she later said. "They were much older than me, far more glamorous." Although Diana did not yet realize it, this was the first step on a road which would ultimately lead to ruin. The end result was that she cut herself off from her friends and became isolated at the precise moment she needed them the most.

That wrong turn was still in the future, however, as Diana did everything in her power to capture the Prince of Wales's notice while she was a guest on the *Britannia*. Whatever he did, she did, too. When he went windsurfing, she took to the water and skied. When he swam, she showed off the swimming and diving skills that had gained her such recognition at school. She was a witty and easygoing companion, doing her best to fit in with the circle which included various German royal relations.

That July of 1980, the Prince of Wales bought, through the Duchy of Cornwall, Highgrove House from Viscount Macmillan of Ovenden. It was situated in the heart of hunting country, at Tetbury near Gloucestershire. Over the years two myths have arisen. The first is that Charles took Diana to view the house before he purchased it. This is not so, as Katharine, Viscountess Macmillan of Ovenden, told me. "He came and saw it one day and literally bought it on the next. He was not engaged or married then and Lady Diana Spencer did not come with him." He paid £800,000 for the Georgian house, set in 340 acres, with four main reception rooms, nine bedrooms and six bathrooms.

The second myth is one which Diana herself helped to propagate once the marriage turned sour and she wanted out of it. This is that Charles bought Highgrove largely because of its proximity to Bolehyde Manor in Wiltshire, where Camilla Parker Bowles then lived. "While it is true that the Prince of Wales had every intention of continuing his affair with Camilla until he found a suitable girl to marry, it is untrue that he proposed continuing a sexual relationship with her once he was married," Lady Sarah Spencer-Churchill said.. "Highgrove isn't even that near to Bolehyde Manor. People ought to remember that Wiltshire and Gloucestershire are neighbouring counties. He would surely have chosen somewhere nearer than a thirty- or forty-minute drive if he wanted easy access to Camilla. No. He chose Highgrove for several reasons, all to do with the property itself. He's an avid gardener and felt its garden had potential. It's small enough to be a cozy home and large enough to have guests and privacy. And it's centrally located. It's accessible to Heathrow Airport, Windsor, London, and the North of England, which are important for someone who travels as much as the Prince of Wales. There's hardly any point in having a home if you can't reach it easily. Yes, it also has the advantage of being in the heart of hunting country, which was important to an avid hunter like him, and was near to Cirencester Polo Ground. He wanted to base himself there, which he does to this day. It was an inspired choice from a convenience point of view."

There is no doubt that at this period of his life Prince Charles was thinking of settling down, not only in terms of having a home of his own, but a wife as well. In the previous year he had proposed to two different women: his cousin Amanda Knatchbull and Anna Wallace. Although he still did not think of Lady Diana Spencer as a prospective bride, he was closer to the transition than he realized.

The decisive moment came a few weeks after Diana's stay on *Britannia*, when she made her second Balmoral trip of the summer. She stayed at Birkhall, the Queen Mother's house on the Balmoral estate, with her grandmother Ruth, Lady Fermoy, who was "in waiting" upon her old friend.

"Diana hadn't been at Birkhall for more than a few days before everyone at Balmoral was saying how lovely she was," Lady Sarah Spencer-Churchill said. "It was a short hop from that to how suitable she was, and how wonderful it would be if the Prince of Wales married someone like her." Once more, Diana's humour, jollity and easygoing manner were winning her admirers.

Diana's objective, however, was to win Charles's heart. This she now did to perfection. "She was abject in her unspoken supplication to him," someone, who was there and does not wish to be identified, said. "You could tell by the way she looked at him, how she spoke to him, how she followed him around, how she laughed that little bit too much and in general behaved towards him. She did not behave badly. Far from it. She was very careful how she trod." Diana agreed. "I picked my way gingerly," she told me. "I couldn't afford to make mistakes. I had to be so careful. I knew from Sarah's example, I couldn't put a foot wrong. I didn't either. I was agreeable as could be. Even said I loved Balmoral and couldn't think of anywhere I adored more," at which point she burst into mischievous laughter, her aversion to Balmoral being well known to both of us.

Diana employed just the right tactics to ensure that Charles would collapse into her arms. An avid countryman who loved Balmoral more than anywhere else on earth, Charles was not one of those men who liked challenges. He liked women who complemented him. Diana made sure she synchronized her tastes and interests to fit in with his. Once the wedding ring was on her finger, of course, Charles would discover that she had no great love of the country or of country pursuits. The one ambition she had realized so far at that point in time was to leave behind the rural way of life both her parents pursued, to live in London. She was a true metropolitan. She certainly had no intention of being "buried in the country," as she put it, for more than a few days at a time.

According to Prince George of Denmark, "What he found appealing about Diana was how harmonious they were together. She was very *sympathique*. He loves fishing. When they were at Balmoral together, she was happy to spend hours by the riverbank with him in companionable, undemanding silence. He has a real need to be in touch with the elements, with nature, and he seemed to think she felt the same way. Of course, we now know differently. Diana's idea of a nightmare was to be torn away from London for more than a day. But, like many women who are trying to hook a man, she was careful to keep her distaste for his interests to herself."

Having fattened the bull for slaughter, Diana sat back and waited for nature to issue the *coup de grâce*. It did. "Things changed at Balmoral," Diana said. "I fancied him something rotten." By this time Diana had awakened his ardour as well, being a pretty and seductive girl who knew just how to egg a man on with a combination of old-fashioned reserve and modern pluckiness. As Sonia Palmer, a former member of the Prince of Wales's staff, said, "The first time he kissed her, she had him where she wanted him. He's intensely sexual, as the Camillagate tapes make plain. Once she'd whetted his appetite, the power shifted from him to her. Thereafter, all she had to do was sit back and make no mistakes, and he was hers for the taking."

This second Balmoral visit was decisive in other ways. "The old story of the two grandmothers conspiring to ensure that their grandchildren married is absolutely true. Queen Elizabeth the Queen Mother went hell for leather to promote the match," Lord Charteris said. "Diana reminded her of herself when she was young. She thought Diana's sweetness and modesty and willingness to fit in made her an ideal personality for the role of Princess of Wales. Ruth Fermoy also encouraged the match. She may well have had reservations about Diana's suitability for the role of royal princess, and may well have expressed them to Diana, but she most definitely gave no hint of any reservations to anyone else. On the contrary, she talked Diana up and took great pride in the fact that her granddaughter might achieve such eminence."

The same former courtier recounted the complaints the Prince of Wales later made about the role Diana's family played in their betrothal: "The Prince found it hard to believe that any family would stand by silently and allow a girl who was so obviously unsuited to the pressure of royal life to marry into the Royal Family. You must remember, her family knew the intense personal demands royal status makes on the individuals concerned. He felt they hadn't been fair to Diana, to himself and to the monarchy. He made it clear to me and to many other friends that he'd never have married her if her family had made him aware of how emotionally fragile she was." At the time of the divorce, Charles went further and said, "They willfully withheld the facts from us."

Charles's comments have the ring of truth. When he proposed to Amanda Knatchbull and to Diana, by her own admission, he qualified his proposal with the rider that he would understand if she said no. "I know how hellish the public and official side of being the Princess of Wales will be. The loss of freedom. Of privacy. All the commitments and demands. Can you bear to take on the task?" Diana herself said he told her.

In the light of all that subsequently happened, it is doubtful whether either Diana or her family fully appreciated how fragile a personality she was, or how detrimental the pressures of royal life would prove to be to her health.

Whatever interpretation an onlooker puts upon Diana's family's behaviour in the run-up to the marriage, one factor nevertheless keeps on emerging. "Ambition, ambition, ambition. The family was ambitious, without a doubt," Ruth Fermoy's old friend Brodrick Haldane succinctly put it. "Who can blame them? Forevermore, they are linked to the Royal Family because of that marriage and the two little princes it has produced."

The ambitions of the Spencer family were the furthest thing from Charles's mind as the protagonists themselves now embarked upon a passionate affair which moved quickly to the denouement the family and Diana wanted. "Within weeks he was asking if we thought he ought to marry her," Charles Palmer-Tompkinson said. "We were all horror-stricken. They barely knew each other. It was obvious they had nothing in common. And I was not alone in thinking that, though Diana genuinely thought she was in love with the Prince of Wales, she was more in love with the idea and glamour of the whole thing than with the man himself."

The Prince of Wales's authorized biography by Jonathan Dimbleby confirms that other friends of Charles shared this opinion. Lady Romsey and Sir Winston Churchill's grandson the Hon. Nicholas Soames both risked his wrath by opining that he was making a mistake by considering marriage at this early stage. "Penny Romsey believed that Diana seemed to be trying out for the starring role of Princess of Wales rather than having the deep understanding of Charles that would make a marriage sustainable," Charles's friend said. "Nicholas Soames simply felt they had absolutely nothing in common and that any future marriage was doomed to failure, and would most likely end disastrously, too. He was a distant cousin of Diana, so you can be sure he was basing his assessment on facts he knew about the Spencer family that he might not even have been conscious of."

Charles, however, did not share his friends' reservations and Diana did not know about them. As far as she was concerned, the romance was proceeding just the way she wanted it to. "He took me to see Highgrove that October of 1980. He asked me to help him do it up. It was a gesture of commitment. I never saw any swatch books until after we were married," she recounted, laughing yet again at her knowing observation, for even at nineteen, Diana was perspicacious and canny, and these were character traits she never lost, her erroneous reputation for lack of intelligence notwithstanding.

Thereafter, the lovers were together frequently. They often had dinner together at Buckingham Palace, or Stephen Barry drove Diana to Highgrove House, which was still unfurnished but where she and the Prince would be served dinner by a footman before decamping to the bedroom. Diana invariably left early in the morning for the trek back to Coleherne Court if she was leaving from Buckingham Palace, or just before dawn if she was leaving from Highgrove. "Obviously, they did what all red-blooded people with the hots for each other do," Stephen Barry used to say. It irritated him whenever people suggested, in the holier-than-thou way they used to adopt with royalty, that Charles and Diana did not become intimate until after their marriage. "As the valet, he was in a position to know," Sonia Palmer said. "He used to say Diana always left with a glow and her hair freshly brushed. Why did she need to brush her hair if they were discoursing on philosophy?"

The Prince of Wales had always included his girlfriends in his life, and Diana was no exception. He had intimate dinner parties at Buckingham Palace with guests who included his closest friends, such as Charles and Patti Palmer-Tompkinson, Andrew and Camilla Parker Bowles, and Nicholas Soames. He took her to stay with his cousin Norton Romsey and his wife, Penny, at Broadlands, Lord Mountbatten's house in Hampshire, and to Bolehyde Manor, where they were guests of the Parker Bowleses for two successive weekends.

"Prince Charles did love her," Charles Palmer-Tompkinson said. "Some of us did have reservations about her, but he didn't. He believed they were extraordinarily compatible. She was so soft and sweet and easygoing. Always such good fun. So jolly. I know the word 'jolly' crops up a lot, but it really is the best description of her during that period. In his opinion, she was as near perfect as it was possible to be. They got along like a house on fire. They were passionate about each other. They shared the same zany sense of humour. They had similar temperaments. They loved country life. And she was from the sort of background he was from. An earl's daughter with links to the Court, who'd been raised on the Sandringham Estate. Impeccable manners. Got along with everyone she met. He felt if he'd set out to invent her he couldn't have come up with anyone better."

The only problem was, Charles was smitten by a mirage. The oasis was infinitely more complex, and, while beautiful in its own way, was so different as to be unrecognizable.

Six

On 8 September 1980, an event took place which altered Lady Diana Spencer's life for all time. Harry Arnold broke the news of her affair with the Prince of Wales in Britain's leading tabloid, the *Sun*. From that date until her death seventeen years less one week later, Diana became the most photographed and written-about person in the world. The effect the tabloids had upon her life thereafter cannot be minimized.

Diana's relationship with the media began well enough. "The publicity made the romance more serious than it might otherwise have been," Prince George of Denmark told me. "He is a very decent and responsible person. The last thing in the world he'd do was romance a nice girl, then dump her."

Diana herself understood this. "It was pretty daunting. Waking up every morning to find all those cameras waiting for you." But Diana was shrewd. "I had to court them. Make them like me. Make them my friends. I may have been only nineteen but I wasn't stupid. I knew from Sarah's mistake what to avoid. I used to go out armed with a smile, say good morning, sympathize with them if the weather was awful and laugh with them if it wasn't. I wasn't pally. Just myself."

This personality captivated the seasoned warriors of Fleet Street. They were smitten by this demure teenaged daughter of an earl. They misguidedly believed she had no need of publicity and therefore her manner revealed the sort of person she was. In this, of course, they were both right and wrong. While Diana was a nice person, she told me, "I understood that the publicity was putting pressure on Prince Charles as well," for Diana, by her own account, was "madly in love with Charles," something she told not only me but many other people, including Lady Theresa Manners.

To fully appreciate how Diana came to seduce a whole team of experienced journalists and photographers, one must remember that few institutions in Britain are more riven with class prejudice and misconceptions than the tabloids. Although they daily write about aristocrats, royals and celebrities, they do so from a great distance. The journalists are usually stationed behind crush barriers for movie premières or balls. While their quarry is inside, they are cooling their heels outside, waiting until the celebrity comes out, at which time they snatch a shot as he or she is between the door and the car. On the odd occasion they are granted access into the houses or functions of the people they are writing about, the subjects of their interest have their guard up; they therefore see only the façade, not the person behind it. Nor do they ever gain true access to the world of these people. They might be able to bribe the occasional servant for snippets of information, but even then they gain merely a glimpse into a way of life. The true concerns and considerations which motivate such people are forever lost to them, for you cannot write with profundity about a world you have never known.

Most tabloid journalists fill these lacunae with misconceptions which they feed to the public with all the authority of the truly knowledgeable. In the process, they shore up prejudices which frequently work against the public figure, but which they hope will appeal to their readers. Hence the distaste which most public figures have for tabloid journalists.

Only occasionally do such gaps in journalists' knowledge work in favour of a public figure. One such occasion was when the journalists doorstepping Lady Diana Spencer assumed that no earl's daughter nineteen years of age would stoop to courting them. Aware as they were that the unwritten rule in royal circles in those days was that no one should cultivate the press, they concluded that Diana's demure friendliness was an insight into her character, not into her *modus operandi*. In that, they misjudged her greatly. Although she always had, and always would retain, a demure dimension, it was a superficial aspect of her personality, not a fundamental indication of her character. Her step-grandmother-in-law, Barbara Cartland, put it perfectly when she said, "Diana had a distinct personality and was not a person, whether she spoke or not, whom one could ignore." Diana herself said, "I don't know where the press got Shy

Di from. I've never been shy." Her own father confirmed the steel lurking beneath the surface when he said, "Diana always gets what Diana wants."

Faced for the first time in her life with the need to cobble together a public image which enhanced her marriageability, Diana showed how remarkably canny she was despite her youthfulness. Her friend Simon Berry asserted that Diana was "an ordinary, terribly nice, unexciting girl who was clever enough to treat the press very well." Issy van Randwyck said, "Even at school, she was very deliberate about how she behaved. What the press mistook for shyness was simply Diana being clever enough to hold her counsel and hide behind a modest demeanour until she was sure how to play things. She always had that tentative quality, the nous to test the water before jumping into the pool, to hold back. She had the willpower of ten devils."

Within weeks of Diana's bursting upon the world stage, the tabloids had christened her Shy Di. Dame Barbara Cartland took issue with that description at a Sunday luncheon once when I was a guest at her Potters Bar home. Diana, she proclaimed, was "not shy. The press thought she was because she tends to look down and hunch over, but she does that because she's so tall. It's nothing to do with shyness." Her old flatmate Sophie Kimball also agreed, "Diana wasn't a scrap shy."

Throughout September and October 1980, as the myth of Shy Di was taking hold all over the world, the determined woman who lay beneath that benign exterior was plotting and scheming how to hook the man she loved. Even with her hairdresser's assistant Vikki she carefully kept his identity secret ("I only discovered it when the engagement was announced," Vikki said). Incredibly, she had managed to convince Vikki that the man about whom she was sharing confidences bore no relationship to the Prince, with whom she was daily linked in the papers. This says as much about Diana's discretion and ability to maintain her privacy even in the midst of worldwide publicity as it does about Vikki's susceptibility to the Princess-to-be's innate charm and plausibility. Diana, of course, already understood how helpful the tabloids could be in exerting pressure upon Charles. Within weeks, she had formulated a straightforward plan of action, one from which she would deviate only occasionally in the years to come. She was charming to all, formed friendly relations with a few, and singled out one for her special attention. The object of her choice, on this occasion, was James Whitaker, then the

Daily Star's royal correspondent. Public-school educated as Whitaker was, the ever-upmarket Diana felt she therefore had more in common with him than the others. On that basis, they formed a relationship which seems, from his point of view, to have been partly opportunistic and partly sincere, and from hers, wholly opportunistic. In years to come, she was particularly scathing about him, "with all the venom of an old friend," to quote Oscar Wilde.

Whatever the sincerity of Whitaker's and Diana's motives, this relationship proved crucial in her endeavour to become Princess of Wales. Whitaker became her most ardent advocate, fulfilling a role that she later sought from me and obtained from Andrew Morton and Richard Kay. On a daily basis, the Fat Red Tomato, as Diana nicknamed Whitaker, wrote reams of praise about her suitability, demeanour, beauty, deportment. Within a matter of weeks Diana was not only on the way to superstardom, but also to revirginization, for the tabloids took to asserting that she had "no past." This, of course, was preposterous nonsense, but the press corps doorstepping her believed, with all of the conviction of the ignorant, that a requirement for becoming the Princess of Wales was that the girl be a virgin. This, of course, could not have been further from the truth. For instance, Anna Wallace had certainly had boyfriends before Charles, but this had not stopped him proposing. The tabloid reporters, nevertheless, were not about to let a little thing like a few former boyfriends ruin a good story. And, though no one could blame Diana for doing everything within her power to achieve her objective and win the man she loved, the future Princess of Wales was right there with them, feeding them the pap that would create the fiction of purity.

Tabloid journalists, as a rule, run in packs and perform accordingly. Where one goes, all the others follow. They seldom, if ever, deviate from this principle, and did not do so where Lady Diana Spencer was concerned. The result was that where James Whitaker led, the others followed. The myth of Shy Di was embellished to make her the most suitable bride for the Prince of Wales: a girl whose charm, graciousness, purity and beauty would prove to be national assets. To the extent that Diana did have some though not all of those qualities, it was a reasonable representation, but it was only a part of the picture, though those journalists did not yet know it.

Ever watchful for signs of the announcement which the tabloids had now decided the Prince of Wales must be encouraged to make, the journalists surrounding Diana were in a frenzy of excitement when she attended Princess Margaret's party at Claridge's in November. That surely was a good sign, as indeed it was.

Behind the scenes, however, the Prince of Wales was proving to be as much a ditherer as he had always been. Although he had recently proposed to two other women in the form of Anna Wallace and Amanda Knatchbull, "He didn't want to get married," Diana told me, and she bitterly complained to Lady Bowker about his reluctance to propose; she said, "Diana herself told me that she had difficulty getting Prince Charles to propose to her". Charles confirmed this to the King of Spain, who told a cousin, "He doesn't want to marry. He feels under tremendous pressure." As well he ought to. The press were not the only source propelling him up to the altar. Prince Philip "made it clear to him that he couldn't dally with a nice girl from a good family like Diana. She had wound the Duke of Edinburgh, who's always been partial to the charms of a pretty girl, round her finger totally," a friend of Charles said.

That November, the Prince of Wales was due to take off for an official tour of India. "Diana was agitated. She was looking for a commitment and none had been forthcoming so far, despite Prince Charles's speaking about the possibility of marrying her to various friends," Lady Sarah Spencer-Churchill said. Luck, however, was on Diana's side. The *Sunday Mirror* published a front-page story stating that Diana had snuck onto the royal train, while it was parked in sidings in Wiltshire, on the evenings of 5 and 6 November for romantic assignations with Charles.

An unholy row erupted. Diana confided in her new best friend, James Whitaker, that she had never been anywhere near the royal train. He published her denials in the *Daily Star*. The rest of the tabloids followed suit, taking the line that there would not have been anything wrong with two red-blooded young people being together in the event that the story was true.

The Spencer family, however, were not about to sit idly by and let the tabloids jeopardize two and a half centuries of hope for a legitimate royal connection. They knew only too well that Diana's position might be undermined if she were seen to have been sleeping with the Prince of Wales prior to marriage. "They had to protect her desirability, her marriageability," Lady Sarah Spencer-Churchill said. The old aristocratic dictum "It matters not what you do, but what you are seen to be doing" was as much in force as ever. They intended to err on the side of caution. They therefore made their outrage known in no uncertain manner, especially within royal circles, where their influence carried the most clout. The result was that the Queen, who had known Diana since she was a child, took the side of her Assistant Private Secretary's sister-in-law – and her mother's Lady-in-Waiting's granddaughter – and demanded an apology from Bob Edwards, the editor of the newspaper. So convinced was he of the accuracy of the story that he declined to print an apology or a retraction. Later, once Camilla Parker Bowles's relationship with Prince Charles became public, she was alleged to be the sandy-haired woman in question. Quite how anyone could have confused Diana with Camilla is a mystery, since Diana's hair was not yet the same colour as Camilla's. But the upshot of this little drama was that Diana's stock in Fleet Street rose even further. If the Queen had come out batting for her, she had to be taken seriously.

Charles's departure for India left Diana in a real quandary. She knew he was considering marrying her, but she also knew that he was fighting shy of a commitment. Every day she had to run the gauntlet of the press corps packed outside her front door. Later, she would say how arduous it was, forgetting that she had also found it useful, and had indeed forged relationships with several of the journalists that could well have been called friendships, but for the gap in rank and background. To the last man and woman, the press corps wished her well. They wanted her to marry Prince Charles, and made no secret of it, either to her or to each other. Whenever she made mistakes – and she did – they suppressed them, telling her, "You can't say that, Lady Diana," or "Let me ask that question again, Lady Diana; I didn't hear that answer." There was a tremendous degree of complicity, and while it is understandable how Diana came to forget it, the fact is, the journalists and photographers deserve recognition for the kindness, decency and consideration with which they showered her.

This is especially true of Roger Taverner, the respected journalist who represented the Press Association News Agency, and whose career Diana and her family came close to damaging. What ended up as a mêlée began as a harmless enough attempt to further her cause. On 28 November, Diana in pensive mood admitted to Roger Taverner, "I'd like to marry soon. What woman doesn't want to marry eventually? Next year? Why not? I don't think nineteen is too young. It depends on the person." When asked if Charles had proposed, Diana blushed and giggled before replying, with all the canniness characteristic of her, "I can't say yes or no to that. I can't confirm or deny it."

After Roger Taverner filed his story and it was published by the papers, the most tremendous row broke out at the instigation of Diana's family. They appreciated, in a way few of the journalists did, how ruinous the story was. Diana had done a Sarah. "She had broken the cardinal rule of speaking to the press about her private life. She had revealed her wishes and hopes. She was exerting pressure on the Prince of Wales in a none-too-subtle attempt to force his hand into proposing. It was an unmitigated disaster. Something had to be done, and done quickly," Lady Sarah Spencer-Churchill said.

In ordinary circumstances, Ruth, Lady Fermoy, and Robert Fellowes would have been the most appropriate members of Diana's family to hop to her defence, due to their influential positions within the Royal Household. But it was those very positions, taken in conjunction with the story involving a member of the Royal Family, which precluded them from playing any part in salvaging Diana's romance. That left other close relations. Earl Spencer, who slurred his words as a result of the stroke from which he had only partially recovered, would not have been taken seriously, his impediment running the risk of being confused with drunkenness. That left only Diana's feisty and highly charged mother, who wrote an indignant letter of denial to *The Times*, protesting Diana's innocence, excoriating the innocent journalist, and managing in the process to reaffirm how suitable Diana was for the role of royal bride. The possibility that a reputable professional who had been acting in good faith, might have his career destroyed or at the very least tarnished by the questions now raised about his credibility, seems not to have occurred to any of Diana's family.

Mrs Shand Kydd's course of action was another first that would be repeated in the future. Diana and her family were getting their act together in a way that would make her the most effective media personality of all time. Diana, too, now began to lay the ground for what *The Times* would call "her manipulative approach to all publicity" (Saturday, 27 December 1997). She therefore hid behind her mother, who was not present for the interview with Taverner and therefore did not really know what had taken place. The ploy had the desired effect. The Royal Family, who know, as all public figures do from bitter experience, the tendency of the tabloids to invent quotes, were happy to accept as fact Diana's disclaimer, made more vociferously in private than in public, where she was careful to let her mother do the talking in case the tactic boomeranged.

What the royals did not seem to appreciate was that Roger Taverner was not a tabloid journalist, but a bureau member of the Press Association News Agency. It was rather like accepting that ducks are swans simply because both swim in ponds. Later, they would have cause to regret not having heeded the warning sign this first media débâcle created, but it let Diana off the hook, not only with them, but with the press as well. Because the attack had come from her mother, the press corps, who were still in favour of the marriage, continued to cover up her errors and enlarge upon her virtues. To the last man and woman, they were willing Lady Diana Spencer to become the Princess of Wales.

Charles, meanwhile, was fighting a battle with himself. On the one hand, he was convinced that he and Diana would have a harmonious marriage, and that he would be able to love her even more fully given time. On the other hand, he would have preferred, if he did not have a duty to the nation and the institution of the monarchy, to remain single.

To Charles, the issue was not merely the loss of his freedom, bearing in mind his belief that he would never be able to divorce, but also the fact that he could not make a mistake. "I have to get it right. If I don't, it will be a disaster," he often said, with a prescience that time would illustrate. Privately and publicly, Charles averred that, as his marriage would have to last a lifetime, he would prefer to base it upon more profound values than being in love. He wanted a wife who would be a companion for him privately. Someone who was a suitable consort. Someone who would not mind too much the sacrifices and official demands placed upon a Princess of Wales. A woman whom he could start out loving, and through shared values and a harmonious existence, end up loving even more. In other words, he was being old-fashioned and careful, as well as sensible and mature.

Diana had no such reservations. "I worshiped him," she told me, and I have no reason to doubt that she did. Everyone who saw them together agreed that she was totally in love. Even if some of those witnesses believed she was more in love with the position than the man, she would have been annihilated if she had not married him, for the heart does not understand the difference between pure and mixed motives, and it breaks just the same in either instance.

To Diana's horror, Charles's actions at the end of his Indian visit led her to wonder whether she would ever win the prize of matrimony. While he was away, "he didn't phone me once. Not once," she told me. Worse, instead of flying straight back to her, as she expected a man in love to do, he embarked upon a three-day trek in the Himalayas. Then, when he returned to London, he did not telephone her. "He was very undecided about what to do," Sonia Palmer said. "He was in a difficult position. Sure, he liked her a lot and recognized how suitable she was in many respects. But he wasn't sure that what there was between them could ever develop into something that justified a radical and irreversible commitment. You must remember, the more he saw of her, the more difficult it became for him to extricate himself if he concluded that this relationship wasn't right. On the other hand, he's always put duty above everything else. He's always been very concerned about what people think, of fulfilling their expectations, doing the right thing, that sort of thing. He knew what practically everyone wanted of him. He could see both sides of the question, which made it awkward for him. He really didn't know what to do. He wanted to be fair to everybody – possibly too much so."

The press, who were now laying on Diana's love of children with a trowel to further enhance her suitability as Charles's bride, played a crucial role in overcoming his hurdle of indecisiveness. According to Prince George of Denmark, "If it hadn't been for the press, the Prince of Wales would never have married Diana. They turned a perfectly ordinary, though attractive, girl, with a pleasing but quite unexceptional personality, into a media superstar. To give her her due, she rose to the occasion magnificently. But it was the press which glamorized her. They presented her as an object of great desire. They have a penchant for hyperbole, and they couldn't resist portraying her as being more desirable than she was. This, in turn, only made her more desirable. The image wasn't her creation. It was the press's. And it's what finally hooked the Prince of Wales."

Keen to please the nation and his parents, Charles finally decided to telephone Diana some time after his return from India and his trek in the Himalayas. "I was spitting with anger," Diana said. "I knew he'd call. So I took the receiver off the hook. And left it off for days. I did it to teach him a lesson. Let him chase me a little." In that, as in so much else, Diana's instincts served her superbly. Her ploy rattled Charles. Faced with the prospect of being eluded by Diana, whom the world was now saying was perfect for him, he became more eager.

By Christmas, the romance was going from strength to strength. Meanwhile, Diana and the whole Royal Family were under siege from the press. Although Charles had edged closer towards making up his mind, he was still vacillating. "Prince Philip made him know in no uncertain terms that the press speculation couldn't drag on much longer," Prince George of Denmark said. "It was torture for all concerned." Right after Christmas, the Court moved to Sandringham. Even the normally equitable Queen got in on the act. She seconded the Duke of Edinburgh on the question of the Prince of Wales making up his mind at the earliest opportunity. But she did not pressurise him to stay in or get out of the relationship. She had strong reservations about Diana. She felt she didn't have the right sort of character for the job. She was concerned that Diana had never stuck to anything she had undertaken. She also felt that they did not have anything in common, that once the thrill of their newfound passion wore off, they would have a problem. Not even she envisaged how big a problem it would become, but she was the only person who spotted the weakness."

The Queen, however, was the sort of mother who did not interfere with her children's freedom. Having had her say, she did not press her case.

Another person close to Charles who was now opposed to the match was his Private Secretary. The Hon. Edward Adeane "didn't think about liking or not liking her," Sonia Palmer said. "He thought about suitability. She was too young. She'd never finished anything in her life. She wouldn't be a stayer."

Diana, who had spent Christmas with her family, now joined the Royal Family at Sandringham. "I felt at home. I went for walks to Park House. Did that bring back memories," she told me. Diana sensed that she only had to play a waiting game before Charles, who was due to go to Klosters at the end of January, popped the question. But she was intensely nervous, as she made clear to Lady Bowker. To prod Charles into action, as soon as she left Sandringham she arranged a holiday with her mother and stepfather at his ranch in Australia. She was going to get Charles to propose the way Raine Dartmouth had done with her father, by following her stepbrother William's advice of disappearing from view.

As events would prove, however, Diana did not need to resort to such tactics. Charles returned from Klosters and told her that he had something he wished to speak to her about. "I knew what he wanted to ask before he did," she told me. Over a romantic dinner at Windsor Castle he popped the question. As her mother had done when Johnnie Althorp had proposed, she accepted before he could even get the words out of his mouth. Charles, however, advised her to think things over while she was in Australia. He explained to her how horrendous some of the pressures and the loss of her liberty through royal life would be, and suggested that she give her acceptance careful thought. It was not going to be an easy life. He did not want her to believe it was. Diana brushed his warnings aside. She had achieved her objective. She was going to be the Princess of Wales. She loved her man and he loved her. Nothing could spoil their happiness. Or so she thought.

The announcement for Diana and Charles's engagement was set for 24 February 1981. Before it could be made, Diana discovered that *Private Eye*, the satirical magazine which frequently runs stories about establishment figures that the national and more respectable publications deem too risky to cover, was ferreting around trying to get some dirt on her past boyfriends. "Rory Scott and George Plumptre's names kept on coming up," a *Private Eye* contributor told me. "There was no threat that they'd talk. They're too well-bred. But who could tell which airhead friend might bleat?"

Once more, Diana went to her perspicacious family and they came to the rescue. They decided to stare down the threat by going on the offensive – yet another tactic Diana and her family would employ with the media, and through it with her adversaries, in the years to come. Her maternal uncle Edmund, Lord Fermoy, therefore gave James Whitaker an interview, in which he asserted that Diana was a virgin, that she had never had a lover, that she was pure and unsullied by human hands. It was an extraordinary thing to say, even in 1981, for which uncle – especially one who saw a niece as infrequently as Lord Fermoy saw Diana – could speak with any authority about a young lady who had been living on her own for nearly three years? Needless to say, his statement caused a sensation.

As with the Roger Taverner incident three short months before, the media, who were eager for the marriage to take place, formed a solid phalanx behind Diana, effectively routing the possibility of *Private Eye* or any other publication scuppering her chances of marriage by claiming that she "had a past." Thereafter, any writer who wished to say that Diana had not walked up the aisle a virgin would not only be going against the tide of received opinion, but would also be accusing Lord Fermoy of lying. The result was that everyone fell in with the doctored version of the truth, until *Diana in Private* was published in 1992, at which time this writer called time on that tall tale. By then, however, the myths surrounding Diana had eaten deep into the public consciousness. Fact and fiction were almost irretrievably intermingled in a glorious fantasy figure known as the Princess of Wales. The only problem was, Diana had started to choke on it. Or, to be more accurate, on parts of it.

This mirage, of course, could not have existed without the collusion of both Diana and the media. "It is an undisputed fact that the Princess connived with the media and exploited it for her own interests, just as much as we exploited hers for ours," Sir David English, editor-in-chief of Associated Newspapers, affirmed on 28 December 1997. "Editors, and TV and radio controllers, always knew that. But within that symbiotic relationship, there were things that we did not know or chose to ignore." Sir David was in an unimpeachable position when speaking about Diana. Associated Newspapers is the parent company of the *Daily Mail* and the *Mail on Sunday*, employers of Richard Kay, the journalist who was proud to be Diana's friend as well as the conveyor of her point of view. English was also her media advisor. Day after day, from shortly after meeting him on her trip to Nepal in 1993, Diana caused stories to be published about herself written by Richard Kay. Indeed, he was one of the last people she spoke to on the evening before her death.

By then, of course, Diana had become the most written about and popular human being on earth. "You're the finest PR operator, man or woman, I have ever met," Sir David English told her shortly before her death. She was indeed. A true genius at the art of media presentation.

The image, however, was only a part of the story. Brilliant work of art though it was, it was only a partial reflection of the woman behind the mask. One without the other is incomplete. Only by capturing both can we begin to understand the captivating creature that was Diana – and how she got from being the "perfectly ordinary" girl whom Simon Berry knew to a media myth.

Seven

The engagement of the Prince of Wales and Lady Diana Spencer was announced, as planned, by Buckingham Palace on 24 February 1981.

Before the announcement was made, the Palace moved Diana from the exposure of Coleherne Court to the safety of Clarence House, the Queen Mother's London residence, where she remained for two nights, before transferring to Buckingham Palace. There, despite having her own suite of rooms, she more or less lived with the Prince of Wales, the way Sophie Rhys-Jones would later more or less live with his youngest brother, Edward, but in the early 1980s such sleeping habits were adjudged to be dangerously *risqué*, so Diana and the Palace maintained the pretence that she was still residing under the care and control of Charles's moralistic grandmother, Queen Elizabeth the Queen Mother. The unspoken message, received as fact by hundreds of millions all over the world, was that the virginal Lady Diana would remain untouched by masculine hands until the wedding ring was safely on her finger.

As Diana recounted events, she was even allotted her own private detective – Paul Officer, a handsome and personable royal protection officer who had once saved the Prince of Wales's life and had been one of his detectives. "This is the last day of freedom you'll have for the rest of your life. Enjoy it," he told her, trying to be helpful. Diana, believing that he was exaggerating, developed a dislike for him from that moment. Only later, after she had insisted that he be removed from her detail, did she begin to understand that she had destroyed the messenger when it was the message that was the problem.

Although no one yet appreciated what was happening, before the engagement was even announced the problems were starting. "I hate it when I'm not in control," Diana admitted. "And I hate being watched. Christ, I couldn't even have a pee without someone watching me going in and coming out of the loo. Talk about being a prisoner."

For someone who felt so strongly about control and liberty, Diana was bound to have problems marrying into a way of life which dictated that she be subject to twenty-four-hour-a-day security. The IRA, above all, was then an ever-present threat to the lives of the British Royal Family, having assassinated Lord Mountbatten a year and a half before, but even without that terrorist organization, this was the standard lifestyle for all top-ranking royals and politicians, whether European, Asian, American, South American or Australian.

For the next decade and a half, Diana's protection officers would be a double-edged sword. Some were friends. One became a lover. But, without exception, she would have liked to live without being watched by one and all. Only when she was separated did she achieve her wish, though at a higher price than she could ever have envisaged. As John Kennedy, Prince Michael of Kent's former Private Secretary said, "Diana would never have died if she'd had her royal protection officer with her. He wouldn't have allowed Henri Paul to drive at that speed. Those officers are trained to evaluate risk. A horde of paparazzi trying to snatch a photograph is not a life-or-death threat. Going at [high speed] on a street in Paris is." He also said, "I've been in a car when a protection officer overruled his boss on security grounds. The royal wanted to do something stupid in the Mall. Was a complaint made? Of course not. You can't complain about someone doing their job properly. The Commissioner of Police would've commended the officer and the Palace would've carpeted the royal, who wisely decided to keep quiet about it all."

Two other problems which would colour the remainder of Diana's life surfaced within hours of the engagement being announced. She and Charles gave a television interview and posed happily for photographs at Buckingham Palace. The interviewer asked if they were in love. The ever-romantic Diana, who never got over her addiction to novels written by the likes of Barbara Cartland and Danielle Steel, answered yes. The unromantic though loving Charles qualified by saying "whatever in love means." "The Prince of Wales, who has a real problem dissembling, was simply trying to be honest. Everyone who knew him knew that he believes in love, not in being in love. He regards the former as real, the latter as illusory. What he was trying to do was answer a complex question in a sound bite," Prince George of Denmark said. "He's certainly lived to rue the day." While most profound thinkers, philosophers, psychiatrists and psychologists agree with Charles's estimation of what some scientists call "limerence," or infatuation, Diana's ears perked up. "It made me wonder," she told me.

Diana's doubts about Charles's feelings towards her, which began at that moment, might not have overtaken her had the next problem not come hard on its heels. Diana was wearing a blue Cojana suit. Despite being nearly six feet tall, with long and elegant limbs, Diana looked chubby in the rather bulky suit, which she and her mother had bought at Harrods. Neither woman was used to the camera, so neither knew that you automatically gain fifteen pounds before the lens. Nor did they appreciate that sleek lines provide a flattering picture, while the blousy effect only adds additional weight photographically.

After the interview, Charles and Diana went inside. They turned on the television to watch themselves. "My God, I look so fat," Diana said she commented. Charles distractedly put his hand around her waist and, squeezing it, said, "It's just the television. Don't worry about it. You look fine."

Later, she would rewrite that scenario for the benefit of Andrew Morton, and accuse Prince Charles of setting off her bulimia by squeezing her and commenting on a roll of fat he felt. This was Diana at her most resourceful, intent on gaining sympathy while at the same time shifting responsibility for her actions onto someone else, but the fact is, she had no roll of fat around her waist, even at that time, and the story as recounted to me bore no relationship to her subsequent and damaging account she created so that Andrew Morton could pillory her husband on her behalf.

The day following the announcement of the engagement, in what would emerge as another pattern, Diana pored over all the newspapers as any other excited girl in her position would have done. Where she was less characteristic was in her reaction. Always a perfectionist, always competitive, always determined, Diana took one look at the rather unflattering photographs and decided then and there that she was going on a diet. She wanted to be svelte and sleek. "I want to look my best as a bride," she said to several people at the time, in what they took to be a perfectly ordinary ambition for any young woman. Even then, her wit was in evidence, such as when she declared to one member of the Royal Household, "I'm not walking up the aisle waddling like a duck."

For three days, Diana starved herself. When she complained to a member of Charles's Household that she was so hungry she was light-headed, the person in question advised her to be less radical about the diet, to eat, but eat less fattening foods in smaller quantities than she normally did. Diana, however, was always an all-or-nothing person, someone of extreme appetites and reactions. "But I might not lose all the weight I need to," she said plaintively, "the child within her very near the surface," as the person to whom she was speaking describes with affection.

As Diana would discover in the years to come, the battle she now waged, and would thereafter wage, was between two conflicting aspects of her own self. On the one hand, there was the steely Diana, intent on gliding up the aisle like a swelte swan. On the other hand, there was the voracious Diana, who had never been able to control her appetite, and who had therefore gained a reputation for gluttony at school and among her friends. Which aspects of her identity won in the long run remained to be seen, but afer three days of self-inflicted starvation, Diana's self-control gave way to her appetite. At lunch she gulped down the meal she had only intended to pick at. Still ravenous, she went to the office she would thereafter share with Michael Colbourne, but found it impossible to settle down to the letters and lists she had to deal with. She left the Palace through a side door, crossed the street and went into the souvenir shop almost opposite Buckingham Palace. Once there, she bought dozens of candy bars. She took them back to the Palace, intending to leave them in her room for the odd occasion when she could not sustain her diet any longer. "I wolfed down the whole lot in one go," she told me. Afterwards, "I couldn't believe what I'd done. Thinking only of the pounds I'd gain if I didn't get rid of all those calories, I went to the loo and made myself sick."

At first, Diana was elated to have found such a foolproof way of dieting, while satisfying her appetite at the same time. As she told a Royal Household member who happened in on her a few weeks later, shortly after she had made herself sick, "I'm fine. It's nothing. I've discovered this great way of dieting. Eat all you want, then aagh." She giggled, opening her mouth and pointing her finger downwards.

Bulimia, of course, is no joke, but Diana did not appreciate that what she had triggered off was a serious eating disorder. Her sister Sarah had had anorexia nervosa badly enough to need hospital treatment, but Diana did not associate the expulsion of excessive intakes of food with the starvation that had nearly wrecked Sarah's health. "I was more frightened of dieting than of overeating," she said, failing to understand that overeating, then vomiting, was not a "great way of dieting" but a life-threatening illness which was the flip side of the same coin as anorexia.

According to Anna Lady Brocklebank, who is a medical doctor, bulimia is a complex condition but it also has a standard effect upon its victims. The act of vomiting rids the body of minerals and nutrients while also releasing a chemical which creates a high. As victims become addicted to their own endorphins, they gain a compulsion to make themselves sick several times a day, to achieve the high which only comes when they vomit and release further endorphins. This throws the body, which naturally seeks to maintain a pH balance, into overdrive, as it replenishes the minerals and nutrients which have been depleted by the latest bout of vomiting. Physical chaos is the result, but it is only a part of the problem, for in its wake comes the emotional effects of the body's chaotic attempt at equilibrium. Emotional upheaval in the form of massive mood swings, depression, anxiety, fear and self-loathing about the inability to control the compulsion to gorge and expectorate, become the order of the day.

Emotionally healthy people do not become bulimics. Anyone who does already has an underlying problem, which might have been manageable before the advent of bulimia, but which cannot be dealt with once the illness takes root. Once the victim is in the grips of the eating disorder, the underlying emotional problem spirals out of control and becomes compounded by a host of new problems. These are frequently difficult to manage, because a characteristic of bulimia is that the sufferer usually denies that she has a problem until the condition has so eroded her physical, emotional and mental condition that her personality becomes affected.

During Diana's first weeks at Buckingham Palace, as the disease took hold, no one noticed anything amiss. This in itself was nothing unusual. Bulimics share a characteristic of being able to mask their condition well, or, as her brother Charles Spencer noted to her, she became, like other bulimics, practised in the "art of deception." Also, in its early stages, bulimia has few noticeable effects. These become more and more pronounced with time, but Diana had not yet reached that stage. Moreover, this was a busy time for her. She had countless details to deal with as she prepared not only for the wedding of the decade, if not the century, but also for life as a royal princess. She had invitation lists to compile. Congratulatory letters to reply to. Other letters to write. Presents to choose. Dresses to order in quantity, for once she was the Princess of Wales, she would be expected to work the way the other members of the British Royal Family did, fulfilling public engagements several days and nights a week. "It was beyond the scope of any nineteen-year-old, no matter how clued up she was," Diana told me. Although "they (the Royal Family) couldn't stand my mother, she came in and helped out," Diana said. "Frances was magnificent," Sonia Palmer told me in 1991. "She is wonderful with people, warm and charming and so capable and elegant. It was a pleasure having her around." She drafted letters and dealt with the myriad choices which were beyond the scope of her teenaged daughter.

This was a period of transition for Diana. She was on the way from an ordinary and undemanding existence of middling privilege and liberty to an extraordinary and demanding existence of hyperprivilege and extreme restrictions. Lady Susan Hussey, a lady-in-waiting to the Queen and one of Prince Charles's closest friends, was delegated to teach Diana the feminine side of royalty's public face. "She (Diana) was terribly eager to please," Sonia Palmer said. "It was touching to see Lady Susan putting her through her paces. Teaching her how to wave the royal wave. To smile at imaginary crowds. To converse with imaginary dignitaries employing the royal technique of asking question after question before moving on to the next person, where they repeat the whole process of question after question again. At first Diana was way over the top in her eagerness to please." As Jan Govett had stated when Diana had gone into her office for an interview, "She smiled much too much. Lady Susan had to get her to modify the smiling."

Charles also got in touch with Oliver Everett, a high-flying career diplomat who had been seconded, as was the custom, to Buckingham Palace for two years in 1978 as the Prince of Wales's Assistant Private Secretary. The prince asked him if he would be willing to come and work as Diana's Private Secretary and Comptroller. Oliver Everett was young, approachable, charming and fun to be with. Beneath a benign exterior lay a powerhouse of capability and efficiency. Charles thought he was perfect for the job. They had got along well, and the indications were that he and Diana would also get along. As indeed they did at first. Everett agreed to take the job, which was conditional on the Foreign Office permitting another secondment. However, it refused to release him a second time, and he had to make a choice between a career at the Palace or at the Foreign Office. Although the prospects of being in charge of Diana's Household were less financially rewarding, the prestige and perks of living at the Palace as a leading courtier more than made up for the downside, and, because he got along well with Charles and Diana and would thereafter be an integral part of their lives, he agreed to make the move after assurances that the job was his for life.

Thereafter, Diana and Oliver Everett became a team. Inevitably, royal private secretaries and their bosses spend more time together than either does with the spouse. In later years, Diana refused to speak about Oliver Everett, but her silence could not obliterate the fact that "they were great friends in the early days." "She adored him at first," Sonia Palmer told me. "They were very, very good friends. They had a great time together. There was a lot of laughter between them. He has a lovely sense of humour and she loved a good laugh. They worked well together as personalities, but he had a heck of a time getting her to buckle down to any of the serious stuff. She didn't want to read any of the biographies and books on the constitution and other heavy-duty stuff she had to learn if she was going to do her job well. 'I didn't leave school to do bloody homework,' she used to complain. She thought she could coast through on the sweetness of her demeanour. Which, of course, is precisely what she did. In the early days, you couldn't get two intelligible words out of her. Later, of course, she was different. But in the early days it was all smiles and no substance. She made life very, very difficult for Oliver, but he was a real sport about it. He felt she was young and inexperienced and, I believe, secretly sympathized with this young girl being made to assume middle-aged responsibilities. The royals get used to it as they grow up. For someone carefree like Diana, it was an ordeal. He understood that and tried to jolly her along."

When Diana was not in the office she shared with Michael Colbourne working on the wedding, or being put through her paces by Susan Hussey and Oliver Everett, her time was her own. This she filled in various ways. Exercise had always been important to her. She "needed it to relax," to quote her, and it remained so. There is evidence to support the theory that she was already an exercise junkie, addicted to the release of endorphins that come with vigorous, prolonged exercise. According to her cousin Luke, the late Lord Annaly, she used to roller-skate for hours through the corridors at Buckingham Palace with a Walkman clamped to her head, listening to her favourite pop music. She also quickly became a religious user of the Palace swimming pool, establishing another habit that would last until she left the royal fold. She was proud of the way the weight was falling off her, and called in the old dance-teaching team from West Heath, Lily Snipp, the pianist, and Wendy Vickers, the dance teacher, to put her through her paces and tone up her muscles. Because she also loved dancing, "I hated it when they had to leave," Diana said. According to Miss Snipp, "She lived for the ballet. Lessons helped her get away from the pressures of being a member of the Royal Family."

There was much about this new way of life that still perplexed Diana. One thing, however, did not. She had already succumbed to the temptation to sacrifice her old friends in the interest of fitting into her new way of life. She cut herself off from them as soon as she moved in. This, of course, is a common phenomenon when people are moving up in the world, as Diana now was, but it is seldom advisable, and would ultimately prove disastrous in her case. According to her, she was trying to please the "Palace crew." While this is undoubtedly so, fair play alone compels that it be pointed out that no one at the Palace – neither royal nor courtier – had made the suggestion. "I got the vibe they saw my friends as baggage. I could never see them alone. So I stopped bothering to see them." Kinty Wake-Walker substantiated the barriers that sprung up for Diana's old friends: "It became very difficult because her friends couldn't get to see her. It was very hard to see her alone."

It was a different story for the new friends Diana was making from within the royal circle. A case in point was Sarah Ferguson. Diana met Sarah around this time because Sarah's father, Major Ronald Ferguson, was then Prince Charles's Polo Manager. They became fast friends and were often together. Diana also became very chummy with Princess Margaret's daughter, Lady Sarah Armstrong-Jones, and son, David Viscount Linley, as well as with Prince Andrew and Prince Edward, and the same rule applied. "I had control of my diary," Diana confirmed. With that went determination of her day-to-day activities until her marriage, at which point she was expected to begin working as a full-time royal. There can therefore be little doubt where responsibility lay for the decision to give up her old friends. Though it was the innocent mistake of a young bride eager to please her future husband and his circle, Diana could not have made a worse choice at a worse time in her life.

Diana's personality was fracturing. According to the eminent psychologist Dr Basil Panzer, "When she moved into the Palace, when the relationship was formalized with an engagement, she underwent her first psychosocial transition. To move from a flat in Chelsea with two girlfriends into the Palace, where all of a sudden all kinds of things are expected is a major change for anyone. Demands are made on her. She must change her behaviour. Things are expected of her. Looking at her as a subject of a psychiatric history, we know that following this change she develops symptoms of mental illness. She develops an eating disorder. A substantial case of bulimia. As she tells us in her own words, she's vomiting four times a day, stuffing food. From being a chubby teenager she becomes skinny and probably underweight."

Worse now followed. While the bulimia was making inroads into Diana's psyche and behaviour, she was discovering that there was much about the royal way of life that was onerous. "This is a girl who is not used to having duties. She likes having fun, living with girlfriends and having a good time," Dr Panzer said after I provided him with reams of comments and information which Diana herself had imparted. "She doesn't have a strong-enough character to cope with the pressures. She can't cope. She cracks under the pressure."

Although Diana had always kept herself busy even as a young girl-about-town, she was not busy enough at the Palace. When she was occupied, it was the wrong sort of occupation to bring her satisfaction. She didn't want to be reading learned works on the British constitution, or the lives of past Princesses of Wales. She had hoped that, by agreeing to marry Charles, she would be escaping from all the pressures and mundane demands of ordinary life. Now she found herself subjected to more pressures and demands, some of the indefinable kind that come with transition, some of the definable and ordinary kind she had hoped she had shed when she had agreed to become the Princess of Wales. To a young girl not yet twenty, preparing for a life of charity work and greeting dignitaries was "sick-making. Borinnnnnnng," she said.

Occasionally Diana would join the Queen for lunch or dinner. As Diana herself told me, "I got on well with the Queen. Not that it was all smooth sailing. Once I went to lunch, I made the mistake of wearing red tights. I was sitting there and the corgis were yapping all around me. You know how much I like dogs (not at all!). Suddenly I realized they were fascinated by my red tights. I thought, My God, what if they think my legs are steak? I had visions of the whole lot tearing into me and devouring my legs. I nearly burst out laughing but managed to suppress it. I wish I hadn't worn those wretched tights, though. I couldn't wait to get out of there."

According to Lord Charteris, who knew both women well, Diana "was a lot more relaxed with the Queen at first than later. Once they actually started to have a relationship, the gulf between them grew and grew. They were such different personalities that, once they'd got the niceties out of the way, there just wasn't (much) common ground."

Family socializing aside, "I was amazed by the number of dinner parties they had. There were just too many," Diana said. A courtier, who prefers to remain anonymous, confirmed this: "Diana was often present at dinner parties. In fact, she complained to friends that there were too many dinner parties at the Palace for her liking." She preferred intimate and informal entertainment to the formality in which she now found herself engulfed. Or, as Dr Panzer put it, "This may suggest that her human relations, her interpersonal skills, were lacking." He believed "that is in the range of a normal character, a normal personality which has not developed." In other words, like most nineteen-year-olds, she was still immature.

Dispiriting as the formality and socializing were, they were nothing compared to how Diana felt once she had the opportunity to witness at first hand how busy her future husband was. Charles's diary of appointments and official engagements had been set prior to the announcement of the engagement. These still had to be honoured. The result was that the newly engaged couple saw less of each other than either of them would have liked. Although Diana, through her grandmother's rota of forthcoming duties as a lady-in-waiting, was no stranger to the custom whereby royal engagements are fixed six months in advance twice a year, after which the royals have to zip around the country, and sometimes the world, in a dizzying array of duties which she herself would eventually sparkle in, she became increasingly agitated. "It was one thing when her grandmother was doing it," Sonia Palmer said.

"She didn't mind old Ruth running herself ragged following in Queen Elizabeth's wake. That brought her family prestige so it was OK for the two old ladies to work crowds till they dropped. But it was another story when the Prince of Wales was similarly engaged. She felt his position was taking him away from her. She didn't like it one bit, I can assure you."

The sting in the tail aside, there is no doubt that this former courtier's observation contains an element of truth. "Duty, duty, duty. That's all he ever thinks about," Diana complained to a cousin at the time, to me later, and to countless other people until her death. Dr Basil Panzer, however, found her objections typical of an emotionally hungry young woman. "He might have been a rich businessman with obligations and it would have been the same story. There is nothing very exceptional about the dynamics of the Prince and Princess of Wales's relationship. It had nothing to do with royalty. It's an everyday story of the prestigious man with obligations – some of which he might even enjoy – and the wife who feels she's not getting enough attention."

Although Diana was not yet Charles's wife, by June 1981 she was firmly convinced that she was not getting the attention she needed from him. While this was undoubtedly so, the rational side of her character should have told her how busy the Prince of Wales is. She could not reasonably expect him to dishonour commitments made six months in advance to various organizations and charities just because she wanted to see him. "He left me on my own too much," she nevertheless complained to me of those days, a refrain she echoed with others.

As the wedding neared, the fracturing of Diana's personality became more perceptible and the very serious problems that were already in existence began to surface. She started having "crying jags," as she put it, bouts of uncontrollable crying which would hit out of nowhere, for no apparent reason. One overcame her at polo just before the wedding in full view of the media. She had to be taken home. Everyone accepted the explanation that the stress of the forthcoming wedding was taking its toll. Prince Charles and the rest of the Royal Family were not alarmed. "They said it was the pressure," Diana told me. She thought so as well, though it was one of the first symptoms of her other mental illness – on top of bulimia – and one moreover which would claim her uncle three short years later when he committed suicide due to clinical depression.

There is no doubt, if you examine what Diana said at this point in her life, as well as the independent evidence, that she was experiencing an identity crisis. She told Lily Snipp something she told many other people, who would prefer that their names are withheld. "I won't be me once I'm married," she said with virtually no deviation to one and all. Stripped bare of the panoply of royalty and aristocracy, that is a peculiarly telling comment for any bride to make. It means that she associates marriage with the loss of her identity. This fits in with Dr Panzer's evaluation that Diana "was a typical young woman with a disturbed childhood. Young women who have had unhappy childhoods frequently have a fantasy that some handsome prince or knight or the modern-day equivalent is going to come along and rescue them from all the pain and unhappiness of their past. He's a magical figure and his wand is going to change their lives. Make all the old problems disappear. Transform them into a new person. Replace all the old unhappiness with new happiness. The problems really begin when they realize that their fantasy figure hasn't rescued them from their past. Can't rescue them."

There is ample evidence to suggest that Diana was the living embodiment of this syndrome. Not only did she say repeatedly, "I worshiped him (Charles). He was like my god," but she was also by her own admission "romantic. I believed dreams can come true. I thought love cured all. I'd read too many Barbara Cartland novels, I suppose."

As the date of the marriage in July neared and Diana's awareness of the enormity of what she was undertaking increased, her mental and emotional condition deteriorated. So, too, did her physical condition. Though she was fit and slender, she was now tightly encased in the jaws of barely controllable bulimia, and would remain so for most of the decade. Perplexed at what was happening to her, and not understanding that she was undergoing a breakdown, she was convinced she had found the reason for all her troubles when the Prince of Wales, thinking he was clearing the slate for a marriage where openness and honesty would be the order of the day, committed the cardinal error of telling Diana about his affair with Camilla Parker Bowles. "He made it crystal clear to her that it was over," a friend of his told me. This echoed what Diana herself said, "Can you believe he thought I was dumb enough to accept it was over? He took me for a fool. But he doesn't now. Not since the separation and, you know, since. . .since I've gone public."

Seizing upon Charles's confession as an explanation for her own problems, Diana became daily more convinced that the affair was ongoing. "She started asking the most probing and inappropriate questions about the Prince's relationship with Mrs Parker Bowles," Sonia Palmer said." She wouldn't leave it alone. She was like a dog with a bone. Day after day she came back to the same old thing. We didn't know what to make of it all. We marked it down to premarital nerves. With hindsight, it's obvious this was the beginning of her obsession."

"I know he was having an affair with her," Diana told me. When asked what led her to such certainty, she said, "I just knew it. If he'd really loved me he'd have found more time for me. He was just too fucking considerate of that Rottweiler to not be having an affair with her. He even told me he still loved her and always would." When pressed, Diana did admit that Charles had qualified his feelings by saying "he would always love Camilla as a friend because she had always been there for him. He thought she was marvellous. What man, about to get married, tells his future wife that he will always love his ex-mistress unless she's still his mistress?" a furious Diana demanded. She would not accept Charles's explanation, that he was merely telling her about his past because he wanted them to be able to speak freely, without forbidden areas.

The upshot was that Diana, who had more hands-on control of the guest list for the wedding than Charles, insisted that Andrew and Camilla Parker Bowles be removed from it. Since Charles had also confessed to an old affair with Dale Tryon, she also struck Lord and Lady Tryon off the guest list. The Prince of Wales then found himself in the position of having to persuade Diana, whose guest list included several former lovers, to adopt the same standard for him that she was applying for herself. "She took that tussle as confirmation that she was right. She didn't buy his explanation, that it would embarrass and demean him to humiliate the Parker Bowleses and the Tryons in front of the world," Sonia Palmer said. Only when Charles dug his heels in and remained adamant that his friends were going to be asked whether Diana liked it or not, did she relent and agree to allow them to come to the church. "Not to the wedding breakfast, though," she gloated to a friend. She was denying them the sanctum sanctorum, creating just enough media conjecture to satisfy herself that she had succeeded in humiliating them.

This was the first time anyone at Buckingham Palace saw Diana's vengeful streak. It caused consternation among the Prince of Wales's staff as she used the power she had over the invitation list to exclude not only people she disliked but those whom she feared or should have felt gratitude towards. Chief among these was Barbara Cartland, mother of her stepmother Raine and the author of those romantic novels which she had read so avidly since her girlhood.

The inimitable Barbara Cartland "is brilliant with publicity," my stepmother-in-law, Margaret, Duchess of Argyll, a lifelong friend, explained. She had turned herself into a hugely popular British institution, so was bound to receive attention as she arrived at the church and Palace for the wedding. No more so, however, than Nancy Reagan, Princess Grace or the various crowned heads who would be attending. Notwithstanding that Barbara had been kindness itself to Diana throughout the years, Diana's competitiveness got the better of her and she struck the octogenarian author's name off the list, right in front of Michael Colbourne and other members of the Prince's Household, including Sonia Palmer, with the comment, "I don't intend to have her upstage me." No amount of persuasion enticed Diana to relent. "She had the power and she was wielding it," Sonia Palmer said.

Because the Household and staff of the Prince of Wales were the people who saw Diana every day, they were the ones who were privy to her daily changes. Having fought and won her battle to exclude Barbara Cartland entirely and the Parker Bowleses and Tryons partially, Diana turned her attention to digging for information about Camilla. She was looking for confirmation of her suspicions. The most logical source was from the people around her. "It was highly embarrassing," Sonia Palmer said. "You'd be speaking to her about something completely different when, out of the blue, she'd come up with something like, 'How often does the Prince see Mrs Parker Bowles on his own? He does still see her, doesn't he? Come on, you can tell me. I won't tell.' It made for a distinctly uncomfortable atmosphere at times, I can assure you."

Convinced that Charles's household and staff were covering up for him, Diana took to inspecting the presents and wedding invitations. "I got to the bottom of it, too," she proudly told me, referring to her discovery that Charles had bought Camilla a bracelet with the initials GF, which he proposed handing over to her before the wedding in a final good-bye meeting. "He said it was a token of appreciation for all she'd given him during the past," Diana spat out contemptuously. "He said GF was for Girl Friday, because she'd been like a Girl Friday to his Robinson Crusoe. I told him I didn't believe him and never wanted him to see her ever again – with or without me. He said he couldn't do that. Can you believe, he had the gall to say Camilla deserved a face-to-face good-bye and he couldn't give me his word? He was going to see her to hand it over no matter what I said." Diana remained convinced that GF stood for Gladys and Fred, Charles and Camilla's pet names for one another, and no amount of disclaimers to the contrary from Charles and his staff could change her mind.

Possibly in Diana's circle, the mark of a man's character was not determined by the way he ended a relationship, but in the Prince of Wales's, as in mine, no gentleman, who wished to be known as such by his peers, would ever dream of telling a long-standing girlfriend good-bye except person-to-person. When I pointed this out to Diana, she genuinely seemed astonished. The idea had never occurred to her before. Finally, she said, her tone a mixture of regret and disbelief, "No. No. That wasn't the reason." Her voice then hardened and she continued dismissively, "And if it was true, it's too late now."

"I know some men are pathological philanderers," Princess Margaret of Hesse and the Rhine said, "and it doesn't behove a woman to believe a word they say. But Prince Charles really isn't like that. Everyone who knows him can confirm that his outstanding traits are his sincerity and an inability to dissemble. Of course we all tell little white lies, but he is unusually truthful. Diana's tragedy is that she refused to accept that she'd found a prince with princely virtues. She was convinced that everyone lied and deceived and dissembled and betrayed and used one another. I'm sure it was a result of her parents' divorce. Her refusal to accept that some people might be genuine and sincere and kind and thoughtful cost her dear. Not only the love of the one man she truly loved, but ultimately her marriage, her position, and friendship after friendship. It really was a tragedy. And one that was born out of the pain of her childhood."

Charles's refusal to dump Camilla unceremoniously was the first real crisis between Diana and himself. Coming as it did days before the wedding, which was scheduled for 29 July 1981, Diana had little room for manoeuvre. She could either go through with the wedding or she could call it off. She told me, "I spoke to my sisters. They said I had to go through with it. My face was on the tea towels. Sarah even said, 'You'll look a right mug to go along with all those mugs with your face on them.' I loved him. He said he loved me. I figured I'd better believe him." And you wanted the fairy tale to come true, I suggested. "Yes. I wanted the fairy tale to come true," she agreed.

I did not suggest, nor did Diana say, that she also went through with the ceremony because she would have caused a worldwide sensation by cancelling at this late stage. That was the unspoken truth hanging obviously between us. That and the fact that she would have been disappointing her family, whose ambitions were riding on her doing the sensible thing. So she did it, paid a high price, but, it must be said, never regretted it. "I'd do it all over again," she confirmed when I put that question to her.

It is comforting to know, in the light of what was to come, that she had no regrets about marrying Charles, even if she would have preferred to have been a pain-free Princess of Wales.

Eight

The wedding of the Prince and Princess of Wales was watched by more people on earth than have ever watched any other wedding. The Archbishop of Canterbury spoke about fairy tales coming true, and everyone, the bride and groom included, hoped that that would be so.

Unlike many bridegrooms, Charles had taken pains with the service. He confidently expected it to be the only time he would be married, and he wanted it to be ideal. With his love of music and architecture, he chose St. Paul's Cathedral in the City of London over the traditional Westminster Abbey because it was more beautiful, could hold a full orchestra, and had a world-famous choir. He called in Sir David Willcocks, Director of the Royal College of Music, to oversee the musical side of arrangements, and selected a programme of music by Purcell, Handel and Jeremiah Clarke that was both joyous and moving. There were three orchestras, the Bach Choir, and the world-famous soprano Kiri Te Kanawa, who was made a Dame shortly afterwards upon the recommendation of her native New Zealand.

Both Charles and Diana were moved by the occasion. He said, "There were several times when I was perilously close to crying from the sheer joy of it all." Diana said, "It was heaven, amazing, wonderful, though I was so nervous when I was walking up the aisle that I swore my knees would knock and make a noise."

After the hiccups of the last weeks, the newlyweds were determined to settle down to a happy married life. Although wrung out from the excitement of it all, they enjoyed their wedding breakfast for 118 guests at Buckingham Palace. When it came time to leave, they did so in high spirits surrounded by their two families and all of Europe's royal families save the King and Queen of Spain. Juan Carlos and Sofia had had to cancel their participation when it emerged that Charles and Diana proposed to board the royal yacht, *Britannia*, from the disputed territory of Gibraltar for a two-week cruise in the Mediterranean and the Aegean seas. This blight aside, everything seemed perfect as they left Buckingham Palace in a horse-drawn carriage for Waterloo Station and the short train ride to Broadlands, the late Lord Mountbatten's home in Hampshire where the Queen and the Duke of Edinburgh had spent the first part of their honeymoon, and where Charles and Diana would spend the first two days.

"I was so wrung out I spent most of the time sleeping," Diana said. While she did so, Charles fished in the River Test or read, enjoying this rare opportunity to luxuriate in peace without the demands of courtiers and citizens.

Two days later, Charles and Diana flew to Gibraltar to board the *Britannia*. There was only one other woman aboard: Evelyn Dagley, Diana's dresser. While Charles was reading Jung or Laurens van der Post – he had suggested to Diana that she might have a look so that they could share thoughts on the subject, but such reading matter had to wait until she was well into her thirties – Diana swam, tanned herself, and beckoned to him seductively, in front of several crew members, to "come and do your duty."

Diana's appetite for sex, as her lover James Hewitt later confided to a mutual friend, was as huge as her appetite for food. "She couldn't get enough. She always wanted more." The sex, of course, was only part of it. She wanted the contact, the intimacy, the affection, the attention that went along with making love, and this she also used to speak about with another mutual friend of ours, Joseph Sanders, from 1991-1996 her financial advisor and accountant, and one of her main confidants (in the pure meaning of the word), to whom she spoke virtually every day of her life until her death.

Because she had no interest in Charles's intellectual pursuits, when they were not making love or swimming and picnicking together in one of the many bays and coves they stopped at, they had little to share. He would read while she drifted about the boat, chatting to the hundreds of ratings, who didn't quite know how to respond in the hierarchical world of the Navy to this friendly young woman who was not supposed to be talking to them as if she were their friend. Some liked it; others did not. But Diana, hungry for human contact, needed to relate to whatever human being was nearby. Once, she even barged in on several of the ratings showering. Some had towels wrapped around them; others were naked. To cover her embarrassment as much as theirs, she saucily said, "It's all right. I'm a married woman now, aren't I?" One rating evidently said, as soon as she'd left, "Yes, but you're royal and we're ratings. Why don't you stop pestering us and go back to where you belong?"

Although Diana would have preferred to skip the formal dinners with various officers invited to join their table each evening, she otherwise took to the billionaire lifestyle of yachts and private planes the way Ivana Trump took to Manhattan. "That's the way to travel," she said with endearing alacrity. Travel she did. The honeymooners passed the Algerian coast, Tunisia, Sicily, Santorini, Crete and other Greek islands before heading for the Red Sea via the Suez Canal. They stopped off at Port Said, where they entertained President Anwar Sadat of Egypt and his half-British wife Jehan on board the royal yacht.

By this time Charles, who did not have the bustle of engagements to distract him, was becoming aware that there was something seriously wrong with Diana. Although the cruise would prove to be the happiest and most harmonious period of their lives, barring the birth of their sons, nothing could mask the fact that Diana's personality was disintegrating. She had massive mood swings. She still had her "crying jags." She was constantly sick, throwing up several times a day, without being seasick. Moreover, her wit, which had been so pronounced in the early days of their romance, seemed to be withering along with her breasts. At the dinners with the officers, Diana seldom had anything to contribute any longer. This was even more marked at the dinner Charles and Diana hosted for the Sadats on board the *Britannia*, which proved to be something of an embarrassment. Where formerly Diana had sparkled conversationally, always throwing in appropriate and witty asides irrespective of the illustriousness or maturity of the company, now she merely sat like a crumpled marionette, repeating "Oh, I do like mangoes." The Sadats pretended not to notice anything amiss, but Prince Charles realized there was a problem. And that the problem needed a solution. However, he misdiagnosed the malady. Instead of understanding that Diana was regressing mentally as her bulimia and depression increased, his assessment was that she needed more substantial reading matter than she had.

Whatever Charles's observations about the way Diana had comported herself, she had liked the Sadats, who came to see them off at the military airfield at Hurghada from where their RAF VC10 was leaving to take them back home. As the President and his wife were descending the gangplank, an ebullient and overaffectionate Diana touchingly blew kisses and waved like an excited child. Diana, who did have a big heart and only wanted to be liked, had forgotten all Lady Susan Hussey's lessons about regal dignity and restraint.

The Prince of Wales, though moved by his bride's childlike effusiveness, appreciated that something had to be done. The Sadats had taken a generous approach to Diana's conduct, but others might not. As much for her as for the dignity of the British state, she had to be provided with a solution. Charles, however, was already wary of how Diana would respond to anything that smacked of criticism. He already understood that she was hypersensitive, that she reacted badly and furiously to anything that was not praise of the highest form, and that her vengeful streak meant that he had better keep himself out of the frame as a target if he wanted his marriage to work. So when he got back to Britain, "the Prince had a word with Oliver Everett. He asked him to take steps to improve her mind," Sonia Palmer told me.

"There was a severalfold purpose in this. There was the fact that she had made a fool of herself with the Sadats, but, more important, he wanted her mind improved for himself. The Prince of Wales, you must remember, is a thinker, a very deep thinker. He is well informed on a variety of subjects, and has many, many interests, some very profound. He'd already realized they'd never have a meeting of minds – which, to him, is an important aspect of any relationship – unless she had something in her mind. But all she thought about was romantic nonsense à la Barbara Cartland, clothes and the childish antics of her Sloaney friends. If he was going to have something to speak to her about, aside from how much he loved her and how much she loved him, if he wasn't going to expire from boredom before the end of the honeymoon, something had to be done, and quickly."

To expedite the maturing process of the twenty-year-old, Oliver Everett provided Diana with suggested reading material. This caused no end of trouble. Eager as Diana was to please, her cooperation did not yet extend to areas which failed to interest her, though, it must be noted, in years to come she would rectify that and become an assiduous reader of the briefs and material presented to her. Before she evolved into the consummate professional, however, she saw no reason to do anything she did not wish to. According to Sonia Palmer, who witnessed one of the scenes, "Oliver brought in a pile of books and gently suggested that she might like to have a look at them when she had a moment. She thanked him, but as soon as he had shut the door behind him, she picked up the books and hurled them one by one at the door."

Trouble started in a big way as soon as the plane bringing Charles and Diana back from their honeymoon cruise touched down in Britain. Nor was it limited to conflict about Diana's distaste for the suggested reading material. The royal couple were scheduled to stay at Balmoral for the remainder of their honeymoon, which was to cover three months. Within days of arriving at Charles's "favourite place on earth," Diana started agitating to return to London. "It's a graveyard," and "It's borinnnnnng," were two of her more agreeable comments. Charles's initial response was, "But you told me you loved Balmoral. You said it was your favourite place on earth." "That was before we were married," was Diana's devastating response. Charles's feelings, upon realizing that Diana had misled him about her preferred way of life, can only be guessed at, for he is not on the record in this respect. I understand from a cousin, however, that he has privately admitted to having been "dispirited" at the realization. "He'd never have married her if he'd known that she couldn't stand country life."

Faced with another problem to add to the mood swings, the crying jags and the throwing up, the Prince of Wales explained to Diana as gently and kindly as he could that the Court was now at Balmoral. She had married into the Royal Family and had to comply with the way things were done, in much the same way that he, and indeed all other members of the Royal Family including the Queen, had to do. The institution was greater than its individuals, and it would not last unless the individuals in question remembered that and made the necessary personal sacrifices. She was welcome to have friends to stay, but she and he could not hive off and do their own thing. The responsibilities of royalty were such that even on honeymoon, they had duties to execute, and they could not let down people who were depending upon them.

"His words went in one ear and out the other," Prince George of Denmark said. "She was back the following day, hoping to persuade him. When that didn't work, she lost her temper and screamed that he was putting his duty before her. 'If you loved me, you'd put me first,' she railed. When his appeals to reason failed, he simply walked off, leaving her to cool down." This, of course, is a common enough mistake for men, who frequently fail to understand that the worst thing they can do is walk away from a row.

Diana's response to a husband who refused to row – at that stage, at any rate – was not particularly exceptional. She simply started screaming the house down. "You couldn't help hearing the rows," someone at Balmoral at the time said. "Her voice carried throughout the castle. It was truly incredible how loudly she shouted. He didn't respond in kind, at least, not then. That came later."

By September, Balmoral was in turmoil, the Royal Family riddled with anxiety. What was happening? Why was Diana so upset? Where had the jolly, easygoing girl of a year ago gone? The pressure of the wedding was off. Life had returned to normal. Why was Diana acting so strangely?

Diana's response was to increase the Royal Family's anxiety. Once she accepted that she had to stay in Scotland for the appointed duration, instead of settling in, she gave vent to another reason for being upset. Charles was leaving her on her own too much. She did not accept that she ought to conform to the traditional way of life whereby the men went out shooting and the women joined them for lunch. Nor did she wish to join Charles fishing (by her own account, "borinnnng"), or to go on one of his long walks with him ("Am I a camel?" she wittily asked, alluding to what she called "his treks"). She wanted him by her side all day. "She would've been perfectly happy to stay in her room all day, looking at television, reading Barbara Cartland while he lay beside her reading his books and they took the odd break to make love. That's what she wanted," a close friend of hers said Diana told her. Charles, however, found such a sedentary way of life dull and uninteresting. He'd had two weeks rest on board the *Britannia*. A sporty countryman at heart, he wanted to savour all the delights that one of the greatest estates in Scotland has to offer. Penelope Romsey, Nicholas Soames and the Queen had been right in their assessment that Charles and Diana had nothing in common except a strong physical attraction.

Within days, the scenes had escalated. In one drama, Diana screamed at him sarcastically, "What am I supposed to do all day while you're off enjoying yourself? Die of boredom? You call yourself a husband? Some husband you are." In another, Charles was witnessed driving away from the castle in one of the royal Range Rovers while Diana ran alongside clutching the door and shouting furiously, "Yes, dump me like garbage. Leave me on my own again. Run off and have lunch with your precious Mummy."

"You must convey the effect Diana's behaviour had upon everyone at Balmoral," Prince George of Denmark said. "The people surrounding the Queen are always models of discretion and decorum. No matter what family crisis is taking place within the Royal Family or the Royal Household, it takes place behind the scenes. In public – and by public I mean in front of the other guests – the order of the day is civility. You cannot have people screaming abuse when you have prime ministers, secretaries of state, various kings, queens, princes, princesses and foreign dignitaries staying at the castle. It lets down the dignity of the Court and the nation as well as the person doing it."

Although writers would later misinterpret Diana's behaviour as a consequence of a young girl being mercilessly isolated in a royal castle without anyone to support her, the facts tell another story. She had her sister Jane, whose husband Robert remained a Private Secretary to the Queen. She could ask friends to stay as guests, and did. Her problems, contrary to popular myth, were not due to having been hijacked and abandoned to a lonely fate by a cruel and callous Royal Family which wished to use her as a brood mare, but because she was now in the grips of two serious mental illnesses, both of which ran in her family – the eating disorder anorexia/bulimia, and clinical depression. While there is no doubt that the Royal Family did take the view that Diana should fit into their way of doing things, rather than change those ways to accommodate her – which was what Diana wanted, and would continue to want – they cannot be justifiably blamed for the faulty upbringing and troubled family history of the Spencers and Fermoys. Sadly, neither could Diana be blamed, for the disintegration of her personality was not intentional, and was beyond both her control and indeed her awareness.

As Diana's downwards spiral continued, her honeymoon was coming to an end and the date of her first official engagement since the wedding loomed. She had already gone on one official engagement following the announcement of her betrothal to the Prince of Wales. That had been an outstanding success.

This was the memorable occasion at the Guildhall when Diana turned up wearing a black Emanuel ball gown with her *embonpoint* served up as a feast for admiring eyes. Later, she would complain that Charles had criticized her for wearing black, a colour the royals wear only for mourning, and one which Diana was seldom out of once she gained her separation. Although Charles might well have pointed out to her the *faux pas* in the belief that she would wish to learn the rules of royalty, he did also proudly say to the assembled throng of photographers and television cameramen, "Get an eyeful," as Diana delivered up herself and her ample bosom for public inspection and approval.

Diana's first postmarital official engagement would prove to be as great a success as her premarital one had been. A month after her first lady-in-waiting, Anne Beckwith-Smith, was appointed in September 1981, Diana set off for a three-day tour of Wales with Charles. From the moment he presented her to the Welsh people from the balcony of Caernarvon Castle, where he had been invested as Prince of Wales twelve years before, the tour was an outstanding success. This was partly due to expert planning, and partly to Diana's demeanour, which she later attributed, with both fairness and modesty, to her husband's guidance, though her own natural warmth and charm must also be given credit.

In keeping with the royal tradition of adopting a dress motif suitable to the place being visited, Diana was attired in red and green, the Welsh national colours. As she and Charles went on a walkabout, she happily pumped flesh, squeezing the hand of this old lady, that child, shaking hands or touching fingers with the ordinary people of the principality with a refreshing lack of royal reserve. Diana was innately tactile. She could no more prevent herself from making contact physically than she could turn off her breath. She liked people and she wanted to be liked by them. They sensed this and returned the feeling in kind. Allied to this was an inbuilt dignity which meant that she did not cheapen herself, nor did she patronize people while conveying the milk of human kindness. She was simply a warm and tactile person who was using her hands and smile to communicate what was in her heart.

What also endeared her to the Welsh, and helped to make the tour the success it became, was her refusal to shelter from the weather. The Prince of Wales had always had a policy of shrugging off the inclemencies of the British climate, taking the view that he ought to share being wet with those who had become soaked while waiting to see him. He, however, was a man. No one expected Diana to share this robust approach. But she did. She refused an umbrella when it rained. As the feather in her hat drooped along with her hairstyle, she said to those who had been standing shivering in the driving rain, "Poor you. I feel cold myself. My hands are freezing, and yours must be much worse. Thank you for waiting for us," or "You're soaked to the bone. You must be freezing. I am. Thanks for coming to see us," or "Doesn't that wind cut right through you? Thank you so much for putting up with it."

In behaving as she did, Diana not only endeared herself to the people she met but also to the British nation as a whole, who saw her performance on television and read about it in the newspapers. Her warmth and kindness were much commented upon, as they would be in the years to come, and she wisely made no attempt to conceal either quality.

The success of this first official engagement was crucial, not only in establishing Diana as a figure of warmth and compassion, but also in giving her the confidence to retain behaviour characteristics that protocol required her to discard. Until Diana's advent, it was not regarded as acceptable for royalty to touch or be touched in public, except in the rarest of circumstances. Although the Prince of Wales, prior to his marriage, was frequently being kissed by strange girls in overeager displays, he was perceived as the innocent bystander who was simply too kindhearted to spurn their advances, so accepted them without demur, before moving on as quickly as possible. Diana's, conduct, however, was another issue entirely. She was the initiator. "No one ticked me off," she told me. "I think they (the courtiers) thought I'd grow out of it. By the time they realized I was never going to, I'd already changed the way things are done." The consequence, as we all know, was that Diana endeared herself to hundreds of millions of people all over the world, and the Royal Family is today far more demonstrative and tactile than it used to be.

Another consequence of the visit was that the Prince of Wales was knocked off his perch as the most popular young royal. Up to that point, Charles had been a figure of adulation for fifteen years. He liked it. He had gone from derided childhood and tormented adolescence to the pinnacle of public approval as an adult. The man valued his popularity all the more because the child within had never expected to be liked, admired or given blanket approval by anyone except his nanny, his granny and a very few friends and relations. Although he had no means of knowing it, his days as the ascendant royal were over, not to return until the tragic morning of 31 August 1997.

At this stage, Charles was not jealous. "He was proud of me," Diana admitted. "And I was thrilled to see that proud look in his eyes." Later, those positive emotions would be sullied by baser ones, but for the moment the newlyweds were content to return to Balmoral and pick up the threads of their life after the tour ended with Diana being presented with the Freedom of the City of Cardiff. She was the second woman to be honoured in this manner, the first being the Queen.

All of this was heady stuff for any twenty-year-old, especially one with a personality as fragile as Diana's. "Of course it affected me," she admitted. "How could it not have affected me? I'm a human being. I'm not made of stone. And I was only twenty. It was all too much. The whole shooting match – all that publicity, the attention – it was just too much to deal with."

Daunted by the responsibilities that awaited her, Diana was "terrified" about the full programme of official duties that were being pencilled in for her. She had no interests, but she was used to old people and children from her community visits at West Heath and her kindergarten work, so the Palace decided to focus on those two groups until she had gained experience and developed areas of interest. According to Dr Panzer, the evidence suggests that Diana's "interpersonal skills were lacking and so when she had a choice, she chose people under her who would be weaker and dependent." Dr Panzer did not consider Diana's preference for the underdog to be an aberration or a sign of a deep-seated malady, however, as some people have implied it might have been: "That is in the range of a normal character."

Whatever the degree and cause of her infirmity, there was now no doubt in the mind of anyone close to her that the new Princess of Wales had major problems. Just when concern was turning to terror that she might actually be mentally ill – a fact not yet confirmed – salvation came in the form of a simple and happy explanation. Diana was pregnant.

"The relief was palpable," Sonia Palmer said. "Everyone, including Diana, seized upon hormones as the difficulty." The fact that Diana had not been pregnant between February and September seems not to have occurred to any of the terror-stricken ostriches who were now either participants or onlookers in what was evolving into a great personal tragedy.

Pregnancy did not break the cycle of bulimia. At least, not at first. "I had the most terrible morning sickness all day," Diana said, blaming her repeated bouts of vomiting on the pregnancy. "From the very beginning the Princess understood that what she ate, how she felt and behaved would affect her unborn child," Barbara Cartland said. She therefore limited herself to white meat, pasta, vegetables, salads and masses of fruit. Never a big drinker, she cut out alcohol entirely. But she could not rid herself of the urge to purge.

As the pregnancy progressed, Diana fulfilled only a limited number of official engagements. Her health, especially her mental health, remained brittle. Knowing that Diana preferred beach to skiing holidays, Charles decided to forgo his annual break at Klosters and in February 1982 took his five-months-pregnant wife to Lord Brabourne and Countess Mountbatten of Burma's house on Windermere Island in the Bahamas. There are many photographs of that stay, which tell their own story. Charles and Diana are invariably intertwined in shows of deep physical passion. Diana looks happy, though, like most bulimics, she had the ability to "put on my smiling face." Her only audience, however, was the members of the house party.

The stay was marred by two of the British tabloids flying out photographers who snapped the pregnant Diana cavorting in the surf in a bikini. This justifiably enraged her and the rest of the Royal Family, for the Queen had already taken the unprecedented step of asking the press to give her daughter-in-law space – an act that might very well have been interpreted as monarchic abuse of press freedom had the victim been anyone but the already popular Princess.

Shortly afterwards, Argentina occupied South Georgia, beginning what became known as the Falklands War. By April 1982 Britain was heavily engaged, the whole country on tenterhooks, the Queen included. Prince Andrew, her favourite child, was a helicopter pilot, flying missions tracking Exocet missiles and doing other dangerous work.

Although with the passage of the months Diana's pregnancy had seen her health improve, with a lessening of the vomiting, the emotional outbursts and the crying jags did not disappear entirely. She was still ill enough that she sometimes sat curled up for hours in the foetal position in a chair, crying uncontrollably. Michael Colbourne, hoping to shake her out of what he mistook for the mood of a spoiled brat, suggested that she read about the losses of life in the daily papers. "Sometimes we all need to stand back from ourselves to gain a sense of perspective," he suggested, placing *The Times* in her hand. With a roar of anguish Diana slapped the paper away, saying, "Don't tell me about their suffering. What about my suffering?" As her friend Rosa Monckton would observe after her death, Diana did indeed have a tremendous capacity for unhappiness.

Despite Diana's bouts of misery, everyone who knew her at the time confirms that she also experienced great happiness during this period. She was overjoyed at being pregnant. She was looking forward to being a mother. She was desperately in love with her husband. And, when she was not hounded by doubts about his feelings for her, she was a loving, affectionate and happy wife. "It was frightening to see how contradictory she could be," Sonia Palmer said. "In the morning she would be happy with Prince Charles, in the afternoon doubtful, in the early evening in despair, then ecstatic the following morning. I would say her positive feelings outweighed her negative ones by a factor of four to one. By and large, though, she seemed happy." The Duchess of Kent, the devoutly religious wife of the Queen's first cousin Edward and a close friend of Diana's until her death, also said that the Princess's letters to her confirm that this was a happy period.

It is therefore ironic that the damaging story that Diana tried to hurt herself and her unborn child in a fit of pique at the Prince of Wales has been accepted as factual. According to this myth, first recounted, upon Diana's instigation, by Andrew Morton in his 1992 book *Diana: Her True Story*, she hurled herself down a flight of wooden stairs at Sandringham in January 1982 to spite Prince Charles for leaving her alone. What actually happened, as she herself subsequently confirmed to me, was that she slipped and fell. She was seen doing so by a member of the staff. The doctor was called, pronounced Diana unhurt by the accident, and Prince Charles, who was due to go out for the day, duly departed. Later, when Diana wanted her liberty, she turned that incident into something it was not, then lived to regret having done so. "I don't know how people can believe that I would ever have done anything that might hurt my baby. You were right when you said I'd slipped, though wrong when you said I deliberately waited for someone to come and find me. I didn't. I really was very shaken up and terrified about the baby until the doctor gave me the all-clear," she said in 1995, alluding to the version of events I recounted in the paperback edition of *Diana in Private* in 1992 and in *The Royal Marriages* in 1993. When pressed about how Morton could have come by the story, she sidestepped responsibility for planting the story with him and spat, "That creep. Everyone knows how much I love my boys. What sort of mother would I be if I endangered the life and health of my unborn child? Only a man could come up with a story like that and expect women to believe it. No mother who loved her children would ever do anything that might harm them. I really resent that story. It makes me sound like a madwoman in a third-rate opera." While Diana's estimation of the way she appeared, as a result of the version in the Morton book is correct, the fact is, she had only herself to blame for it, as he did not make it up. She did. He simply recounted her invention.

Although Diana's prevarications and rearrangements of facts were still in the future, the fracturing of her personality had an effect upon her marriage during its early days. While kind and indulgent towards her, Charles avoided being alone with her whenever he could. Sonia Palmer said, "We used to encourage him to spend more time with her. 'She's alone in there (the bedroom), sir,' we'd say. But he'd say, 'No, no. I have nothing to say to her.' It was very sad, because we knew she wanted him with her, and we knew he'd have wanted to be with her more if only he could've been sure what reception he was going to get. The trouble was, she was so unpredictable he could never be certain whether she was going to drape herself around his neck affectionately, or lambast him. You could see him retreating into himself more and more each day. Each of her outbursts drove him deeper into his shell. He can't handle emotional outbursts and she, poor dear, couldn't help herself. If only she could've pulled herself together and reverted to the girl she'd been before the marriage. But she couldn't, and he couldn't stand riding on the emotional roller coaster."

In the final months of her pregnancy, Diana's health and frame of mind underwent a welcome and dramatic improvement. The bulimia, or all-day morning sickness as she preferred to describe it, disappeared. She gained weight. She kept down food. The depression lifted. Her mood swings reduced. By the time Prince William of Wales was born, one day after the end of the Falklands War and two weeks early, at 9:03 p.m. on 21 June 1982,

Diana was as close to being the woman Charles had been captivated by as she would ever be again. The nation had a double cause for celebration: the end of the war and the birth of an heir to the throne.

Happy days seemed to be here again.

Nine

"The first time I experienced true happiness was when I held William in my arms," Diana said. "I'd never been that happy before. And I've never been that happy since, except when I had Harry."

William's birth, which the Prince of Wales witnessed, coincided with a brief period when all the signs pointed towards a resolution of the problems that Diana had been experiencing. She and Charles were genuinely happy together. They were both absorbed in their son. Much to the disapproval of Prince Philip, the doting father even wiped his diary clear of engagements in order to spend more time at home with the baby. Finally, they had something in common: their son, their pride and joy.

Diana breast-fed the baby and at first it looked as if her problems were at an end. She had a good nanny, Barbara Barnes, known as Baba, who had reared the children of Princess Margaret's close friends, Lord and Lady Glenconner. Although Papa and Mummy cared for William themselves much of the time, with her wealth of experience, Baba was an invaluable safety net for the new parents.

As genuine peace and happiness settled upon Kensington Palace, Diana heaved a sigh of relief at leaving the difficulties, some of which were not emotional, behind. To her, one of the major problems had been their lack of a London home. Throughout the pregnancy, she and Charles had been bunking at Buckingham Palace while their apartments at Kensington Palace were being done up. "I hated being at Buck House," Diana said. "It's like living in a mausoleum."

This was a sentiment shared by all the other royals, but what made Buckingham Palace especially odious for Diana was the access that living near the office afforded the courtiers. "She hated public engagements," Sonia Palmer said. The result was that Diana found herself engaged in a running battle with the Household about her official duties until 1987. "I felt awkward, uncomfortable. I was petrified I'd have nothing to say to the various dignitaries I met. That they'd think I was a silly young girl. That they'd see through to the frightened doe I really was. That I'd let myself and the side down," Diana said. This was confirmed Sonia Palmer, who said, "On the way to an engagement, she'd have the most ghastly attack of nerves. Like an actress with stage fright. She'd be crying, protesting that she didn't want to do whatever it was she had to do, saying how much she hated it all. Once the car stopped and she stepped out, though, the consummate professional took over. She'd be charm and graciousness itself, letting everyone know how much she wanted to meet them, how happy she was to see them."

Official duties were a war fought on two fronts. The first front was the occasion itself, before which Diana's supporting troops would have to rally to her aid so that she actually arrived on the scene. The second was the background material which Diana was obliged to read before an engagement. "I remember once, I was in her bedroom with her," Sonia Palmer said, "Oliver Everett, her Private Secretary was trying to reach her on the squawk box, which connected the office to the bedroom. He was chasing her up about some reports which she was meant to be reading. By then he knew she wouldn't even look at them if he didn't keep at her. If he did, she'd at least give them a cursory glance. That was better than nothing. Anyway, to cut a long story short, as soon as he came on to the squawk box, she took some pillows off the bed and buried it to block out the sound. She had a determined look on her face. Her jaw was set, her eyes spitting daggers.

"Her attitude was, 'The public already think I'm marvellous, so why should I waste my time boning up on boring subjects?'"

With such feelings of aversion towards the official side of being a princess, it is no wonder that Diana hated living at Buckingham Palace. The Waleses' private apartments and offices were in easy reach of each other, which meant that she had no escape from the courtiers who were exerting what she took to be "excessive pressure" upon her.

Five weeks before William's birth, Charles and Diana resolved the problem by moving into their official London residence, Apartments 8 and 9 Kensington Palace. To her relief, the move made Diana less accessible to the courtiers responsible for her public life. There was no dreaded squawk box, and she could hide away far more effectively in her new home, which was a large, L-shaped, three-story house with twenty-five principal rooms and many subsidiary ones. Their nearest neighbours were Prince and Princess Michael of Kent, at No. 10, with whom they shared a courtyard. Close by were Princess Margaret and the Duke and Duchess of Gloucester, the royal cousins who had accompanied Charles on that ill-fated ski trip to Klosters which signalled the end of his romance with Sarah Spencer. And of course Diana's sister Jane lived there, in a cottage called the Old Barracks, with her husband, Robert Fellowes.

Charles had left the decoration of both Kensington Palace and Highgrove House to Diana. It is a testament to his trust in her, and to her confidence, sophistication and energy that she was able, at the tender age of twenty and despite health problems, to steer Dudley Poplak, the South African-born interior designer she inherited from her mother, into executing her ideas. Diana had well-developed likes and dislikes. For instance, she refused to have any sheets but traditional white Irish linen. She wanted cheerful and tasteful rooms in the aristocratic, country-house mould. Her ideas did not always coincide with the Prince of Wales's, who nevertheless gave her her way (a compromise he reversed at Highgrove as soon as they separated. Within weeks, the rooms were being changed, all traces of Diana's handiwork eradicated).

Pregnancy and illness did not impede Diana in her quest to fashion for herself an environment in which she could be happy. "I'm a hands-on sort," she used to say, and many of her staff can attest to the accuracy of that statement. She also had the highest standards possible. Her houses had to sparkle. As soon as she or the Prince had left a room, it had to be vacuumed. After resting, beds had to be remade, crumpled sheets ironed. Her clothes had to be cleaned and pressed after each wearing, and woe betide any maid or dresser who did not iron every collar and cuff, every hem and crease, just so. She was as hard a taskmistress with staff as she was with herself, leaving no room for failure or foible.

Diana was also a hands-on mother, to such an extent that Barbara Barnes sometimes found herself with little or nothing to do. While Diana was breast-feeding William, her health, weight and state of mind stabilised. Her pH balance was restored, her moods levelled off, and she enjoyed one of the two most fulfilling periods of her life. She was no longer the svelte bride who had walked up the aisle. She was more reminiscent of the voluptuary whose embonpoint were, as Lady Diana Cooper had wittily observed on Diana's first public engagement, "a feast to set before a king."

Charles was also happy to have back the girl he had asked to marry him. "He relished the harmony, the peace, the joy of a happy family life," Prince George of Denmark said. "This is what he'd married for. He was also thrilled to have a woman with something to grab hold of. His taste has always been for well-endowed women."

William's christening was arranged and his godparents chosen in this atmosphere of harmony and cooperation. Diana, having chosen her son's name, was happy to step aside and let Charles have the greater say. The godparents, all appropriate for a future king, were the exiled King Constantine of the Hellenes, head of the former Prince Philip of Greece's family and a close friend of Charles's; Lord Mountbatten's grandson Lord Romsey; Sir Laurens van der Post, the South African writer and philosopher; Princess Alexandra, Charles's cousin and great friend; Lady Susan Hussey, another friend of the couple and the lady-in-waiting who had taught Diana the feminine side of the royal role; and the Duchess of Westminster, another recent friend of the couple.

As soon as Diana stopped breast-feeding William, she resolved to lose the weight she had gained. Clothes had become something of a passion for her, and she aimed to achieve the slender elegance of the models who already fascinated her. Within weeks, unfortunately, she was back in the grips of both anorexia and bulimia. It was only a matter of time before she had once more lost control over her actions and was purging herself four and five times a day, expelling the food which she could not resist eating. Her pH balance askew, it was inevitable that her moods and behaviour would follow suit.

This time, Diana's problems were clearer to those closest to her. Having seen the pattern of bulimia, clinical depression, and emotional outbursts once more, Charles, his family and advisors were able to understand that she had a major problem, and that that problem needed treatment.

The Royal Family is frequently portrayed as being out of touch with their human feelings. The impression given is that they are so repressed that they wouldn't know an emotion if it hit them. They are meant to have a deep and abiding loathing not only of emotion but also of anything associated with it. Psychiatry, individuality, even normal displays of joy and pain are supposedly anathema to them. The truth is at variance with that image. The Queen, Princess Margaret, the Duchess of Kent, Prince Charles and Prince Andrew have all, at some time, consulted psychiatrists. Moreover, the more senior royals all did so at a time when psychiatry was regarded with deep suspicion by even sophisticated Britons. Their attitude is more intelligible if you know that Prince Philip's Aunt Marie (Princess George of Greece, née Princess Marie Bonaparte), with whom he and his family lived at St. Cloud outside Paris after they were exiled from Greece, was one of the most eminent female psychoanalysts in the world. Trained by Freud, she and his daughter, Anna, were two of the very few accredited female practitioners of Freudian psychoanalysis.

With a background steeped in psychiatry, it is hardly surprising that the first thing Charles did was suggest to Diana that she see a psychiatrist. "There is nothing wrong with me," she insisted, and continued insisting for the next several years. This denial is standard fare when dealing with bulimics, but Charles persisted, realizing that he would never have the sort of marriage he wanted as long as Diana remained ill. Finally, she agreed to see Dr Allan McGlashan, who came highly recommended by Laurens van der Post and who has a particular aptitude for analysing dreams as a means of putting the patient in touch with his or her unconscious. Charles also saw him. While Dr McGlashan's techniques proved compatible for the Prince of Wales, who continued to see him regularly at his office near Sloane Square, Diana had no wish to poke around in her unconscious, whether by means of dream analysis or any other form of therapy. "My problems had nothing to do with my past," she maintained. "I was fine until I got sucked into the royal way of life. That's my problem." In this assessment, she was both correct and blinkered, for the fact remains that she would never have broken down the way she did, if she had not had a troubled family history. She would never achieve a state of genuine healthiness until she accepted that she had her own problems. This she was not yet ready to do, though she would do so later. So she demanded that Dr McGlashan stop coming to see her.

With Charles's psychiatrist out of the way, Diana was seen by Dr David Mitchell, who went to Kensington Palace in the early evening for his consultations. His focus being more on cognitive therapy than on

Diana's unconscious, he used to ask her to recount what was happening in her life, especially in her marriage. According to Diana's account of these sessions, she would start to recount an exchange with Charles, the tears would flow, and the remainder of the session would be dedicated to Dr Mitchell's watching while she cried uncontrollably.

Not surprisingly, Dr Mitchell made no more headway with his uncooperative patient than Dr McGlashan had done. So began the long parade of psychiatrists and psychologists in and out of Kensington Palace.

The Society psychiatrist Dr Michael Davies told me, "In the early eighties, the doctors were not sure whether she was merely mentally ill or psychotic. There's an important distinction between the two conditions. If you're mentally ill but basically normal – in other words, your everyday, seriously disturbed neurotic – you're treatable as long as you want help. With cooperation, you may even be curable. But if you're psychotic, that means you're insane. That makes you a lot less treatable, and the cure rate is not encouraging.

"She was exhibiting symptoms which could be interpreted either way. There was the bulimia, which is a serious mental illness and can lead to death. There was the clinical depression, which is another serious mental illness and led to her uncle's suicide. There was the self-mutilation, which was not severe and struck me as histrionic rather than serious, but which nevertheless had to be classified as a mental illness and had to be taken seriously. More worrying, she was exhibiting symptoms of paranoia and schizophrenia – symptoms, incidentally, which she continued exhibiting, in varying degrees of severity, until her death. So the question everyone wanted to know was: Is she a bulimic/depressive/self-mutilating neurotic, or is she a paranoid-schizophrenic whose symptoms are manifesting in those terms? Her behaviour certainly indicated that she was, if not a fully fledged paranoid-schizophrenic, suffering from a borderline personality disorder. The question the doctors had to ask was, Is this a girl who cannot fit in and cannot take responsibility for her actions, so projects her incapacity onto others, or is she someone who has unwarranted suspicions, who imagines plots and schemes where there are none, who has a fractured personality and wavers between seeming reasonableness and overt irrationality?"

Once the Royal Family and their advisors became aware that Diana was not only mentally ill, but might also be clinically insane, they were struck with horror. While they tried to keep a sense of proportion, they also swung into action to ensure that no one would ever find out about the Princess of Wales's condition. The one reassuring aspect of her condition was that she did not seem to be suffering from classical schizophrenia, a condition that is sometimes hereditary. At least William and, later, Harry were spared the prospect of Diana doing to the royal genes at the end of the twentieth century what Queen Victoria had done at the end of the nineteenth to the Russian and Spanish Royal Houses by passing on the recessive gene for haemophilia. The consequent turmoil had resulted in both monarchies collapsing under the strain.

The true nature of Diana's condition was never resolved satisfactorily. Two couples, however, who reluctantly came to the conclusion that her emotional problems extended far beyond the norm were Nicholas and Catherine Soames, and Peter and Hayat Palumbo. Neither couple was unintelligent or unsophisticated, nor did any of the four parties wish Diana anything but the best. Nevertheless, with the passage of time, they all came to view Diana's mental state as desperate.

Nicholas Soames was the first to become convinced that the diagnosis of paranoia was correct. He had been a friend of the Prince of Wales for years, as well as having been his equerry from 1970 to 1972, so he knew the public and private faces of the man. Moreover, his knowledge was extensive owing to the extreme incestuousness of the circles in which he moved. Not only had he been on the spot for Charles's first and second affairs with Camilla Parker Bowles in the early and late seventies, due to his friendship with the Prince, but also his sister Charlotte had been Andrew Parker Bowles's girlfriend during the late seventies. Indeed, when his father, Lord Soames, became Governor of Southern Rhodesia in 1979 prior to the hand-over of power from the breakaway state of Rhodesia to the legitimate authorities of Zimbabwe on 18 April 1980, the scene was set for an incredible display of musical chairs. The Prince of Wales flew to Rhodesia as the official representative of the British nation for the independence celebrations. Camilla Parker Bowles was his official hostess, while Charlotte Soames Hambro was in attendance upon Andrew Parker Bowles, who was also a member of the official party. To say it was incestuous would not only be accurate, but also shows why Nicholas Soames had such an inside track on the realities of the relationship between Camilla Parker Bowles and the Prince of Wales.

With such firsthand knowledge, Soames knew that Diana's continuing suspicions about the nature of Charles and Camilla's relationship were unfounded. He also had experience of the way the royal system works, and could see that Diana's suspicions that the courtiers were out to break her spirit and wreck her life could not have been further from the truth. They wanted a strong and successful Princess of Wales, if only because that was the sort of princess who was best for the institution to which they had dedicated their lives. They had no motive in destroying her, and her imaginings to the contrary were, in Soames's view, evidence that she was indeed paranoid.

Nicholas Soames's ex-wife, Catherine, took longer to come to the same conclusion. Indeed, for many years she did not agree with her ex-husband's assessment. She and Diana became close friends. Her son and the Wales boys, being of similar ages, became good friends as well. Diana and Catherine, with and without their kids, spent a great deal of time together. They went to lunch. They had dinner parties. They spent weekends together. They even went on holidays abroad together. Then in 1995, out of the blue, Diana dumped Catherine. "I'm positive she's leaking information about me back to my husband through her ex-husband," Diana said. Catherine, of course, was doing no such thing, but once a suspicion of that nature entered Diana's head, it assumed the status of fact and that was the end of the matter.

When the Palumbos got to know Diana well, they also came to the reluctant conclusion that her mental illness was more serious than it appeared to be upon first inspection. They became close friends with Diana through Lucia Flecha de Lima, the wife of the Brazilian Ambassador to the Court of St. James's who became Diana's surrogate mother. When her husband was posted to Washington, she asked her good friends Lord and Lady Palumbo to keep an eye on Diana, who was then between her separation and her divorce. This they did, striking up a quick and close friendship. Diana and Hayat Palumbo could often be seen lunching at fashionable clubs such as Harry's Bar. The Palumbos had her for dinner, to dinner parties, and even took her to Paris on their private plane.

It was in Paris that Peter and Hayat Palumbo first became aware that Diana was seriously ill. On the first day, she was her normal self: witty, engaging, fun, agreeable, civilized, pleasant. The following morning, however, she came down for breakfast in a "black mood." She "refused to speak to anyone." She was encircled in gloom, uncommunicative, uncooperative, unapproachable. No matter what they did to try to break through the wall, Diana repulsed them with imperviousness. She only came out of this "terrifying state" when they all left the house and some strangers came up to speak to her, having recognized her. In a dramatic shift of mood, she responded normally and cheerfully. The incident was edifying for the Palumbos, and illustrative of the depressions to which Diana remained prone, albeit with a slight improvement, until her death.

Even Vivienne Parry, Diana's close friend who would subsequently become a member of the Diana Princess of Wales Memorial Committee, confirmed that Diana, "though not mad, as she has sometimes been portrayed," "was certainly mentally ill at times in her life."

In the early and mid-eighties, while therapist after therapist trooped through Kensington Palace, assessing her mental state, Diana's attitude to them was simple. "How can they understand what I'm going through when they've never gone through it themselves?" she asked, as she spurned their help and tried to gain control of her life through more overt means.

As far as Diana was concerned, her problems could not be solved until she had altered the basic structure of her life. She wanted a life that she had fashioned herself. She could not abide the way the royals themselves are steered and directed by their advisors and officials, having little or no control over vast aspects of their existence. She saw no reason why she had to put up with a system which cut into her liberty. She intended to try to change it.

Diana had always been a nonconformist beneath her seemingly conventional exterior, even at school, and now she began giving this streak its head. Her assertiveness seems at odds with the fact that so many people found her to be insecure, but Dr Panzer resolves that anomaly. "People who are afraid or insecure, people who are out of control, often seek to impose control externally. Insecure people often overreact. The more insecure they are, the more they assert themselves in order to cover their insecurity. In other words, if I am secure I don't have to fire my wife's cook, but one of the ways to show I am the boss – because I am insecure – is to fire my wife's cook."

When she married Charles, Diana could easily have stepped into his way of life, limiting her sphere of influence to the decoration of their town and country homes, taking care of her baby, planning their social life, and doing her royal duties. She could have taken the view that much of his life was already set up, and that she would concentrate on setting up her own or upon their joint life together. She did not do so, however. She had always been energetic and romantic, with strong ideas of what the role of wife entailed. She had ambitions to leave her mark upon every aspect of their life together. In her view, a husband and wife should be inseparable, which meant that there was no area of Charles's life over which she should not hold sway. The only exception was his official role. That held even less interest for Diana than her own official obligations did. She was therefore only too happy to give that a wide berth.

In Diana's view, Charles's life needed a good "shake-up." "He was surrounded by hangers-on," she told me, dismissing people whom he regarded as long-standing and loyal friends with the contempt she felt they deserved. William's birth had given her the confidence of being the mother of the future king, and she used it to eradicate people whose presence she deemed detracted from the quality of life. The Parker Bowleses she had already seen off during the first year of marriage, suspicious that Charles might still be hankering after his former mistress. The Tryons she also refused to allow Charles to see, for the same reason. With the pre-marital royal mistresses safely out of the picture, Diana turned her attention to Charles and Patti Palmer-Tompkinson, Nicholas Soames, Penelope and Norton Romsey, and, while she was about it, his parents John Brabourne and Patricia Mountbatten of Burma. It was her considered opinion that Charles should replace these people with friends whom he and Diana made together. The Romseys and Nicholas Soames she wanted out because she had got a whiff of their disapproval of her, but the Brabournes she cut out simply because she did not want the awkwardness of having to face the parents when she had frozen out their son and daughter-in-law.

Charles's response to the culling was hardly commendable, but understandable. "He was so desperate to keep Diana happy that he dropped us all," one of his friends, who does not wish to be identified, said. "We understood he was being forced by circumstances beyond his control to choose between us and his wife, but it hurt nevertheless."

Keeping Diana sweet was a goal Charles shared with his mother. Even before Diana had been diagnosed as being mentally ill, the Queen had counselled patience and indulgence. "She needs time to get used to all of this," Elizabeth II told Princess Margaret of Hesse and the Rhine, waving her arms to take in the palatial surroundings.

"The Queen has a reputation for being dour and unsympathetic, but, if anything, she's too indulgent as a mother and mother-in-law," John Kennedy, Prince Michael's former Private Secretary, said. "She's so used to looking at the world through the eyes of African presidents and West Indian prime ministers, she's developed this capacity for putting herself in other people's shoes. That's a tremendous strength politically, though not everyone thinks it's a virtue in terms of dealing with her family. It makes her too understanding. The result is they get away with what the public regards as murder."

Once Diana's malady was known, however, the Queen's approach made sound sense. Diana must be accommodated. The system must find a way of being flexible enough to absorb her without exacerbating her condition. Humanity and the interests of the monarchy dictated that a certain amount of appeasement be employed. After all, she was now the Princess of Wales. She was the mother of the future King William V. She was a permanent part of the Royal Family, or so, at any rate, the thinking went at the time. A *modus vivendi* had to be found which protected her, both from the public gaining knowledge about the true state of her health, and from the worst effects of her illness. Diana must not therefore be weighed down with official duties which were anathema to her. It was important that she be seen, not only because the public adored her, and because official duties are the work which the Royal Family undertake to fulfill their end of the monarchic bargain, but also because the surest way for the public to realize that something was amiss was for Diana to retire or fulfill too few engagements.

Faced with a measured number of engagements, Diana fulfilled them ably but painfully. She was willing to please, however, and never once sought to avoid any official obligation. Even when she had to leave a dinner table at a state banquet to be sick, she would always return to her place.

Work was only a minor part of Diana's life at that stage. Having done what she could do to sort out Charles's and her own social life, the Princess next turned her attention to his staff. All the major positions were occupied by people who had been with him for years, some since he was a teenager. Feeling at a disadvantage because most of them knew more about her husband than she did, Diana decided to rid herself of those whose presence made her uncomfortable. The first to go was Chief Detective Paul Officer, the six-foot former public schoolboy who had saved Charles's life when a rating on a Royal Navy training exercise at Poole, Dorset, had gone berserk and tried to crack open the Prince's skull with a chair. With no thought for his own safety, Officer had jumped between his charge and the assailant, wrestling him to the ground before he could injure Charles. Charles had sacrificed his favourite protection officer for Diana, but she could not stand the control he sought to exert over her, and she forced him out. According to her, her method was simple and effective. "If I don't want someone around me, I freeze them out. I act as if they're not there. I won't talk to them. I don't listen to them, respond – nothing. It works every time."

Having tried and succeeded with Paul Officer, Diana next used the technique on Charles's valet, Stephen Barry. Even though they had got along well in the early days, while Charles was courting her and Barry had to drive her on assignations, she claimed to have developed a dislike of him because he had once, before the wedding, refused her access to the Prince of Wales with the words, "HRH says no one is allowed in, Lady Diana. I'm sorry, but orders are orders. I hope you understand."

While Diana was infuriated whenever crossed, this incident seems to have been the catalyst, as opposed to the cause, which brought a power struggle to a head. Until his marriage, the Prince of Wales invariably allowed his valet to choose what he wore for him. Stephen Barry would therefore make a selection of shirt, tie, suit, socks, handkerchief, and shoes from the extensive array of clothes which Charles had. He would lay his selection out on the Prince's bed, and, whenever necessary, help him get dressed. Diana, however, wanted a say in what her husband wore. "You look like a stiff. You embarrass me in front of my friends," she told him, hoping to induce him to change his mode of attire. Barry, in her opinion, "had too much influence." He had been with the Prince of Wales ever since he was an adult. He and Charles were genuinely fond of one another. They valued one another's opinions. Moreover, he had seen every girl come and go. "I wasn't the only one he fetched and carried," Diana told Sonia Palmer, who got the impression that she wanted to put space between Charles's past and herself. What sealed Barry's fate was that he did not concede to Diana's authority. As far as he was concerned, Charles was his boss, Diana only the boss's wife. "He was always crossing swords with me," Diana said. "He didn't know his place."

Diana resolved to replace the valet with Ken Stronach, Barry's assistant, who had been valet to Earl Mountbatten of Burma until his assassination in 1979. John Barratt, Lord Mountbatten's Private Secretary, had then arranged for him to go to work for Charles. Where Diana was concerned, Stronach was easier to handle than Barry. He was subservient where Barry was opinionated. He was easygoing where Barry was punctilious. He was polite without being as friendly as Barry. In other words, he knew his place and was happy to concede that Diana was also his boss. "Although not pompous, she did insist upon subservience," Sonia Palmer said, and Diana, who, quite truthfully, said as much herself: "I don't mind if they forget the occasional Ma'am, as long as they remember that they're here to fulfill my wishes."

Barry responded to the deep-freeze the way Diana expected. After trying to ignore and rise above it, he became so disturbed by it that he tendered his resignation to the Prince of Wales. He was not dismissed, as the tabloids would later claim, nor did he and Diana have a row. "One day he simply decided he'd had enough," Sonia Palmer said. "The atmosphere was too unpleasant. Life was too short. But he and the Prince remained on good terms, even after he wrote his memoirs. He'd never signed the Official Secrets Act, you see, and he didn't violate HRH's trust. He was discreet enough to take all the choice morsels to the grave when he died of AIDS."

With Barry out of the way, Diana turned her attention to Oliver Everett. She was fed up with her Private Secretary. "She went off Oliver for a variety of reasons," according to Sonia Palmer. "She blamed him for the professional pressure she felt was ruining her life. Of course, he was not to blame. Even though she did not see it, she was not exactly overworked." She had more time off than most working mothers. "He had a difficult time with her from the very beginning. First there was the never-ending battle of getting her to read the reports. Then once she settled into the role of being Princess of Wales and read the reports he distilled for her onto cue cards, she wanted an unacceptable amount of flexibility. You know the royals' diaries are filled six months in advance. Well, one of Diana's friends would ask her for lunch or dinner, she'd say yes, then she'd want Oliver to rearrange her diary. But that was not possible. He couldn't very well let people down when they'd been waiting four or six months to see the Princess of Wales, just because she wanted to see a friend instead. So he'd put his foot down and tell her no, she couldn't do what she wanted, and she had to honour her commitments. She didn't like that. Not one bit.

"Oliver had to put up with a lot, but he took it all in his stride. His attitude was, 'She's young.' He never forgot that no twenty-or twenty-two-year-old likes being burdened with responsibility, and he never allowed her turns to affect their relationship."

Diana, at first, seemed to respond in the same mature manner. One day towards the end of 1983, however, she stopped speaking to Oliver Everett without warning. Notwithstanding that Charles had promised the former high-flying diplomat a lifelong career as Diana's Private Secretary and Comptroller, and that a change of position within the royal hierarchy would be a demotion, Diana decided to rid herself of him by freezing him out. This she did as effectively as she had done with Stephen Barry and Paul Officer. "I left the Prince and Princess of Wales in December 1983 and came to Windsor in January 1984," Oliver Everett, who became the Queen's Librarian at Windsor Castle, told me.

The Oliver Everett saga did more damage to Diana's reputation both at the Palace and in the media than anything before and few things since. She took the view, however, that she should not have to be stuck with a Private Secretary whom she did not wish to have. And she much preferred damaging his career to having his presence in her life affect her peace of mind. Looked at from her point of view, it was a rational decision and one she had the courage to implement, irrespective of the disapproval of just about everyone surrounding her.

Thereafter, there was a vigorous turnover in Diana's household. Barbara Barnes, Victoria Mendham, Jane Atkinson, Geoffrey Crawford and Patrick Jephson were the tip of the iceberg. All left suddenly, harmony shattered at the end of what had seemed to be enduring relationships.

The first to go was Barbara Barnes. Their relationship had been somewhat checkered. Baba, as she was called, was used to being an integral part of a harmonious and bohemian family. She had worked for fifteen years for Colin Tennant, now Lord Glenconner, and his wife, the former Lady Anne Coke, whom Johnnie Spencer had thrown over for Diana's mother. She was used to being a valued part of their family, but coped well with the hot-and-cold, in one-minute-out-the-next atmosphere that prevailed at Kensington Palace.

Coping with Diana's mood swings was difficult for everyone, but Diana, always a devoted but jealous mother, seemed to have Nanny Barnes too much in her sights for comfort. "It was as if she had to exert her authority whenever she saw how fond the children were of their nanny," Sonia Palmer said. "It was as if she was saying, 'Don't encourage them to love you too much. I'm their mother and I must come first.' She had done the same thing with the Prince of Wales, when he wiped his diary clear to take care of William. He didn't make the mistake of doing that again with Harry, because she used to have such goes at him over William. 'I'm his mother,' she once snapped at him right in front of me. 'He doesn't need two mothers. Why don't you go back to work and get out from under my feet?' She certainly could be protective of her position *vis-à-vis* her children." That is undoubtedly so, for, as everyone knows, Diana loved her boys more than anything else on earth, and had an almost atavistic connection with them, showering them with kisses and cuddles, sleeping with them, as she told me, until they reached puberty, and generally making sure that the mother-child bond was so strong that she was the foremost influence in their lives.

With a Nanny who was used to being treated as part of the family, and not as good-friend-in-the-morning and hired-help-in-the-afternoon, and a mother who was as protective of the bond between her sons and herself as Diana was, trouble was bound to loom sooner or later. The fact that it took five years is a testament to the two women's tolerance.

The rupture took place as a result of Barbara Barnes using her holiday time to attend Colin Glenconner's elaborate birthday celebrations in Mustique. Treated as an honoured guest, she received almost as much media coverage as Princess Margaret, Mick Jagger, Jerry Hall and Raquel Welch. She returned to Kensington Palace with a glow and a tan, only to be confronted by a glowering Diana, who had already complained to another member of her staff, "It's time for her to go. She's forgotten who the star turn is around here." Of course, Miss Barnes had courted publicity no more than Jane Atkinson later would, but Diana did not consider the fact that they were both victims of attention rather than instigators of it. As soon as Baba Barnes returned, Diana "accepted" the resignation she had not tendered.

Victoria Mendham was another one whose position was scuppered after a West Indian sojourn. Diana's loyal assistant, she was such a close friend that they travelled to the West Indies together not once, but twice. Then they had a rancorous falling out in the year before Diana's death, when Diana discovered that Miss Mendham had not been footing her own travel bills, but had been passing them on to the Palace for payment. "I will not be used," Diana insisted, even after being told by more than one friend that she was being naïve in expecting an employee to foot expensive travel bills which could have gobbled up her annual salary. Joseph Sanders told me, "I dropped the subject when she turned bright red and said, 'Are you taking her side?' I knew Diana too well to say anything but 'Of course not. I was just trying to put her point of view across.' 'Well, don't,' Diana said. 'Users don't have a right to a point of view.' She could be unbelievably naïve. She'd never had to budget in her life, so she didn't understand that secretaries can't write cheques to match the Princess of Wales's. And she demanded 110 percent loyalty. If I hadn't dropped the subject, she'd have dropped me for not being loyal to her. That's how she was. Loyalty meant a lot to her. More than friendship."

Because she had such exacting standards, Diana did not always appreciate when she was asking too much from employees. Jane Atkinson was a case in point. Her media advisor when Diana was making the transition from royal wife to ex-royal ex-wife, "Jane Atkinson was fantastic," according to Joseph Sanders. A part of Atkinson's job was to brief the press, to establish good working relationships with its members, and to get them to put a positive spin upon Diana's activities and interests. Of necessity, that called for cultivating journalists in a spirit of cordiality. Unfortunately, Jane Atkinson was such a success that one or two stories appeared attesting to the excellent job she was doing on behalf of her boss. There were two versions of what happened next. The first is that Diana became disenchanted with Atkinson because "I don't see why my media advisor has to be written about almost as much as I am," Joseph Sanders told me.

Atkinson, for her part, was becoming disenchanted with a charge who never took her advice. For instance, at the time of Diana's loss of the title Her Royal Highness, Atkinson strongly counselled her against resigning from the hundred charities she supported, warning her the media would interpret it as vengeful pique. Diana ignored her, resigned, issued a statement linking her decision to the loss of the title, then was upset when she received the adverse publicity Atkinson had warned her about.

Diana's response to the divergence of opinion and style between her media advisor and herself was to pile on the pressure to encourage Atkinson to depart. "Jane told me that the pressure became too much," Joseph Sanders said. "She had no time for anything else in her life. Diana, a notoriously early riser, would start phoning her from six o'clock in the morning. Once, Jane was having a dinner party. Diana phoned her so many times she didn't have time for her guests. It wasn't an emergency either. Just something that was on Diana's mind, and she wanted to work it out. She was devouring Jane. It became too much."

To Diana's detractors, this behaviour was indicative of a self-centred woman who thought of no one but herself. To her admirers – and most of her staff were admirers for much of their time with her – it was reflective of Diana's inability to turn off her emotions. "She was always being engulfed by her feelings," Joseph Sanders said. "She couldn't help herself. People understood. Ultimately, though, it made working for her and having your own life impossible. You had to sacrifice one or the other. Naturally, people ended up choosing themselves. Her behaviour wasn't deliberate. Her feelings used to get the better of her."

This tendency to alienate the people closest to her was a problem Diana had had to struggle with ever since she had first become ill. Regrettably, it is one which many people suffer from when they are in the throes of a serious mental illness. "The fact is, the people closest to her knew she was ill and made allowances," Lady Sarah Spencer-Churchill said. Even then, Diana was often bitterly disappointed when employees departed. Three over whom she cried were Evelyn Dagley, her dresser; Geoffrey Crawford, her Press Secretary; and Patrick Jephson, her longest-serving Private Secretary.

"Evelyn had been with her from her earliest days," Joseph Sanders said. "She even went on her honeymoon with her. Finally though, she couldn't cope with the volatility anymore. One minute Diana would be her normal self – the person the public knew and loved – then something would happen and her stress level would rise. Whoosh. Diana would be screaming down KP (Kensington Palace), throwing her dresses about the place, finding fault where there was none. Evelyn has always publicly denied that that's why she left, but I can tell you categorically, that's the real reason. She didn't go public because she liked Diana and understood that she often didn't mean to say or do the things she did. Whether she meant them or not, she did them, and it became too nerve-racking having a boss with a volcanic temperament."

Geoff Crawford's and Patrick Jephson's resignations had nothing to do with personal relations between Diana and themselves, and therefore were a shock to her when they came. Diana had gone behind their backs and arranged the *Panorama* interview with Martin Bashir which was, according to her good friend Rosa Monckton, "Diana at her worst." Crawford, who had loyally followed her after her separation, resigned as her Press Secretary as soon as he learned of the interview's existence. Jephson, who had been her Private Secretary for years and was her most loyal supporter, resigned a few weeks later.

"He loved her," John Kennedy said, speaking about Jephson. "Even though the clever career move would have been to take the Prince of Wales's side at the time of the divorce, he chose her. He would never hear a word spoken against her. But when he saw the *Panorama* interview and saw for himself the lengths to which Diana was going to deprive the Prince of Wales of his right to the throne, he finally understood that, no matter how much he liked her personally, she really could be extremely vengeful and destructive. His view was that, as long as things between the Prince and Princess were personal, he could take her side. But once her behaviour was damaging the monarchy, the time had come to resign." Amid tears from Diana, he did.

It would dishonour Diana's memory not to close on a note that took account of the many kindnesses she showed her staff. When her dresser Fay Marshalsea and her private detective Inspector Graham Smith had cancer, she could not have been more solicitous. She visited them in the hospital. She wrote them notes. She sent them flowers. She even took "Smudger" Smith along as a guest on a Mediterranean cruise in 1991. And Paul Burrell, who had started out as her butler and ended up effectively her personal assistant, still thinks the world of her. The final word belongs to him. This man, who was the only nonfamily member to attend her burial, said, "She was truly marvellous."

Ten

The period between the births of Prince William on 21 June 1982 and Prince Harry on 15 September 1984 seemed to Diana to be productive and painful but reassuring and hopeful.

Desperately in love with Prince Charles, she aimed her efforts at laying down bricks in the courtyard of her personal life with the view that these would be permanent. The marriage of the Prince and Princess of Wales was reckoned to be indissoluble. Diana did not mind the sacrifices she was making, for she genuinely believed that her efforts were being rewarded. Although the relationship between the Prince and herself was not perfect, she believed she was "training my husband" and would eventually achieve the sort of marriage and family life she wanted.

Despite those positive feelings, Diana also felt that the marriage was not bringing her the personal satisfaction she craved. Charles was not attentive enough. He was not emotional enough. He was not demonstrative enough. He was not affectionate enough. He was not sufficiently highly sexed, or he was, as she put it to me and to many others, "Dead below the waist."

For the first, but by no means last, time in her marriage, Diana took a measured view of her predicament and came up with a worldly and traditional response. The 17th Earl of Pembroke was a tall, slim, dashingly handsome movie producer, "with the ideal looks for a romantic hero," according to Barbara Cartland. His ancestral home, Wilton House near Salisbury in Wiltshire, was one of the most beautiful houses in Britain, boasting a double cube room with Van Dyck ceilings among other treasures. While the Spencers were, in aristocratic terms, middling, Henry

Herbert, Earl of Pembroke and Montgomery, was top drawer. He and the rest of his family had always mixed in royal circles, as I can personally attest to, having first met him in 1975 at a party given by Princess Elizabeth of Yugoslavia, a royal cousin, at her house on the King's Road in Chelsea. Moreover, his aunt, Viscountess Hambleden, was a closer friend and higher-ranking lady-in-waiting to Queen Elizabeth the Queen Mother than Ruth Fermoy.

When Diana first became captivated by him, Henry Pembroke was anything but a stuffed shirt. The ultimate aristocrat, he was refreshingly unpretentious, with a mind and a direction of his own. In fact, to the more stuffy members of the aristocracy, he was almost *risqué*, though they never held that against him, not when they might receive invitations to so famous a stately home as Wilton House.

Pembroke had produced *Emily*, a film co-starring a seventeen-year-old American actress named Koo Stark, who cavorted around semi-nude. This would later haunt the unfortunate Miss Stark when Prince Andrew fell in love with her. Notwithstanding that the Queen was much taken with the elegant, intelligent and discreet Koo, the press never mentioned her name without describing her as a "soft-porn actress," which she was not really, but which had the effect of scuppering her chances of becoming the Duchess of York.

Mixing in overlapping circles, it was only a matter of time before Henry Pembroke caught Diana's eye. Even though he was a decade older than Charles, in 1983 the recently divorced celebrity earl was still so strikingly handsome in the Clint Eastwood mould that his age did not deter her.

Much has been made over assertions by certain writers over the years that Diana had difficulty getting pregnant a second time. This was not actually so. Both the Prince and Princess of Wales wanted a two-year gap between their children. Moreover, she was hardly going to be trying for a second baby, the "spare" to insure against anything happening to the "heir," while she was interested in another man. Whatever criticisms her detractors would later make of her, no one could accuse Diana of ignorance of the royal way. She, above all, understood the importance of producing children whose paternity could never be called into question, even though, by a strange irony, her second son's paternity would later on be, once she had confirmed her love affair with James Hewitt and people thought they discerned a resemblance between her declared lover and her second son. This, however, is not the time to address that issue, though address it I will later on in this work.

Diana's relationship with Henry Pembroke has remained a closely guarded secret within the upper echelons of aristocratic circles. Not one word of it has ever leaked out. No journalist or gossip columnist has ever known about it. It was not love. Pembroke gave her what she needed: a feeling that she was desirable, that she was not stifling within her marriage, that life still held out possibilities and the prospect of fun and games with fascinating men. "Not a stiff like Charles," as she described the handsome earl.

Diana's relationship with Henry Pembroke did not last long. By the time she was ready to try for another child, the divorced producer/aristocrat was a happy, ego-boosting memory. Fortified with the positive feelings the relationship had given her, she returned her attention to her husband with a new softness. The result was that Diana considered the run-up to Harry's birth an especially harmonious period between the Prince of Wales and herself, and she said, "We were getting along better than ever."

Throughout this second pregnancy, Diana made sure she did not gain weight as she had done with William. She was still bulimic, still prone to emotional outbursts, still a victim of mood swings, still a prisoner to crying jags, still inordinately suspicious. Intent on placating his pregnant wife, Charles more or less let her do as she pleased, agreeing even when he did not wish to do so. For that reason, Diana was under the illusion that her "training," to use the word she employed about shaping her husband, was working. Charles was finally becoming the obliging and facilitating husband she wanted.

The day after Harry's birth, at 2:30 on Sunday afternoon, Charles picked up his elegantly attired and beautifully made-up and coiffed wife and infant from the Lindo Wing of St. Mary's Paddington and took them back to Kensington Palace. Diana did not want to stay in the hospital longer than necessary for several reasons, one of which was that she did not propose to give the medical staff an opportunity to observe her bulimic habits.

Charles left Diana to rest at Kensington Palace while he headed for the Guards' Polo Club at Smith's Lawn, Windsor, to play in a match specially arranged to celebrate his second son's birth.

Although Diana felt that she was finally moulding Charles into the sort of husband she wanted, she was about to receive a big disappointment. Regrettably, she had misinterpreted her husband's attitude. Remaining in the grips of bulimia throughout her second pregnancy, with all the attendant traumas, she did not understand that she was alienating him by making him feel, as Princess Margaret of Hesse and the Rhine put it, "that he had no rights in his own palace. She believed that the way to keep him by her side was to subjugate him. He kept on appeasing her because he knew she was ill, and because he is the sort of person who will do anything for a peaceful life. But she wasn't training him up, as she once put it to me. She was alienating him. Making him withdraw from her. Killing all the love he had for her."

This opinion is borne out by Lady Theresa Manners. Both Charles and Diana used to ride out with her family hunt, the Belvoir. Both stayed at Belvoir Castle as guests of the family. She knew both since childhood, as well as the rest of their families. She once told me, "I like Diana. She's a very nice person and she's made a great success of being the Princess of Wales. But she's made a big mistake with Prince Charles. It's easy to see why anyone would fall in love with him. But she's gone and become anti-everything he likes. If he wants to fish, she's anti-fishing. If he wants to shoot, she's anti-shooting. If he wants to hunt, she's anti-hunting, even though she'll turn up at Belvoir with her sister Sarah the following week and ride out to hounds with us. You can't make a success of your marriage if you're anti-everything your husband stands for. Her trouble is, she's become too domineering."

Domineering as she appeared to be to some onlookers, the real Diana nevertheless remained insecure within herself, especially about her husband. "Sometimes I felt he loved me. Other times, I was sure he didn't," she admitted. This insecurity became the basis, not only for greater and greater attempts at controlling Charles, but also for the jealousy she felt whenever his attention was directed away from her. One fateful incident involved his Labrador Sandringham. "The Prince loved that dog," a lady-in-waiting said. "One day Diana decreed that he had to get rid of Sandringham. She said she didn't want it messing up her house. I felt the real reason she wanted to be rid of the animal was that he loved it too much. 'He pays more attention to that blasted thing than he does to me,' she complained shortly before she began agitating for him to give it away, which, in my opinion, was a dead giveaway of her true feelings. He fought her over the dog, but in the end she wore him down. I know this will sound ridiculous to people who aren't dog-lovers, but I believe that was a defining moment in their marriage. I think she killed something within him."

In his authorized biography of the Prince of Wales, Jonathan Dimbleby states that the marriage of the Prince and Princess of Wales did not break up because of any one incident, but that it gradually disintegrated. The process, in other words, was cumulative. That point of view reflects Charles's opinion, which accorded with Diana's as well. "I didn't even know it was breaking up until I woke up one day and discovered that I no longer had a marriage," she told me, still smarting from the shock.

It is impossible to understand how the marriage unravelled without examining the conduct, attitudes, personalities and characters of the Prince and Princess of Wales. They were hopelessly incompatible. Where Charles was idealistic but practical, Diana was romantic and naïve. While she thrived on conflict, he shied away from it. He found it difficult to dissemble, while she, like most bulimics, was so adept at masking her true feelings, that people often left with the opposite impression of her true position. Despite an innate dignity, Diana did not mind anyone – friend, relation, staff, stranger – being privy to the most personal details of their lives, even confiding in a Concorde flight attendant whom she saw only once. Charles, on the other hand, had an abiding loathing of "display" and prized his privacy.

Beneath the differences, there were crushing similarities. Both had had damaging childhood experiences which had left them sensitive and self-protective. Each wanted a partner who would put the other first, who would bestow the love, understanding and support which they felt they had not had as children, so needed all the more as adults. Each really wanted the unconditional love of the other. Each wanted the other to be subservient. Each wanted to be in the driver's seat, to call the shots, to become the dominant partner. Charles felt this primary role belonged to him as a right, not only because he was a royal, but also because he was a man. Diana, as a Spencer, believed the dominant position belonged to her. "All the Spencers have strong personalities," Barbara Cartland told me, opining that "Diana was not a person one could ignore." To Diana, being a Spencer meant being the person who had a birthright to call the shots.

Charles and Diana were bound to have problems even if she had not become mentally ill. Her illness, however, blew everything out of proportion. It aggravated the underlying personality conflicts and affected her behaviour in ways that Charles found "a real turn-off," to use the expression he employed. "He hated the way she used to fly at him for no reason, how she would respond to a difference of opinion by shouting or crying, how she would kiss him for something one minute and kick at him about it the next. He never knew where he was with her, what would please her. And she hated it when his response to her response was to walk out, leaving her alone to stew in her own juice," a friend of both said. This Diana herself confirmed, telling me, "I know I rubbed him up the wrong way. I couldn't help it. I couldn't control myself."

After Harry's birth, relations between the Waleses deteriorated rapidly and irrevocably. "Something happened in his head," Diana told me. What happened, according to Princess Margaret of Hesse and the Rhine, is that "one day he'd had enough. It was as simple as that. One day – a day neither he nor she nor anyone else can identify – she pushed him over that invisible line. He didn't realize it at the time, but she'd goaded him past the point of endurance. After that, he retreated into himself."

Charles's withdrawal from Diana was both subtle and obvious. Although he was still polite to her, he was no longer there. He had pulled up the drawbridge emotionally, withdrawn his willingness to cooperate in the marriage being conducted along the lines she had been laying down since 1981.

"I suspect the marriage would still have stood a chance if she'd been able to give him his head some of the time," Joseph Sanders said. Incapable of doing so because of her insecurities, these very demons now rose with fresh vengeance to undermine Diana's marriage further. All her old suspicions about him loving someone more than her resurfaced. This scenario, according to Dr Basil Panzer, was a typical response to a marriage in difficulty. As he put it, speaking about the archetypal husband and wife, "She gets worse. He goes out more innocently. And she gets suspicious of this. 'Does this man have a mistress?' she asks herself when he does not come home from the office on time. This is normal enough. So, too, is the young woman who finds herself suspicious when her husband stays at the office, even though he may well be there because he has a lot to do. The first explanation most wives come up with when there is a change in their husbands' behaviour is that he's having an affair."

At first, Diana was not sure whether Charles had returned to Camilla Parker Bowles or whether his eye was travelling elsewhere. "I didn't particularly suspect the Rottweiler," Diana told me through clenched teeth. "I just knew he had to be having an affair. My instincts told me he was."

For one year Diana could find no proof one way or the other. "I had disturbing clues," she said. Charles had now taken to spending nights away with friends when he was on official duties far away from home. He often did not come back from work when she surmised he ought to. And their sex life, which had always been passionate, dipped dramatically.

In 1985, however, through the simple expedient of pressing the recall button on his telephone, Diana discovered that Charles had telephoned Camilla. This was all the proof she needed to become convinced that he had returned to his former mistress. "Within days she had convinced herself that he had never severed relations with Camilla, and that he'd been deceiving her all along," Lady Sarah Spencer-Churchill said. "This was not so. But there was no getting her to see anything to the contrary. Once Diana's mind was made up, it was made up!"

The already disintegrating marriage now came under even more severe strain as Diana, inflamed with jealousy, started hounding Charles about Camilla. "She could not accept that her behaviour had alienated him," Princess Margaret of Hesse and the Rhine said. Diana herself concurred. "He tried to lay a head trip on me, saying that my behaviour drove him away. My behaviour had nothing to do with it. He was having an affair with that woman all along. That was the problem. That's what caused my behaviour. Wouldn't you have been disturbed if your husband was having an affair? No wonder he couldn't give me the love I needed. He was giving it all to bloody Camilla fucking Parker Bowles." Although Diana conceded that there had been a period between 1981 and 1985 when she had not seriously believed that Charles and Camilla were still conducting their old affair, she rationalized that her unconscious had known of the affair all along, and that those unrecognized instincts were what had led her to become ill. In her eyes, that, and of course the pressure and restrictions of being a royal, or, as she put it, a "prisoner" of the "men in grey suits".

The stage was now set for some battles royal. Whatever her weaknesses, no one could accuse Diana of lacking the courage of her convictions. Sensing that she had an invisible opponent, and being a fighter whose goal was victory in any contest, she acted out her distress, not only in accusations and quarrels, but also in symbolic gestures. "Self-mutilation is a sign of feeling worthless," she said. "I was acting out those feelings of worthlessness – of despair. I never did anything to actually hurt myself, though." This was certainly so. She took a lemon slicer and grazed her thigh, drawing little blood and leaving no scar. She passed a penknife over her wrist, neither drawing blood nor leaving a mark. She threw herself at a display cabinet, making sure not to hit it.

Those gestures of distress would later, at her instigation, be blown out of all proportion, and would be distorted as cries for help which constituted suicide attempts. At the time, however, neither Charles nor Diana regarded them as anything of the kind. They were howls of despair; nothing more, nothing less. They were not cries for help; she did not want help. She wanted her husband's love, and she was acting out, in the middle of rows over whether he had another woman, the anguish that losing him was causing her.

Against this backdrop of turmoil and illness, Diana's life was about to change with the advent of an ally and competitor. Sarah Ferguson had become one of Diana's closest friends, if not her closest friend, ever since meeting prior to Diana's marriage in 1981. Sarah used to drop in to Buck House, then Kensington Palace once Diana moved there, for lunches and chats. She is great fun, with a breezy sense of humour and a personality which, in those days, sparkled even more brightly than it now does. She had been embroiled with Paddy McNally, a multimillionaire a generation older than herself, for years. He refused to marry her, however, and she was increasingly unhappy about her romantic life.

Diana decided to help her friend out by playing matchmaker. She thought her brother-in-law Andrew, whom she liked enormously and felt was "the best of the whole lot of them," would like Sarah. She therefore arranged for Sarah to be asked as a houseguest at Windsor Castle during the four-day Royal Ascot race meeting in 1985. Over lunch, the playful Fergie and the amorous Andrew engaged in a seductive exchange about a profiterole prior to setting out for Ascot racecourse. By the end of the day they were well on their way to becoming a couple.

Seven months later, Andrew proposed. Sarah accepted, and the engagement was announced when the Queen returned from another of her tours of Australia and New Zealand in mid-March 1986. "She will have a great effect upon all our lives," Princess Michael of Kent predicted. "She's a very strong personality. They (the dreaded courtiers, or, as Diana and Sarah called them, the 'men in grey suits') won't be able to control her. Through her, things will change for the better." In some ways, that prediction came true, though royalists everywhere, and Sarah York especially, must sometimes wonder if the cost was worth the improvement.

Fergie's presence also seemed to bode well for Diana. The first and most immediate effect was that the tabloids supplanted the Princess of Wales with the future Duchess of York as the media's darling. Sarah was universally praised for being a "breath of fresh air," for being "natural," for being a "delight."

From the British tabloids' point of view, Sarah Ferguson had not come along one moment too soon. In the three and two-thirds years since Diana had been the Princess of Wales, she had changed from cooperative and obliging Lady Diana, who was always game for a laugh and a chat, who would brief journalists unofficially and help them with their stories – and whom they would protect in return – to the smiling but elusive Princess of Wales who seldom spoke to them, whose wit extended to stay-in-your-place remarks such as "I'll tell the jokes" in answer to jocular quips, and who made her dislike of media coverage obvious to them. As a rule, she did still slow down and smile for photographers, which made the less charitable members of the media accuse her of being contradictory, but there were times when she did not bother to do even that. Because news editors did not want glum photographs of the Princess of Wales, this was a foolproof way for Diana to limit newspaper coverage. Sometimes, however, she behaved like that even on official photo calls. One such occasion was when she was on a skiing holiday with the Luxembourg ruling family and the Prince of Wales. She remained sullen while the remainder of the party smiled, "spoiling the photographs for the tabloids", as Judy McGuire, editor of the *News of the World Magazine*, put it to me.

In the view of the media, the Royal Family had a duty to provide them with photo opportunities. This was a view which the Royal Family, recognizing the value of publicity, shared up to a point. Diana was therefore opening herself up to a charge of not discharging her obligations fully. Though many other royals had ambivalent attitudes towards the media, and her stance was bound to gain her a degree of private sympathy with them, she was also perilously close to losing their support as well. Whatever their ambivalence, the Royal Family held up as icons to be emulated the two previous queens dowager, Queen Mary and Queen Elizabeth the Queen Mother, both of whom had lived by the inflexible rule that a consort had an absolute duty to smile for the press at all times, funerals excepted, irrespective of how she was feeling. So Diana's public face of dourness was antithetical to their expectations of the way she, and they, were supposed to acquit themselves publicly, and there was only so much rope they would allow her before they too lost all sympathy with her.

At first, Diana was relieved to have the glare of a thousand neon lights shift away from her. Her health and her marriage were a mess, and she did not know how to straighten out either. Naturally enough, she was looking for some sort of relief from the pain and anguish she was enduring. This came in an unexpected but enduring form.

One evening early in March 1986, Prince Andrew and Sarah Ferguson were guests at a dinner party hosted by his close friend photographer Gene Nocon, and his wife, Liz. Another guest was Penny Thornton, the British astrologer who is the author of several popular books on the subject, and whose specialty is helping people develop their potential and reduce the effects of their weaknesses. Upon hearing that Miss Thornton is what Mrs Henry Ford II calls "a very gifted astrologer. . .one of the best," Prince Andrew asked her if he could pass her telephone number on to his sister-in-law. Penny Thornton replied, "I'm finishing off a book. I can't see her until I've done it." Diana nevertheless telephoned a day or two later. Upon being told that she could not be seen immediately, Diana said, "I just wanted to see if there is light at the end of the tunnel." Realizing that the Princess was in deep distress and needed help immediately, Penny Thornton dropped everything and agreed to see her at Kensington Palace at 4 p.m. on 6 March 1986.

According to Thornton, "She really was in desperate straits and needed someone she could talk to, someone she could trust. She was at the end of her tether. She was oppressed by the misery within her life, by the terrible state she was in because of her marriage.

"She was not a dilettante and she did not go into this lightly. I used to go to see her at Kensington Palace. I saw her a lot in 1986 and 1987 especially, when things were really very bad. Things got better in 1989 and 1990 was all right," but by 1991 they were "not very good again." By then their sessions were conducted mostly over the telephone.

"Diana's problem was that she had no sense of control over her own situation. She felt powerless, imprisoned, and could see no way out of resolving her problems except by escaping them. More than once I had to talk her out of leaving. Once she actually had packed her suitcases when I spoke to her over the phone. I managed to talk her out of leaving. The Prince of Wales thanked me. So did Prince Andrew.

"I enabled her to get some of her power back, to see that the situation wasn't insoluble, that this period could be replaced by great happiness and that she'd eventually find great happiness and fulfilment. That she could use her suffering to make her more substantial, that it had a purpose that was strengthening."

Penny Thornton found Diana to be "a spiritual person" She felt herself to be merely "a facilitator who helped Diana to get in touch with the spiritual side of her personality.

"Diana was in deep distress. She was open to any help, which made what she heard all the more powerful. What she gained from me was hope and strength.

"We were together for two and a half hours during the first meeting. What was important in that meeting was my message that her role as Princess of Wales was important, that she must realize that her role was something that would lead her out of the abyss she was slipping into.

"She was very open, very needy. We established great trust. An astrologer has great power when someone is in distress."

Where Penny Thornton was especially helpful was in making Diana "aware of her own spiritual path, to encourage her in her increasing spiritual development." The accuracy of that statement is supported by something she said to me in 1991: "This is now showing up in Diana's interest in healing. She is now firmly on her spiritual path. She lives her beliefs. She doesn't pontificate about them. There is no split intellectually. She simply lives her beliefs. She has this charisma. She can go into a hospital room, and bring light and joy and comfort." As this was a sentiment which many other observers shared, including Peter Bowring of Help the Aged and John Coblenz of CRUSAID, both of whom sang her praises to me, there is no doubt of its accuracy.

"Those were the darkest days of my life," Diana told me in 1991 and again in 1995. The two people who gave her a lifeline were Penny Thornton and Sarah Ferguson. Sarah's attitude was, "You only live once. You mustn't accept misery docilely. Do whatever it takes to drag yourself out of the hole."

Sarah's presence had, as Princess Michael had predicted, a tremendous effect. Though it did not eliminate the power of the courtiers, who would ultimately be the rock upon which the Duchess of York's own ship foundered, Sarah preached the importance of fun and also offered Diana hope and encouragement. This was especially true in the development of her social life. Sarah encouraged Diana not only to renew old friendships but also to form new ones, including with men.

Diana started by getting in touch with her old friends and ex-boyfriends, writing to people such as Adam Russell, who happily resumed the friendship which had been shelved with Diana's elevation. She also availed herself of Sarah's wide and occasionally *louche* circle of friends, cultivating the less controversial ones such as newsagent heiress Kate Menzies and Julia Dodd Noble. Soon the perennially athletic Diana was to be found at the Vanderbilt Racquet Club in London's Shepherd's Bush, a convenient seven-minute drive from Kensington Palace, playing with one or the other of these two socialites. Indeed, Kate Menzies soon supplanted the Duchess of York as Diana's closest friend, and remained so for several years to come.

Once the novelty of having her best friend as a sister-in-law wore off, however, Diana's relationship with Sarah shifted fundamentally. Sarah was no longer Diana's perpetually nurturing supporter, the way she had been in the days before she had also become royal. They were more equal. Sarah was now one of the most senior royal ladies, ranking fourth behind the Queen, the Queen Mother and Diana. She was now a star in her own right. In fact, she was now the foremost royal media superstar, having supplanted Diana as the most popular and written-about royal. These realities introduced an element of competitiveness which drove a wedge between the two of them. Although they did remain friends, "I resented the way the whole family was always telling me I should be more like Fergie. 'Fergie's a sport. Fergie doesn't take things to heart the way you do. Fergie doesn't get upset. Fergie rolls with the punches. Fergie doesn't have a problem with FOOD (Diana's emphasis, not the writer's).' It was always Fergie this, Fergie that. I still liked her, but did they cram her down my throat!"

To add insult to injury, Sarah's reign as the fairy on the top of the royal Christmas tree meant that Diana was now either ignored or criticized in a way the media would never have dared to do previously. From Diana's point of view, it was one thing to enjoy a respite from the harsh focus of worldwide tabloid attention, but the break had degenerated into something altogether less salutary. Diana, whose self-protective instincts were finely honed, therefore moved to stem the tide of adverse publicity which was undermining her popularity and leading the public to believe she was nothing but a spoiled and moody clotheshorse. Where formerly she had maintained a regal distance from the reporters, smiling for the photographers only when the mood took her, the Princess now reverted to Lady Diana's tried and tested methods. "She started speaking to the reporters she knew," royal correspondent Robert Jobson told me. "Her car would pull up, she'd step out smiling happily, walk slowly into whichever engagement she was on, the essence of cooperation. To those of us who had to stay outside, she'd say a quick word. Inside, she always found time to have a quiet chat with the correspondents she knew. If someone new came on the scene, she'd introduce herself and thereafter include him. She could be so gentle and thoughtful. No one held the past against her. It was back to business as usual – a monumental relief to all of us, I can tell you. The Duchess of York was not as photogenic or glamorous and you can only have so much of a breath of fresh air before it becomes stale. And stale and dumpy is no substitute for svelte and sexy, which is what Diana was."

In person, Diana was astonishingly flirtatious. Like the Queen Mother before her, she seemed unable to restrain herself from parading the choicest of her feminine wiles as soon as she was within range of a man or a camera or both. Although some people criticized her for this, the fact remains she could no more help the seductiveness of her manner than the colour of her eyes. Both were essential features of her identity and, as she was not misusing either for personal profit, there is no reason why she should not have given free rein to such an appealing quality. And she did. There is countless television footage of the Princess of Wales inspecting a submarine; sashaying past a parade of officers in her capacity as Colonel-in-Chief of this or that regiment; being shown how to fly an aeroplane or tour a ship; touring a building; meeting a line-up of dignitaries. In most of them she is coquettish. She exulted in being a woman, and in using her femininity as a foil for a man's masculinity. Both men and cameras loved her as a result.

With her marriage in a mess and her romantic needs as strong as ever, Diana needed no encouragement to embark upon romantic adventures. As Penny Thornton witnessed from personal observation as well as from Diana's chart, she was "a very sexual person, very sensual and sexual."With Charles's withdrawing his sexual and personal interest from her, it was now more imperative than ever that the Princess look elsewhere for the love and affection she craved.

Diana's first foray during this period was also her biggest miscalculation, though she did not understand this until it was too late. Royal circles were awash with stories about how Princess Anne had conducted an "over-familiar" relationship with her private detective Peter Cross. Of how she had telephoned him after the birth of her daughter, Zara, before even speaking to her then husband, Captain Mark Phillips. Two other British princesses of the Blood Royal (one of whom was Princess Margaret) were also reputed to have had long-standing affairs with their private detectives, one of which was then supposed to be still in full swing, so Diana can be excused for jumping to the conclusion that there were ample precedents for having an affair with her own private detective. Moreover, she believed that one of the reasons affairs between princesses and private detectives were accepted in Court circles was the discretion inherent in such an arrangement. Private detectives go everywhere their royal charges do. If the royal is attending a ball, the detective hovers behind, to the left or the right of his charge in black or white tie. If the royal is visiting a hospital, the detective is once more hovering behind, in a business suit this time. Going to dinner? The detective is at the adjoining table. Going for a drive? The detective is on the passenger seat. Detectives even follow their charges to the door of the lavatory, though they do not enter it, for obvious reasons. Because a princess and her private detective are together constantly, people expect them to get along well and do not comment when they do. Indeed, one of the yardsticks for the relationship is that they strike up a good rapport.

When you put two human beings together, who get along well and enjoy intimate (in the pure, nonsexual meaning of the word) relations, it is hardly surprising if sexual desire is sparked. This is especially true if you stop to consider that most royal protection officers are chosen for two qualities. First, they must be at the peak of their physical powers. And second, they have to be versatile enough to fit into any surroundings. These men are therefore frequently handsome, intelligent, superfit, tall, well-built, personable and presentable. As most of them are posted to their charges when they are in their early thirties, they are also at the pinnacle of their sexual desirability.

Throwing the young, attractive and sexually needy Princess of Wales together with Sergeant Barry Mannakee, who joined Diana's staff in November 1985, was tantamount to bringing together gasoline and fire and being surprised that flames erupted. With the slightly reddish hair of the Spencers, a handsome face that could have belonged to an earl's son, and a taut and rugged body that could not, this married man found himself thrown together day and night with Diana. Although he was not lonely, she was. Moreover, they were compatible personalities. He was fun-loving and easygoing, intelligent without being intellectual. He was also sexy. "He'd tell me I looked good. Something my husband no longer did," Diana explained. Soon Diana was modelling dresses for him, asking his advice on which dress, hat or earrings to wear, parading fully clothed openly seeking his approval. "Hot stuff" was only one of the more contemporary terms he employed to describe the coquettish Diana as she sought his approval.

Over the years, many people have wondered whether Diana did have an affair with Barry Mannakee. Several things point to the fact that they did.. One is that she herself told me that she was sure the Palace "wiped him out because they were worried he was going to talk," and it is patently obvious that that meant that he had something worth hearing. The second is that she started to create opportunities for being alone with him. But, most tellingly, she told friends, including Joseph Sanders, that they did indeed have an affair.

Being the Princess of Wales meant that Diana was subjected to twenty-four-hour-a-day security. Snatching undetected moments of passion was not that easy. In the country, Highgrove House was extensively covered by security cameras in just about every public room and in the passages leading into the bedrooms and bathrooms. Kensington Palace afforded lovers more privacy, in that the main focus of the security cameras was on the exterior, but there were always staff and children around. Although Charles was relatively relaxed about people jumping to conclusions about his behaviour, which was discreet but not secretive, Diana was not. It was treason for any man to go to bed with the wife of the Prince of Wales: an offence punishable by death. Moreover, Diana had the prejudices of her family, who had been heavily influenced by Court attitudes to morality. It mattered not what you did, simply what you were seen doing. As long as you denied, you could indulge. But you must never be caught out. Such behaviour was "untidy." "Tidiness" meant simulating purity, not possessing it. And Diana, whatever her failings, was always "tidy."

The upshot was that Diana and Barry Mannakee were frequently seen going for long drives. This was especially true at Sandringham House, where he joined Diana for the usual stay after the Christmas celebrations, and Balmoral Castle, when she was in residence there. They would disappear for hours on end, re-emerging with the unconvincing explanation that they had been for a long drive.

Not surprisingly, their behaviour became the subject of chatter within the palaces, starting with the staff and filtering upwards through the Royal Household to the Royal Family itself. Diana did not care. She genuinely believed she was abiding by an unwritten royal code – that it is acceptable for royal women to take their private detectives as lovers – quite misunderstanding that she was not a royal by birth, only by marriage, and that what was acceptable for a blood princess was not for princesses whose status derives via matrimony. In fact, what she was doing was dishonouring her husband, conducting a relationship with the hired help. In British terms, it was an Upstairs, Downstairs union, something which defied the conventions of a society still governed by class divisions. Far from being appropriate, there were few things more inappropriate. "If she'd been sleeping with a gentleman, no one would've minded," a royal says. "But taking up with the private detective? I ask you."

Matters came to a head in July 1986. According to a supporter of the Prince of Wales, he stumbled upon Diana and Barry Mannakee engaged in "overly familiar behaviour," a euphemism for conduct which was so unbecoming that the sergeant was immediately transferred from the Royal Protection Department to ordinary, indeed obscure, police duties. He had been banished to the police equivalent of Siberia.

Diana also paid a heavy price for her miscalculation. Charles, humiliated and deeply offended, withdrew from her entirely. Any hope of a reconciliation was removed.

The marriage was over in all but name.

Eleven

The point at which the Waleses' marriage suffered an irreversible rupture is clearer with hindsight than it was when it occurred. Throughout that summer of 1986, life seemed to go on as normal for both the Prince and Princess.

Ever since Charles had started withdrawing from Diana after Harry's birth, both of them had been testing the waters with other partners. "They're both all-or-nothing types," Penny Thornton said, and their behaviour certainly supported that contention. Marital fidelity was a thing of the past. While Diana was going on her long drives with her lover, Charles re-established contact with Camilla Parker Bowles, of whom he had remained inordinately fond despite not seeing her throughout the early years of his marriage. "He was not yet in love with her the way he now is. Camilla was only one of many women he saw," a friend said.

There is ample evidence to indicate that Charles was not devoting himself exclusively to Camilla at this stage. His taste had always run to older, glamorous, sophisticated and attractive women. Some were just friends, others he took a more personal interest in. Now he started shooting off to spend time with them on their estates or in their *palazzi*, visiting beauties such as Marchesa Bona di Frescobaldi, and, in the process, exciting chatter.

One relationship that caused comment within social circles and never filtered through to the press or the public at the time was the one with Eva O'Neill. A tall, slim and beautiful blonde with a good sense of humour and such flair that she has been voted one of the most elegant women in the world by the French society magazine *The Best*, Eva used to sit a bit apart from everyone else at the Guards Polo Club and watch Charles play, as I myself saw on more than one occasion. As he gripped his mare with manly legs and hurtled down the field, mallet swinging from his hairy and muscular arms, Charles exuded sexuality through every pore. Nor was this just an illusion. As Sonia Palmer told me, "The Prince is an intensely sexual man. Diana herself told me so."

There is no doubt that Charles and Eva were close friends, and though she herself has denied to me that their friendship is now anything but innocent, word in fashionable circles two decades ago is that things were different then.

Confirmation of this fact came in the form of a comical scene enacted one Sunday afternoon when Diana drove over from Windsor Castle unexpectedly after polo. "She was doubtless on the prowl, looking for evidence that he was up to no good," socialite Liz Brewer told me. This was so, as Diana herself confirmed to me. She very nearly succeeded in catching Charles red-handed. At the very moment that she was approaching the changing rooms, he was busily engaged with Eva inside. Anthony Taylor, a well-known figure on the social scene, had been delegated to stand guard outside. Upon seeing Diana approaching, he fled to the back to inform Charles and Eva. While Charles headed towards the door to deflect his wife, Anthony helped Eva crawl out of a window in the back before 'innocently' joining Charles, who had had to plead with Diana that she could not barge in because there were men changing (even though none actually was). Although Diana did not actually catch Charles out, she certainly knew that he had been up to something, and with whom.

The response of Anthony Taylor, when confronted, is indicative of the way people surrounding Charles conduct themselves, and how Diana ran them ragged. When I asked him for his account of what had happened, he said, real panic in his voice, "I can't speak about that incident. They'd know it had come from me if I said anything. Anything I say they'd trace back to me. God, Georgie, you're asking me about the hot stuff. If you wanted who was at dinner, that sort of thing, I could talk. But not this." What the loyal Anthony did not know was that Diana herself had been the source of much of the information. There had, after all, been only four people present that Sunday afternoon in the changing room at the Guards Polo Club: the Prince of Wales, the Princess, Eva and himself. As he, Eva and Charles had not done the talking, who did that leave? But I did not say so to Anthony, leaving him to figure out the mystery for himself.

This period was as uncertain for Charles as it was for Diana. Neither of them envisaged that their marriage would actually end in divorce. They were groping in the dark, seeking a *modus vivendi* which would allow them to find satisfaction outside their marriage while tolerating one another within its framework, if they could not turn it into a satisfying and satisfactory union. "Prince Charles still hoped that something would happen to make Diana change," Princess Margaret of Hesse and the Rhine said.. "She had the same hopes," Penny Thornton told me. Even though Charles had lost sympathy with her, and was so obviously irritated by her that he mocked her opinions and habits, including her inability to keep down food, "there were still times when he would see her by herself. . . I remember once, in the grounds of Highgrove House, he went up to her and rubbed her neck. Another time, he stroked her shoulder in a gesture of affection. Diana spurned him. There were other times when she'd make similar gestures of spontaneous affection. He'd rebuff her. They just didn't seem capable of synchronizing," a friend who does not wish to be identified, said.

Neither in nor out of the marriage, Diana was no more ready for a big romance than Charles was. Just as he had not yet settled down to the serious commitment he would eventually have with Camilla, Diana had not found love either. She was not in love with Barry Mannakee, as demonstrated by an incident which transpired around the time Charles forced his removal. She was at a party to celebrate Sarah Ferguson's impending nuptials to Prince Andrew. Once more the venue was the Guards Polo Club, which Sarah's father, Ronald Ferguson, then headed. Diana spent half the evening wrapped around a financier and man-about-town who, regrettably, cannot be named for legal reasons. Sophisticated and attractive, like Diana, he was definitely married.

John Rendall, who subsequently became social editor of *Hello!* magazine, also attended that party. Shortly after midnight, he went outside for a cigarette. "I heard sounds coming from the bushes. I nearly choked with astonishment when I looked over and saw the Princess of Wales with this man. They were necking. I moved away, finished my cigarette quietly, and went back inside. They didn't return for ages."

The following month, Charles, Diana and their boys headed for the Marivent Palace in Majorca, where King Juan Carlos and Queen Sofia played host with their three children. Born a princess of Greece and the sister of King Constantine, Sofia was and remains a close friend of Charles as well as his cousin. The Prince was also and remains on cordial terms with Juan Carlos, but not as close as he was or is to Sofia.

What started out as two families linking up together for a holiday quickly turned into something else. "The King is well known to have an eye for the ladies," a European princess, and a cousin of the King, told me. "The Queen has spent her whole married life ignoring his interests, shall we say?" At some point, while the families were cruising on Juan Carlos's modern yacht, the *Fortuna*, swimming by some of the stunning Mediterranean beaches and coves around the Balearic island, enjoying water sports, picnics and forays to places of interest, the unthinkable happened. Diana and Juan Carlos connected. "Obviously, the relationship that they now embarked upon could never go anywhere. There was no possibility of it developing into marriage, or indeed into a serious arrangement," the princess said. "From his (the King's) point of view, it was nothing but a fling and, I believe, from hers, a convenience as well as a fling. I'm pretty sure she was using him to make Prince Charles jealous, but it didn't work. He couldn't have cared less. In fact, he upped sticks and left them to get on with it, and went to Puerto Andratx, where he stayed with Jose Luis de Villalonga (the Marques de Castelvell). I do not believe Queen Sofia knew anything then. If she had known, she would not have welcomed Diana back." Rather than complete his stay at the Marivent Palace with Diana and the boys, Charles then flew back to Britain without them.

The following year, Charles and Diana did return to stay with Juan Carlos and Sofia yet again. This time, the trip was not quite the success the previous one had been. "They picked up where they'd left off. This time Queen Sofia took a less tolerant view of what she had previously dismissed as Diana's innocent flirtatiousness," the princess said. "There is no question about it. They were having an affair."

Independent corroboration came to me from an unlikely source. An executive then working for Bijan, the upmarket jewelers, confirmed to me that King Juan Carlos bought Diana a watch costing more than $200,000. A gift of that scale, when it is not a wedding present paid for by the State, is indicative of only one thing, especially when the donor is a man who is not, in royal terms, rich.

While the King of Spain might have been good for Diana's self-esteem and was a handy tool with which to prod her indifferent husband, he was incapable of meeting her needs. What the Princess of Wales wanted, as she made clear to Penny Thornton and other friends, was "someone to love her, someone whom she loved". Diana herself told me, "I only want a man who loves me, who (sic) I love, who'll be there for me." As her most enduring lover, James Hewitt, would later confirm to a mutual friend, "She needed constant attention and reassurance. Ten minutes after I'd left, having spent most of the time making love to her, she'd be on the phone needing to be told how much I loved her. She'd phone five, six, ten times a day, always needing to hear the same thing."

This craving for emotional sustenance was obviously deep-seated within Diana. It also limited the scope of the men who would be able to satisfy her. Had Diana been more independent, with her looks, humour, wit, seductiveness and status, she could have had her pick of men. As it was, she began learning a lesson which would be repeated time and again until she and Dodi Fayed became a couple: "Most men don't want women with baggage," to quote her.

The effect of Diana's individual needs was to rule out a whole category of males who would ordinarily have seemed to be the perfect type for her. Whether as Lady Diana Spencer or as the Princess of Wales, Diana should have been attracting successful men. Men of status, position, power. Men of accomplishment and commitment. Men who were on a par with her.

Successful men, however, frequently like the challenges and nonpecuniary rewards of their careers. They do not want a woman who demands too much of their time or attention. Their idea of the perfect woman is someone who is independent and capable. This sort of man cannot be bothered with a woman to whom he has to speak on the telephone five, six and ten times a day; who wants to have lunch and dinner with him every day. He is not a nurturer. To him, a woman who needs nurturing is a living nightmare, a suffocating and claustrophobic drain in the guise of an adult female, the personal equivalent of a secretary who expects her boss to type his letters and do his filing for her.

Bearing in mind the limitations which geography, status and her own emotional needs put on her relationship with King Juan Carlos, it was inevitable that Diana would cast about for a more suitable lover. Private detectives, she now knew, were out of bounds. This was a pity, for Barry Mannakee had been perfect in many ways, and it is possible that the affair could have continued, providing her with the sustenance she needed, without anyone outside Court circles knowing about it. However, Britain being Britain, the class difference was a factor, so Diana avoided making the same mistake twice.

Diana's eye was now caught by the handsome brother of her friend Millie Dunne, later the wife of Sir Winston Churchill's grandson, the Hon. Rupert Soames (Nicholas Soames's younger brother). Philip Dunne was a Clark Kent look-alike, a strapping and sexy Old Etonian who was also a successful merchant banker with Warburg's. "All the girls were after him, and I could see why," Richard Szpiro, the eminent merchant banker, told me. "He's very good-looking, charming and intelligent. The classic tall, dark and handsome type. But there's a lot more to him. He's street-smart as well as civilized. He's got it all."

This description was no exaggeration in 1986 and 1987. The son of the Lord Lieutenant of Hereford and Worcester (the Queen's representative for those counties) and the godson of the monarch's first cousin Princess Alexandra, Philip Dunne became the focus of Diana's attentions and the relationship quickly gathered pace. They were seen lunching and dining in fashionable restaurants such as Ménage à Trois, where a famous socialite observed them "playing footsie under the table. It was quite funny really. They must have supposed no one could see them. Well, we could."

The Prince of Wales knew about the relationship and endorsed it by asking Philip Dunne to join their skiing party at Klosters. To people within Court circles, who knew about the dates of the Princess and the handsome banker, this was the signal they had been waiting for. Charles had issued a semiofficial stamp of approval.

Diana certainly took advantage of the hallowed status her confidant now enjoyed. She weekended with Philip Dunne at his parents' house, Gatley Park, near Leominster in Herefordshire, exciting comment when it emerged that his parents had been away skiing in Meribel. The Prince of Wales, not surprisingly, was nowhere to be seen. As the weeks became months and the relationship continued, the banker and the Princess continued seeing each other privately and publicly.

The full measure of the Prince of Wales's approval of his wife's latest distraction became even more evident when Philip Dunne was included in their party for Royal Ascot 1987.

By now, Diana was lulled into a false sense of security. She seems to have forgotten the golden rule by which her courtier antecedents lived and prospered: It matters not what you do, but what you are seen to be doing. Previously, her exemplary sense of discretion had always ensured that she made a sharp distinction between private reality and public perception. For the first, though by no means last, time in her life she now allowed the boundaries to slip. She started getting careless. It was one thing to play footsie in public, but quite another to take to the dance floor at the largest society wedding of the year and behave as if no one else but her handsome banker was in the room. This, nevertheless, is what Diana did at the dance following the marriage of the Marquess of Worcester to the actress Tracy Ward. "It was unbelievable," a fellow guest said. "She took to the dance floor with him and wrapped herself around him the way a creeper does around the trunk of a tree. Indiscreet as that was, it was nothing compared to what then followed. She started combing his hair with her fingers and nuzzling his ear. Then she pushed her tongue down it. The effect upon the witnesses was tremendous. You must remember, this was 1987, not 1997. Everyone still expected the Prince and Princess of Wales to present a united face to the world. To behave with decorum. Of course, we all knew they weren't getting along but none of us expected the Princess of Wales to take to the dance floor and flirt – I'm being polite here – so outrageously."

Whether Diana was trying to make Charles jealous or had simply thrown caution to the winds, or both, no one can now say. However, if she did it for the first reason, she wasted her time. Throughout her display, the Prince of Wales remained huddled in conversation with Anna Wallace, the girl to whom he had proposed before Diana. Not once throughout the evening did he look in his wife's direction. At two o'clock, he departed without her, leaving her to continue the floor show that precipitated the end of her relationship with the sexually appealing Philip Dunne.

Naturally, Diana's conduct set tongues wagging. Within days, the gossip columnists, who are sometimes fed stories by penurious socialites in exchange for pin money, were aware of the sensation she had caused at the Worcester wedding dance. There was an air of inevitability as stories about her and Philip Dunne started appearing in the press. When these continued, the Palace swung into action to prevent Diana's reputation from being tarnished. "He got a telephone call from the Palace instructing him to stop seeing Diana," a relation of his told me. "He was instructed not to contact Diana again. To discourage her from contacting him. He was ordered to disappear from public view until the speculation had died down." Confirmation of this was provided by the banker and novelist Richard Szpiro, who told me, "At the height of the Princess of Wales sensation, we had a meeting arranged. I got a telephone call from him asking that I meet him, I forget where. He was in hiding at the time. He'd gone to ground."

The stories linking the Princess of Wales to Philip Dunne could not have come at a worse time for her. She and Charles were barely on speaking terms and did not spend their sixth wedding anniversary together on 29 July. She was still struggling to re-establish herself, not only as the pre-eminent royal in terms of media coverage, but also as the unblemished figure she had once been. The newspapers were full of speculation about the state of the Wales marriage, especially after Charles and Diana spent most of the summer apart and did not get together for even one night. The last thing Diana needed was to be blamed for the breakup of her marriage, so from that point of view, the death of the stories about Philip Dunne was welcome. However, there were rumours that Barry Mannakee was getting ready to sell the story of his affair with Diana to one of the downmarket tabloids.

To Diana's horror and relief, she was spared that ignominy. Within weeks of these rumours gaining ground, Barry Mannakee was dead. He was killed in July when the motorbike, on which he was riding pillion, swerved to avoid a Ford Fiesta car driven by seventeen-year-old Nicola Chopp. His police partner, who was riding the Suzuki, survived, but Mannakee was thrown, suffering fatal injuries.

The innocent circumstances notwithstanding, Diana did not believe that her former lover had died accidentally. "MI5 wiped him out," she told me and many of her friends, including Joseph Sanders. According to him, "She believed that MI5 opportunistically used the accident to rid itself of a threat to the monarchy. She remained terrified that they would target one of her other lovers if they also regarded him as a threat."

Those who considered her paranoid seized upon this as yet another instance to prove her state of mind, but, in the light of the manner in which Diana and Dodi Fayed died, and the widespread publicity her theories of Mannakee's death excited when *Diana in Private* was published in 1992, her opinions need careful examination. Between 1987 and 1992, she was firmly convinced that the accident was no accident. She revised her opinion only when this writer made it clear in *Diana in Private* that the accident had to be genuine. It could not have been planned by MI5 for the simple reason that the precipitator of the crash had been a novice driver who had come out too far from a side road into the path of the motorcycle, forcing the rider to swerve. Mannakee had been thrown at this juncture. It strained credibility to suppose that MI5 had seventeen-year-old girls as agents, or that a police officer would have been delegated to remain on the lookout for a likely excuse to cause a traffic accident. Aside from the unpredictability of such an event, the consequences were also unpredictable. Innocent bystanders could have been killed. Furthermore, the rider of the bike could have been killed himself. It was simply not credible that an MI5 agent would risk killing himself just to protect the Princess of Wales's reputation.

Confronted with the bald facts, many of which Diana did not even know until I informed her of them, she revised her opinion about the accident. It had been a genuine accident, she conceded, but then alighted upon the theory that MI5 opportunistically used the event to "wipe out Barry because he was a threat to the monarchy." Diana's new explanation also deserves to be shared. "I bet MI5 reached him before the doctors and pumped him full of drugs to kill him." Nor did she limit the explanation to this writer. She elucidated upon the theory to many friends, including Joseph Sanders, and remained convinced to her dying day that Barry Mannakee had really been eliminated.

There were two consequences of Diana's conspiracy theory. First, she remained "nervous that they could target one of her other lovers in the future, were they also to be regarded as a threat." Second, the senior courtiers at Buckingham Palace saw it as further proof of her emotional instability. These courtiers knew that the system might discredit people with a judicious leak to a friendly journalist here, and a well-planted poisonous story there, but that it would never assassinate a policeman just because he might sell a story which could always be denied. After all, Peter

Cross, Princess Anne's bodyguard, had sold his account of their relationship to a downmarket tabloid, and he was still alive. Taking a measured view, these courtiers decided that Diana's conspiracy theory was yet more proof that she was not merely neurotic, but psychotically paranoid.

The turmoil throughout the summer of 1987 extended further than the difficulties within Diana's marriage, the severance of relations with Philip Dunne, and the aftermath of Barry Mannakee's death. To Diana, nothing was more important than love. It was a quest she pursued because "life is pointless without love." Her sons were her first loves, but she also had the physical and emotional needs of a woman, in stronger measure than most. Although she had experienced another rebuff, she remained optimistic that she might still find what she yearned for. It will doubtless come as a shock to those who believed that Diana's interests stopped short of adult fulfilment, to discover that throughout 1987, she had not one man as a point of interest, or two, but three.

The second man who figured in Diana's life at this time was a distant cousin. David Waterhouse is another of the tall, good-looking, dark-haired, muscular Army-officer types to whom Diana gravitated. He is also a grandson of the previous Duke of Marlborough, the true head of the Spencer family, his mother, Lady Caroline Spencer-Churchill, having been a daughter of that duke.

"David was viewed as a safe pair of hands by the Palace," Lady Sarah Spencer-Churchill, his aunt, told me. "No attempt was ever made to break up the relationship. He's never confirmed or denied whether he and Diana did have an affair. He won't speak about her at all. Gentlemen don't."

What has been confirmed, and by her most public and established lover, James Hewitt no less, is that he was jealous of Waterhouse and did not believe Diana's protestations that they were just friends. There were good reasons for his skepticism. Diana's technique, whenever confronted by an awkward fact, was to deny it. Inevitably, of course, the truth would come out, but it would take time. And in the interim, she would blithely preserve her liberty and privacy with disclaimers.

Diana used to have David Waterhouse over for dinner at Kensington Palace and go out with him on dates to the cinema, dining and dancing. She frequently went to his bachelor flat for bridge games as well. Her private detective would remain in the car while the distant cousins were supposed to be inside playing cards for hours on end. The trouble was, bridge requires a quorum of four and Diana and Waterhouse were the only two bodies in the flat.

What preserved Diana's relationship with David Waterhouse, which continued for some time, was his innate discretion; the lesson in discretion she had learned from flaunting Philip Dunne; and the confusion which the newspapers created over his identity. The Princess and David Waterhouse had been photographed side by side at David Bowie's Wembley Stadium concert that turbulent summer. Princess Margaret's son, Viscount Linley, was also sitting beside Diana, but he was not featured in the published photographs, only Waterhouse, who was identified as Philip Dunne. This mistake, coupled with the fact that journalists were fearful they would strain the public's credulity by asking them to believe that Diana had supplanted one beau with another so quickly – or, worse, that she was conducting relationships with two men at once – led the press to tread lightly. This was just as well, for within weeks photographers observed Diana leaving the Odeon Cinema at Kensington High Street with Waterhouse and Julia Samuel. In an attempt to avoid giving them a compromising photograph, he unwittingly provided an even better story by jumping over the traffic railings and hotfooting it into the night.

Despite these two incidents, David Waterhouse continued to pursue his relationship with Diana without bother from the Palace. This time she was careful not to compromise herself by making a spectacle, the way she had with Philip Dunne. She could, and did, say that they were just friends. With no evidence to the contrary, the media, avid for proof, and the courtiers, avid to avoid a scandal, and James Hewitt, avid to continue his affair with her, soon let it go at that.

There is a postscript to this, however. When Jonathan Dimbleby published his biography of the Prince of Wales, David Waterhouse was not only listed as a "confidant," but as someone with whom the Prince of Wales wished Diana well. Because Dimbleby had unprecedented access to Charles and his circle, there can be no doubt that his information was authoritative. Moreover, he makes Charles's attitude to Diana's "confidants" – the accepted euphemism for relationships within royal circles involving more than mere friendship – clear: the marriage was over and he wanted her to lead her own life, to develop satisfying relationships with men. In royalspeak, this was tantamount to an admission that the major and his pretty cousin had been romantically involved – and that he had behaved so impeccably that only honour would devolve upon him.

Throughout Diana's relationships with David Waterhouse and Philip Dunne, she was also conducting an affair with another man. And this was a torrid one. She first met James Hewitt in July 1986. Another of those tall, well-built, athletic, muscular, good-looking, Army officers to whom she was attracted, he was, like most of her other love interests, a captain in one of the prestigious Household regiments. They met at a party in Mayfair. He was a well-known equestrian, and once Diana decided she liked him, she proposed that he give her riding lessons. This, despite the fact that Diana was vociferous in declaiming to one and all that she had a morbid horror of horses.

Within days of the meeting, Diana was on the telephone to Hewitt repeating her request for riding lessons and firming up arrangements. At first, Diana and her handsome riding instructor went for early-morning rides in Hyde Park accompanied by Hazel West, a lady-in-waiting, and/or Major-General Sir Christopher Airey, who became the Prince of Wales's Private Secretary, as well as the inevitable private detectives, all of whom kept a respectful distance behind Diana and Hewitt.

Within the social circles that Diana moved, this new development raised questions. She had always made such a "thing" of her terror of everything equestrian that people who knew her waited to see where this change in attitude took her. Captain Hewitt was known to be an accomplished polo player as well as rider, and one member of the Royal Household said, "The day she chooses to watch Hewitt play polo is the day I'll know he's bonking her."

One of Diana's pet peeves was having to watch polo. Within Court circles, it was a known fact that soon after she married the Prince of Wales, she started agitating for him to give up the game, to spare her having to watch it. Or, as Lady Theresa Manners put it to me, "Diana was anti-polo, anti-hunting, anti-everything he liked. She was used to hunting, the family she comes from. How could she expect her marriage to be good when she was anti-everything he was for." The joke going the rounds had been that he had told her the two activities, playing and watching polo, were not necessarily linked. He did not need to forgo a sport he loved, nor was she obliged to watch something she found boring and distasteful.

Hewitt described the progression of his relationship with Diana. For four months, he and Diana remained pupil and teacher. She frequently telephoned him under the guise of "fixing up lessons," even finding time to fit extra ones into her busy schedule. He observed that most of her calls were not "necessary," but was delighted to receive them nevertheless. At this stage, he could not believe that she was cultivating him with a view to making him her main lover. He was sure he was imagining things, that she was merely being friendly, that he was detecting a frisson of sexuality which was not actually there.

Hewitt, of course, was wrong. In November 1986, he and Diana were following their custom of having a cup of coffee and a chat after the riding lesson. The Princess informed him that her marriage was a sham and that she and the Prince of Wales had been leading increasingly separate lives for years. She plaintively told him that she was so alone, though surrounded by people, and took his hand in hers. "You are not alone," he assured her. "You have me."

No sooner had Diana returned to Kensington Palace than she was on the telephone to the dashing captain, issuing him an invitation to join her for dinner.

In the evening, Hewitt turned up at Kensington Palace and was shown into Diana's sitting-room. There a radiant Diana was waiting for him with a bottle of champagne. Although she did not drink frequently, she did this evening. She wittily recounted tales of a banquet which she had recently attended with the Prince of Wales on his thirty-eighth birthday in Oman, when the Emir waived the rule of no women and allowed Diana and her lady-in-waiting, Anne Beckwith Smith, to attend. Diana brushed her hand against Hewitt's and the air crackled with sexuality until dinner was announced.

Dinner was served by a footman on the circular dining table in the dining-room, where they sat side by side. After the meal, Diana and Hewitt repaired to her sitting-room for coffee. The captain sat in the corner of the sofa nearest the fireplace. Diana sat opposite. She poured coffee into his cup, handed it to him, and, as he took it, seductively stroked his hand with hers. To his surprise and delight, without further ado, she crossed over to him, slipped into his lap and cupped his head with her hands.

Even though he was thrilled to have Diana in his arms, Hewitt was astonished by the assertive way she had taken control of the situation. Although they had been building up to this moment for four months, when it came, it was nevertheless a shock to discover how aggressive

Diana was when she wanted something. She did not pretend to be a weak and delicate flower. She looked deeply into his eyes, invited him to kiss her with lips slightly parted, and responded with vigour when he did. As soon as he stopped, she took his hand, got up from the sofa, indicated that he should follow her, and led him into her bedroom, into her marital bed. There they made love for the first of many times.

Fortunately for his relationship with Diana, James Hewitt was good with children, as I can personally attest to, having seen how he treated my two sons when they were little boys. That meant she could include her boys in some of her activities with her main lover. The Prince of Wales, who was happy for her to have her own life while he pursued his increasingly serious relationship with Camilla Parker Bowles, had no objection to Diana arranging for "Uncle James" to teach his sons to ride. This uncle was fun. Not only did he make their riding lessons a joy, but he also played games with them while their mother stood by beaming approval. He could also be thoughtful, such as the time he arranged a tour of Combermere Barracks at Windsor and provided the two excited little boys with their own miniature uniforms – flak jackets, Army regulation-green trousers and berets.

Through the debâcles with Barry Mannakee and Philip Dunne, Diana had learned the value of discretion. However, that did not prevent her from leading a relatively normal life with Hewitt. Approximately one weekend a month he stayed with her at Highgrove House while Charles was away. They invariably slept together, not in the master bedroom, but in the guest bedroom. She visited him at his mother's cottage in Devon, sharing his bedroom with him. Ken Wharfe, her discreet but friendly private detective, or Detective Sergeant Allan Peters, took the guest bedroom, while the back-up police officers slept nearby in the local hotel. In London, the lovers also used to go out normally. I often used to see them at San Lorenzo, the fashionable Italian restaurant in Beauchamp Place owned by her friends Lorenzo and Mara Berni. They usually sat at the back right-hand corner table in the conservatory, taking care to respect the proprieties of polite society, in which lovers do not kiss or fondle in public. Nevertheless, the air between them was always suffused with intimacy. They would remain huddled together in deep conversation, breaking off their discourses only when joined by Mara, who was always telling them that the future looked bright for them. So established and accepted did Diana's relationship with Hewitt become that he was asked to the ball at Buckingham Palace to celebrate Prince Charles's fortieth birthday in November 1988. The following May, Diana's stepmother, Raine, issued an invitation to Hewitt to attend the sixtieth-birthday ball her husband was giving for her at Althorp House. This event was particularly memorable for Hewitt, not only because Diana proudly took him on a tour of her family home, but also because she led him to the poolhouse shortly after midnight. There, in what was effectively a public place, they made love, at her instigation, forbidden fruit and the threat of discovery making the act all the sweeter.

Despite the lovers' usual discretion, word had spread within Court circles about Diana's latest lover. She was being seen so much with Hewitt, and in such inconsistent places, that observers would have had to be blind not to come to the correct conclusion. One such event took place in the summer of 1989. Hewitt was playing polo for the Life Guards against the 13th/18th Royal Hussars, of which Diana was colonel-in-chief. This was at Tidworth, where she had broken down in tears while watching Charles play polo shortly before their marriage. Diana told Hewitt she wanted to come and watch him play. She said no one would suspect her true motive in being there, for everyone would assume that she had come to cheer on her regiment. This, of course, was not so. Diana did not ordinarily sacrifice private time to cheer along her husband, much less her regiment, and everyone knew it. Nevertheless, she arrived with her sons, which in itself would have excited comment, if only because she ordinarily refused to allow them to watch their father on the field. The *coup de grâce* came when Hewitt's team won and Diana presented him with the cup. "I don't know who she thought she was fooling," stated the courtier who had said that he'd know she was sleeping with Hewitt the day she elected to watch him play polo. "She was so coy and seductive, her body language screamed sex. I turned to my wife and said, 'You see, I was right. She is bonking that riding-instructor chappie. She's here of her own volition and she can't stop smiling at the ground.'"

Both Hewitt and Diana have admitted that there was a time when they dreamed of having a life together. This was during the golden period of their romance, between 1987 and 1989. Although he realized that this was a pipe dream, like most men in love he hoped against hope that the fantasy could materialize into reality. Diana felt the same way, and began agitating for a separation, though she was always careful not to link her desire for one to her ambition for a new life with her lover. With an innate canniness which made her wise beyond her years, she understood that she would never be able to leave the marriage with her status and reputation intact unless she laid the blame squarely at her husband's door and emerged as the innocent party.

Yet Diana also tugged in the opposite direction. "I really want to get back with my husband," she told me in 1990. I did not doubt her sincerity then and I do not doubt it now, though there is also no doubt in my mind that the only way she would have found her much-reviled husband acceptable would have been by making him over into someone he was not, and could never become. In other words, no matter the degree of her desire, she was bound to fail, for she wanted a successful marriage with a Prince of Wales who did not exist, not with Charles as he was.

One of the keys to Diana's personality, and the main reason why she was frequently so unhappy and misunderstood by even those who knew her well, was that she was a creature of conflicting desires and directions. There can be little doubt that, given the choice, she would have opted for a happy marriage with the Prince of Wales. For the remainder of her life, she struggled to accept that her marriage was over, that Charles no longer wanted her, that there was no hope of a reconciliation, because he would never want her again. "I fought him tooth and nail to save my marriage," she told me. "He wanted Camilla and not me. Look at her. It doesn't make sense."

Regrettably, it did. The Prince of Wales obviously saw an inner beauty in Camilla that he could not find in Diana. The fact that he preferred an older and less-attractive woman to his glamorous wife should not have been a source of mystery, but confirmation of the extent of the flaws within his marriage and the depth of the feeling within his relationship outside marriage.

This was the period when Charles and Diana's scenes reached crescendo level. Although she had her own lovers, she became obsessed with Camilla Parker Bowles. "It is not true that she was jealous of Camilla before," Joseph Sanders, to whom she spoke virtualy every day of her life on just about every topic under the sun, said. "Her jealousy increased in direct proportion to his love for Camilla. As long as she was one of many, Diana didn't care that much. She didn't like it, of course, but she wasn't like a woman possessed. She became like that slowly, as it dawned on her that Prince Charles was never coming back to her, and that he'd developed an alternative relationship elsewhere."

Always competitive, Diana became crazed with jealousy. She, to whom beauty and appearance were so important, could not understand how Charles could fail to desire her, yet loved the "Rottweiler". "There's no secret why the Prince feels the way he does about Mrs Parker Bowles," Lord Charteris said. "She is a constant, reliable, mature and loving woman. She has genuine generosity of spirit. She puts him first. She has no interest in a public life for herself. She is not ambitious. She does not wish for the public accolades that being the Princess of Wales brings to anyone who occupies the role. She is a discreet and private person who relishes Prince Charles for the man he is. They have settled into a fulfilling relationship in the autumn of their years. It's hardly surprising he'd value her. She's the first woman he's had such contentment with. What they have now is quite different from the lighthearted affairs they had when they were younger. They are older and wiser than they used to be. It's profound and they treasure the uniqueness of what they have."

"Nothing's worked," Diana told me plaintively when I was writing *Diana in Private*. "No matter what I've done to get him back. Nothing." She tried seduction. According to her, "I went into his dressing room. I was wearing this fabulous eau-de-Nil silk nightdress, low-cut and slinky. He was reading. I sat down on the bed beside him. He was reading one of those deadweight books by Laurens van der Post. I said something nice and touched his fingers. They were wrapped around the book, which was propped up on his chest. He winced when my fingers brushed past his. I've never been so hurt in my life. The idea that my own husband can't stand me touching him. That's just one of the things that have shown me how futile it is to try breathing life into this marriage."

When seduction did not succeed, Diana tried playing upon the Prince's sympathies. Once, she threatened to commit suicide. She told Charles she had emptied a bottle of paracetamol. This was true. There had been only two tablets left, and she had taken them both. However, since he had been the one to reduce the four remaining tablets to two, her ploy did not have the desired impact.

"The fact is, I've never tried to commit suicide," Diana told me in 1996, having told me the opposite in 1990 and 1991. "I would never leave my boys motherless. What woman who loves her children would?" That is undoubtedly the voice of the real Diana, the woman shorn of wiles, inducements, enticements and threats. The woman who put her "boys" before any man. Undoubtedly, she had a propensity for acting out her feelings. When she was frustrated, she howled. When she was happy, she laughed. When she was loving, she bewitched. And when she was angry, or desperate, she threw scenes. Once, she picked up a penknife and threatened to stab herself with it. When that did not produce the desired effect – for Charles to give up Camilla Parker Bowles and start to love her again, or to continue loving Camilla Parker Bowles and release her from her gilded cage – she then threatened to stab him with it. Threatening to do something and doing it are two different things, however. All of Diana's scenes ended up with her either failing to carry out her threat or implementing it in so slight a manner that she defeated her purpose.

"I was desperate," she said. "I had to try everything." On the off chance that yet another drama might reduce the crisis within her marriage, Diana cried wolf so often that "she turned off the Prince of Wales completely. He's basically a compassionate guy and he wanted her to be happy. But he was not going to have her browbeat or blackmail him into loving her when he no longer did. She'd killed his love with her antics and she should've been counting her blessings that it took four years instead of four weeks. She was lucky he's a decent guy and the monarchy did not want a divorce. Most men would've walked out on her after a month," Lady Sarah Spencer-Churchill said.

One particular scene of which Diana was inordinately proud took place at Ormeley Lodge, Lady Annabel Goldsmith's home on Ham Common near Richmond. This formidable dowager, who subsequently became like a second mother to Diana during the last years of her life, was hosting a party to celebrate the fortieth birthday of Camilla's younger sister Annabel Elliot. According to Diana, "My husband didn't expect me to attend. He couldn't believe it when I started getting dressed. I made sure I looked my best. That night, the adrenaline flowed, I can tell you. I felt great. I walked up to Camilla, who was chatting to a load of the Highgrove hangers-on (her description of Charles's friends). I slipped my hand under her elbow and steered her to a quiet corner. 'I want you to know that I know what you're up to with my husband,' I said, as composed as could be. I wasn't upset at all. 'You've been a malignant presence throughout my marriage. I don't care any longer. You can have him if you want him. I don't. I just want him to leave me and my boys alone. I just don't want you to think you can swan around my house Highgrove playing the hostess when I'm not there, and think I don't know what's going on. I do and it disgusts me. You're both ridiculous, with your snatched meetings and childish telephone calls. Just so you know where I stand,'" Diana ended, walking off with a rush of satisfaction.

Although controlled in that situation, despite Diana's claims to the contrary, she was not always in control of her emotions or her actions. Her conduct during this period must be viewed in that light. Her bulimia was rampant, her mood swings frightening to behold. Even people who disliked her feared for her, wondering how she would end up. Because her behaviour was assessed through the prism of her illness, much of the anger that she would otherwise have triggered was diffused.

One antic, however, which caused great consternation, was the use which Diana now began to make of the telephone. "She would call Camilla countless times a day," someone who knew all the parties said. "In the evening, whenever she suspected that Prince Charles might be with Camilla, she would ring the house and either leave the phone off the hook thereby blocking the recipient's line or then breathe heavily, make ungodly sounds, or just hang up. Believe me, when you have months and months of harassment like this, you want to pull your hair out. Camilla, however, kept her own counsel, the way she still does. I believe she genuinely felt sorry for Diana. You see, she knew how sick she was. I believe that prevented her from condemning her."

Although Diana's obsession with and jealousy of Camilla is now widely known, the myth can be discounted that this ruled her life, virtually to the exclusion of all else. This was a fraught period of her life, but it was not fraught for only negative reasons. Her sons were growing up and she was taking an active part in their lives, moulding them so that they would become informal lovers of humanity rather than formal products of the royal system she so hated. She was changing her attitude towards her public duties, developing herself spiritually and turning a duty into something which would become a life-enhancing joy, not only for herself, but for the countless people whose lives she touched. She had a busy social life. And her sex life, always busy, was about to become even busier.

Twelve

As the 1980s drew to a close, so, too, did Diana's twenties. She was no longer a young lady. She was a woman quickly approaching her prime. Looking at her life, it was, on the one hand, a wonderful accomplishment earned at and against tremendous odds, and, on the other hand, it was a mess.

The Princess of Wales was carrying an unbearable burden of pain. She had tried blaming her problems on the adjustment from privileged and irresponsible upper-class girl to even-more-privileged but weighted-with-responsibility royal princess. She had also blamed the royal way of life, with its onerous restrictions. These would have wiped out all the benefits of royalty but for the monumental fame and adulation which had come in its wake, and to which the Princess of Wales was addicted. "I read everything that's written about me," she told me, and this was corroborated by Paul Burrell in his memoir, *A Royal Duty*, as well as by film-maker and television presenter Tim Willcox, who wrote and presented a documentary of Diana while she was still alive. He told me, "She was extremely concerned with her image. Every morning one of the first things she did was pore over everything that had been written about her in that day's editions. If the stories were positive, she was ecstatic, but if they were negative, she would tailspin and bemoan the cruelties of the world. Then she'd hit the telephone, and make sure that the journalists she had in her pocket put her side of whatever story she felt needed to be re-spun in the following day's papers."

Diana's extreme protectiveness of her public image was a factor which would influence her actions, moods and behaviour to an unusual degree until her death, complicating her life in ways that it need not have done, had she been capable of taking a more measured viewpoint of her fame. She enjoyed being the most famous woman in the world, and felt that it not only afforded her an invaluable platform, which was true enough, but also provided her with personal validation, which is open to question.

Nevertheless, as she approached her thirties, Diana had every reason to be delighted with her public image. Her face was on more newspaper front pages and magazine covers than any other person's on earth. She was the only royal who featured regularly on television. She was universally acclaimed as beautiful, glamorous, gracious, sweet-natured, kindhearted. As her tentative start gathered pace along the path of converting the boredom of official duties into the spiritual quest of genuine charity, her public image also benefited. Stories surfaced of Diana going beyond her royal duties to visit or write letters to the sick and injured, of doing work that many people associate with saintliness.

Behind the scenes, she was developing a quest. "I needed to. I was the Princess of Wales, with two wonderful boys, and I still felt worthless and miserable," she told me.

Diana was now actively seeking out charitable causes which provided her with an emotional or spiritual spark. "I wanted to find charities I could grow with," she said. Her approach was refreshingly quixotic, and eventually brought Mother Teresa into her life, via Pida Ripley, an old friend of mine.

Pida Ripley was one of the most eminent charity fund-raisers in the world. For over two decades she had been a powerhouse behind the United Nations Association, raising funds for worthwhile cause after worthwhile cause. Then, in the mid-eighties, she founded WomenAid, a charity in which women in the first world help women in the third world to help themselves. This might be by providing the funds and technical know-how to enable women in the Kenyan countryside to build a well, or by helping in the purchase and setting up of an electrical generator in India. As someone who had sat on Pida's committees since the mid-seventies, and who had helped Pida in her commendable fundraising activities, I am in a position to personally state that she is truly an exceptional woman, and someone for whom Diana had the utmost respect. Pida recounted to me how Diana came into her life, "She had seen a leaflet about WomenAid, I believe lying around at one of her friends' houses. She asked about it, heard that it was women working for women, and said that's something she'd like to get involved with. We'd just started, and the Foreign Office said she couldn't become a patron yet, not until we were more established and had more of a track record."

When Diana heard that WomenAid was hosting a luncheon at which it would distribute Women of the World Awards, she offered to attend and present the awards. She was most excited about her involvement with the project, as I can attest to, for I was a committee member and was present at the VIP reception prior to the luncheon where Diana was in full flood, rallying the troops and making it obvious how much she admired our work.

"She chose us," Pida said. "She wanted to become involved in something that was making a meaningful contribution, something that was small and had just started, the way she did with Birthright.

"I was surprised by her. She was a lot deeper and more knowledgeable than I had been led to believe she would be. I found her a real delight. I think the secret of her success was her approachability, her informality and her sense of humour."

One of the winners of the Women of the World Award instituted by WomenAid was Mother Teresa. Although she was too ill in Calcutta to fly over and collect it herself, she sent three of her Sisters of the Missionaries of Charity. These nuns were truly impressive, and Diana told them and Pida of her desire to meet Mother Teresa. Pida promised to do what she could to help, and the outcome is known to all.

What is less well known is that Mother Teresa's order was the catalyst through which Diana developed an interest in the homeless. Much of the work which the Sisters of the Missionaries of Charity do in Britain, as in India, is related to homelessness. In time, Diana started accompanying the Cardinal-Archbishop of Westminster, Basil Hume, on visits to the arches and tunnels throughout his archdiocese, which had, and still has at the time of writing, one of the greatest homelessness problems in Great Britain.

Another charity which Diana sought out and associated herself with at this time was the English National Ballet. Being a balletomane whose childhood fantasy had been to become one of the world's great prima ballerinas, this was a natural choice for Diana. "She was wonderful," Jamie Jeeves, the fund-raiser, told me. "She was great at saying the right thing to the right person at the right time. She could get people to loosen their purse strings like no one else." He "couldn't sing her praises highly enough" and felt that her "lack of airs and graces" and her "informality" made her a "delight to be around".

Certainly, Diana involved herself in areas which went beyond royal patronage. She used to attend rehearsals casually dressed in jeans, as if she herself were a dancer and not a princess, taking note of everything and thoroughly absorbing the atmosphere of a world she had long wanted to be a part of.

Slowly but surely, she was finding ways and means of nurturing herself, of gaining pleasure and fulfilment while doing good, and there is no doubt whatsoever, as I can attest to from personal observation, that she was utterly sincere in her desire to do as much good as possible for the disadvantaged. It was my opinion then, and is my opinion now, that she was on a genuine spiritual quest, that she was not necessarily playing to the gallery, and that she was not actually trying to garner public accolades for herself. Nevertheless, one also had to acknowledge, after three decades in the charity world, that the less worthy element ego-gratification, the recognition from others that one is doing good, is also a natural part of the whole package of doing good, for no human being is purely good or purely evil, nor is any one human being entirely free of the egotistical element of altruism. As far as I could see it, however, the acid test, for Diana and anyone else who is involved in charity, is whether they would do what they were doing without any recognition at all. There is no doubt in my mind that she would have done so, because many of her activities remained and still remain unrecognized and unsung by the world at large. And, if she wanted people to view her as a good and kind person, a person of compassion who related to and sought to relieve the suffering of others, who can fairly criticize her for that, when all she actually sought was to gain recognition for her genuine motivation and accomplishments?

Some of Diana's areas of identification were not immediately apparent to outsiders. Her interest in AIDS and AIDS sufferers is a case in point. When I asked her why she was so drawn to them, she said, "Maybe it goes back to when I was a little girl." She explained that there were times as a child when she wanted her mother's love but could not have it, because her parents' separation meant that she was stuck with her father during the week. She felt this had created within her an ability to "love people no one else wants to love."

Undoubtedly, Diana developed a commitment to AIDS sufferers, and at a time when AIDS was not the popular cause it became. Her sincerity is therefore apparent. John Coblenz, then of the charity CRUSAID, told me, "The first thing she did for us was open the Kobler Centre in September 1988". Thereafter, she did a plethora of engagements for them, including "visiting many of the wards in the hospices". He felt that her greatest accomplishment was "to show the public that you can't catch this disease by normal physical contact," by touching AIDS victims in front of photographers. He found her "very helpful, willing to devote as much time as we needed." She also avidly attended fund-raising events, "realizing that her presence at something would enhance the occasion." Her appreciation of her status was now paying dividends that others could reap.

So began Diana's hospital and hospice visits. Sometimes she took William and Harry with her, telling them they were going to see cancer patients. "She would drop in late at night without warning and go from bed to bed, talking to patients," a nurse at St. Mary's Hospital, Paddington, told me. "She undoubtedly gave some of them a real fillip. You must remember, many of them were young men who were dying, often without a friend or relative in sight. It's frightening how many families cut themselves off when they discover that their son or daughter, usually son, is dying of AIDS."

Diana's approach to getting her life onto a more profoundly satisfying footing was two-pronged. On the one hand, she aimed to nurture her spirit and develop interests that would benefit herself as well as others. On the other hand, she actively sought assistance from other people. This was a new and encouraging trend, for which much of the credit must go to Carolyn Pride, her West Heath School friend who became a Coleherne Court flatmate. By this time the wife of brewery heir and party-planner William Bartholomew, Carolyn had been appalled by the state of Diana's health ever since they had resumed the intimacy of their friendship, which had been interrupted in the early days when Diana was adjusting to her step up in the world.

Carolyn knew the marriage of the Prince and Princess of Wales was over. She and her husband often went away for weekends with Diana and James Hewitt, her main lover. Painfully struck by the disparity between the public myth of the Princess of Wales and the private reality, she had been begging Diana to get help for some considerable time before she hit upon the winning formula. She threatened to go public if Diana did not seek medical treatment for what she considered to be her friend's number-one health problem: bulimia. "She felt if she didn't take desperate steps, I'd eventually die," Diana told me.

Confronted with the knowledge that Carolyn did intend to expose her to prevent a worse fate, Diana agreed to act. She chose Dr Maurice Lipsedge, a psychiatrist whose hourly rate was £200 and who had successfully dealt with her sister Sarah's anorexia. Although he had never suffered from either anorexia or bulimia any more than the many other doctors whose opinions and advice she had dismissed upon the grounds that they were only worth listening to if they had suffered themselves, Diana was prepared to give Maurice Lipsedge a chance. Partly, this was because she knew Carolyn Bartholomew would expose her if her condition did not improve, and partly because she had reached the stage where blaming others was scant comfort for the suffering she was still enduring.

"He helped," Diana said of Maurice Lipsedge, whom she saw regularly, though she gave him only limited credit for the turnaround which her health now took. She assessed Stephen Twigg's contribution to be even more significant. A holistic therapist whose treatment included massage, diet and positive thinking, Twigg started paying professional visits to Kensington Palace at the end of 1988. At first, he was primarily Diana's masseur, utilizing a Swedish form of deep tissue massage which she found relieved the physical tensions to which she had always been prone, and which she had sought to release throughout much of her life with vigorous, sustained and sometimes violent exercise.

Gradually, Twigg made Diana aware of the needs of her body. Certain forms of exercise did not release stress; they created tension. What Diana needed was a more balanced and respectful approach to her own body, to her own needs.

"He struck a chord within me," Diana said, explaining how she came to rely upon Twigg. As Twigg conveyed the principles of balance, harmony and respect to his eager pupil during their hour-long consultations, she became curious to understand the thinking behind what he was propounding. So Twigg began telling her about the necessity to harmonize the emotional, intellectual and spiritual aspects of her nature. Gradually, he showed her that she could cope far more effectively with her problems if she replaced negative attitudes with positive ones.

Sometimes, his tips were remarkably simple, such as when she was bemoaning going to Balmoral, which she found a sap on her energy because she was "stuck with the Royal Family." "They're stuck with you, too," he counselled, appealing to her vengeful side and making her see for the first time that her presence could also be a thorn in their side: an observation, it must be said, which she thereafter relished.

Twigg's greatest contributions to Diana were in helping her to become more positive and in giving her the means to eat as much as she wanted without gaining weight. In some ways, this latter gift was the magic wand which threw new light on everything else. To someone whose appetites had always been unmanageable, but who insisted upon remaining slim, this truly was "eating your cake and having it." Twigg was a follower of the method of eating whereby you consume as much protein or carbohydrate as you wish, but do not mix them. Called the Hay Diet when first introduced, it allowed Diana to eat to her heart's content without having to worry about gaining an excessive amount of weight. Utilized in conjunction with vitamin supplements, which she worked out with Twigg, for the first time in years Diana was able to satisfy her cravings for food without needing to expel them afterwards. Although "I wasn't cured of bulimia overnight," Diana did start "keeping down food" and broke the cycle of "despair, self-hatred, self-disgust" after "overeating then making oneself sick." This was the single most significant step along the road to recovery, and it is one which has never been adequately acknowledged.

Once Diana discovered how good professionals could make her feel, she did not limit herself to Penny Thornton, Maurice Lipsedge or Stephen Twigg. In 1988 she acquired a second astrologer. Where Penny Thornton steered Diana on the voyage of spiritual self-discovery, Debbie Frank dealt with her everyday concerns. "Astrology has great value," Diana said. She used it to check on everything, from matters connected to minutiae of her work and lovers to the outcome of her marriage, Penny Thornton having told her that she would never be queen. No problem was too big or too small to be addressed, with the result that she was constantly on the telephone to Penny Thornton and Debbie Frank. She also consulted with the astrologer Felix Lyle beginning in 1991 and continued using him intermittently for the next few years.

Astrology, however, was only one of the esoteric fields in which Diana and her sister-in-law Sarah York took an abiding interest. Both women were obsessed with fortune-tellers, especially after Diana discovered the benefits Penny Thornton could offer and Sarah's marriage to Prince Andrew started to unravel in 1990. Spiritualists, palmists, tarot card readers, numerologists, crystal gazers and crystal users were just a few of the occultists who came and went from Kensington and Buckingham palaces, or were visited by the sisters-in-law.

Diana's favourite psychic between 1987 and 1992 was Betty Palko, a sixty-two-year-old grandmother to whom the Princess paid frequent visits at her house in suburban Surbiton. In 1992 Sarah recommended Rita Rogers so highly that Diana gave her a chance. Thereafter, she stayed with Miss Rogers, who says, "I do some amazing work. I'm not a fake. That's why I never get into the papers. I think anybody who seeks that, well, they are not good at their job, are they? I enjoy my work, but there is no way I would discuss my clients. I am very loyal. Very loyal. My job is like being a priestess."

So reliant did Diana become upon Rogers that she took Dodi Fayed to see her, via the Harrods' Sikorsky helicopter, on Tuesday, 12 August 1997, at her Victorian house in Little Pilsey, near Chesterfield.

Sarah was also reliant upon Rogers, and even went to the lengths of having her spokesman make an announcement in 1996: "I can tell you that this woman is definitely not a conwoman." Sarah's other medium, Madame Vasso, had written a turgid little book revealing what she labelled Sarah's secrets.

So enthusiastic did Diana become about this voyage of self-discovery and therapeutic satisfaction, upon which she had embarked with encouragement from Sarah, that she branched out into other fields as well. Knowing now that many of her problems lay within her own head, she tried to sort herself out by altering her perceptions with the help of hypnotherapist Roderick Lane. Meanwhile, she was still seeing Maurice Lipsedge and Stephen Twigg, both of whom were also dealing with matters relating to her head. Later, she would replace Lipsedge with Susie Orbach, an American psychotherapist whose ethos and values were more in keeping with the maverick Princess's ambitions than were those of the more traditional psychiatrist. Orbach was a feminist, and Diana gave her credit for "empowering" her.

There was overlap in the physical as well as the mental fields. While Stephen Twigg was kneading her muscles, Diana also embarked upon another form of massage. Aromatherapy involves the use of essential aromatic oils to soothe away the stresses and strains of life. Most people find and stick to one masseur or masseuse, but not Diana. Failing to see why she should limit herself to one form of massage if two gave twice as much relief, she availed herself of the expertise of Sue Beechy, who would pack up her oils and take them to Kensington Palace, where Diana eagerly awaited the relief afforded by hands with two decades' experience. James Hewitt's and Diana's chart as outlined by Thornton were indeed right: she had strong sensual needs. Or, as Diana herself put it, "Touching is one of the most important things you can do."

Yet another regular Kensington Palace therapist administering to Diana's strong physical needs was Oonagh Toffolo, an acupuncturist and trained nurse. From Sligo in Ireland, she had a sensible and sensitive approach which appealed to Diana, who happily submitted her body to the stimulation and release afforded by the minute needles which Toffolo placed along the meridians, or invisible energy lines. "Acupuncture really works. You should try it," Diana said to me. "It frees your energies."

It was around this time that Diana engaged Carolan Brown, a fitness trainer, to come to Kensington Palace three times a week for workouts. These took place in the Princess's sitting-room. The butler or a footman would shift the furniture, and the two women would start a vigorous but sensible workout for an hour. For five years Brown and Diana worked together. Although she asserts that she left when she became pregnant, her departure coincided with the release of a video she made using Diana's name.

From 1990 until her death, Diana used another fitness trainer as well. Jenni Rivett, who overlapped with Brown for a period of about three years, helped the Princess tone and reshape her body. Her figure was important to her, as was feeling good through exercise, and it was typical of Diana's approach to life that she would avail herself of the services of the two women at once. According to her reckoning, if one was good, two must be better, especially if they had new suggestions, new ideas, and the payoff was feeling good or improving her figure.

Diana used to suffer from backache, a relic of slouching and balancing William and Harry on her hip while they were babies. She therefore used Michael Skipwith, a cranial osteopath, who relieved the pain when it was there, and otherwise kept her back and head in good shape with cranial manipulation.

Sandwiched among these other forms of therapy was an unconventional one which Diana swore by. Colonic irrigation is the method whereby the body is cleansed of toxins with a deeply penetrative enema. Chryssie Fitzgerald was her colonic irrigator, reflexologist and healer for nine years. "It sweeps you clean," Diana told me, trying to convince me to have a session at the Hale Clinic in London's Marylebone area, where she was a frequent visitor. "It leaves you feeling light and floaty." This was doubtless factual, though the more conventional branches of the medical profession might attribute that effect to the loss of essential fluids and bacteria, crucial to maintaining the body's ability to fight disease, which poured out of her system along with the "toxins" colonic irrigation is supposed to purge. Diana also used a second colonic irrigator, Ursula Gatley.

Although conventional medicine frowned upon this treatment, criticism from the medical establishment did not perturb Diana. An avid health-food shopper, she merely replaced the essential bodily agents swept away by colonic irrigation with store-bought supplements. Although this was not the ideal way to maintain the body's balance, it did possess the advantage of allowing her to experience some of the physical effects of a good purgative without perpetuating the bulimia which had caused such havoc, and which she had under relative control as the 1990s dawned and she approached thirty.

The progress Diana was making in regaining her health was only one area of her life, albeit the most important, into which she now channelled her considerable energies with a view to improving her quality of life. "I want to be known as a workhorse, not a clotheshorse," she announced, and set about changing her professional style to match the new, vocational approach she was taking. Hitherto, the focus had always been on what she was wearing. While this was an excellent promotional point for the British designers she employed, such as Murray Arbeid, Bruce Oldfield, Victor Edelstein and Zandra Rhodes, "It detracts from my work," she decided. Shrewdly, on official engagements she cut out wearing clothes by all others designers but her favourite, Catherine Walker, thereby bringing the feverish speculation that had long been a feature of her public appearances – "There she is in a blue Jacques Azagury/peach Yuki," etc. – to an end.

Thereafter, until her death, Diana's style of attire become simpler and simpler as her humanitarian work became more and more admired.

Although she was still frequently, indeed usually, photographed in couture, it was always Catherine Walker couture in Britain, whether she was visiting a hospital for sick children in Central London or attending a gala in an exotic shalwar kameez. In doing so, she retained all the elegance and beauty which helped to make her such a glamorous and desirable photographic icon, while taking the focus off the clothes she was wearing, for the one thing no publication was prepared to do was give daily publicity to the inevitable Catherine Walker. Only when she was in Europe or America did she switch to designers such as Versace and Lacroix. And, of course, when she went to Africa or the West Indies, she limited herself to simple cotton shirts and trousers, which were also flattering and photogenic, but which had the virtue of being over-the-counter and not worthy of mention in coverage, except to confirm the simplicity of their wearer's approach.

Diana was only too aware that one gift she lacked was that of public speaking. After her marriage, she had been given lessons by Sir Richard (now Lord) Attenborough, and while these had enabled her to deliver a few words under duress, she realised she needed to enhance her skills if she was ever to be taken seriously as a humanitarian. She therefore called in the speech therapist Peter Setterlen, who had once been an actor on Britain's most enduring soap opera, *Coronation Street*. Gradually, she learned about breath and delivery, space and comfort, pause and passion. Although she never did become a great orator, the lessons did enable her to become reasonably proficient at public speaking – "To get the message across," as she put it.

As Diana gained control over her health and image the way she had previously done over her staff and the structure of her life, she had cause to reflect upon how well deserved her rewards were. Nothing had come without a struggle. But she was shaping her life and her self the way she wanted them to be, and indications were that she was succeeding.

Diana was now effectively separated from the Prince of Wales. He lived at Highgrove House; she lived at Kensington Palace. They got together just enough for him to see the children. Otherwise, whenever he was at Kensington Palace, she was at Highgrove House and vice versa. Unless, of course, the purpose of the visit was for him to see the children. This was the primary reason she now went to Gloucestershire for weekends. On such occasions, Diana ventured forth from her bedroom, where she watched television and talked on the telephone to friends, only to swim in the heated pool or to play with the children. If she was in an especially good mood, she would join Charles and the children for dinner, but more usually she dined with the children or on her own upstairs off a tray. The result was that a whole weekend might pass by without Charles and Diana saying anything to one another but hello and good-bye.

"The Prince of Wales hated the state of affairs," Princess Margaret of Hesse and the Rhine said. "He desperately wanted to have a friendly relationship with Diana. Sometimes she met him halfway, but more often she simply didn't want to know. She was very much an all-or-nothing type, and since he was now nothing to her, she frequently acted as if he didn't exist." Diana herself confirmed this in a roundabout way when she said, "I didn't see why I had to be all sweetness and light when I had nothing to say to him."

Once a month, Highgrove House danced to a different beat when Charles vacated it so that Diana could entertain her lover in peace. She and James Hewitt had known each other for three years and been together for much of that time. Their relationship had grown into a settled and passionate union with a strong fantasy element. Diana often told him how she dreamed of being with him for the rest of her life; how she wanted to have babies with him, especially the daughter she had not yet had; how the fortune-tellers who proliferated around her had predicted that something sudden and violent, like an avalanche, would remove Charles from her life; how she would then be free to lead a life of her own choice. Like many men in love, Hewitt hoped they might have a future together, but he was too skeptical to expect one. Exclusivity was not even a feature of the relationship. Although neither party admitted it to the other, both Diana and Hewitt consistently dabbled with other partners. Nevertheless, he confidently expected their relationship to continue to their mutual satisfaction.

In the summer of 1989, however, Diana went to a party given by Julia Samuel. There she saw a man who had eluded her in her youth. James Gilbey was yet another tall, handsome and well-built scion of yet another established family – this time, the gin family. A great-nephew of the Roman Catholic *éminence grise* Monsignor Alfred Gilbey, he had been someone the youthful Diana was crazy about. His interest had never matched hers, however, and he had thrown Diana over after she had damaged his car when he had stood her up on a date. They had not spoken since that episode, but ten years was long enough to let bygones be bygones.

They got along extremely well. He was much smitten by the glamorous and exotic princess who was now the world's number one media superstar. Diana's feelings towards him were substantially cooler, though she was human enough to enjoy gloating at this reversal in positions. Gilbey gave her ample opportunity in the weeks and months that followed. He went after her like a man possessed. Diana, who had been very keen on Gilbey before her marriage, blew hot and cold. By her own account to a friend who does not wish to be identified, she took to leading him up to the point of penetration, before changing her mind "leaving him high and dry." This she did practically every time she saw him, varying the torment only with absolute abstinence. "She enjoyed playing cat and mouse with him. It was her way of getting back at him for having rejected her all those years before."

What provoked a change in the direction of Diana's relationship with James Gilbey was James Hewitt's being posted to Germany for a two-year stint starting at the end of 1989. "He told her as soon as his superiors told him," his friend Alison Demuth confirmed to me prior to James Hewitt himself doing so. Her reaction shocked him. She chose to interpret the posting as a betrayal, a personal rejection. Up to that point, she'd been on the telephone to him five and six times a day for a period of three years. She'd always been eager to receive his calls and had always taken every one. Now, she stopped calling and always found some excuse for not being able to speak to him. He was stunned. Shattered. He couldn't believe it. He tried to be understanding, and persisted in calling her. When they did speak, she was invariably cold and could never find the time in her packed diary to squeeze him in. This from a woman who had spent the last years juggling appointments so that she could see him at every opportunity.

He did not confront her. He knew to do so would be pointless. Diana had made her position very clear. She didn't need words to do so. She was very good at nonverbal communication. She conveyed to him in no uncertain terms that the relationship was at an end. That it was over because he had chosen to accept a military command from his superiors, instead of refusing to accept the command and staying with her in England. She didn't care that he could have been court-martialled for refusing a direct command, or that he would ruin all prospects of further promotion even if he got off without a court-martial.

Diana's reaction provides an invaluable insight into her personality and the way she functioned. She never saw the other person's point of view if it conflicted with her own. So James Hewitt left for Paderborn without seeing her, convinced that the affair was over. It was a bad time for him because he really did love her.

Although the affair truly had ended, they did have one last lovemaking session. This took place when Hewitt returned to England just before Christmas 1990. The Gulf War was expected to break out at any time, and Hewitt naturally wanted to see his family and loved ones before being posted to the Gulf. Diana rang him up and asked him to Highgrove. He was nervous about going because there had been no contact between them while he was posted to Germany. After a rather stilted tea, she came and sat with her back pressed against his shins. Having initiated intimacy with that gesture, she allowed the passion to build until they could no longer contain themselves. Then she led him into the bedroom, where they had one last lovemaking session. It was her way of sending off one of the troops with a smile on his face. In case he didn't return. And it gave her a reason to become absorbed in the drama of having a beau in the line of fire who might be killed at any time.

Diana had become an excitement junkie.

Hewitt flew back to Germany on Christmas Eve and left for the Gulf with an advance party right after Christmas. Throughout the Gulf War, Diana remained in touch with him, writing him affectionate and encouraging letters. He hoped they would remain friends if they could not return to being lovers, but for her, a fit Hewitt who had survived the war unscathed had significantly less appeal than one who might die or be maimed during it. Upon his return, she consigned him to the past.

As 1989 and the decade hurtled towards an end, Hewitt's torment turned to James Gilbey's advantage. Hewitt's absence from her bed and her life had created a void which needed to be filled, and the cat-and-mouse games with Gilbey came to a gratifying end.

Having avenged herself on the dish best eaten cold, Diana now warmed up to become the passionately sexual and sensual powerhouse who was, as James Hewitt observed, "always ready for more." Night after night her easily recognizable car was parked outside James Gilbey's flat in

Lennox Gardens, causing comment by residents and visitors. Squidgy, as Gilbey nicknamed her, seldom left before the early hours of the morning. With the passage of time, she became more reckless, leaving later and later. One morning, she was even stopped for speeding by the police at 6:45 a.m. and let off with a caution. The newspapers who picked up the story asserted that Diana was on her way back to Kensington Palace from Buckingham Palace, where she usually went for an early-morning swim. While she did often avail herself of the pool there, she did so later in the day, and was fresh from the pool of passion, not swimming, her car having been seen parked in Lennox Gardens that whole night. As the Prince of Wales wished her well in her independent quest for gratification, as long as the press did not make awkward connections, she was all right.

Diana, however, was about to trigger one of the worst crises of her life. This would result in the termination of her relationship with James Gilbey and would ultimately surface as the Squidgygate and Camillagate scandals.

For more than two years, Diana had been agitating for a separation if Charles would not reconcile with her and make the changes within himself and his life that she required of him. While agitating, she also accepted the status quo and sought to improve her lot within the royal way of life. "She loved being the Princess of Wales," Penny Thornton noted, an opinion Diana confirmed to me and to many others. Contradictorily, Diana also tugged in a third direction. Although she did not actually want a reconciliation with the Prince of Wales under any terms save her own, she also let it be known that she would be happy to have her husband back. Partly, this position was backed by a genuine streak of romanticism. By her own admission, Diana sometimes saw herself wafting off into eternal marital bliss with a Prince Charles who no longer cared about Laurens van der Post, philosophy, architecture, churches and the myriad things which bored her; who now cared about what she cared about, and wanted to do what she did; who loved her so much that he was happy to sacrifice his interests as the proof of this great love which she had managed to generate within him, against all the odds. Unrealistic though this dream was, it did exist. What was far more realistic was her other motive for preaching the virtues of reconciliation. As long as she continued to be seen as the welcoming and rejected partner, the blame for the breakup of the marriage could be shifted solely onto the Prince of Wales. This was a clever position to adopt, and one which Diana did with increasing aplomb, especially during her *Panorama* interview in 1995. The fact that this stance was untenable did not alter its tactical advantageousness, as Diana knew only too well. "Brill, don't you think?" she asked Joseph Sanders when ticking off the points in her *Panorama* interview which she had clearly adopted for expedient rather than sincere purposes. Although that friend was shocked, there were others who were not, myself included. It was tactically brilliant for Diana to have made herself into the victim; to have ignored that there were considerably more than "three" in the marriage; that her contribution had made it rather more crowded than Charles's. The stance served her purposes well, as would become apparent at the time of her divorce.

As 1989 was coming to an end, Diana, already anticipating the uses to which she would put the evidence of Charles's adultery, sought evidence of his adultery. She hoped to "use it the evidence against him as leverage for a separation," a courtier, who cannot be named for legal reasons, said. So she approached a friendly male in the grey world of the protection services and asked him, "Can you help me win my husband back?" Faced with a plaintive Diana casting her wonderfully limpid eyes at him, he naturally answered in the affirmative, little realizing what her real agenda was. So Diana seduced him with a plan which she claimed was simple. She said that all she needed was proof that Charles was committing adultery with Camilla. Once she had that, she could confront him with it and precipitate a crisis that would force him to surrender his mistress and return to her loving arms. Could her friend please intercept and tape a sexually explicit conversation between the Prince and Mrs Parker Bowles?

On 17 December 1987 this man locked onto and recorded the amorous conversation that became known as the Camillagate tape. In it, the lovers exult in their passion and love for one another and repeatedly make it clear just how strongly they feel.

Diana now had what she needed. There was a problem, however. She had to be in a position to say that she had happened inadvertently upon the tape. That meant that it had to be broadcast, for a possible scanner to pick it up. To fulfill that requirement, the tape was duly aired on the evening of 18 December. This, however, presented genuine scanners with a striking inconsistency. Camilla speaks about her son Tom's birthday being "tomorrow," that is, the day the tape was broadcast, not the day the conversation took place. This lacuna would come back to haunt Diana. It was the vital giveaway, for no genuine radio buff would have taped then rebroadcast something he had happened to pick up by accident.

In fairness to Diana, the mere fact that she was prepared to go to such lengths shows how trapped she felt. "I can't just pack and leave. I'd tried that and it didn't work," she said to me in 1990. The adulterous tape worked no better, however. Waving it around and issuing the ultimatum that Prince Charles must change into a man who'd make her happy and abandon Camilla, or give her a separation, resulted only in her being told, as Charles himself described to a courtier, "Don't be so ridiculous. Your marriage is for life," after which the secret services laid a trap for her. This was sprung on New Year's Eve, when Diana was having another of the long, erotic telephone conversations to which she was prone with all her lovers. Interwoven among Gilbey's protestations of love, her fears of becoming pregnant by him, and several minutes of explicit eroticism (cut out of the version broadcast by the *Sun* tabloid in 1992) were topics as varied as the Queen Mother's fascination with her; the Bishop of Norwich's enquiry for her secret when dealing with the infirm; and her resentment of "this fucking family" despite "all I've done for them" by becoming the most popular person on earth.

Although the information I received from the courtier in 1993 was that the secret services broadcast the Squidgy tape three times in a two-week period after it was made, they did not alert Diana to the fact that she had been stymied. They did not need to. They expected a radio buff to pick it up on his scanner and sell it to a newspaper. This is precisely what happened. Cyril Reenan, a radio buff, happened upon the conversation while operating his scanner. He then sold it to the *Sun*, Britain's tabloid with the largest circulation.

According to a senior executive of the Murdoch organization, who asked me to withhold his name, "We sent around two reporters to Gilbey's flat in Lennox Gardens. They stopped him in the street as he was about to leave. They confronted him with the tape and asked for his comments. He literally turned white and started to jabber and shake uncontrollably. He couldn't comment. He couldn't say a word. He was in shock. But his response did confirm that the tape was genuine, which was all we were interested in." For the next two and a half years, the *Sun* locked their gold mine away, bringing it out only after "public opinion was ready for it. Diana was so revered in 1990 we could never have used it. We'd have been killing the goose that laid the golden egg. But after *Diana in Private* and the Morton book, it was a case of anything goes."

Once Gilbey told Diana that the *Sun* had the goods on them, his fate was sealed. While she had been crazy about him at seventeen, at twenty-nine she was significantly less ardent. In any contest between a plaything and her public image, the latter was bound to win. So she gave him up as a lover.

Despite this, Gilbey remained on cordial terms with Diana and a good friend of her brother, Charles, to whom he had become increasingly close as the relationship with his sister had intensified. Viscount Althorp, as he then was, often asked Gilbey and his girlfriend of the moment to join him and the model he had married that year, Victoria Lockwood, for weekends at Althorp. Indeed, Gilbey, his girlfriend Lady Alathea Savile and the Althorps were conspicuously plastered over the tabloids in 1992 at the height of the sensation about Diana's part in the Morton book. Gilbey and Spencer were both sources.

By January 1990, therefore, Diana was no nearer to achieving the separation she wanted, and was now aware that she was sitting on a powderkeg. The question was: Would it blow her sky-high, or could she somehow turn the disadvantage to her advantage?

Thirteen

Stuck in a marriage and a way of life she wanted to be free of, Diana told me she "despaired for the future. I couldn't see a way out. But there had to be one. Had to be."

Hope presented itself in an unexpected form. Fund-raising for charity had undergone fundamental changes since the recession had started towards the end of the 1980s. Gone were the halcyon days when the ladies who lunch could get together and effortlessly albeit energetically organize lavish balls which the great and the grand clambered to attend. "Even my rich friends no longer have any money," Jane Hartley, née Princess Martin Lubomirski and Lady Edmonstone, accurately stated at a committee meeting at the Red Cross headquarters in 1990 when we were organizing a gala for that worthy organization. The result was that many of the established functions on the London social scene withered on the vine, along with the charities which still needed money even though no one had any to spare any longer.

At that time, one of the main purposes of my life was to raise funds for humanitarian charities. Being single, childless and with a reputation as a well-known socialite, I had plenty of scope, and had exercised it sufficiently throughout my adult life to be named third in a list of the top-forty British charity fund-raisers by the *Sunday Express* magazine. My path often crossed that of the Princess of Wales, for the world of which I had been a part since she was a teenager was one with which she was increasingly occupying herself.

Although Diana and I were not close friends, we did enjoy cordial relations. It must be said, however, that we had little in common, on the face of it, aside from our joint interest in charity work. I was twelve years older than she. My circle of friends was international, while hers was then overwhelmingly British. Of course, she would later change that as she came to appreciate how much more colourful, stimulating and enriching London's international community is than its British upper-class counterpart. Whenever we met, we had little to say except hello, how much we liked one another's dresses and jewels, and what excellent work our charities were doing.

Those meetings, however, were the root of the inspiration that struck in 1990, and which altered both her life and mine irrevocably. I was already an established author and social columnist. Why not capitalize upon that by writing an official biography of the Princess of Wales, focusing on her charity work, as a means of raising funds for three of our mutual charities? The book was bound to sell well. If I donated all profits to the charities, each of them would make a fortune, far outstripping anything that charity balls could raise. I decided to approach the charities to ask if they were interested in receiving the donations, conditional upon the Princess's cooperation. They all unsurprisingly said, "Yes, please."

In royal circles, the normal way to gain official cooperation is to first approach the royal in question unofficially to see whether an official invitation will be met with a favourable response. If the answer is no, you save yourself and the royal embarrassment, for neither of you will be particularly comfortable if you run into one another following an official refusal. On the other hand, an unofficial rejection can be presented in such a way that everyone saves face. An unofficial acceptance is always, but always, an agreement that the official approach will have an affirmative response.

Once I had the green light from the charities, I put out feelers to the Princess of Wales through mutual friends to see what her attitude would be if I made an official approach. The reply was a resounding yes, so I wrote to Patrick Jephson, then her Private Secretary. Dickie Arbiter, the Prince and Princess of Wales's Press Secretary, answered inviting me to attend Buckingham Palace for a meeting. In royalspeak, that meant that Diana's yes remained yes.

In the interval between Arbiter's writing his letter and my showing up at the palace that August of 1990, Diana had a change of heart. The result was that what had been a green light now turned amber. I was not only perplexed, but annoyed, and asked a mutual friend to get an explanation.

Shortly afterwards, I received a telephone call from Diana herself asking if we could meet at the house of that friend. "Everyone says you're one of the most discreet people in London. I can trust you, can't I?" she said, meaning that she was placing confidence in me and didn't want it violated.

When I met Diana at this mutual friend's house, I was astonished by her conduct. Up to this point, the Diana I had encountered was a princess who behaved very much in keeping with the forms and traditions of royalty. In social situations, she was as circumspect as the rest of them, as indeed all ladies are. Although her style was more relaxed than the other royals, there was nevertheless that expected degree of formality. Although this semiprivate, semipublic face was dignified and composed, I had never felt any affinity with the woman behind it. Now, however, she was the antithesis of circumspect. Throwing caution and reserve to the wind, she said that she wanted me to write the truth about her life "because I feel as if the whole fairy tale is crushing whatever's left of the real me. I need to get out from under . . . to get away. If you write what my life's really like, that'll make it possible for me to find a way out."

To say that I was shocked and surprised does not even begin to convey how I felt. The nearer someone is to royal circles, the more reverential people surrounding the monarchy are. Although I was neither an intimate nor a personal friend of the Princess of Wales, we moved in overlapping circles, where everyone expected the royals to conduct themselves the way royalty always had behaved. That meant that I expected Diana to play the game, to keep up appearances with everyone except her closest friends (which meant with me as well, for I was most emphatically not one of her closest friends), to continue living out the charade that she and the Prince of Wales were still a couple, even though people like me had known for years that they were not. I was sufficiently old-fashioned to deplore people washing their dirty linen in public, unless, of course, someone else had thrown it into the public arena first, in which case you addressed the subject as minimally as possible, then shut up about it, as I had done for nearly two decades.

Now here was the Princess of Wales sitting opposite me pouring out how unhappy she was: How the Prince of Wales was "a perfect beast" who had "never loved" her; how he had "callously used" her to "produce the next generation then thrown" her aside for the "woman he loved"; how she had been so unhappy she had "hurt" herself several times; how she wanted a separation; how she had been made ill by the demands of the "men in grey suits" (the courtiers); how the strain of royal life and the pain of her marriage had driven her to bulimia; how she "knew" she'd die if she didn't get away from the royal way of life.

At the end of what seemed like a weekend but cannot have been much more than two hours, Diana departed, asking me to please consider helping. "I want what my life's really like to be out there published for public consumption," she said. "Not the fairy tale. The fairy tale's killing me. If you'd just write about the real Diana, it would make all the difference."

I could hardly believe what I had just heard. Was that really any member of any royal family, any person of breeding, much less the Princess of Wales? In all the time we had been together, she had not evinced one ounce of circumspection. On the contrary, she had been direct to the point of painfulness. Amid the outpouring of anguish, frustration, hopefulness, and desperation, every semblance of reservation had been washed away. The Princess of Wales had poured her heart and ambitions out to me as if we were twins, yet we were nothing more than social acquaintances. I could not make up my mind whether to be flattered or appalled, and remained a bit of both. She had certainly sprung a surprise upon me, and I had to go away and give careful thought as to whether it was welcome or not.

One natural consequence of the change in the status of the book was that it could not be a vehicle for raising funds for charity. Inevitably it would be a sensational book. No British charity would accept donations from any source that dragged the Royal Family into public controversy. Obviously, I stood to make a considerable amount of money from publication of what was bound to be, and indeed did become, a worldwide best-seller. But did I want the hassle? To write such a book would undoubtedly put my social connections in Britain in jeopardy. Did I want to take that chance? Indeed, did those connections matter very much to me?

The conclusion I came to was that they did not. My friends were my friends and I had no doubt most would remain so. If a few did not, it would be useful to have them weed themselves out, so, rather than deplore their absence, I would welcome it.

Of course, I was in a stronger position than the average British lady. To begin with, I am not English. My social position was not based upon my

British connections. It was founded upon the family of my birth, their connections, the fact that I was an established public figure of many years' standing. My circle of friends was too wide, too international in flavour and too independently wealthy or situated, some being royal themselves, to take a lead from the British Royal Family if they decided to ostracize me.

Diana's suggestion that I write her biography could not have come at a more opportune moment for me for one reason. I had been considering adopting a baby. It was one thing for me to rely upon the benevolence of my family to help me maintain my lifestyle while I was a woman on my own, but quite another to do so with a child, or children, to support. Choosing to look at the opportunity Diana was offering as enabling me to afford a baby without family help, I decided that jeopardizing future relations with the British royals would be a small price to pay, if pay it I had to, for financial independence and motherhood.

With Diana's complicity, I therefore set about placing the biography via my agent with a publisher. She asked me to keep her part in the book confidential, because it would damage her life, and of course I was only too happy to do so. While the book was being sold, we continued meeting at our mutual friend's residence. On each occasion, her outpourings were as unreserved and overwhelming as they had been the first time. Naturally, I felt a tremendous amount of sympathy for her. It was obvious she was a deeply unhappy woman. She was also impatient. She wanted the book written before a book deal had even been signed. This I was not prepared to do, partly because I had a prior commitment to organize a charity ball in aid of the Chemical Dependency Unit and SSAFA (Soldiers' Sailors' Seamen's Forces Association) with the Duchess of York as guest of honour.

It was while I was putting the six months of hard slog into bringing the Maypole Ball to fruition that I realized how complicated Diana's relationship with Sarah was. They were friends and supporters, but they were also competitors. Diana certainly seemed to relish any discomfiture Sarah experienced, and later I would discover that this competitive element was reciprocated in full by her sister-in-law.

Only after the Maypole Ball was held on 30 April 1991 did I settle down to writing *Diana in Private*. Diana, I had already discovered, was a thorough and cooperative subject. We were hamstrung, however, by the need to meet at our mutual friend's residence. I could not show up at Kensington Palace for meetings without her help with the book becoming obvious upon publication, nor could she see me at the Cundy Street Flats, where I lived. Half the Royal Household, several royal cousins and relations of Diana's, as well as friends of hers and of Prince Charles's, lived there. Hugh and Emilie van Cutsem, for instance, were not only members of the Prince of Wales's inner circle ("my sworn enemies," according to Diana), but also my immediate neighbours. I could look out of my windows into their flat, and they could do likewise. Obviously, it would be fatal for her to be seen coming and going, so we agreed that Diana would telephone me regularly instead.

After four meetings, most of our contact was over the telephone – approximately thirty-five conversations in all. As the book took shape, I used to ask her to enlarge upon specifics. This, it must be said, she did not always like doing. I got the distinct impression that she also did not like being pinned down, especially when her statements were contradictory, or had the potential to mislead. Two examples spring to mind. One of these I have already mentioned: Critical though she was of her mother's "legging it," she admitted that Frances had had no choice in the outcome of the custody battle and had been a devoted and loving mother. She conceded that Frances had always maintained that Johnnie had been brutalizing her, and that, when she had originally left, she had set up home in London with Diana and Charles. It was Diana who told me that her father had created the custody battle simply to get back at her mother for leaving him, and that once he had scored his point, he had thereafter shared custody with Frances. Yet she persisted in maintaining that Frances had abandoned her children, and stated that both she and Charles felt that Frances should have stayed no matter what. Only by doing so would Frances have spared her children the agony of missing her when she was not with them.

This attitude frightened me then and has frightened me since. Diana seemed to be saying that her mother was selfish in trying to make a clean break from a wife-beater, and that she should have gone back to him when Johnnie refused to let the children return to London with her after that Christmas of 1967, instead of taking the chance and losing custody of them through the courts. "I would never take the chance of losing custody of my boys," Diana said with such determination that I had no doubt she would prefer to die rather than find herself in the position in which her mother had been placed.

Another area where Diana's statements needed reconciling was her claim that she had repeatedly tried to hurt herself. The very first time she alluded to these events, I noticed that she used a word which could lead one to conclude that she had tried to commit suicide, without actually saying so. On each subsequent occasion the subject came up, I noticed even more strongly her choice of words. Never once did she say that she had tried to commit suicide, or kill herself, yet I had no doubt that she was hoping that I would draw that inference from her statements. The scenarios she described, however, did not constitute suicide attempts. Picking up a penknife of your husband's in the middle of a row and passing it over your wrists without grazing yourself or drawing blood is not the same as "slashing your wrists." Threatening to use it against him or yourself is a dramatic statement, one that even has threatening overtones, but that is all it is. So, too, is hurling yourself in the direction of a display cabinet, taking care to stop short lest you cut yourself on the glass and mar your beauty. As for picking at one's thigh with a lemon slicer, could Diana have been seriously hoping that any rational person would believe that she was peeling herself to death?

There was a sound reason for Diana making these statements, however, and for hoping that I would misinterpret them. "I live in terror that the men in grey suits (the courtiers) will take my boys away from me if I push too hard for a separation. That family (the Royal Family) are stuck in the 1930s. They're convinced separation lowers them in the eyes of the public. As for divorce, it's *beyyyyyyyond* the pale. They still act as if my mother is only a bit better than the devil and Wallis Windsor. They just don't get the hang of it. They'll never allow me to leave without trashing me even worse than they trashed George Harewood. He was the Queen's first cousin, for fucksake, but that didn't stop them from throwing him out of the family like he was a dead rat. If Tony Snowdon hadn't been as clever as he is, the public would also be convinced he's a stinker. He clawed his way back after the divorce from Princess Margaret. He was not even informed when the announcement of his separation was being made. I bet Mark Phillips won't, though (he and Princess Anne had been separated only a year at that point, and would not be divorced until 1992). They've turned him into a figure of derision, even though he hustles like hell to bring home the bread."

It should be noted, in both the interest of Diana and the Royal Family, that her criticisms and fears were levelled against the courtiers, not the family itself.

Diana, of course, was accurate in her observations about the fate awaiting royals who sought a separation or divorce. Proof of this was not long in coming either, as the campaign of vilification and abuse orchestrated by the Buckingham Palace Press Office against Sarah, Duchess of York, proved when she sought an amicable separation from Prince Andrew in 1992. That does not mean that Diana was accurate in her assessment that these same courtiers would have taken her children from her. Indeed, I tried to point out to her that her fear, while understandable, was based more upon the experiences of her mother than upon her own situation. "You don't know what they're really like," she said the first time, but when she realized I did have some inkling what the courtiers could and did get up to, she held to her position firmly. "I'll never take a chance on losing my boys," she repeated time and again like a mantra.

Although I tried to allay Diana's fears by pointing out that the Royal Family were so afraid of adverse publicity that they would never strip any royal mother, even one who was patently unsuitable, of access to or custody of her children, she said, "I can't take that chance. I can't let what happened to my mother happen to me." Even though she continued fearing that her children might be taken from her – a fear she instilled in Sarah York as well – the fact of what happened at their separations in 1992 and their subsequent divorces proves that their fears were groundless.

Diana, of course, knew only too well that the Royal Family had ammunition that they could have used against her if they wished to do so. First, there was the Squidgygate tape, which she had learned about from James Gilbey after his alarming encounter in the street with two *Sun* reporters, and which left no doubt that Diana was an adulteress. Then, there were the many occasions upon which she had slept with James Hewitt and been in compromising situations with a variety of men. To put it bluntly, should the truth about her activities get out, the roll call of her lovers would do her no credit, especially when placed beside the relative abstemiousness of her husband. Last, and possibly most important of all, was the state of her mental health. Had Diana been married into her own family, this would doubtless have been employed against her the way her brother, Charles, opportunistically and gratuitously brought his wife Victoria's medical history into their divorce. "The Royal Family had no intention of using Diana's mental problems against her in a divorce,"

Princess Margaret of Hesse and the Rhine said. "Not only would that have been a low blow, and the Queen and Prince Charles do not go in for low blows, but the whole thing would've been too mortifying for them. They're only human, after all, and who wants to parade such distasteful problems before the world?"

People frequently measure others by their own yardstick, however, and Diana, being a Spencer, was afraid of what she would have done to anyone who found herself in the position she was now in. Nevertheless, she took brilliant methods to combat the perceived threat. Her first foray was to leak to me her eating disorders and emotional turbulence, which I placed in context and retold in 1992 in *Diana in Private* in as constructive and unsalacious a manner as possible. "I want my public to know what I've been through," she said, but her reason was not purely to maintain a mystical relationship between the great unseen public and herself. Vulnerable though she might have been, she was undoubtedly a mistress of the art of public relations, and understood that once people knew she was suffering, and had been for some time, they would not question the causes of that suffering overmuch. She was therefore neutralizing the use to which the courtiers could put the issue of her mental health in the event of a custody struggle, for once the public knew she had been ill, they would be less interested in the label than in the person to blame. Being born a nonroyal, Diana was the natural repository of sympathy as the misunderstood – especially from the British public, which is well known to have a natural proclivity towards underdogs and views the Royal Family as the ultimate top dog.

Diana's fears led to a falling-out with me before *Diana in Private* was published. (This, it must be said, was not a permanent state, for we made up in 1995.) I had committed two cardinal sins. The first was that, after getting Diana's side of the story, I referred back to friends and relations of the Prince of Wales who were friends of mine and asked them to fill in the picture Diana had been painting. Even to a fool, which I hope I am not, it would by then have been apparent that Diana had so slanted the picture of her life in her own favour that it could not possibly have been a balanced account of the facts. Although the Prince of Wales was not a personal friend of mine, I knew well enough that he was not the unfeeling monster Diana had depicted. Indeed, the criticism most frequently levelled against him in royal circles was that he was too "sensitive" (HRH

Princess Alice, Duchess of Gloucester, among others) or "soft-hearted" (the Duke of Edinburgh, who actually used the word "wimp" and was forever criticizing his son for not being harsh and confrontational enough). Charles was known to be too much of an idealist, and was roundly condemned in certain political circles as a "wet." None of this tallied with Diana's portrait of a callous bastard wickedly snatching the heart of an innocent young girl whom he turned into a brood mare before discarding on the refuse heap of the Crown Jewels, so that he could philander with his ageing mistress. I was also convinced – having heard it from many people, including friends and cousins of Charles and friends of Camilla and Andrew Parker Bowles, who were upset at being "dropped," as well as from reports by one of Camilla's neighbours (Lady Caroline Waterhouse, sister of my good friend Lady Sarah Spener-Churchill and mother of Diana's beau David Waterhouse) that there were no royal cars near her house during the first years of Charles's marriage – that Charles had not seen Camilla Parker Bowles at that time and had, moreover, enjoyed friendships with the likes of Eva O'Neill before his return to Camilla resulted in the strong union it had become by 1991.

A further consideration was that Diana had been trying to sell me the bill of goods she eventually had Andrew Morton purvey to an unsuspecting public: that she was a sexual innocent who had known only the Prince of Wales. While I had every sympathy with Diana for wishing to keep her private life private, the scales of justice decreed that she either extend the same consideration to her husband, or, if she wished to unmask him, she should also come clean, if only in part, about her own activities. Diana was a very sharp lady, or instinctive, as she would have put it. It didn't take much for her to see that I was not convinced by her version of events. Yet she remained adamant that the only man with whom she had ever had sexual intercourse was the Prince of Wales, and equally adamant that it was Charles's infidelity with Camilla Parker Bowles which had broken her spirit. As I knew this to be untrue, I decided not to press the issue with her, but to balance out her claims in *Diana in Private* with tasteful references to some of her love interests. I chose Barry Mannakee, the King of Spain, Philip Dunne and James Hewitt, limiting myself to those four because the public was simply not ready to accept the reality that Diana had a voracious romantic and sexual appetite and had been unfaithful to Charles from shortly after Prince William's birth.

187

In my opinion, every ethical writer has a duty to provide the facts in as acceptable a manner as possible for his or her readers. If readers then wish to ignore what is being placed before them, that is their prerogative. With that view, and bearing in mind that I sympathized with Diana's basic objective of being able to attain a dignified and well-protected separation, I informed her that I intended to write a balanced account of her life that did not "rubbish" the Prince of Wales but could be used as a platform for separation. This, to Diana, was not good enough. To her mind, I had committed the second, even more unacceptable, sin, for she was afraid if she was not perceived by the public as being the innocent pseudo-virginal victim of an unfeeling Prince of Wales, a cold Royal Family and a heartless way of life, she could be stripped of her children and her privileges. For that reason, as she confirmed to me in 1995, she set in motion the chain of events which led to the Morton book. Andrew Morton, she said, "doesn't have your sensibilities."

At this point in her life, Diana's fears were so overwhelming that they led to rifts with others as well. To use her friend Rosa Monckton's description in another context, she was like a trapped animal, lashing out in all directions, hoping to protect herself regardless of whom she mauled. This was never clearer than in March 1992. "Duch and I had it all planned. We were going to split together," Sarah York said.

Confirmation of the complicity between Diana and Sarah comes from an unexpected source. John Kennedy, Prince Michael of Kent's former Private Secretary, said, "I think from a personal point of view that if the Duchess of York had not been there none of what happened would have happened. I think they fed off each other in the early stages, and I think the Princess of Wales would have realized her role and accepted the sacrifices that had to be made – and one of those might have been happiness – and that she would have done her job properly in that regard, had the other one (Sarah) not been there. But I think they were there, egging each other on, saying that these people (the courtiers) are all rotten, and what a ghastly family we've married into, why should we put up with it? The combination of the two women was bad news."

Sarah had already been to see the Queen, and was waiting for Diana to get herself together to do the same. Then serialization of *Diana in Private* started that March of 1992 with the assertion that Diana had had a series of lovers during her marriage. This caused a worldwide sensation, with tabloids and television programmes devoting rather too much attention to it for Diana's comfort. Her reaction was to sacrifice her friend, sister-in-law and companion-in-escape with a masterful two-pronged attack. First, she told Andrew Morton that Andrew and Sarah were about to separate, encouraging him to take the story to the *Daily Mail*, which published it over the protestations of its gossip columnist, Nigel Dempster. Then she set about encouraging Sarah to depart without her. "She suggested I leave on my own," Sarah said. "She said the time wasn't right for her to go. But I should. I had no idea she was using me." Using her, Diana certainly was. First, she rightly assessed that the news of the Yorks' separation would knock speculation about her love life off the front pages of the world's tabloids. Second, she was using Sarah as a canary, to test the air of separation, so that she could make all the mistakes while Diana sat back in the relative safety of Kensington Palace and learned from them.

By the time Sarah realized what Diana was up to, it was too late. Her separation was announced; she was being roundly trounced by the Buckingham Palace Press Office; she discovered that her beloved Diana had leaked the news of her separation to Morton to save her own skin. So she stopped speaking to her sister-in-law, accusing her of betraying her.

While Diana does not come out of this episode with much credit, she was motivated by fear more than anything else, and with time Sarah came to forgive her. The two women then resumed their friendship. In the run-up to her divorce, Diana used to go and have Sunday lunch with Sarah and her daughters, Beatrice and Eugenie, every week. They even took their children away for a summer holiday in 1996, after Diana's divorce *nisi* was granted. Then Sarah wrote her autobiography and mentioned that Diana had given her verrucas, or warts. Diana, who had been chafing for some time under the restrictions she felt Sarah's commercial activities had caused to be written into her own divorce agreement, stopped speaking to Sarah. Doubtless, there was also an element of levelling the score. Diana did not like being in the wrong, and must have also been rubbed the wrong way because Sarah had found her out and therefore been placed in the position of forgiving her. To Diana, who liked being ascendant, this must have been galling. Until she had the chance to turn the tables on Sarah.

Diana could be a lot harder than Sarah. When David Tang, a friend to both sisters-in-law, suggested to Diana asking Sarah for lunch, Diana said, "Anyone but her." Doubtless, they would have kissed and made up with time. But time ran out before they could do so. This was a great pity, from a personal point of view, for Sarah York, who has been left to reconcile feelings and conflicts that Diana's premature death ensured would remain unresolved forever.

Such situations as took place between Diana and Sarah were far from rare for Diana, who was always falling out with people. Aside from Sarah, before the year was out she would also no longer be speaking to either Rosa Monckton or James Hewitt. Monckton's crime was to tell Diana, while she was playing the pathetic on an official tour of Korea that October of 1992, that she ought to know better than to drag her personal life into her public role when she was representing her country. After that, Diana did not speak to Monckton until the following year, when she one day telephoned out of the blue, acting as if nothing had happened. Monckton was big enough to forgive her.

Diana dumped James Hewitt in even more remarkable circumstances. She asked him to give a story to the *Daily Express* refuting the claim in *Diana in Private* that they had been lovers. Notwithstanding the fact that she was asking him to lie, and there were letters and photographs of them making love to prove it, Hewitt, who had had no real contact with Diana since his return to Britain from the Gulf, but who was motivated by gentlemanly protectiveness, agreed to do as she asked. According to Alan Frame, then deputy editor and someone I have known for many years, he delegated a staff writer named Anna Pasternak do the story. She met Hewitt, and settled down with him to write the fictional account of his nonsexual relationship with the Princess of Wales, and this was duly published in the *Daily Express*. The tabloids, who hover around anybody connected with the Royal Family, intent on milking any story they can to their own advantage in the fierce circulation battle each publication wages against its competitors, duly pounced on Hewitt. The unfortunate man, whose actions had been at Diana's own request, was accused by them of exploiting his relationship with her for personal gain. This, of course, was untrue and unfair, for Hewitt had not at that juncture made one penny out of the story, and was moreover merely complying with Diana's request for him to deny the truth of what I had stated in *Diana in Private*. Moreover, Hewitt's career was already in danger, as his Commanding Officer Gordon Birdwood had previously mentioned to me over dinner one evening in 1991 "because of his relationship with the Princess."

Hewitt knew that if Diana did not do something to roll back the tidal wave of criticism that was engulfing him, his reputation would be irreversibly damaged, thereafter making success in any future undertaking more difficult than it would otherwise have been. Yet when he asked Diana to issue a simple statement making it clear that he had gone public at her request, she refused to do so and never spoke to him again. Thereafter, as far as the public was concerned, James Hewitt was the cad who had sold Diana out. The fact remains, however, that it is Diana herself who sold James Hewitt out.

Of course, James Hewitt's critics will argue that he did himself no favours thereafter. He embarked upon a relationship with Anna Pasternak, who had been rather smitten by him. She encouraged him to allow her to write a book about the truth of his affair with Diana. Using Diana's love letters to provide an authentic voice, she wrote *Princess in Love*, which, upon publication, was, ironically enough, roundly slated as being untrue owing to the overblown language attributed to Diana!

Whatever mistakes James Hewitt made after 1992, the fact remains that it is Diana who placed him in the invidious position he found himself in. It was her refusal, to rescue his reputation by the simple expedient of issuing a supportive statement on his behalf, once she had manoeuvred him into destroying it to protect hers, which thereafter rendered him unemployable; which assured him of revilement as a cad; which perverted his kind and gentlemanly action of coming to her rescue when she asked for his help. Sadly, there are two instances in Diana's life when it is difficult to find an excuse for her conduct. Sacrificing James Hewitt is one. And the other comes later, when she sought to deprive her husband of his birthright, when she tried to bounce him out of the order of succession, so that she could enjoy a clear run as Princess of Wales while he stepped aside, pressurised into doing an "Uncle David", and thereby cutting his own throat while she remained on the world stage enjoying acclaim that was, and wasn't, her due.

Having scarified both Sarah York and James Hewitt, Diana had now set the stage for the publication of the book she had fed to the willing Andrew Morton. Without realizing it, however. Diana had sown the wind – and would reap the whirlwind. The book, which she was so confident would help her achieve the separation she wanted, would prove to be a disaster that very nearly ruined both her life and her reputation.

Fourteen

The man Diana chose to act as her Minister for Propaganda was a journalist with considerable experience of the yellower segments of the press. For years Andrew Morton had been knocking around Fleet Street, working on royal stories for various downmarket publications. He had also written a series of books on Diana, none of which was a best-seller, but all of which were admiring and had caught the eye of their subject, who still read, as she would continue to do until her dying day, everything published about her.

Morton was proud of having had the distinction of meeting Diana once, when she was on an official visit and was introduced to the journalist by his squash partner, and her old love interest, Dr James Colthurst. Dr Colthurst was one of the many people from whom she had withdrawn after her marriage, only to resume contact when she realized she preferred her old circle of friends to the grander and more influential strangers she had met with the Prince of Wales.

Now Diana put her friendship with the aristocratic scion of Blarney Castle to good use. She instructed James Colthurst to arrange for Morton to place, then write, the book she had wished me to pen for her. This time she was careful not to be involved person-to-person with the author, electing to use Colthurst as her intermediary. He would ride his bicycle to Kensington Palace, collect the tapes which Diana had made, then hand them on to Morton, who in turn distilled them into book form.

Behind the scenes, Diana was the orchestrator of the piece. With a book contract in place, she organized for her friend Carolyn Pride Bartholomew, her former lover James Gilbey, and her brother, Charles, to be sources. The information they imparted was selective, to say the least. Bartholomew, whose main contribution was Diana's problems with bulimia, conveniently managed to ignore the number of times she and her husband, William, had been present while Diana, portrayed in the book as faithful to a faithless Prince Charles, was sleeping with her lover, James Hewitt. Gilbey also managed to forget how fearful Diana was of becoming pregnant by him as he shored up her version of events by stating that the faithful Diana had been driven by the abject misery of her husband's infidelity to attempt suicide on several occasions. Only her brother, a true Spencer, managed to sting while he was supposed to be supportive, pointing out that Diana had a track record as a liar going back to childhood, and that her inability to differentiate between fact and fiction had even been commented upon by her teacher.

Diana was nothing if not shrewd, and I was filled with admiration for the way she went about rebutting the contents of *Diana in Private*. Because *Her True Story* (called *Her Untrue Story* in fashionable circles) was published four months after *Diana in Private*, the book's subject, author and publisher were able to wait until publication of my book to see what inconvenient themes and information it would be in her interest to rebut. Chief among these were my contentions that Diana was even guiltier of infidelity than Charles; that she shared responsibility for the breakup of the marriage; and that she was so emotional she was not always in control of her actions.

I learned of Diana's reaction to *Diana in Private* from mutual friends at the time and later, after we had kissed and made up, from Diana herself. While Diana was pleased that I had made her unhappiness clear, she was disappointed that I had been decorous in describing her bulimia. It was not enough that I had said she was ill. She wanted the world to have graphic descriptions of her struggle with the eating disorder, so that she could employ the sympathy generated by the public's knowledge as a vehicle for separation. Moreover, she was upset because I had not described the scenes in which she had played at hurting herself as suicide attempts. While I had naïvely believed I was protecting Diana's reputation by omitting such sensational claims – and had even gone on *This Morning*, Britain's most popular chat show, to take the sting out of subsequent claims by stating, before my own book was published, that I had been fed the suicide stories but had been forced to discount them – Diana was sitting there in Kensington Palace hoping the public would believe she had been driven to kill herself.

Morton's book went beyond the fiction that the Princess of Wales had tried to commit suicide. It falsely asserted that Diana's bulimia had begun after her marriage, ignoring the tremendous weight loss between the engagement and the wedding, in favour of the contention that she had been driven to starvation and gluttony by discovering after marriage that Charles and Camilla were still lovers. It asserted that Diana had been a virgin at marriage, once more ignoring the fact that she had had several lovers before she knew Charles, and, moreover, had been living at Buckingham Palace with him after their engagement. It claimed that Diana had never been given any advice about how to make the transition from aristocrat to royal, discounting the efforts of Lady Susan Hussey, Oliver Everett, Michael Colbourne and others. It accused the Royal Family in general and Prince Charles in particular of being callous and heartless, in defiance of their many attempts to gain medical treatment for Diana. Of course, as the book did not admit that Diana was disturbed, it ignored the patience the Royal Family had exercised in dealing with someone who had had tremendous difficulties, and had created tremendous difficulties, in making a successful and healthy adjustment to a way of life that should not have come as a surprise to someone from her background.

Credit for the masterful way in which the Morton book was presented, and the seriousness with which it was therefore taken, does not go primarily to Diana and her co-conspirators. It must be directed at Andrew Neil, the anti-establishment journalist who was then editor of the Murdoch organization's British flagship, the *Sunday Times*. Rupert Murdoch had long been regarded within British establishment circles as anti-monarchist, and this view was certainly substantiated by the brilliant and highly political way in which Neil set about promoting the book. Serializing it over a three-week period prior to its publication in book form in the summer of 1992, Neil gave Diana's untrue story a gravitas the contents lacked by aggressively asserting that it had to be true because the stories came from her close friends, and because it was being serialized in a publication with as prestigious a reputation as the *Sunday Times*. These arguments were not sound, of course. Diana's friends could twist the truth, and did so until it was no longer recognizable as anything but shameless propaganda.

Despite the complicity of Diana's friends, Neil had some discordant moments to contend with. Gilbey had asserted in the book that the Princess had tried to commit suicide. But Bartholomew was adamant, once the claims were made in the serialisation, that she had never once, in all the years she had known Diana (and, being a school chum from West Heath, she was one of her oldest friends, and in a position to know), heard anything about her friend trying to kill herself. Neil coped with the contradiction brazenly, ignoring it as the British public was treated, on a virtually daily basis for the next six months, to his distinctive tones on practically every television and radio talk or opinion show, asserting that every word was both true and fair, and that Diana had been badly used by the hated establishment. He refrained from saying how it was possible that one could believe both Gilbey and Bartholomew, when their statements conflicted so absolutely. Instead, he authoritatively pushed the contradictions into being accepted as fact by insisting that both Bartholomew and Gilbey were accurate. Thus did the myth of the suicidal Diana join the pantheon of stories about her.

Neil's aggressive promotion of the Morton serialization meant that the Prince of Wales's reputation was in shreds along with the Royal Family's prestige before the book was even published. The world now believed that a pseudo-virginal Princess of Wales had been driven to suicide by the coldness and heartlessness of the family she had married into.

"They're pulling their hair out at the Palace," Diana laughingly told Joseph Sanders, high on the drama and the hope of freedom. One of the royal private secretaries, who was sympathetic to her, John Kennedy, said that she felt "in order to survive, she had to start manipulating things to her own ends and probably didn't know where to stop and didn't actually look at the broader picture. I think when people feel isolated, they don't look at the broader picture. They look at a very narrow response to what they think is going on around them, and they don't look at what the consequences are."

Finding themselves involved in the gravest royal scandal since the Abdication Crisis of 1936, the Royal Family and their advisors, chief among them the Queen's Private Secretary, Diana's brother-in-law Robert Fellowes, did stop to consider the consequences. "Bellows," as Diana called Fellowes, suspected Diana of being behind the book. "Robert Fellowes asked her point blank if she had a hand in the writing of the Morton book," Lord Chartiers said. "She said no. He took her word for it, then was made to seem a fool within weeks when Diana posed for photographs outside of Carolyn Bartholomew's house in what was obviously a staged scene to convey her approval of the contents of the book. From that day onwards, Robert Fellowes deplored her." Thereafter, the relationship between them was antipathetic, with Fellowes considering her a "traitor," according to Diana, and with her viewing him as "my greatest enemy", though they did manage to maintain sufficient civility to speak to one another.

Meanwhile, not only the courtiers were trying, albeit ineffectually, to stem the tide of stories damaging to the monarchy. The Royal Family themselves swung into action. On 12 June the Queen met with the Prince of Wales to discuss his marriage. Although she had long known about the problems, and sympathized with her son because he was stuck with a sick wife, and with her daughter-in-law because she could not help being ill, Elizabeth II nevertheless addressed a problem that had started to threaten the security of the institution to which she and her ancestors had dedicated their lives. "She wanted the nightmare to stop," Princess Margaret of Hesse and the Rhine said. "She was repulsed by the scandal, the sensationalism, the sheer horror of it all." For that, she needed the co-operation of her son and daughter-in-law.

Three days later, after the Garter Ceremony at Windsor Castle, there was another meeting, at which only the Queen, the Duke of Edinburgh, the Prince and the Princess of Wales were present. According to a friend of the Duke of Edinburgh, Diana pretended that she had not had a hand in the Morton book, which caused the Duke of Edinburgh, who takes the lead in family matters, to point out to her that the time for game-playing was past. He was angry with her. He was especially annoyed because she had painted an unfair picture of the way the Queen, the Royal Family and the Royal Household had treated her at the time of her marriage, claiming that she had received no help in adjusting to the royal role, when this was patently not the case. He had called her a "fifth columnist" to a cousin only a few days before, pointing out its appropriateness for someone who went around telling tall tales about her husband and in-laws. The purpose of the meeting, however, was not to cast recriminations but to find a solution, so they asked Diana what she wanted. "A legal separation," she said.

The Duke then warned Diana that she must be very careful. If she achieved the separation she was pushing for, divorce would be an inevitable consequence. That brought her up sharply, because the Princess had naïvely thought she could remain a semi-detached member of the Royal Family, with her liberty and her own Court, as the separated but legal wife of the Prince of Wales. Only if someone else came along whom she wished to marry would she then require a divorce; otherwise, she would maintain the status quo. "This eating-your-cake-and-having-it approach to life is typical of the immature and unrealistic point of view of bulimics," Dr Michael Davies said.

The three born-royals all preferred that the marriage remain intact formally, but that the Prince and Princess of Wales go their separate ways privately, so Diana, uncertain of what she was unleashing if she did achieve her treasured separation, and understanding the necessity of continued amity with her mother-in-law and monarch, agreed to a show of unity for six months. On the other hand, what she was really doing was buying time. She fully intended to depart when the probationary period was up, and intended to do so on her terms, which meant no divorce unless she wanted one.

Secretly pleased that June of 1992 that she was creating a groundswell of public opinion in her favour as a result of the publicity surrounding the Morton book, and hoping that that would wash her upon the shores of a favourable separation, with custody of her boys and her royal status intact, Diana was about to receive the rudest awakening of her life. "Up to that point, she believed that the Murdoch organization was in her pocket," Joseph Sanders said. She learned to the contrary when the *Sun*, the sister tabloid of *The Times* broadsheets, waded into print revealing the existence of the Squidgygate tape. Plastering the story of Diana and her confidant James Gilbey's indiscreet telephone conversation over several pages of the paper, the *Sun* did have the good grace to edit out the most sexually explicit minutes, while making sure to leave in Diana's concerns about pregnancy. The Morton book had not even been properly published, yet one of its main planks, Diana's sexual fidelity, had been exposed as the hoax it was.

According to one of her advisors, the Princess then asked him to organize a meeting with Rupert Murdoch, the head of News International, which is the parent company of *The Times*, the *Sunday Times* and the *Sun*. This he eventually did. "I arranged for her to meet Rupert Murdoch, but he kept his distance. He didn't want her phoning him twice a day trying to influence his editors through him."

Under strain because of the unremitting attention to which she had been subjected since early March, when *Diana in Private* had been serialized, Diana's bulimia returned in force once the Morton book was out and her hand in its creation was established. "This time," a courtier, who does not wish to be identified, said, "no one in Palace circles sympathized. Everyone was heartily sick of the scandal and we all felt, if you bite off more than you can chew, don't complain when you choke." Another, John Kennedy, summed up the attitude of people within royal circles by saying, "The whole point of being in the Royal Family is that you go along like a procession of swans, keeping your webbed feet under water, not bobbing up and down all the time, saying 'Look at my feet. I've got webbed feet. Look, webbed feet.' Ruining the grace of the spectacle."

This loss of sympathy was not limited to the courtiers. The British establishment, which had hitherto admired Diana and had sympathized with the fact that a young woman wanted her freedom but was condemned to live out her life as a royal princess, now split into Diana supporters (a small segment) and Diana detractors (a larger segment). One duchess, distantly related to the princess, summarized the prevailing mood, "I do wish the Spencers would get over their habit of washing their dirty linen in public. It is an unedifying spectacle."

Where Diana lost the most sympathy was within the Royal Family. "In varying degrees, they were appalled," Princess Margaret of Hesse and the Rhine told Burnett Pavitt. "The Queen was beside herself with worry. She also felt badly let down. An element of watchful distrust definitely became a feature of the relationship thereafter, though the Queen ensured that the tone remained friendly and accessible. I'm sure in her heart of hearts she would have preferred not to have to bother with what she had to see as a tiresome girl, but since she was stuck with her, the Queen got along with the business at hand. She's very good at getting on with the business at hand. She's disciplined and understands the concept of self-sacrifice in a way that neither Diana nor Sarah did. If they had, none of what happened would have happened."

John Kennedy, Prince Michael of Kent's former private secretary, agreed with that. He knew Diana well because she shared a courtyard with the Kents and "often would come and have a chat. She was lonely. A perfectly nice girl but out of her depth." He believes, "It was a family row and she didn't notice the harm of the newspapers plopping through the door every day." He felt "Diana was just a simple girl who got caught up in something that she didn't understand fully and it all ended disastrously and in tears. Nobody had ever told her that you can't have everything. You've got security. You've got a family. You've got a position. You can't necessarily have absolute bliss as well. I don't think she ever understood that."

Diana's lack of comprehension was not something the Duke of Edinburgh sympathized with. "Prince Philip felt that Diana had betrayed the Queen, the whole family, and the monarchy. He was incandescent with rage, but there was very little he could do," according to Princess Margaret of Hesse and the Rhine.

"Queen Elizabeth the Queen Mother, who seldom agrees with Prince Philip, backed him up completely. She was bitterly disappointed that the girl, whose suit she had pushed, could turn around and shake the monarchy to its foundations without even realizing what she was doing.

"The Prince of Wales was beside himself with fury and hurt. In some ways, the effect upon him was cruelty personified, not that she set out to be cruel. Without realizing it, Diana unleashed forces which catapulted him back to the terrible days of his youth, when he was reviled and bullied and accused of being all sorts of things he wasn't. In terms of public perception, he was right back to square one, all the good work and years of dedication forgotten as the bullies in the press ganged up to level metaphoric blows into a tripped-up Prince of Wales. It is to his credit that he said, 'She's the mother of my children. She's sick. We will not retaliate.' He felt to do so would be unhelpful. It would exacerbate the situation and 'God knows where it will then end,' as he put it. It was a dreadful, dreadful time for him, but one couldn't help admire the way he coped. Even Diana later had to admit he is a truly noble man."

The less personally affected members of the Royal Family took less wounded points of view. Although Princess Anne would thereafter avoid Diana, Princess Margaret remained somewhat cordial. Prince Andrew and Prince Edward, who had never been close to their brother, still remained pleasant to Diana when they saw her, as did the deeply religious Duchess of Kent. She blamed Diana's childhood for the terrible mess, and, understanding that Diana's battle was not actually with the Royal Family, but with the ghosts of her past and her inability to accept the regimentations of the royal way of life, she was able to sympathize with Prince Charles while treating Diana with the kindness she deserved.

Always sensitive to the feelings of others, Diana picked up the fact that many people, who had formerly admired her, now reviled her. This made her acutely uncomfortable. "It was one of the worst periods of my life," she later told me – and, as she looked around for solutions, found herself shedding or being dropped by loved ones.

The saddest and most important casualty of Diana's involvement in the Morton book was her relationship with her middle sister, Jane. Placed in the painful situation of having to choose between supporting a husband she loved and admired for his rectitude and integrity, and a sister she loved but no longer agreed with, Jane took her husband's side against Diana. "They did not speak for years," Lady Sarah Spencer-Churchill said. "Even after they mended fences enough to talk, there was little trust there. The sisterly spark was a thing of the past. Jane couldn't trust Diana, while Diana, whose virtues did not include lack of vindictiveness, couldn't quite bring herself to forgive Jane for not taking her side. It's very sad really." Jane paid a terrible price because of Diana's untimely death. "But she understands there's no reason for self-recrimination." Diana, moreover, wouldn't want it.

The second casualty from within Diana's immediate family was her grandmother. Ruth, Lady Fermoy, died without forgiving Diana for what she had done to the Prince of Wales in particular and to the monarchy in general. "She was appalled, absolutely appalled, that her own granddaughter could behave like that," Brodrick Haldane said. Recognizing the injustice of Diana throwing Charles to the wolves so that she could escape from the control of the hated courtiers, Lady Fermoy refused to see her granddaughter until she was dying. Then, and only then, did she receive the Princess whose elevation she had worked so hard to achieve.

A surprising casualty was Carolyn Bartholomew, whom Diana kicked from the first to the third division once the book was out. According to a mutual friend of mine and the Bartholomews, "William Bartholomew couldn't stand Diana after she edged his wife out. He felt she'd used Carolyn badly. Having been all over them like a bad rash, to use Diana's favourite phrase, while the book was being prepared, she practically never saw Carolyn afterwards. She'd served her purpose. While they remained friendly in a distant sort of way, there was no longer any closeness there."

While that might be William Bartholomew's interpretation of what happened, Diana's was radically different. She felt that Carolyn had let her down badly by publicly stating that Diana had never tried to commit suicide. Caught up as she was in the struggle, the Princess failed to appreciate that her friend was simply speaking the truth, without realizing that Diana herself wanted the public to believe a fiction which Carolyn, like all reasonable people, found so damaging that she would have suppressed it even if it had been factual.

Another contributor to the book to bite the dust, in even more naked fashion, was James Colthurst. As soon as Diana was informed that he stood to make between £300,000 and £400,000 from the book, by virtue of having been her intermediary, she cut him out of her life permanently. "I will not have my friends making money out of me," Diana said. "The fact that he had only done what she wanted didn't matter to Diana," Joseph Sanders said. "She felt he should've run her errands for nothing. She couldn't forgive him for doing her a favour and profiting at the same time. Even though he needed the money and she knew it. She was very protective of herself like that."

Nor was Colthurst the only contributor named James who found himself discarded by Diana as a side effect of the disastrous book. Gilbey she also edged out with finality as soon as the Squidgygate tapes were published.

Reeling from the unexpected effects of a book of which she had had such high and naïve expectations, Diana battened down the hatches for the stormy weather ahead. According to John Kennedy, "The idea that she sat down and calculated every stage of the plot is fanciful. I think she got herself into a situation she could not get herself out of and was way out of her depth and didn't have anyone sensible she could trust to advise her. So she swam in the wrong direction. You know, she spoke to people for hours on the telephone, different people, friends, supposed advisors, acquaintances, then dropped them to speak to other people and got different advice from them. Many of them wanted to live in reflected glory and didn't give her particularly responsible advice." To my certain knowledge, those who did, like Joseph Sanders, were listened to without her acting on their advice.

For the first time in her life, the Princess of Wales was truly controversial. Her public image was now mixed in a way she could never have envisaged. Her motives, integrity and behaviour were seriously questioned for the first time since her advent upon the world stage in 1980. On the one hand, segments of the media accused her of being manipulative and insincere, of being a publicity seeker and egocentric, of putting her private, short-term interests before the longer-term interests of the family she had married into, of undermining the monarchy and, with it, her sons' birthright. On the other hand, there were segments of the media which praised her for going public with her private problems, of being open and approachable, of letting daylight in upon the magic of monarchy and showing the world that the fairy tale had its nightmare aspects.

Whatever anyone's point of view, *Diana in Private* and *Her True Story* had focused public attention on Diana's character, personality and private life in a way that nothing had hitherto. Until then, her image was largely a superficial one, as the glamorous, photogenic Princess of Wales. Now she was fascinating. People no longer necessarily knew what to believe about her, but that was part of the fascination.

Thereafter, until her death, the column inches and television coverage Diana enjoyed were monumental. Through controversy, she had been catapulted from the realms of regal fame into the league of living icon, of vulnerable demigoddess, of mythical figure given flesh.

Diana's reaction was typically contradictory. As Sarah York opined to a friend at the time, "She loves the attention. She might not like all they're saying, but she gets off on the idea of everyone talking about her all the time." This was undoubtedly a true if incisive assessment, but it was only half the picture. As Diana herself would say in 1996, "The Morton book was the biggest mistake of my life. He made me out to be a bitter, twisted crackpot. I hate having to cope with all the bitterness and suspicion that's directed at me because of that Morton." What Diana did not say, and what would not emerge until after her death, however, was that the Morton book contained *her* words. She, not Morton, was therefore responsible for the bitterness and suspicion she was having to cope with. It was, after all, *her* message in *her own words*. He was simply the purveyor.

By then of course, Diana was painfully aware that there were elements in the book that had been a grave mistake. One of which bothered her was the claim that the Prince of Wales had married her without loving her. "He did love me. He didn't always show his love the way I wanted him to. But he did love me. I can't have my boys growing up believing their father didn't love their mother when he did," she told me.

The other claim that perturbed her was that she had hurled herself down a staircase while pregnant with William. "How must any child feel if he believes his mother was prepared to kill him?" she asked, hoping that one day I would write that the story was untrue. Even though I had made it clear to her, time and again, that I had written all the books I intended to about her, and would write no more. Nor would I have done, had she lived.

By 1996, of course, the Morton book was a thing of the past. It had served its purpose and proven to be too mixed a blessing for Diana's comfort. Morton, she knew, disparaged her. Indeed, only two weeks before her death he wrote about her claiming that she was a "fruit" (nut) and implying that any man who was married to her would want to run into Camilla Parker Bowles's arms.

What Diana had no means of knowing, of course, was that after her death he would reveal that she had been the source of *Her True Story*. He then published an updated version of *Diana: Her True Story* which bore no resemblance to the original work, though its contents were frighteningly similar to *Diana in Private*, thereby proving the fashionable wits correct when they had dubbed his and Diana's joint 1992 enterprise "Diana: Her Untrue Story."

And the tapes, which she had made and handed to James Colthurst (the contents of which she was so keen to rebut as lies, and blame Andrew Morton for inventing in the years between the publication of the first Morton book in 1992 and her death in 1997), ended up being played on American television, for the naïve and gullible to believe and the knowledgeable to wring their hands in despair about, as Diana's voice reverberated from the grave with destructive and unfair untruths.

At the time Diana was reviling Morton to me and to others, she had no means of knowing she would face a premature death in a year or two. By then, she had left behind the bitterness and uncertainties of the early 1990s. She had gone a long way towards actualizing her real self, towards reconciling the opposing and conflicting demands of her nature and of her way of life. That Diana, the real Diana, was infinitely more constructive and admirable, less pathetic and pitiful, more likable and purposeful. She was right to be embarrassed by the portrait in Andrew Morton's book, for it did her no justice.

Fifteen

From the summer of 1992 until her separation that December, Diana experienced one of the most turbulent and anxious periods of her life. Having been descended from many generations of courtiers, "I knew they were plotting to keep me on side," she said. In this, Diana was correct, though not even she could have imagined the circuitous route they would take to issue their warning.

The month after publication of the Morton book, Sarah York informed the Queen's Private Secretary that she wished to go on holiday to France with her daughters, Princesses Beatrice and Eugenie of York. Her lover Johnny Bryan, officially her financial advisor, and two Scotland Yard private detectives would also be accompanying her.

By this time, Sarah as well as Diana regarded Robert Fellowes as her greatest enemy. Sarah held him principally responsible for forcing her to seek a separation. "He was always bellowing at me. 'Look at what you've done,' he'd say, waving that morning's newspapers at me, as if I was to blame when the papers made up things about me or had a go at me about my weight. The way he carried on, you'd have thought I was in cahoots with them. Day after day after day it was the same story. He never let up. Even when I was pregnant. Once he upset me so much I thought I was going to miscarry."

One of the other royal private secretaries, John Kennedy, who was well used to Fellowes's bellowing down the telephone at him about his charge, said, "Anyone who has Robert Fellowes after them, in full flight, is either going to be barking mad or turn out to be an assassin. You know, it's not a pretty sight. He was incredibly hectoring. I mean, that was his style, very hectoring to everybody really. If there were messages saying he needed something, we thought, Oh, Christ, what have we done now? And there was lots of clearing of throats and shuffling of feet. He was known as Bobby Bellows or Ruffled Feathers. I think it's just that he is a pompous twit about forty years out of date really. He was an ideal courtier for the thirties, but not the nineties. He had the Queen's support because he's loyal and discreet. Well, I don't think he knows how to react to things."

Sarah's relationship with Robert Fellowes was complicated by family connections, just as Diana's was. In Sarah's case, it was not a sister who was his wife, but her grandfather who was his mother's brother. That made Fellowes her father's first cousin, and her first cousin once removed. "He's jealous of us because we're royal and he's not," Diana said. "He'd love to be a member of the Royal Family, too. Instead, he's just a glorified flunky."

Fellowes, of course, took a different view. He was a very able, traditional private secretary, who felt that his sister-in-law and his cousin should both stop their antics and start behaving in a more responsible manner. "He deeply deplored the havoc both girls created, demanding separations and rocking the monarchic boat," Lord Charteris commented. "He felt they should start counting their blessings and stop complaining about not having everything. No one has everything, and when you're as overprivileged as Diana and Sarah were, it's criminal to want more. His viewpoint might have been old-fashioned, but you can't deny it has merit."

Be that as it may, after informing Fellowes of her travel plans, and getting the necessary permission to take her daughters out of the country, Sarah, the girls and her party set off in a private plane for a week's holiday at Le Mas de Pignerolle, a pink villa in the densely wooded hills above St. Tropez on the French Riviera. She was careful not to tell anyone where she was going, because she had been too much in the news, and was ensuring that no one could tip the press off about her plans.

The standard practice when members of the Royal Family are staying in France is for the British authorities to inform the gendarmerie, who police the outer perimeter of the property where they are staying, in order to assure their safety. In 1992, when the IRA still presented a terrorist threat to the British Royal Family, all of whom had been declared to be valid targets for liquidation, this was especially necessary.

Extraordinarily, when Sarah and the Queen's granddaughters landed in France, the British authorities failed to inform their French counterparts of their arrival. This omission was not made known to the Duchess or to the Scotland Yard private detectives accompanying her, who laboured thereafter under the illusion that the property where they were staying was secure against intrusion. In fact, it had been left exposed.

Diana felt that this omission was deliberate. As anyone who had come into the briefest contact with Sarah York socially knew, she was open to the point of innocence and pleasure-loving to the point of childishness. It was no secret in royal circles that Johnny Bryan had become her lover. A safe bet for anyone wishing to set up Sarah was that the frank and sybaritic duchess, lulled by the Mediterranean sun and the feeling that she was secure behind a protected and heavily wooded property, would be so unguarded that her behaviour could then be interpreted as unbecoming. All that was needed was a photographer hidden in the bushes to capture her antics.

Daniel Agneli was the hit man's hit man, the paparazzo who was known for his ability to snatch shots no one else can. With a reputation like his, he had unparallelled connections with photo agencies around the world, all of whom gladly pay top dollar for the fruit of his labours. He was the photographer who received a tip-off that the Duchess of York was ensconced in Le Mas de Pignerolle with her lover and her children. The message could not have been clearer. All Agneli needed to do was get his camera within range of Sarah, Bryan and the kids, and exercise some patience, and his fortune would be made, compromising photographs of the Duchess of York then fetching six figures. With syndication, Angeli stood to make possibly seven figures out of a few hours' work.

Sure enough, no sooner had Sarah returned to Britain and flown up to Balmoral with her daughters to stay with the Royal Family, than Johnny Bryan telephoned to inform her that the *Daily Mirror* intended to publish snatched photographs of them kissing beside the swimming pool in their Cote d'Azur idyll. "My world fell apart," Sarah has said, accurately conveying the impact, which included exile from the Royal Family, publication of those photographs had upon her life.

"The Palace set her up as a warning to me," Diana said. "There's no doubt in my mind – or hers – that she was set up. No one knew where she was except the Palace. They were supposed to lay on the gendarmerie and didn't! They'd like everyone to believe it was an oversight, but they don't make mistakes like that. They threw her to the wolves as a warning to me. The message was clear. Leave, Diana, and you, too, will be ripped to pieces. I wasn't intimidated, though I was forewarned."

Believing that her surest route to victory lay in gaining the world's sympathy, Diana set out on an official visit to Korea with the Prince of Wales in October 1992. The purpose of the trip was twofold: one, to drum up business with Korea, and two, to convey a message to the world that the marriage of the Prince and Princess of Wales was not in trouble. In fact, feelings now ran so high between the couple that they could not bear to be in the same room. "We loathed each other with a passion," Diana told me.

When the royal aircraft took off, the Princess of Wales left England with her own agenda. Throughout the Korean visit, whenever she was with the Prince of Wales, she gave off clear and unmistakable messages of pathos, of misery, for the photographers to capture. When she was on her own, however, she presented them with the contrast of her normal, cheerful self. As even her most avid admirers know, Diana had a rare ability to act out her feelings, to convey a subliminal message so explicitly that, had she been born half a century earlier, she could easily have become a great silent-movie star. This had caused her detractors at Buckingham Palace to call her the Actress, and, as she went from engagement to engagement with her husband, her expression perfectly hangdog, the publicity was negative in the extreme and reaction to it back home was one of frustration and cold fury. Even her friends were bemused that Diana could wreck an official tour, with all its hopes of future contracts and jobs. It was then that her friend Rosa Monckton told her to start behaving herself properly, with the result that Diana severed relations with her for several months.

Having set the stage, Diana now yanked the chain of the main player. No sooner did she return to Britain, and go her separate way from the Prince of Wales, than she did the one thing she knew would force his hand into agreeing to a separation. He had arranged a weekend at Sandringham with the boys in November. It was a shooting weekend. She telephoned at the last minute and said they wouldn't be coming. She'd made other plans.

Throughout the year, Diana had been using Charles's access to the children as a means of bringing him to heel. By doing so, she was actually being exceedingly clever. He was a loving and devoted father, contrary to public opinion, and she knew that the surest way of reaching him was to hit him through William and Harry. "He loves those boys every bit as much as she (did)," Princess Margaret of Hesse and the Rhine said. "To get to see as much of them as he wanted took some doing. He'd make space in his diary, or rejig things to take them to something he knew would interest them. On the appointed day, his Private Secretary would receive a call from Diana's to inform him that Her Royal Highness had taken them to McDonald's, or to the zoo, or to an amusement park, or God knows where else. On the weekends that they were together at Highgrove with the children, he would look forward to dinner with the boys, only to turn up and be informed that his wife had ordered the staff to feed the boys and herself in her bedroom, and that they were upstairs eating right then. You can imagine his frustration."

To add insult to injury, the Prince was now acutely aware that public opinion was convinced that he was a cold and aloof father. This, of course, Diana had fostered with judicious photo opportunities and leaks to journalists. Chief among these was when she tipped off the press that she would be staying overnight at the hospital with William, after he had suffered a small wound to the head inflicted by a fellow student at his boarding school. She then highlighted the difference in her attitude and Charles's, by letting the reporters know that he had spent twenty minutes with his son before going on to the opera to honour an official engagement. What she did not say was that the doctors had said William would be fine, and there was no need for either parent to attend upon him overnight.

Diana's motivation, of course, was not malice, but fear born of her mother's experience in losing custody. Always terrified that she stood to lose her children unless she was, and was seen to be, a devoted mother, she was intent on exploiting every opportunity that conveyed the message to the public that she was the better parent. Her tactic worked. By November 1992, the average member of the public, if asked what sort of parents were the Prince and Princess of Wales, would have answered that Charles was a cold, aloof and indifferent father, while Diana was a warm, loving and caring mother.

Having won the public-relations battle, the Princess of Wales finally achieved yet another victory in November 1992. By limiting Charles's access to the children the way she had been doing, she was showing him that, as long as they officially remained a couple, she could, and would continue to, deprive him of his rights to their children. On the other hand, if he agreed to a separation, they would have to arrive at mutually satisfactory access arrangements. In other words, she was saying, "My freedom or your kids. The choice is yours."

That November of 1992, Diana finally drove Charles to making the choice he had been avoiding. "He snapped," Princess Margaret of Hesse and the Rhine said. "He'd had enough. 'I will not have her using William and Harry to score points like this,' he said. He promptly went and saw the Queen and told her it would have to be separation."

Lawyers were now called in. The Prince of Wales consulted first Sir Matthew Farrer, of Farrer & Co., then later switched to Fiona Shackleton of that same firm. Diana chose Paul Butner of Wright, Son & Pepper, switching after the separation was finalized to Anthony Julius of Mishcon de Reya.

Once more, Diana showed her mettle. Insecurity firing her fears while her perspicacity about royal life steadied her hand, she drove a hard bargain against a family known for always emerging victorious at the termination of every marriage. Not this time, though. Neither Diana nor Charles was prepared to relinquish custody of the children, and, surprisingly, this became the easiest issue to resolve. They agreed to share access equally, which allayed Diana's fears of losing custody while appeasing Charles's frustration at not having been able to do enough with his sons.

With that point settled, Diana strove to retain the full panoply of royal privileges, insisting that her side take a tough negotiating position. She demanded her own accommodation within a royal palace, along with her right to continue performing official engagements and to have those engagements listed in the Court Circular. She had learned from the mistakes of Sarah York, who had lost all of these prerogatives in her divorce. In the process, Sarah had become hopelessly *déclassée* to the establishment. Diana had no intention of being "buggered around like that," as she put it. She intended to set up her own rival court and to remain the Princess of Wales for as long as it suited her. If she did not find someone else to marry, she was determined to become queen when Charles inherited the throne. Contrary to what Prince Philip had warned about the inevitability of divorce, she wrung the concession out of her husband, whose stance was to avoid adding fuel to the fire by appeasing Diana wherever possible, that he would not seek a divorce and that she would be crowned queen upon his accession to the throne. In this, as in so much else, Diana's negotiating skills were formidable. She knew that the one thing the Royal Family feared above all else was more scandal. Using the threat of what she might do if they didn't meet her demands, "I made sure they didn't do a Fergie on me," she said, and extracted every concession she wanted before the separation agreement was concluded.

There was a consensus that the announcement would be made in the new year, after Diana had joined the Royal Family for one last Christmas and New Year at Sandringham. Plans were being laid accordingly while parallel arrangements were being made for the second marriage of Anne, the Princess Royal, on 12 December 1992 in Scotland to her lover of several years standing, her former equerry, Tim Laurence. Once more Diana's emotions overwhelmed her. "I couldn't face another Christmas with that family," she said by way of explanation as she swung into action and demanded that the date of the announcement be altered to Tuesday, 8 December. "They have a choice. They give me what I want or I'll make the announcement myself on the day of Anne's wedding," Diana informed Joseph Sanders, who was filled with admiration for the resolute way in which she was conducting herself.

Faced with the prospect of a rout, the Royal Family agreed to the separation announcement being made early. Princess Anne's marriage aside, this was hardly a convenient time, for John Major, the Prime Minister, who had to make the announcement to Parliament, had been due to attend a meeting of the European Union's Heads of State and Government in Scotland. Instead of being there fulfilling his ordinary duties, he had to remain in London, where he read out on Tuesday, 8 December 1992, the carefully drafted announcement of the official separation of the Prince and Princess of Wales. It ended with Diana's final demand, that she would be crowned queen in the fullness of time.

Careful though Diana had been to counter the courtiers, who she suspected would find a way of dishonouring this condition unless she tied the Royal Family to it publicly with the Prime Minister's announcement to Parliament, she had no means of predicting Parliament's reaction. It was adverse in the extreme. Before the words were even out of John Major's mouth, there was an audible rumble of disbelief and disapproval. By the following day, there was general agreement that Diana had no right to be queen if she did not wish to remain the true wife of the Prince of Wales. She could not eat her cake and have it.

Diana was shocked and shattered by Parliament's reaction. "She was devastated," Joseph Sanders said. "She cried and cried and cried and cried. You'd have thought one of the boys had died. She really felt the loss that acutely."

"I'd have made a good queen," Diana contended, and there is no doubt that she would have fulfilled the public and humanitarian sides of the role with all the cachet for which she was justly admired. There were other aspects to it, however, and it was her reluctance to fulfill these that brought about Parliament's disapproval. Their attitude was, If you don't want to act out your part in the fairy tale, don't expect to be asked to the enchanted banquet.

Once more, Diana's vengeful side came to the fore. "I don't see why my husband doesn't step aside and let me and the boys carry on the Wales name," she told Joseph Sanders and other friends, who understood she was saying that Charles should renounce the position of Prince of Wales and, with it, his rights to the throne. "We'd've been a good team as monarch and consort, but if I can't be queen, why should he be king?"

Thereafter, until shortly before her death, Diana did indeed try to manipulate public opinion in favour of Charles stepping out of the line of succession in favour of Prince William. Although many monarchists were of the view that tampering with the succession would be the surest way of undermining the monarchy, Diana did not agree. She believed that there was no danger in skipping a generation, and contrived through sympathetic journalists to have the subject become a source of serious debate.

"She was suffering from an acute case of what psychologists call envy," Dr Basil Panzer says. "It's the rage of the frustrated child. If I can't have it, you can't have it either. It's not creditable, but there's nothing abnormal about it. All sorts of normal people suffer from envy."

As 1993 dawned, the one bright spot in Diana's life was the publication of the Camillagate tapes in the newspapers that January. "She felt vindicated," Joseph Sanders said.

Vindication proved a transient comfort as the newly separated Princess of Wales adjusted to her new life. She was horrified to see that liberty, which she had thought she was buying for herself with a separation, did not materialize. Diana had truly expected that she would have a free run. She had envisaged high-profile foreign trips in aid of charitable causes, using her fame to focus world attention on issues – the way she ultimately did in the months before her death, after the Labour Government came into power. Under the Tories, however, most of her suggestions were blocked, including her request that she visit British troops in Bosnia or undertake a private visit to the Irish President, Mary Robinson. She was told she could not go to Bosnia because the Prince of Wales planned to make a similar trip, and that the Irish visit was out of the question due to security. She was later allowed to attend a Remembrance Day service in Enniskellen in Northern Ireland, where security did not become a problem.

Despite these setbacks, Diana did actually make a trip to Nepal with Linda Chalker, the Foreign Office Minister, who was a great supporter of hers, and who told me, "She acquitted herself admirably." But even that turned out to be something of a public-relations disaster when the press noticed that Diana was no longer accorded the National Anthem and many of the other perks of royalty. On this trip, she struck up the friendship with Richard Kay, the *Daily Mail* royal correspondent, which would turn out to be a propitious meeting from her point of view.

This was a nerve-racking period for Diana. Invitations she had expected from charities no longer flowed as fast and furious as they used to before the separation. Organizations that had once sought her out now were afraid of offending the Palace, of jeopardizing their relationships with the other members of the Royal Family, of possibly embarrassing the Queen or the Prince of Wales. As Frances had learned to her cost at the time of her separation from Diana's father, and Diana was now learning, the Establishment always goes where the power is. And with royalty, the power is with the born-royal.

Increasingly disheartened as the year 1993 progressed, Diana could not even console herself with the thought that her marginalization remained private. That summer, a dozen books on her or the Royal Family were published in the space of a few weeks. In varying degrees, all gave her mixed notices and all acknowledged that her days in the premier league of royalty were numbered. Only one, *The Royal Marriages* by this author, went as far as to spell out how she would be marginalized. Diana read it and later told me, "I wish I knew who your sources were. Every word you wrote was spot on." For someone who was as status conscious as Diana, such public winding down was supreme humiliation.

There was one bright spot in her life, however. She had begun a relationship with Oliver Hoare, a cultivated art dealer and Middle Eastern expert whose wife, Diane de Waldener, was the daughter of the Queen Mother's close friend, Baronne de Waldener. In fact, so close was the family to the royals that Prince Charles usually stayed each year at the Waldener château in France. Twice the paparazzi photographed him standing nude at a window looking out onto the château's magnificent view.

Hoare was not only a friend of the Prince of Wales, but was also his contemporary. "Oliver is a charming, debonair, exciting man," Vanessa Hoare, a member of the Hoare banking family, said. "He's not an immediate member of the banking family, but he's a successful art dealer and of course is married into an immensely rich family. The girls have always liked him. It was hard for Diane to act as if the Princess of Wales didn't exist. She's French, though, and she made up her mind she was going to sit this one out, no matter how long it took."

While Diane Hoare was doing her level best to ignore the developing relationship between her husband and the Princess of Wales, Diana was becoming more and more attached to Oliver Hoare. "She used him as a lifeline," Joseph Sanders said. "She needed his warmth and companionship. She was terrified her world was collapsing and that her enemies at the Palace would shove her out the way they'd shoved Fergie out."

From Diana's point of view, there was ample evidence to support her suspicions. Aside from the downgrading of her royal role by the palace, the press now uniformly questioned her motives and integrity, and she was firmly convinced the courtiers were behind this new attitude towards her. That summer, for instance, she took an extended holiday in Bali before flying to America with Prince William and Prince Harry. As she trotted them around one Disney spectacular after another, the British press photographed them, then asked, "Is this woman for real, or is she using her children to score points?" Cut to the quick that anyone could believe that she would use her children in that way, Diana said, "I can see which way this is headed. From now on, no matter what I do, I'll be turned over for inspection like porcelain that might or might not be Meissen."

Worse was to come. No sooner did she land in Britain than Diana discovered that Charles had appointed Alexandra Legge-Bourke, known as Tiggy, to act as his sons' adult female companion when they were with him. The newspapers were full of how Tiggy would be the boys' surrogate mother, which drove Diana, always prone to jealousy, to paroxysms of rage. "They don't need another mother," she said – shouted, actually – in deep distress. "They've already got a mother." Refusing to accept that Charles, like most busy men, would find it easier to cope if he had a glorified nanny in the background, Diana remained firmly convinced that Tiggy Legge-Bourke's appointment was a ruse to undermine her relationship with her children. In fact, Diana became so obsessed with Tiggy's role in her husband's and her children's lives that her existence drew Diana's attention away from Camilla. Thereafter, the woman who remained firmly in her sights was not the Rottweiler or the Presence, as she called Camilla, but Tiggy.

Nor did the passage of the years lessen Diana's antipathy. If anything, it grew, for she convinced herself that Charles would end up dumping Camilla and marrying Tiggy. The prospect of another tall, attractive, glamorous Princess of Wales – one who was younger than Diana and capable of giving the heir to the throne more children – was enough to drive Diana to extremes of emotionalism.

Such a highly charged situation could not last indefinitely without something giving, and at the Wales staff party three years after Tiggy's appointment, Diana went up to her and said, in her most acid tone, how sorry she was to hear about her abortion. Of course, there had been no abortion. Tiggy was not having an affair with Prince Charles, who took his employee's side when she publicly threatened to sue Diana for defamation of character. Diana had to back down, though she did succeed in having Tiggy's role in her sons' life wound down in the year before her death. Ironically enough, now that she is dead, Tiggy, who has always had an excellent relationship with both boys, has returned into the frame. This, everyone who knows Diana agrees, is something she would be happy about, for while she hated being replaced when alive, she would want comfort from any quarter for her sons now that she is no longer here to provide it herself.

Diana could not have discovered about Tiggy's appointment at a worse time. She and her brother, Charles, had always shared a unique relationship due to the experiences they had shared when their parents separated. As if this needed any reinforcement, both of them often said how similar they were. Although brother and sister had not seen as much of each other after her marriage as they had before it, Diana's attitude was that she was always there for Charles, and that he would always be there for her. This seemed to be confirmed in April 1993 when he offered her the use of the Garden House, a four-bedroom property on the Althorp Estate. Diana happily got in touch with Dudley Poplak, who was once more instructed to ferret out swatches and designs for her approval. Three weeks later, however, Charles telephoned her and withdrew the offer, stating that her presence would result in an unacceptable level of intrusion for him as a result of the additional security required. "I felt betrayed," Diana said. "Even though his reasoning was plausible, it hurt. He loves me so much he can't even put up with inconvenience that wouldn't affect him!" She didn't speak to him for a long time after that.

Feeling that she could no longer rely upon even her own brother, Diana's fears about the way she was being marginalized by what she called "my husband's side" were reinforced in November 1993 when she got wind that her official engagements were to be pared down to such an extent that her December diary planning session, at which her royal duties would be fixed for the following six months, might as well not take place. Days before, the *Sunday Mirror* had published photographs of her taken secretly by Bryce Taylor, the manager of her former health club. In them a fully made-up Diana is seen exercising on machines. Remarkably, she does not sweat. Taylor later tried to imply that Diana had colluded with him in taking the photographs, but she refuted this by swinging into action with a lawsuit for breach of trust engineered by Anthony Julius of Mishcon de Reya. This was settled with rich friends of the Princess paying off Taylor with a six-figure sum, to "spare her the indignity of entering the witness box."

While the Palace officially supported Diana, there had been sufficient times in the past when she had manipulated her public image for there to be doubt about whether she was innocent or guilty. Behind the scenes, they were no longer supporting her. On the contrary, throughout the year there had been press briefings in which courtiers, including Robert Fellowes himself, had made it clear that they regarded Diana as a loose cannon. Diana felt "they were slitting my throat." In one briefing in particular, published that autumn, an unnamed courtier was quoted as saying, "Diana is headstrong but we must show her love and understanding and bend over backwards to avoid a chasm in the early stages because, if she became bitter and twisted, it would be impossible for the children." Diana was incensed, because she felt the tone patronized her. She confronted her brother-in-law, loudly telling Robert Fellowes that she was sick of being used in the newspapers by the Palace. "It was ironic. She who had taken her dirty linen to the public for a good airing, complaining that they had no right to say she must be treated with love and understanding," Lord Charteris said. "Of course it was patronizing, but it was a damned sight nicer and fairer than any of the accusations she'd made against the Prince of Wales and the rest of the Royal Family."

Once more, Diana's canniness and innate ability to outfox her adversaries saw her through the crisis. Realizing that she had better jump before she was pushed, Diana chose to announce the retirement from public life she suspected was being forced upon her. On Friday, 3 December 1993, at a charity luncheon in aid of the Headway National Head Injuries Association, Diana, dramatically employing the techniques taught her by Peter Setterlen, announced that she was retiring from public life and begged for "time and space" to pursue her life in private.

It was a masterful performance and Diana's many admirers were sorry to see her go. Especially the many charities of which she was patron. She had raised their profiles and helped them raise tens of millions of pounds. Alan Sievewright, the opera impresario who had worked on charitable projects with Diana, spoke for all her charitable colleagues when he said, "She was marvellous and she'll be sorely missed."

Having cleared the decks, Diana was now confronted by a life that was often frighteningly empty. Although she still remained true to her spiritual quest of healing and being healed through ministering to the infirm, and kept up her private visits to AIDS patients and the homeless, her life had yawning gaps. John Kennedy, who got to know Diana as a result of sharing that courtyard with her, told me, "She often poked her head round for a chat. You could tell she was at a loose end, lonely and with nothing to do and no one to see. The weeks were bad, but the weekends were worse. We used to live in Gloucestershire and would come up on a Sunday afternoon into London, and pop into KP (Kensington Palace) to see if there was anything in the tray. Her house was next door to Prince Michael's, where I worked, and she would often come in, usually 4:30, having been out to lunch with friends. That would be it for the night.

She'd be all alone in the house, sometimes with the butler Paul Burrell, sometimes with nobody. I think she was lonely. I mean, you got the impression she was very much alone. There was nobody there, everybody else had gone off to the country, the place was in darkness, and there she was, on her own. During the week, you could see her sitting in the window of her sitting-room for hours on end, her mobile phone clamped to her ear, despite the fact that we'd been warned that there were people with scanners in the park (Kensington Gardens) and it wasn't safe."

It was John Kennedy's observation that Diana was not only lonely but had been forced, by circumstances, into being something of a loner. "I don't think she felt she could trust anybody, to be honest. She was just an ordinary girl but she had been turned into an icon and she wasn't one. She certainly from '94 to '95 started to just go out by herself to places. Before, she had been using the driver Steve a lot, now she got rid of him. He spent half his time washing cars when she went out by herself. Sometimes you would see her wandering off into High Street Kensington by herself. Once I saw her going off in leggings and dark glasses. She was a loner by then, I think."

Worst of all, from Diana's point of view, was Christmas. The Royal Family, which had once split itself between Christmas at Windsor Castle and the New Year at Sandringham, now congregated at the Queen's Norfolk estate, where Diana had been born, while Windsor Castle was undergoing extensive repairs. Diana refused to avail herself of a standing invitation to join the Royal Family for Christmas – a privilege denied Sarah, Duchess of York, who was relegated to a cottage on the estate without access to the big house, where her husband and children stayed. "It would bring my bulimia back full force," she explained, going on to state how acutely uncomfortable she was around the Royal Family. If it had been bad before they thought her manipulative and disloyal, in the light of her complicity with Morton, now that her secret was out, it was unbearable.

Diana therefore started what became something of a tradition. After a pre-Christmas Christmas with her sons, she saw them off for their stay with Granny, then boarded a flight, usually across the Atlantic, where she stayed with her close friend Lucia Flecha de Lima, wife of the Brazilian Ambassador to the United States and previously to the Court of St. James's. "It's the only way I can cope with Christmas," she said.

During this time, Diana's life was full of uncertainty. She did not know whether she would remain married or be divorced. Charles had made no move, nor had she. She did receive a word of warning when this writer penned a series of articles for the *Sun* in January 1994, the first article stating that Buckingham Palace intended to strip her of her title at the time of a divorce. "That was the first clue I had of what they'd do," Diana later told me. Unsettled by this revelation, she coped by concentrating on getting her life together. Every morning she rose at seven, ate breakfast, which was usually muesli, and drove herself to the Harbour Club, where she worked out for an hour before returning home to shower and receive her hairdresser, Sam McKnight, who would comb her hair while she spoke to friends on the telephone and made her daily plans. If she had somewhere special to go, she called in her make-up artist, Mary Greenwell.

Although Diana could be remarkably unguarded, she could also be remarkably discreet. Her butler Paul Burrell has opined, "She could never keep a secret," but that is not accurate. To my certain knowledge, she kept several secrets from him, including the fact that she and the Prince of Wales were planning to separate, the taping of the *Panorama* interview, and her intentions regarding Dodi Fayed. Indeed, Diana kept secrets very well when she had to, or believed that she ought to. If she didn't want anyone to know about a man she was seeing, she was careful not to reveal his identity even as she spoke about the fact of his existence to friends. She was also careful not to breathe a word about her part in the Morton book to anyone save her co-conspirators, and maintained a similar level of discretion with regard to her collusion with *Diana in Private*, letting, to the best of my knowledge, only the mutual friend in whose house we met in on the secret.

One secret Diana certainly kept from Paul Burrell and most of her friends was that in 1994 she became pregnant. Very few people knew about it. Aside from an earl's daughter, who told me at the time, and Joseph Sanders and his wife Anita, this was one secret that Diana did not share with the myriad people she telephoned on a daily basis for advice and guidance. According to the earl's daughter, in whom she confided, when Diana found out, "She freaked out. She freaked right out. She wanted the baby. 'Suppose it's a girl,' she said, distraught at what she knew she had to do."

What Diana "had to do" was to have an abortion. "How could she have a baby?" the earl's daughter explained. "She wasn't divorced. What could she do? She couldn't have an illegitimate baby. The very idea of a hugely pregnant Princess of Wales marrying the father of her third child was enough to make her see the futility of the whole thing. She couldn't do that to William and Harry. The scandal would've been too much."

So Diana, tearfully and in distress, made arrangements, used an appointment with Joseph Sanders as a cover, and sacrificed the baby she wanted. Afterwards, she returned to Kensington Palace and took to her bed, crying.

"When she got pregnant is when the telephone calls to her friend, Oliver Hoare, started with a vengeance," this earl's daughter said. "Diana was almost unhinged with grief and misery. Before and after the abortion. She wasn't responsible for her actions. She couldn't help herself. Day and night, day after day, night after night, she'd sit on that telephone, calling Oliver's house thirty, forty, fifty times. She'd use her telephone. She'd go out to the call boxes on the High Street. She'd call from her sister Sarah's house. She was desperate."

Diane Hoare called in the police, who traced the calls back to Diana's private line, telephone boxes in the vicinity of Kensington Palace, and Lady Sarah MacCorquodale's telephone. Oliver Hoare then asked the police not to proceed with their investigation, and they closed the case.

When the news became public, a mortified and humiliated Diana admitted making some of the calls, but denied making the majority. "There's a conspiracy against me," she said. For once, no one believed her, nor did anyone sympathize at a time when she needed sympathy, because the reason why she had been tipped over the edge remained unknown.

As Diana recovered from the abortion, she was overtaken with anxiety. "She was terrified the police would prosecute her for making nuisance calls," Joseph Sanders told me. "She'd call every day and say the same thing. I'd tell her, 'Don't worry. The police aren't going to prosecute you. You're the Princess of Wales. If you killed someone they might be forced to take you in, but even then, they'd find some way of letting you off the hook. Public confidence couldn't cope with you being prosecuted. It won't happen. Believe me.' It was ages before she accepted that nothing would happen."

What helped to take Diana's mind off the possibility of prosecution and off the pain of having aborted a baby she would have loved to bring into the world, was the advent of a new man. Will Carling was the burly, masculine, potent captain of the England Rugby team. Engaged to and living with an attractive public-relations girl, now television presenter, named Julia Smith, Carling was nevertheless bowled over by the Princess of Wales's interest in him.

There was no pretence that it was a love affair. He was committed elsewhere and Diana was happy to enjoy the pleasure of a man who was very much her type: a gentleman, athletic, muscular, sexy.

Meanwhile, the thick-necked and handsome Carling married the slender and pretty Julia. Knowing nothing of Diana's existence in her life, Mrs Carling believed that her relationship with her husband was a strong, passionate, exclusive union. Carling, in the interim, was still seeing Diana on a regular basis, dropping into Kensington Palace and meeting up at the Harbour Club, where he had the excuse of advising her on the restructuring of her body, to see her several times a week.

After more than a year of this, exposure came from an unexpected source. Carling and his assistant parted company vitriolically. In the ensuing slanging match, she informed the world that Carling and Diana were more than just friends.

The fact that they were friends at all came as a shock to Julia, who was labouring under the misapprehension that she and her husband were so close that she knew everything about him. She confronted him with the allegations. He denied them, stating that he barely knew Diana, that their relationship, such as it was, was based on the admiration her sons felt for him as captain of the England Rugby team. Convinced by that disclaimer, Julia Carling publicly warned Diana that she "had picked on the wrong married couple to try to break up this time."

Within days, however, Julia Carling was forced to eat her words. Will Carling was spotted by the newspapers entering and leaving Kensington Palace – "with presents for the young princes," he asserted. Before the newlywed Mrs Carling had time to recover from that shock, or to test her ultimatum that he must never meet Diana again, she opened up the newspaper to see her husband and Diana, guilt written all over them, stealthily leaving the Harbour Club after an early-morning meeting. "It would be easy to say she ruined my marriage," Julia said, "but it takes two to tango and I blame Will for getting involved in the first place."

The Carling marriage over, the question that now arose was whether Julia intended to name Diana as corespondent. For a while, she tantalizingly remained silent. This allowed the public to conclude that she did have the option. Subtly, Mrs Carling was wreaking her vengeance on Diana by omission.

Diana, meanwhile, was apoplectic. She had only meant to have fun with Carling. She was not in love with him, nor he with her. To have her pseudo-virginal reputation sullied further than it had been after Diane Hoare's report to the police was, to her mind, cruel and unnecessary punishment.

"Why can't they leave me alone?" Diana asked, blaming the press for her latest misfortune and failing, once again, to take any responsibility for her actions. She had hoped to consolidate her position, yet here she was, even more exposed and vulnerable than ever.

Sixteen

One of the most confusing and complicated areas of the Princess of Wales's life was her relationship with the press. No one becomes as famous as she did, and consistently maintains the level of coverage that she had, without working at publicity. This Diana did. Moreover, she did it with a brilliance bordering on genius. To quote Sir David English, her unofficial media advisor, editor-in-chief of Associated Newspapers, and employer of Richard Kay of the *Daily Mail*, "Diana liked the tabloids. She had no quarrel with any of their staff photographers, most of whom she knew by their first names. She regularly met with tabloid editors. Indeed, she had ongoing contact with all editors. She was – perhaps by necessity – a media groupie."

This assessment, from one of the most eminent editors in Britain, was sound. Sir David's offices abutted Kensington Palace with a gap of maybe three hundred feet. According to him, Diana frequently popped over to see him from Kensington Palace. Once, when they were lunching together after some particular coup she had organized which had got her great tabloid and broadsheet coverage, he congratulated her on her skills. "If you were not the Princess of Wales," he said, "you'd be running your own commercial public relations company. And it would be the best in the world. You're the finest PR operator, man or woman, I have ever met."

Sir David acknowledged that Diana was capable of "scheming, of obsessive manipulation, that whole frightening and distressing picture of a beautiful and terrified creature at bay." He also acknowledged how, after her death, "we editors listened with shock at the stories of how street gangs of paparazzi worked. How they pushed and jostled her . . . if she stepped on to the streets."

Diana's argument, as Sir David implied, was not with the tabloids, or the broadsheets, but with the paparazzi. This was an oversimplification. While Diana did indeed suffer at the hands of certain paparazzi, she also had a running tussle with most newspapers, and indeed authors who wrote about her. "If they wrote anything she disliked, she was furious," a former member of her staff said. "She didn't forgive but she didn't alienate either. She'd try to influence the way they presented her by charming them."

Diana's need to manipulate her coverage, and the convoluted nature of her relationships with people who could provide her with that attention, is something I can personally attest to. Before publication of *Diana in Private*, I wrote to tell her that she did not need to worry. Although I was incisive, I was fair, and she came out of the book creditably, albeit as a human being with failings as well as virtues. When she did not respond, I took her silence to mean displeasure, something confirmed by mutual friends, who said that she was not exactly thrilled by the warts I showed in her portrait. Notwithstanding her constant refrain that "I am not a saint," Diana obviously and rather paradoxically wanted to be admired as imperfect, without any flaws marring her image, ambitions or objectives.

Thereafter, I decided to avoid seeing Diana at social events, lest she cause a scene. I knew of her proclivity to confront, and certainly was not about to put myself in the position of having a slanging match with the Princess of Wales that would most likely be reported in the popular press. For three years, I therefore declined invitations when I knew she would be present. In 1995, however, I was asked to a reception being given by the Russian Ambassador at his residence in Kensington Palace Gardens. Because my sons are Russian and I myself am part-Russian, I decided that I had at least as much right to be there as Diana, and decided to attend.

Once I accepted, Diana knew that I would be there, because the guest list for that type of event is invariably sent to the Palace to be vetted, so that no one unsuitable gains admission. In the ordinary course of life, silence would mean assent, but with Diana, you could never be sure what her reaction would be. I therefore went armed with the attitude that I'd fight fire with fire if she caused a scene, but if she ignored me or spoke to me, I'd respond as my sentiments dictated.

As Diana started her sweep across the three reception rooms, people, including Anna Pasternak's father, Charles, to whom I was speaking, were betting that she would not speak to me. For my part, I could not have cared less, and frankly did not expect her to acknowledge me in such a highly select setting. What we all reckoned without, however, was Diana's gumption and determination to swing everyone into an uncritical fan. Having spoken to Princess George Galitzine and Princess Bassam Salameh, she turned around, walked out of her way to where I was standing, and buttonholed me.

"It's been a long time," she said affectionately and regretfully.

"It certainly has," I agreed.

"You look marvellous. I like your hair that colour (it was lighter than it had been the last time we had seen one another). And I see you're wearing my favourite choker and bracelet (pearls with large, emerald-cut cairngorms)."

"You're looking pretty good yourself. If you want, I can introduce you to the jeweller who made them. She's a one-woman band, and all the better for that."

"I couldn't afford something like that. Those stones are huge."

"Of course you can. If I can, you certainly can. They're only cairngorms. She's really very good and affordable. If you want an intro, let me know."

By this time, I was amused to see people clustered around us gaping in disbelief. Diana had only just started, and as we chattered on, I thought, She's hoping the photographer will come and snap us together so that her photo will be on the front pages of the world's tabloids day after tomorrow with the headline, DI AND LADY C KISS AND MAKE UP.

The one thing that blinds me to my own self-interest is recognition that I'm being manipulated, so, rather than allow Diana to do something that was in both our interests, I decided, in defiance of protocol, to bring the conversation to a halt before he arrived. As we chattered on, I could see him in the other room, oblivious of the photo opportunity but making his way slowly in our direction nevertheless. Diana's back was to him. As soon as I reckoned he was getting uncomfortably close, I brought up a letter I had at home from a lady in the Philippines who had written asking me to forward it to her. "If you'd like it, I'll send it to you," I offered.

"Please do. I'd love to see it."

"I'll send it tomorrow. That's a promise. It's been good to see you, and to see you looking so well," I said, bringing the conversation to a close.

Diana, obviously thinking I was being considerate, said a pleasant goodbye and we moved off in separate directions. I could see her face, and, as she saw the photographer, she turned to me, a wan smile playing around her mouth, as if to say, "Pity he couldn't have shot us."

In interpreting Diana's fierce determination to maximize her publicity, I misinterpreted her ultimate goal. She was not interested in just one photo opportunity. She was still trying to influence what I had to say and write about her. I realized this once I had sent that letter. I did not expect my path to cross Diana's until the next social event. I was therefore shocked when she telephoned me a few weeks later out of the blue. As the charm offensive started and, to my surprise, continued, with further unexpected telephone calls, I realized she was courting me so that I would be more favourable about her than I already was. Then, once I moved from the Cundy Street Flats, she took to dropping in at my house. We must have had six or seven meetings and countless telephone conversations in the months before her death. I was pretty sure she did not believe me when I told her that I did not intend to write anything about her ever again, but I meant it. Nor would I have done, had she remained alive. Only her death, and the unique perspective which she, more than anyone else, was responsible for giving me about her, convinced me that possibly I had another contribution to make.

Diana's actions with me might have been extreme, but they were not atypical. When she was not trying to charm journalists or writers into seeing things her way, she was co-operating with photographers. Hence the cleverness of Rupert Murdoch in keeping his distance from her. Sir David English's observation, that she was on first-name terms with most of the staff photographers on the tabloids and broadsheets, is valid. She was uncannily story-wise as well as camera-wise. A true professional, Diana knew not only how to influence a story being written, but also how to pose so well that she might have been looking through the lens instead of being in front of it.

Diana's secret with photographers could not have been simpler. She made sure she looked good and smiled often. As she said to Sarah York when Fergie accompanied her on a visit to Prince Andrew's ship before the Yorks' marriage, "Just smile. Always smile. No matter how you're feeling, smile." A photograph says more than a thousand words, and that cheerfulness, allied to the glamour and beauty which she made sure she projected at all times, ensured that Diana remained etched in the public consciousness as a beautiful, good-natured, kindhearted and co-operative person. Only when it suited her purposes, such as on her trips to India and Korea in 1992, did she cease smiling. At those moments, she was nevertheless careful to look as glamorous and beautiful as ever, while projecting the pain or displeasure which would waft her to another stratosphere.

Diana's consistent co-operation with the media sometimes broke down with the paparazzi, those freelance photographers who frequently camped outside the gates at Kensington Palace and followed the Princess of Wales from place to place. Although these freelancers had always been a feature of her life, they did not become a problem until after her separation, when she divested herself of the private detectives who were deemed to be a necessary part of her protection, but whom she viewed as potential spies. Although everyone tried to point out to her that she needed the protection, Diana was adamant. "I want to lead a normal life. How can I when half the world's following me?" So, having rid herself of the hated police detail, she was exposed to and followed by a larger number of paparazzi instead.

John Kennedy provided me with a vivid picture of what life was like with the paparazzi on her trail. "We sometimes had to trick them to get her out of the Palace. On more than one occasion, it was needed for all of us to leave at once. If anyone was going, they would say, 'Well, hold on, we need four or five cars to leave at the same time.' And when we got to the gate at the end, we'd all go off in different directions so they wouldn't know who to chase. I think she definitely felt hunted by then, and they (her staff) used to deploy tricks to get her out. She would often hide in the back of the car to get out, so her driver would drive her out." If she made her escape, Diana would drop him off a few blocks away from the palace and continue on her way.

One paparazzo in particular perturbed Diana. Martin Stenning had been photographing her for years, and, according to him, had had a happy and co-operative relationship with her when she suddenly turned on him for no apparent reason. That was the beginning of the end. Once Diana had the bit between her teeth, she ran all the way to court, where she sought, and gained, an injunction preventing him from harassing her.

It is impossible to know how much reliance to place upon what Mr Stenning said. He maintained, with what seems to be the ring of truth, that Diana usually co-operated with him, giving him the poses he needed to sell photographs to the agencies which were then distributed to the newspapers. Moreover, he made the point that she often created photo opportunities for him and for other photographers, which is borne out by everyone else who photographed her.

One photographer who came off shattered by his encounter with Diana was Brendan Beirne. According to socialite Annabel Barrington, "He left England because of what she did to him. They'd always had a cordial, civilized relationship. He's a really nice guy. Not at all intrusive. She used to pose for him happily. Talk to him. They were chummy, without being chums." On Easter Monday, Diana left the Earls Court Gym at about 10:30 in the morning. "She was walking down the street looking happy," Beirne said. "I took a couple of pictures of her and thought that was it. I was about thirty feet away, on the other side of the street, and I put the camera down for a moment. Suddenly she saw me and ran across the road saying, 'What are you doing? What are you doing? Give me that film.' Seeing a strapping stranger in his late twenties passing by, Diana appealed to him. Kevin Duggan waded in for what he thought was the Princess's rescue. He managed to pinion Beirne against the wall, his arm locked behind his back, while Diana shouted dramatically, 'Get the film. Get the film.' "He thought he was going to break his arm," Annabel Barrington said. "He was so distressed by what happened that he chucked in photography here and moved to America." The last word belongs to Beirne, who said at the time, "It's outrageous. She knows I am neither a stalker nor a threat. I've taken photos of her for ten years. But she's very manipulative. She can shout at photographers, but then the next day she is tipping off someone so they know where she is and comes out smiling."

Diana, of course, had a capricious streak in her nature. What seemed unreasonable or a change of heart to others, was, in her opinion, perfectly reasonable, because it answered her own needs. To an onlooker or to the receptacle of her actions, with no access to her thought processes, her behaviour could be baffling, because it bore no connection to what had gone on between them, only to what was going on within herself. That, it would seem, is the explanation for why she turned on the men whom she frequently tipped off one day, then railed against the next.

Diana's inconsistent attitude towards the British paparazzi who were a feature of her life made for intermittently volatile relations. As any royal or public figure knows, the best posture to adopt is one of pleasant blandness. By doing that, you create an atmosphere of steady neutrality, which is ultimately boring and does not make for good photo opportunities. Diana, however, was incapable of this. On the contrary, she provided all the drama and unpredictability that the paparazzi could have wished for. Sometimes she would put her head down. Other times she would be smiling. Sometimes she would do both within seconds, giving the impression that she was answering photographic needs rather than actually conveying her true feelings. Sometimes she would speak to them pleasantly. Other times she would shriek at them. "You make my life hell." "Get lost." "Fuck off." "Piss off." She complained during her *Panorama* interview, "It's become abusive and harassment. It goes on and on and the story never changes." Unfortunately for her, the very photographers she was publicly complaining about, were the ones she tipped off when she wanted publicity.

Mark Saunders, Glenn Harvey and Keith Butler are three paparazzi who used to follow her around. They experienced at first hand her hot and cold attitude towards them. After the *Panorama* interview, for instance, Saunders and Harvey were trailing her up the M4 motorway. According to Saunders, "Diana knew my car well enough and I could see her looking at me in the rearview mirror. She indicated left and pulled across to the middle lane from the overtaking lane. She slowed down so much she forced me to pass. And then, in a moment of insanity which to this day neither Glenn nor I will ever understand, she increased her speed and lurched back into the fast lane, coming up directly behind me. We were travelling at ninety miles per hour when I felt her bumper touch the rear of my car.

"'What the hell is she doing?' Glenn shouted. He gestured wildly at her. 'Back off. Back off.' But Diana made no attempt to slow down. The cars carried on, bumper to bumper. By now I was genuinely scared. I could see Diana's face in the rearview mirror. She was driving with only one hand, with the other gesturing wildly at me. Her car remained just millimeters from mine, putting our lives at risk. I increased my speed, thinking it was the only way to escape her. At about 120 miles per hour I shook her off and managed to slip into the middle lane. Diana sped past."

These car chases were not a rarity, either. In a harbinger of later tragedy, Diana would too frequently become involved in trying to shake off the paparazzi by jumping red lights, driving at eighty and ninety miles per hour on residential London roads, and, at night, turning off her lights. A mutual friend who was with her during one of these chases says, "It was frightening. They were behind her, their bumper practically touching hers. She jumped a red light and they followed suit. She put her foot down on the accelerator and took off like a bat from hell. They were right on her tail. They got alongside her. She swerved into them. I swore we were going to crash. We were going way, way over the speed limit. I was frantic and said, 'For God's sake, let them get their bloody picture. They're endangering our lives.' Her jaw was set with determination but she answered sweetly, Don't worry, this happens all the time. You're not going to be hurt.' I sat back, tried to calm myself and thought, She's right. Nothing's going to happen. She's the Princess of Wales. Of course everything's going to be all right. With hindsight, that's ironic, isn't it?"

Diana felt entitled to behave as she did. She said, "They scream obscenities at me hoping I'll lose my temper and give them a sensational photograph. Sometimes they try to trip me while I'm walking. They want to snap me ungainly, maybe exposing a bit of underwear. The other day one even had the gall to scream, Stop the shit and behave like a fucking princess. You're the fucking Princess of Wales. Stop carrying on like a fucking tart.' He wanted me to lose my temper."

Unlike the other royals, who kept their distance from journalists and refused to get sucked into the media game, Diana, and Sarah to a lesser extent, found themselves in the vortex once they no longer had police protection. This was especially dangerous for them, as well as for the Royal Family, because the negative publicity was feeding upon itself, with sensationalism piling upon sensationalism. Prince Michael's former Private Secretary John Kennedy said, "It is the worst thing that could have happened to the two girls. Certainly the worst to the Royal Family. And the best thing for the media. It was a gift from heaven for them in the circulation wars of the tabloids. It became one of these games like the lottery in the *Sun*. Who was going to come out with the most outrageous story next?

"I think certain elements of the media had an anti-royal agenda, so whatever they (the girls) and the royals had done, they've been clobbered. The Princess of Wales and the Duchess of York were goaded into trying to manipulate the media. But what they didn't realize was that, however powerful they might be, the media was twice as powerful still.

"Certainly the press goaded all sides. They were using them and they were digging a huge elephant trap, but much to their (the press's) surprise, the elephants (Diana and Sarah) hurled themselves into the hole before they had even bothered to cover the traps with leaves. There was a stampede to jump in.

"It was a disaster for the Royal Family, but it was an even bigger disaster for the two girls. It has left one of them dead and the other ostracized."

By now, amid the behind-the-scenes turmoil of Diana courting and fighting the media, the War of the Waleses was firmly underway. Although the Prince of Wales had given his friends and his staff firm instructions not to speak to the press, or to leak stories about him or Diana, those who disagreed with his stance, that Diana should be appeased lest she be goaded to ever-greater damaging heights, ignored him or spoke to their friends, who then passed on information for publication. Diana was convinced "my husband's side are out to destroy me" even though their ripostes were always mild compared with her forays, and usually in response to some initiative from her.

The Princess, meanwhile, was actively courting not only editors and journalists but making friends of them. Chief among these was Richard Kay of the *Daily Mail* and *Mail on Sunday*, whom she met when she went to Nepal in 1993. Being public-school-educated, Kay was a "gentleman," and was therefore uptown enough for Diana to feel that he was "one of us."

Gradually, as she fed him stories and he responded suitably by writing them up in a way she approved of, they become friendly. Tellingly, Diana never befriended, or even met with, Andrew Morton, who was from a working-class background. She truly was an uptown girl.

As story after story leaking private information about the Prince and Princess of Wales featured prominently in the *Daily Mail* and *Mail on Sunday*, word spread among the *cognoscenti*. Richard Kay was Diana's Mercury. Whenever he used the words "friends of Diana said," those in the know understood that this was the code for "Diana herself is the source," a fact he confirmed after her death.

While this was an agreeable position for Kay to be in, it did not enhance Diana's royal status in Palace circles to be leaking private information several times a week during the course of her separation. Indeed, after her death, when it emerged that she spoke to Richard Kay sometimes on a daily basis, and did so even on the night of the fatal crash, to bring him up to date on her affair with Dodi Fayed, the question arose: While Diana might have felt compelled to divulge secrets to gain an advantage in divorce negotiations with Prince Charles, why did she feel compelled to share the most private aspects of her life with the public at large even after there was no necessity or obvious advantage?

An answer to that question is provided by a psychiatrist who knew Diana, is familiar with her medical history, but did not actually treat her. Dr Michael Davies said, "The Princess of Wales was a true narcissist. People think a narcissist is someone who is in love with her own image, but that is not so. In lay language, a narcissist is someone whose sense of self is so shaky that she exists only when others are reflecting their impression of her back to her. That was why the Princess of Wales was so sensitive to criticism and so dependent on the good opinion of others. That was why she needed the constant attention of the media. In the vernacular, that was why she was a media junkie. That was why she had the feelings of emptiness she speaks of. Emotionally, she didn't exist except when she saw her reflection in the opinions of others. It's a frightening condition to have, because sufferers have such voids within their personalities. I am convinced that was her true problem, and that everything else followed as a consequence – the weak sense of self, the feelings of emptiness, of alienation, the maladjustment, the eating disorder, the depression, the fear. As she matured and developed a sense of her own existence, the corollary was a firmer sense of self. That's when her problems started lessening, when Diana the individual started to blossom."

While Diana's motivation for manipulating the media after her divorce might very well have been personal, her interest in doing so before the divorce was practical. She intended to maximize her advantages, to come out of the marriage with a large-enough settlement to be financially independent for the rest of her life, to retain her privileges, and to continue sharing custody of the children with Charles.

For three years, however, Diana remained in limbo, unable to fight for what she wanted, or to pursue her life with the openness that she desired, because the subject of divorce was never raised. This was both reassuring and threatening. On the one hand, she wished to remain the Princess of Wales, with the full panoply of privileges, and, on the other, she wanted to remarry, to have more children, especially a daughter.

"She was definitely on the lookout for men," Joseph Sanders, to whom she spoke every day, said. "She wanted love and she wanted to find someone to share her life with, even to marry. She liked being a member of the Harbour Club because she could meet attractive men there. She told me that. She said it was great to be able to see what you were getting. She meant in terms of their bodies. The fact that they were in shorts and vests left little to the imagination. If she saw someone she liked, she'd go right up to him, introduce herself, and ask him when he was going to ask her for coffee. She met many, many men there and had several flings. Believe me, Diana had more men than anyone will ever be able to figure out. Even me, and she often spoke about her men to me. Her most enduring relationship from the Harbour Club was with Christopher Whalley the tall, well-built, handsome property developer she continued to see until shortly before her death. The press used to criticize her for working out with full make-up. Well, now you know the reason why she wore it. It wasn't, as she said, because people expected the Princess of Wales to be presented with *perfect maquillage*. It's because she was on the hunt for men. And a girl who hunts has to look her best, even as she pumps iron."

As so often happened with Diana, while she was headed in one direction, she was pulling in another as well. The main source of her conflict, and of her pleasure, was a man she met by accident. Diana was visiting Joseph Toffolo, her acupuncturist Oonagh's husband, who had gone into the hospital for a triple-bypass, when she saw Hasnat Khan, then a thirty-seven-year-old heart surgeon from Lahore in Pakistan who was a member of the world-famous Professor Sir Magdi Yacoub's cardiac team. "He's sooooooo handsome," she confided to Joseph Sanders and her two hairdressers, Nathalie Symonds and Tessa Rock.

Smitten, Diana's strong romantic streak came to the fore. To Joe Toffolo's surprise, she started visiting him with unexpected frequency. "She used to pop in practically every day. It was a great morale booster, but I didn't expect to see her so often."

While ostensibly visiting Toffolo, Diana made a point of looking in on patients on the ward, especially when she knew Khan would be making his rounds. "She spent hours every day at Brompton Hospital," Joseph Sanders said. "She set out to get him. She told me so herself. She said she had a thing about doctors. The fact that he helped sick people fascinated her. She really admired him. All the hours he worked, and the sacrifices he made for his profession."

While Diana was smitten, the first time Khan saw the princess, he did not even have any idea who she was. Making sure she rectified that as quickly as possible, Diana set about ensuring that Khan would fall under the spell of the beautiful and compassionate young woman who had so much time for the sick and for him. "He was flattered that the Princess of Wales could take an interest in him," Joseph Sanders said.

By the time Joe Toffolo left the hospital, Diana and Natty, as she called Khan, were getting close. Employing the technique that she had used to win the Prince of Wales, Diana evinced an interest in all his activities. This time, however, she did not make the mistake she had done when she was young. Instead of faking interest, she developed it by reading books on heart surgery and the Muslim religion, and by asking Natty to allow her to look at operations which he and Sir Magdi performed. "Sometimes they make me feel sick to my stomach," she said, "but I swallow hard and watch."

Unfortunately for Diana, intent on looking her seductive best even while the knife was being wielded, she also wore make-up and jewellery in a sterile area, where both are forbidden. This resulted in an outcry when she was filmed by a television news crew, which was doing a piece on Sir Magdi and his team. Diana had on mascara, gold hoop earrings, and her fringe jauntily shot out from beneath her surgical cap. She was accused of self-promotion, of being a ghoul who was muscling in on gory operations just so she could be photographed looking beautiful and seeming wonderful. Naturally, Joseph Sanders said, said, "Diana was upset. She hadn't intended to get publicity. She was looking at her man work."

As the romance with Khan intensified, Diana met his family. She also allowed herself to be influenced by Eastern customs. She started burning joss sticks at Kensington Palace and ordered an array of shalwar kameez, the Pakistani national dress with the exotic trousers, tunics and scarves.

Tangentially, Diana also developed a closer relationship with Jemima Goldsmith, first the fiancée, then the wife of Pakistani cricketer Imran Khan (no relation to Hasnat Khan). By this time, Diana's feelings towards Dr Khan were deep enough for her to consider whether she might ever marry him. There was a major impediment to that: Diana was already married.

In the roundabout way that Diana viewed as necessary to her survival, she came up with a solution in late 1995. She would force the issue of divorce by bringing it out into the open. This she set about doing with all the flair and disingenuousness for which she is rightly respected, using an opportunity which presented itself to precise purpose. Martin Bashir, a BBC journalist and member of the highly-regarded *Panorama* current-affairs programme, had approached her for an interview. He was the latest in a string of telejournalists who had sought to gain her co-operation for a programme on the monarchy. Like Khan, he was from the Indian subcontinent. "This was a bonus, but only a small bonus, I believe," Joseph Sanders said. "It made her feel cosier."

The bigger bonus was that Bashir was prepared to offer Diana total secrecy and a level of control over the contents to be filmed and included if she agreed to an interview. She did, emphasizing that they would have to resort to extremes of subterfuge if the programme were ever to be aired. No one could know about it, including the top brass at the BBC, where the chairman was none other than the then Sir Marmaduke, now Lord Hussey, husband of the Queen's and Prince Charles's good friend Lady Susan Hussey, who had taught Diana the feminine etiquette involved in being the Princess of Wales. If Hussey got wind of the interview, he would probably pull it, on the grounds that it might compromise the monarchy.

Filming was arranged for a Sunday early in November 1995. Because Diana could not trust her staff, she gave all of them, including the ones now trumpeted as people she trusted entirely, the day off. Bashir and his tiny crew smuggled themselves and their equipment, reduced to include compact cameras, into Kensington Palace. There, they set to work with Diana, who took care to apply dramatic, mournful make-up, and wear suitably depressing clothes. They did take after take after take of certain things. Diana intended the effect to be just so, as she portrayed herself as a trapped animal hounded by vicious enemies at the Palace. Cleverly addressing every area where those very enemies might have ammunition, she defused the issue of her mental problems by saying that they considered her to be "mad," but that she was "not mad." They wanted to be rid of her and had made her life a misery. In a *tour de force* of denial, she alleged that she did not want a divorce, but would, of course, consent to one when it was forced upon her. She denied that she would mind not being queen. All she wanted to be, she said, was queen of people's hearts. Making herself out to be the innocent by ignoring her many lovers, she said of Camilla Parker Bowles, "There were three of us in the marriage, so it was a bit crowded." She frankly admitted that her tactic for confounding her enemies was to confuse them. Cleverly, she spoke about her eating disorders, her attempts to hurt herself, and her unhappiness, which she laid firmly at the doorstep of the Prince of Wales and the courtiers, thereby removing any possibility of her mental illnesses being used against her in a divorce. She touchingly revealed the depth of her love for her children, appealing to popular prejudice about the Royal Family being aloof and out of touch, by describing how she took the boys to see cancer patients who were in reality AIDS patients, and to see the homeless, so that they would grow up to be normal kids. She staked out her claim for an official position in the future, stating that she thought she'd be a good roving ambassador for Britain. Shrewdly, she admitted to her affair with James Hewitt, knowing only too well that denial would be folly, for he had a stack of compromising letters he could use against her and there were photographs of them making love in the garden of his mother's house in Devon. Sadly, Diana then allowed her envy to get the better of her, and she went in for the kill, seeking to deprive the Prince of Wales of his right to the throne by questioning his suitability for what she called the "top job." This last action was a step too far, and would have tremendous repercussions in her life.

Later that November, *Panorama* aired the film, and got the highest ratings of any documentary programme ever aired. Everywhere on earth, people watched with morbid fascination as Diana regaled them with confidences about her personal life. In the process, she gained many sympathizers and admirers, and a lesser but equally potent number of detractors. "My heart went out to her," a foreign princess, whose husband is the head of their House and therefore cannot afford to be identified, told me. "I felt very sorry for her. Don't,' Queen Anne Marie of the Hellenes said. Don't believe a word of it. It's all an act. She's a perfect witch.' Only she didn't use the word beginning with w, but another that rhymes with it!"

Once more engulfed in controversy, once more the subject of conversation all over the world, Diana proved yet again how adept she was at cutting her way through the thickets of adversity. Even her discreditable attempt to deprive her husband of his birthright proved to be a winning ploy, at least in the short-term. Although she lost the sympathy of many people over that, she instilled terror into Prince Charles and Buckingham Palace.

This was terror which she then capitalized upon in a most clever and resourceful way. Armed with a tape recorder, she had been to visit George Smith, a former member of her husband's staff who was hospitalized with mental problems. Lavishing sympathy upon him, she winkled out of him the story about how he believed himself to have been raped by her husband's valet. She then skilfully got him to state that he had also seen that man and her husband in a compromising position when he went to serve Charles breakfast. Diana, of course, would have realized, as did everyone else with even the most basic knowledge of how the Palace works, that it would not have been possible for George Smith to catch Charles and the valet in a compromising position while serving his royal master breakfast, for he, George Smith, never took Charles his breakfast. This salient point, however, did not deter Diana from utilizing the tape as a negotiating tool to obtain what she wanted in her divorce settlement. The unspoken but obvious message was, "Give me what I want or I'll involve you all in the most massive homosexual scandal you can think of."

"We finally realized nothing was off-limits to her. She would stop at nothing to achieve her objectives. Who or what she destroyed in the process didn't even enter into the equation," a senior courtier, who cannot be identified for obvious reasons, told me. "It was then that everyone understood what the Princess of Wales was all about." Unless they were prepared to fight fire with fire, which they were not, she had the winning hand.

One consequence of the *Panorama* programme which Diana did not foresee, however, related, and continues to relate, to her admission that she had had an affair with James Hewitt. Since then, an uncomfortably large segment of the public has believed that he, and not the Prince of Wales, is the natural father of Prince Harry. This is a rumour that has circulated far and wide. It has been reported in the press, newspapers even going as far as suggesting that Prince Harry knows all his friends believe Hewitt is his father, but he isn't bothered by the rumour. It circulates freely in conversation after conversation on several continents, as I have discovered. In my limited capacity as a biographer, I have had to endure enquiry after enquiry as people bring up the subject. Always, they point out the supposed physical resemblance between James and Harry, invariably alighting upon their shared hair colour.

Because I am one of the few people in the public eye who knows, and has known since my youth, how painful it is to have to live with distortions about basic elements of your identity – and how a dignified refusal to acknowledge the distasteful controversy does not actually lessen any pain you feel about the unfairness accompanying such invasiveness – I do not console myself with the thought, as do many writers and journalists, that Harry doesn't care. If he doesn't, good on him. But even if he does, he is certainly not going to let on to you or me or possibly even his closest friends. Some pains are too deep, some violations too private, for people to share them with others, unless some external event or situation forces them to do so.

Therefore, this is as good an opportunity as any to state the facts. Harry is not James Hewitt's son. Any resemblance to Hewitt is purely coincidental (to cynics who wish to lapse into denial mode, this is not a whitewash). Harry's hair colour comes from the Spencers. He looks like his aunt, Diana's sister Sarah. He has the colouring of his Aunt Sarah, whose other siblings, Charles and Jane, share, to a lesser extent than she does, the reddishness that runs in their family. The fact that there is a passing resemblance between Sarah and James Hewitt does not support the theory that Hewitt is Harry's father, simply that Diana, like many other people, fell in love with a man who bears a passing resemblance to a relation.

Moreover, James Hewitt cannot have been Harry's father because he did not know Diana at the time of Harry's conception. James himself has told me, "I met Diana through Hazel West after Harry was born. I am not his father." Indeed, he could not possibly be his father, because he did not know his mother until after his birth.

Such an unforeseen consequence of Diana's admission on *Panorama*, however, was in the future at the time of airing. Before the dust settled in its wake, the Queen swung into action. After consulting with the Prime Minister and the Archbishop of Canterbury, she wrote to both the Prince and Princess of Wales advising them, i.e., ordering them, to divorce. The game was up and Diana had won it, though it was not yet apparent to outsiders.

Not even Diana yet appreciated that she now held all the cards in her hand. As she reeled from the strong and opposing reactions to *Panorama*, she had one source of consolation. She had been nominated Humanitarian of the Year 1995 in the United States. In December, she flew to New York to collect her award from Henry Kissinger at the United Cerebral Palsy Gala Dinner at the Hilton Hotel in New York. Never had Diana looked lovelier. She was a study in style and simplicity, in a stunning and sleek black dress, pearl and diamond earrings and bracelet.

The victory of *Panorama* proved to be Pyrrhic where Hasnat Khan was concerned, however, although it did not seem so at first. Diana's relationship with him continued to grow in strength throughout 1996. She made no secret to certain friends how much in love she was, or that she hoped for a future with Khan. She even visited Pakistan twice, ostensibly as a result of her friendship with Jemima Goldsmith Khan, "but really because she saw herself in the same role, as the wife of a Pakistani," Joseph Sanders said.

Between visits, in November 1996, the *Sunday Mirror* published a detailed account of their romance. Khan was furious, believing that Diana had leaked the story to apply pressure on him to make a commitment that he did not yet feel able to make. She managed to dig herself out of that hole with the support of Joseph Sanders, who covered for her as she convinced Khan that she had had no hand in it. Khan, however, knew that Diana used to speak to the press. According to Joseph, "One evening when she had to give an interview to the *News of the World*, she told Clive Goodman she was at the Brompton Hospital when she was actually at Khan's flat."

In May 1997 Diana returned to Pakistan, once more on a charity visit connected to Imran and Jemima Khan, but "really she was checking out the culture while embracing it." During this last visit, she met Hasnat Khan's family. "They love me and I love them," she said with obvious relief to Joseph Sanders.

By this time, an increasingly desperate Diana was pushing for Khan to propose to her. He would not. According to Joseph, "conflict had arisen over his priorities." She was now facing the same problem she had had with the Prince of Wales. "I admire the work he does," she explained. "He saves so many lives. He makes such a difference to people's lives. It's wonderful. But he has so little time for me. It's become a problem. We're always arguing over it. He puts his work before me. If he really loved me, he'd put me first."

As the rows escalated, Diana started being seen in public with other men. Christopher Whalley took her to lunch and Gulu Lalvani, the Binatone Electronics tycoon, took her to Annabel's, the fashionable members-only nightclub in Berkeley Square named after Jemima Goldsmith's mother, Lady Annabel (another good friend of Diana's). "No one wants me," she complained to Joseph Sanders. "I come with too much baggage. Why can't I find a nice guy who loves me and wants me to love him?"

While Diana's relationship with the handsome Whalley excited jealousy in Khan, her friendship with Gulu Lalvani did not. They were just friends, as he has often said publicly, and his first wife, Vimla, an old friend, has confirmed to me.

By the time Diana set off for her first holiday with the Fayed family in July 1997, her relationship with Khan had been strained to the breaking point. Then her path crossed another attractive man who was more able and willing to give her what she wanted than the worthy Hasnat Khan. Although that would end in tragedy, Khan's feelings for her remained such that he had to hide behind dark glasses at her funeral. He might not have wanted to marry her, but there was little doubt that she had inspired his love.

Seventeen

Diana had mettle. She did not care who her opponent was. Once someone became a potential or actual adversary, she stood her ground, her competitive streak propelling her to victory. This trait was never more evident than when she received the Queen's letter instructing her to divorce. Instead of acknowledging it, Diana ignored it, refusing for over a month to reply to it. In ordinary terms, such a failure to respond was discourtesy, but in royal terms, it was *lèse-majesté*. People simply did not treat the Queen of England like that. But Diana did.

While the Queen was left to stew, Diana sent for Anthony Julius, the lawyer who had achieved a victory of sorts for her against Bryce Taylor. Julius had a reputation for pugnacity. Julius did not care whether he alienated the Palace or not. This combination was just what she needed for negotiations with her husband's side.

While Diana had the Palace cooling its heels, she was once more learning from her sister-in-law Sarah York's mistakes. Sarah had agreed to a settlement that was derisory to say the least. After six years of marriage to the Queen's son, she was getting the paltry sum of £1.4 million in trust for the girls and £600,000 for herself, out of which she was supposed to buy a house, support herself in the style suitable to a royal duchess, and provide a regal lifestyle for two daughters, both Princesses of the Blood Royal. Moreover, she had also agreed to forgo the title of Her Royal Highness. Once the divorce was absolute, she would become Sarah, Duchess of York, losing her precedence as the fourth-ranking Lady in the Kingdom, and taking precedence behind the wives of all the nonroyal dukes.

"They've squeezed Fergie dry," Diana said, resolving that the same thing would not happen to her.

While Diana figured out what ploys and tactics to use to bring the Palace to heel, she took secret delight in the discomfort she was causing "the enemy." "Let them stew," she said, and laughed.

Two months after Diana received the Queen's letter, she swung into action. Once more taking the position that offence is the best form of defence, and that once she made a public assertion it would be difficult and unpopular for the Palace to contradict it, Diana suggested to the Prince of Wales that they meet à deux at St. James's Palace under conditions of amity and confidentiality, neither party to divulge what had been discussed or to use it against the other in negotiations between their lawyers. Not sensing that he was walking into a trap, Charles agreed. As she described the meeting on Wednesday, 28 February 1996 to me, Diana said she would agree to a divorce by mutual consent, but that she wished to continue living at Kensington Palace; to continue having her office at St. James's Palace, where the Prince of Wales had his and also lived; to continue having a say in all areas of the children's lives and to share custody of them; and to continue being known by the title Princess of Wales.

Ever since Diana had read this writer's revelation, in the *Sun* newspaper in January 1994, that the Palace intended to change her title at the time of a divorce, she had been worried. "Princess of Wales is the second-best name title in the world," she had always contended, the implication being that only Queen of England topped it. According to Diana, the word on the grapevine was that they wanted to strip her of the title Princess of Wales, and make her Her Royal Highness Princess Diana. This she did not want. "The Wales name means a lot to me," she said. In Diana's calculations, the fact that "there's never been an English princess who wasn't a Royal Highness" loomed large. Why settle for being HRH Princess Diana when she could hold out for HRH Diana, Princess of Wales?

With her own agenda in mind, Diana left the 28 February meeting with the Prince of Wales, returned to Kensington Palace, and, in defiance of her own conditions of secrecy and confidentiality, issued the following statement: "The Princess of Wales has agreed to Prince Charles's request for a divorce. The Princess will continue to be involved in all decisions relating to the children and will remain at Kensington Palace, with offices at St. James's Palace. The Princess of Wales will retain the title and will be known as Diana, Princess of Wales." The implication, that she would remain a royal highness, was so obvious it did not need to be stated.

Confident that she had outmanoeuvred the Palace on all the most important points, including custody of the children and her title as HRH Diana, Princess of Wales, by issuing news of an agreement when none had been reached, Diana had finally gone too far. The Queen issued a chilling rebuttal stating that she was "most interested" to hear that the Princess had finally agreed to a divorce, but that nothing, including her title, future role, or any aspect of the settlement, had been agreed. In other words, the Queen was publicly saying, "Diana is lying."

Humiliated and distressed that she had been rebuked so publicly, Diana channelled her fury through Anthony Julius, who now began negotiations in earnest. "He had them quaking in their boots," she proudly said. "He doesn't give a toss what they think of him. It's brilliant."

As Anthony Julius and his opposite number, Fiona Shackleton, settled down to the serious business of hammering out an agreement, he made Diana's position clear. She wanted tens of millions of pounds in a lump-sum settlement (£35 million). She intended to retain her privileges. She planned to continue sharing custody of the children. She was not prepared to be downgraded in any way, and, if she did not get what she wanted, she would not accede to a divorce by mutual consent, but would drag out the process, forcing the Prince of Wales to wait the five years that the law requires in the event of a divorce without consent. As the other side knew she also had ammunition which she could use to sully the name of her husband and involve him in a homosexual scandal, in the form of the tape she had made with George Smith, and that she was perfectly capable of using it, indeed was likely to use it, if she did not substantially achieve her aims, they were functioning from the vantage point of weakness.

For his part, Prince Charles had finally learned one lesson when dealing with his shrewd wife. Unless she was made to sign a binding confidentiality agreement, not only would each and every term of the agreement find its way into the public arena, but so too would other potentially destructive weapons such as the George Smith tape. A confidentiality clause, in which Diana would never be able to speak or write about her marriage, her divorce, or anything connected to the Royal Family, therefore became one of the inflexible conditions. The only way to protect himself and the institution to which he had raised her was by silencing her, and the most effective muzzle would be the law.

Sarah York's commercial activities, which were deemed in royal circles to be undignified, despite the relative penury in which she had been left (thereby forcing her to act as she was doing), also provided the Palace with its second learning curve. Another precondition was that Diana would be banned in perpetuity from engaging in any commercial activity. "That cow," Diana said. "Thanks to her, I'm having to give up the right to make money." She bitterly resented the loss of that right, but understood the reasons. In this instance, she was furious with Fergie, not the Palace, although it is arguable that Diana ought to have been shouldering some of the blame of the loss of that privilege, for the circumstances in which Sarah found herself were, in part, of Diana's contrivance as a result of the way she had forced Sarah's hand with regard to the announcement of the separation, and had then used her the canary to check out the poisonous fumes of the chimney of freedom.

Diana's relations with the rest of the Royal Family were hardly heartening. "The Queen had lost all patience with her," Princess Margaret of Hesse and the Rhine said. "So had Prince Philip and the Queen Mother, who viewed Diana as the greatest danger to the monarchy – Wallis Simpson included. They were all heartily fed up with her. But the Queen and Prince Philip kept the channels of communication open and remained civil and understanding in their demeanour. ''

For four months, increasingly tough negotiations took place. "The name Anthony Julius is not one you mention at St. James's Palace or Buck House (Buckingham Palace) unless you want to turn the air blue," Lord Charteris said. "He went about his task with rather too much relish. Let's just say, he's no Fiona Shackleton, who is commonly regarded as bright and tough but ladylike."

Finally, negotiations had progressed to the point where Ms Shackleton was able to list the divorce. The Prince of Wales was the plaintiff, Diana the respondent. Among the points agreed were a lump-sum payment of £17 million; Diana's right to continue living in Kensington Palace; the financing of her office by the Prince of Wales, who moved it out of St. James's Palace into Kensington Palace before the ink was even dry on the deed; and one which caused Diana private grief despite her attempt to put a bright public face upon her loss. The Queen took at face value her

28 February offer of being ready to be known as Diana, Princess of Wales and stripped her of the title Her Royal Highness.

There was a precedent for this, of course. Sarah, Duchess of York, who also bore a royal title, had also been stripped of her royal rank in her divorce that May, establishing the principle that the former wives of Royal Highnesses would no longer hold the style and dignity of Royal Highness themselves. And there was the famous Duchess of Windsor, married but ignominiously disallowed from styling herself Her Royal Highness.

The loss of her royal rank and one of her royal titles – the title which she retained, Princess of Wales, is also royal, so it is both untrue and pejorative to say that Diana, Princess of Wales did not have a royal title – hit Diana hard. "I didn't think they'd do it," she said. "Who ever heard of a Princess of Wales who wasn't a Royal Highness?" Reeling from the shock and trying to save face by announcing that Prince William had talked her into accepting a *fait accompli* she actually had no choice in, Diana was inclined to view her diminution in rank as personally motivated.

Charlotte Pike, the former editor of the royal genealogical bible, the *Almanach de Gotha*, did not believe that it was. "Royal life is governed by precedence. If you're the Princess of Wales you rank before the Duchess of York and after the Queen. There's a sense to it, an inevitability. So basically once you're out, your status is demeaned. There is a public process which might seem like humiliation to the person being divested of their status. You're not in the Court Circular any more. You're not invited to things that you would have been before. To somebody like Diana, that probably appeared to be a personal attack, whereas to somebody like the Queen's Private Secretary, it would be the proper way of dealing with things. I just think the two sides were worlds apart and that was also part of the problem. They were living in two separate worlds."

Although Diana believed that the loss of her royal rank was punitive, the precedent established by Sarah York indicates that this was simply the response to an innovation. Royal ex-wives' new titles were identical to those of any other titled, divorced woman.

Diana, however, did not accept that. "They punished me for not settling for HRH Princess Diana," she said, as if being granted your own royal title were somehow a deprivation. If such an offer had been on the table, and we have Diana's word for it that it was, she was misguided in not accepting it. In trying to manipulate the Prince of Wales the way she did, hoping to extract from him and the Queen every last desire she had, she overreached herself. People have limits, and even Diana's greatest admirers must concede that the way she went about setting up the 28 February meeting, then making her announcement in contravention of her own conditions, was enough to make anyone lose patience. Moreover, what Diana failed to appreciate was that she could not convincingly state that the Queen was punishing her when she had taken Diana at her word and given her the title she had peremptorily and unjustifiably announced to the world had been agreed upon.

The irony of the issue of Diana's title is that had she become HRH Princess Diana, she would thereafter have had her own royal title and would have enjoyed a status as if she had been born a royal princess. She would have been free to marry whomever she pleased, and still retain her royal rank. This was not so with the title Diana, Princess of Wales. The loss of HRH aside, if she had remarried, she would have been going against modern custom if she had retained the title. There is a ruling which states that "a woman of superior rank does not have to relinquish that rank upon marriage to a man of inferior rank," but most modern women choose to be known by their present husband's name, and not their previous, even though there are some notable exceptions, including Maureen, Marchioness of Dufferin and Ava (first husband's title despite three marriages) and Diana's own stepmother Raine, Countess Spencer (whose last husband's name is Jean-François de Chambrun).

Diana's reaction to the loss of her royal rank was swift. She immediately announced that she was severing her links, mostly as patron, with more than one hundred charities, including the Red Cross and Help the Aged. According to Joseph Sanders, "Jane (Atkinson, her press relations advisor) strongly advised her not to. She said, It will look like pique. You'll look spiteful. Don't do it.' Diana did it nevertheless. When her mind was made up, it was made up. You could advise her till you were blue in the face. She'd do exactly as she pleased."

Although Diana did receive criticism for what seemed like a spiteful act, the fact is, now that she was no longer a proper member of the Royal Family, she had to shed some of her workload if she were to have her own life. Being royal is hard work, contrary to popular belief. Four, sometimes five, days a week, most royals work from early every morning till late every night, involved in charity work or state duties. Long after the average person is at home relaxing, the royals are out, attending evening functions and getting home when most of us are in bed. By nine o'clock the following morning, the grind has started again—and that's without counting the time it takes to get from their residence to the place of engagement, which can be halfway across the country. While the labour might not be arduous, the hours are long, the pressure to perform intense. It is no wonder Diana was so keen to divest herself of that load.

"Charity is my work," Diana said. Not being lazy, and being motivated spiritually, she retained links with the five charities which most appealed to her: the National AIDS Trust, Centrepoint (the homeless charity), the Royal Marsden NHS Trust (Britain's foremost cancer hospital), the Great Ormond Street Children's Hospital and the Leprosy Mission. She also remained patron of the English National Ballet.

This spring-cleaning had a dramatic effect upon Diana's life. As she returned to public life, she was doing so on her terms. Gone were the days when she would be bogged down in meetings and public duties from early in the morning till late at night. Now, she gave herself time and space to grow into her own life. She still made hospital and homeless visits; still attended high-profile functions associated with her causes; still helped raise funds. However, her work took up only a fraction of her time.

As Diana adjusted to her new status as divorcee, she found herself freer than she had intended to be. She still rose at seven, ate breakfast, made herself up and put on leggings or shorts and a sweat shirt, and headed for the Harbour Club, where she did her day's workout. Returning to Kensington Palace, she met her hairdresser, who still did her hair while she chatted to friends on the telephone and arranged her day.

Diana's days were now mostly filled with the therapists whose skills she called upon to help her overcome her illnesses. Despite prodigious energy, she perpetually felt tired, and had for years. To counter it, she availed herself of the services of Chryssie Fitzgerald, the colonic irrigator, reflexologist and healer. She also regularly and frequently saw Susie Orbach, her psychotherapist, whom she credited with "empowering her." She consulted herbalist Eilleen Whittaker, telling her, as she told all the others, "You're the reason I'm so healthy these days." In addition, the spiritual healer Simone Simmons visited Diana once a week during the last three years of her life at Kensington Palace. And Diana replaced Oonagh Toffolo as her acupuncturist with Dr Lily Hua Yu in January 1996.

Dr Hua Yu worked from the Acu Medic Clinic in Camden, north London. Diana had a standing Thursday appointment. According to the centre's director, Professor Benny Mei, "She felt at home here. Sometimes she would book the whole of the top floor with a group of her friends and they would shout and laugh at each other as their treatment was being done."

Diana viewed Dr Hua Yu as a "miracle worker" because she was able to relieve much of the congenital stress which had perturbed her even as a schoolgirl. The doctor's diagnosis of Diana's health problems was that they were stress-related and a residual effect of the bulimia from which she had suffered for years. She frequently inserted minuscule needles into Diana's ear, where they remained for extended periods. In May 1997, for instance, she put four needles into zones in the ear related to mental activity, the liver, the spleen, and the heart. In June, Diana flew to New York to attend a reception before the sale of her dresses. In her ear were the four minute instruments of acupuncture.

According to Dr Hua Yu, Diana, who had suffered from insomnia even while at school (hence the need to dance for hours after lights-out), had been taking sleeping tablets for five years before coming to see her. Despite this, she continued to suffer from such severe insomnia that she was never able to get a full night's rest. This exacerbated her chronic fatigue, which Dr Hua Yu countered by prescribing ganoderma lucidum. According to the doctor, once she "restored the Princess's inner balance, she no longer needed sleeping tablets."

Dr Hua Yu also had the knack of curing jet lag, which was a considerable boon to someone like Diana, who was now crisscrossing the world regularly. She became such a devotee that she usually went straight to the Acu Medic Clinic from the airport.

Enjoying the benefits she received from Dr Hua Yu's ministrations, Diana devotedly attended the clinic every Thursday. She also built up a warm and touching relationship with Dr Hua Yu. This was typical of Diana, who was more generous than the average royal or celebrity. As Nicky Haslam, the interior designer who was a friend, told me, "She never turned up empty-handed." For example, on 24 June 1997, in gratitude to Dr Hua Yu for curing her jet lag, Diana sent one of the glossy catalogues for the auction of her dress collection with these words, "Dearest Dr Lily. Lots of love from Diana."

Despite the many other forms of therapy that took up some of her time, along with exercising, lunching with friends, or visiting them, Diana did not have enough to do. She was not one for solitary activities. Her whole life revolved around people. Her relationship with the busy surgeon Hasnat Khan was not as all-embracing as she wished. He was constantly working, and while she dreamed of a life with him, the fact is, they were even more hopelessly unsuited for the long haul than she and the Prince of Wales had been.

Another factor that increased Diana's sense of isolation was that she was unable to fulfill the plans she had for herself professionally. As Michael Gibbins, her last private secretary, told Help the Aged when they approached her to reconsider them, "She's only doing high-profile things that get maximum publicity from now on." While this attitude might have seemed vain to some, the Princess understood the power of her fame, the effect it could have, and the usefulness of rationalizing her efforts so that she could expend the minimum of energy and achieve the maximum result.

As Diana saw it, she was uniquely placed to be a roving ambassador for Britain. With her style, fame and marketability, she could focus the world's attention on any cause she became affiliated with. The only problem was, when she approached John Major, the Conservative Prime Minister, and Douglas Hurd, the Foreign Secretary, she was rebuffed because Buckingham Palace regarded her ideas as being more suitable for execution by the Prince of Wales than by his ex-wife.

The chickens were coming home to roost. For years Diana had been deliberately upstaging the Prince. While they were still married and sharing an office, she was notorious for finding out when he had a major speech. She would then schedule some activity or wear an outfit that would grab the headlines away from him. On one infamous occasion, when they were sharing an official engagement, Charles sat down to play the cello. While he was tuning up, Diana crept up behind him, sat down at the piano and played the opening bars of Rachmaninoff's Piano Concerto No. 3. As all cameras swung from him to her, her expression was wreathed in satisfaction, while his was a study in humiliation and suppressed anger. She even allowed her competitive spirit to run riot on the evening the Prince's interview with Jonathan Dimbleby was being aired on television. Despite the fact that Charles's admission of adultery was the major news story of the day, Diana managed to swipe some of his coverage by turning up at a reception at the Serpentine Gallery in an exotic black Christina Stambolian dress, slashed on one side to within inches of her thigh, and looking like a billion dollars.

"People say the Prince of Wales was jealous of Diana's popularity. That's not, strictly speaking, true," Princess Margaret of Hesse and the Rhine said. "When they were first married, he was as perplexed as she was by the extremes of interest the public and the press took in her. But he was her greatest supporter. She herself used to concede that all she learned, she learned from him. She used to mimic him. I suppose no one likes his thunder being stolen, and the Prince must have had mixed feelings as her popularity continued to eclipse his. I think he was proud of her but also somewhat irritated by the reaction of the press. It wasn't a problem, though, until, well, things turned sour, when the marriage started to go wrong. The Princess was a great one for taunting him. She didn't limit herself to doing it in private either. She did it in public as well. She delighted in scoring points against him, in making him and the rest of the world know that she was of greater public interest than he was. What he objected to was her motivation. There was a sense of vindictiveness about it that stuck in the throat. There was also the more serious element that she was undermining his work. For instance, he'd spend weeks preparing a major speech on some matter of national interest and she would come or turn up at her own engagement with cleavage everywhere so that the press would focus on her and ignore him."

Finally able to remove the platform of royalty from the competitive Princess, the Palace hoped that the pendulum of public attention would swing back from the personalities of the Prince and Princess of Wales to the work the heir to the throne was doing. Diana, of course, had other ideas. Resourceful as ever, she took matters into her own hands once she realized that she had been frozen out by British officialdom. If she could not have a platform in Britain, she would create an international one instead.

Earlier, in 1996, Diana had visited Lahore, to stay with Jemima and Imran Khan and raise funds for – and the profile of – the charitable Shaukat Khanum Memorial Cancer Hospital the cricketer had founded in memory of his mother, who died of that disease. This visit had been an outstanding success, focusing attention on that hospital, on Imran Khan, who soon threw his hat into the political ring and announced that he was running for president, and on Diana herself, who looked wonderful in the exotic shalwar kameez couture outfits she commissioned from Catherine Walker.

Armed with the experience of receiving a rapturous reception in foreign parts, and with the British and world press as attentive towards her as if she were still a fully fledged member of the Royal Family, Diana now set about creating her own platform. She accepted invitations for foreign engagements, or organized them herself when no invitations were forthcoming. In July, for instance, a glamorous Diana once more turned up to support her friends the Khans in their efforts to raise money for the Shaukat Khanum Hospital. This time, she did not even need to leave Britain to derive the benefits of her foreign connections. The banquet took place at the Dorchester. The press attention was as outstanding as ever.

So, stymied in her own country, Diana's view was now directed abroad. In September, for instance, she chose to attend the funeral in Greece of Yannis Kaliviotis, a twenty-seven-year-old student she had met on her visits to the Brompton Hospital, with Susie Kassem, a fellow hospital visitor and friend. She was able to give comfort to the parents, who were moved that someone of the stature of the Princess of Wales would bother to attend their daughter's funeral. She also was scoring a point against the Royal Family, who, as a matter of protocol, usually attend funerals only of other royals, while generating column inches which gratified the part of her personality that always yearned for outside reassurance.

As Diana's new path gained her approbation, she became a veritable hive of activity. No sooner was she back in Britain than she flew to Washington to attend a fund-raiser for the Nina Hyde Center for Breast Cancer Research. From Washington, Diana flew to Chicago to visit Northwestern Memorial Hospital. Once more, her presence served the dual purpose of focusing public attention on the cause she was supporting and feeding her need for public approval. This was also the case when she crossed the world to attend a dinner in aid of the Victor Chang Cardiac Research Institute in Sydney.

As Diana had suspected, her fame and her cachet were sought after everywhere. She was now getting a glimpse of a far more dynamic and intriguing world than that of the Sloaney set she had been raised in or the royal set she had married into. Whether a tycoon like Hong Kong-based David Tang, an ambassadress like Lucia Flecha de Lima, a photographer like Patrick Demarchelier, or the Anglo-French Sir James Goldsmith's exotic harem of wives, mistresses and children, Diana's new circle of friends had one foot in a foreign camp, and were all the more interesting and open-minded for that. She, who was now an international icon, was finding her niche away from the land of her birth.

Eighteen

Now that she was single, and free of the shackles and restraints of royalty, Diana was creating the sort of life she wanted. This she did with the courage, resolve and creativity which she possessed in splendid measure, and which is an aspect of her character seldom given the credit it deserves.

In the final months of her life, after years of turbulence and acrimony, hostility and controversy, illness and anguish, Diana had come into her own. Her sons, the one constant, were growing into handsome and charming young men, whose unaffected enjoyment of ordinary pleasures she was rightly given – and took – credit for. Her relationship with her ex-husband had improved dramatically. And through her campaign for the victims of land mines and her nomination as Humanitarian of the Year in December 1995, she had elevated her position, removing much of the dross with which the controversies surrounding her divorce had polluted it.

Diana had never felt better. "I'm over the worst," she told me and many of her friends, exulting in a state of good health she had not enjoyed since her teenage years.

The bloom of well-being added luster to a Princess who looked more beautiful than she had ever done before. Coming into her own was reflected, not only in the vibrantly healthy glow she now had, but in a sense of style that was superb. Although Diana had always dressed well, gone was the conservative Princess look. In its place was the pared-down, sleek, elegant woman of purpose who looked as comfortable with Tom Cruise and Katharine Graham, publisher of the *Washington Post*, as she did with European royalty or on the front cover of *Vogue*.

With her profile raised, especially in the United States, by her travels, it was hardly surprising that the Princess would gain the recognition she cherished. In December 1996 she repeated her previous year's coup and crossed the Atlantic to attend yet another high-profile American event as guest of honour. This time it was the ball benefiting the Costume Institute of the Metropolitan Museum of Art. Her choice of dress showed the extent of her growth, from *jeune fille* aristocrat through conventional princess to confident *styliste par excellence*. She chose a figure-hugging royal-blue evening dress with a nightgown effect created especially for her by John Galliano of Dior. Set off with the pearl, diamond and blue sapphire choker originally given to her by Queen Elizabeth the Queen Mother, the attire was inappropriate for an ordinary princess, but was perfect for the woman who was now both flesh and myth.

By this time, Diana fully appreciated how much in her interest it was to re-establish amicability in her dealings with St. James's and Buckingham palaces. She therefore started to be more co-operative with the Prince of Wales when arranging their children's schedules. She stopped leaking information detrimental to him or the Royal Family. When they encountered one another, for instance at Eton for Prince William's carol service in December 1996, she even kissed the Prince of Wales in greeting, to his and all onlookers' consternation. No longer the surly, awkward Diana who was able to find fault even with compliments, she was rewarded by her ex-husband's commenting upon how good her legs were looking.

The Prince of Wales had long hoped that, if he did not retaliate when Diana attacked him, they could settle down to a civilized, hopefully amicable, relationship. His tactic was based not only upon his natural tendency towards nonconfrontation, but also upon the assessment that he and Diana would have to rub along together for their natural life spans, which could well prove to be another forty or so years. It therefore made sense for them to establish some sort of *rapprochement*. Now, as she waved the olive branch, he met her halfway. Soon, they were floating the possibility of going on a joint official engagement, to be tied in with the decommissioning of the royal yacht *Britannia*, and he was hearing from the children and unexpected sources that she had made favourable comments about him. "He was pleased beyond measure to see his years of patience finally rewarded," Lady Sarah Spencer-Churchill said. "It had taken over sixteen years, but he was once more getting glimpses of the girl he had first been attracted to. The jolly, easygoing, co-operative Lady Diana, before illness overtook her and distorted her basic personality."

Diana's change in attitude "was a supreme relief to them (the Royal Family)," Princess Margaret of Hesse and the Rhine said. "You must remember they had taken a compassionate stance from the very beginning of the problems, until the Morton book, *Panorama* and her other antics forced them to take a firmer line." Delighted that harmony was being re-established, they rewarded Diana in a most meaningful way. They gave her permission to travel on behalf of the Red Cross.

Upon returning home from wowing the New York fashion elite in December 1996, Diana had got in touch with Mike Whitlam, Director General of the British Red Cross. Notwithstanding her resignation from that charity, she asked him if there were any international projects she could help with. When they met, he told her she was ideally situated to turn the public's mind to the Red Cross Anti-Personnel Land Mine Campaign, which had been in effect for some time. This was a two-pronged effort. On the one hand, the Red Cross was trying to get land mines cleaned up from places such as Angola and Bosnia, where they cause such damage to the civilian population now that the wars had ended. On the other hand, the Red Cross was also campaigning for a ban on land mines altogether, which the Ottawa Treaty in 1997 was intended to seal.

This sort of campaign was indeed ideally suited for Diana. She readily agreed to help, but first permission had to be gained from official sources for her involvement to be allowed. Unlike many other of her ideas, which were blocked while she was spearheading the War of the Waleses, this request was granted and arrangements were swiftly made by the Red Cross and the Princess of Wales's office for a fund-raiser and for a visit to Angola in January 1997.

As Mike Whitlam told it, Diana was co-operation itself. On the flight over, she even asked his advice on what clothes to wear, anxious that her attire not detract from the working nature of her visit. Of course, she had already packed, but he was suitably flattered when she wore the clothes they had conferred about (and which her unfailing instinct for appropriate attire had directed her to bring from Britain): simple blouses, cotton trousers, flat shoes.

There is no doubt that Diana's involvement with the anti-land mine campaign raised its profile considerably and made easier the final push in, what had been for the Red Cross, a long campaign. By this time Diana was the consummate performer in the most positive meaning of the word. With her unique mixture of charm, grace, compassion, simplicity, camera awareness and vanity, during her four-day visit she provided the assembled media with photograph after photograph that was potent, heart-rending, beautiful, expressive and, above all, usable for publication. The counterpoint of the beautiful, immaculately presented Princess of Wales sitting on a wall with and touching the face of a young Angolan girl whose leg had been blown off by a land mine as she walked about her everyday business was just what the Red Cross needed to get its message across. Nor was either Diana or the Red Cross in danger of alienating the arms manufacturers' vested interests, which came up with a plan whereby the armaments industry could make as much money cleaning up the mines as they could make in future selling new ones. It was an inspired denouement for an inspiring project.

Inevitably, anyone as busy and open to possibilities as Diana was bound to run into squalls when even the most cautious and closed-off do so as well. No sooner was the Princess back in London than she became involved in two controversies. The first involved certain Tory MPs, who were concerned that her pronouncements in favour of the anti-land mine campaign could adversely affect Britain's vast armaments industry. She was accused of being a "loose cannon" and a "self-publicist" who would go anywhere and promote any cause to get her name in the newspapers. Her detractors seemed not to be aware that she could not have left the country without the permission of the Queen and the Government.

Diana's response to this criticism was disarming and truthful. "I was only trying to help," she said. While accusations of self-promotion and vanity sometimes did undoubtedly contain a kernel of truth, the fact remained that the Princess of Wales was a complex individual who did genuinely have a big heart and profound humanitarian instincts. Only the most bigoted of her detractors could fail to see that, but Diana had not helped her case by making remarks implying that the Government's track record was not as good as the opposition Labour Party's stand on the issue.

No sooner had that mini-storm blown over than another burst upon Diana. This one involved one of her new international friends, Gianni

Versace. Elton John, a good friend of the Italian designer as well as the Duke and Duchess of York, had organized a plan for her to write a foreword for Versace's coffee-table book, *Rock & Royalty*. He had also obtained her agreement that she would attend the book's launch at a fund-raising dinner for his Elton John's AIDS Foundation on 18 February. More than $400,000 worth of tickets had been sold by 10 February, when Diana saw an advance copy of the book. Photographs of nude males were juxtaposed with those of royals, including the Queen. Although not tasteless in contemporary terms, the book did stretch the boundaries of old-fashioned sensibilities. Diana, already nervous of the shakiness of her position with the Royal Family, and intent on building bridges with them now that there was nothing more to be gained from hostilities with them, promptly severed her links with the book and the gala. "I am extremely concerned that the book may cause offence to members of the Royal Family," she said in a statement. "For this reason I have asked for my foreword to be withdrawn from the book, and I will not attend the dinner on February 18, which is intended to mark the book's launch."

This was an unmitigated crisis, from Gianni Versace's and Elton John's point of view, as it would have been from any other charity fundraisers', and Diana, being experienced by now with the ways of the charity world, must have known this. Once she pulled out, other guests were bound to follow suit. Versace and John therefore had no choice but to cancel the gala or face the odium of a public rout. Although the designer had the grace to make good the lost revenue to Elton John's AIDS Foundation, the Versace camp were incensed and the pop singer stopped speaking to Diana. They had no doubt she could easily have weathered the storm by asserting that the book was artistic, which it was.

The Princess, however, felt fully justified. As far as she was concerned, there was more at stake here than an AIDS benefit. Indeed, this was yet another opportunity to improve further relations with the Royal Family. By behaving as she had, Diana did indeed accomplish her goal, for her actions sent a clear message that she was now being co-operative and was respecting royal rules of conduct. In doing so, she continued her realignment *vis-à-vis* the powers-that-be. This was of crucial importance to her. The terms of her divorce restricted her freedom to leave the country, and if she intended to develop her international platform for humanitarian work further, she would need the Queen's consent.

As Diana was scoring points at the Palace with her co-operativeness and handling of the Versace affair, she honoured the second part of her commitment to the Red Cross. She attended as guest of honour the gala première of Richard Attenborough's new film *In Love & War*, to raise funds for that organization. Prior to the film, a shortened version of the BBC documentary of her visit to Angola, and of the Red Cross land mines campaign, was shown. Although Diana was still being prevented from realizing her wish of becoming an official roving ambassador for Britain, she was being allowed to become one, out of the country, on behalf of her causes. The *rapprochement* with the Prince of Wales and with the Palace, not to mention the 'men in grey suits', was paying dividends indeed. All she needed to do was remain 'on side,' and she could pursue her interests and her life without interruption or interference. In the process, she would also be establishing herself as an ambassador of sorts, thereby gaining the role she had stated on *Panorama* she wished to have.

With the decks cleared for constructiveness, Diana dedicated the rest of February to her next high-profile project: the sale of a collection of her clothes at Christie's in New York, in aid of the British charities AIDS Crisis Trust and the Royal Marsden Hospital's Cancer Fund, and the American ones, the Harvard AIDS Institute and the Evelyn H. Lauder Breast Cancer Center at Memorial-Sloan Kettering. Princess Margaret's ex-husband, Lord Snowdon, was commissioned to photograph her in some of the dresses, after which Diana and Lord Hindlip, Christie's chairman, unleashed their public-relations expertise, taking the decision to print 170 catalogues autographed by Diana for sale at $2,000 each, and another 5,250 unsigned for $265 each. There were parties in both London and New York to promote the event and the public's interest in it, and in June Diana flew to New York, acupuncture needles in her ears, for a reception preceding the sale.

By a happy coincidence, from Diana's point of view, the Conservative Government had been voted out of power the month before. Although she had enjoyed excellent relations with both John Major, the Prime Minister, and Douglas Hurd, the Foreign Secretary, there was so much "history" there that the backbench Members of Parliament often misread her burgeoning relationship with officialdom. A clean start with a new government and new MPs was preferable.

Especially a government headed, as the new one was, by the husband of Cherie Booth Blair, Queen's Counsel and renowned feminist and supporter of victims.

By another of those happy coincidences which now seemed to be cropping up with such regularity, as Diana was relaunching her harmonious and newly energized self on independent seas, she had the invaluable help of Maggie Rae, one of her legal advisors during her divorce, who was the former flatmate and good friend of the Prime Minister's eminent barrister wife. Through Maggie Rae, Diana was able to develop a relationship with Cherie and Tony Blair that would otherwise have been more difficult to achieve.

The Prime Minister immediately saw the uses to which his Government could put the Princess of Wales's extraordinary combination of gifts, if she continued to enjoy good relations with the Royal Family. A consummate politician, Blair understood on practical as well as ethical grounds the desirability of having Diana return, if only in part, to the fold. Blair, as well as his wife, is not only a highly successful worldly practitioner but also a Christian fundamentalist whose ethical stance is that he must help others in pursuit of their rights and freedoms. Diana was therefore given hope that her ambassadorial role might yet transmogrify, but she was in no doubt that it rested upon her good behaviour, especially because the most powerful member of the new Government, the Minister Without Portfolio, Peter Mandelson, was a close friend and advisor of the Prince of Wales. Even this, though, had its reassuring element. As Diana herself knew only too well, Blair would not have been making the sounds Diana said he was, without the sanction of the Prince of Wales. This was therefore yet more proof that her bridge-building was working.

Diana, however, was not relying upon unspoken promises for the future. She had made sure her present was filled with the activities that would provide her with the responses she required. On 22 May she flew to Lahore on Sir James Goldsmith's private jet for a two-day visit to his son-in-law Imran Khan's cancer hospital. While there, Diana made the time to visit Hasnat Khan's parents and other relations. Unused to the ways of the press, his aunt Ghasia and cousin Naeem Tareen then made unguarded comments, the former saying "Oh, my nephew and the Princess are in the throes of an Eastern love affair," and the latter asserting, "She wants to marry Hasnat. They are in love." Even though his parents were prompted into issuing denials, the fact is, Diana did wish to marry him, as she told many friends, including Joseph Sanders.

From Pakistan, Diana flew back to London to catch up on her personal life, address a meeting for the anti-land mine campaign, see her children, and prepare for her next trip. This was undoubtedly a boon time for the Princess, who was coming into her own as never before. Free of the restrictions under which she had chafed when a full-fledged member of the Royal Family, she gained strength from the success she was encountering on the world stage, and was healthier than ever, her bulimia under control, her depression at bay, the signs of what some called her paranoid and schizoid behaviour taking a welcome retreat into the background.

On 16 June, Diana was back in the United States to attend the eightieth-birthday celebrations of Katharine Graham, the *Washington Post*'s publisher. The following day, she spoke movingly at an outdoor news conference with Elizabeth Dole, president of the American Red Cross, about the "deadly legacy of 15 million land mines scattered around a country with 10 million people," proclaiming, "I am committed to supporting in whatever way I can the international campaign to outlaw these dreadful weapons."

That evening, Diana pulled out all the stops to look drop-dead gorgeous in a beaded red evening dress as she attended a dinner for 400 also attended by Elizabeth Dole and the British Ambassador, John Kerr, to raise funds for the Red Cross. Once more she was less like a traditional princess and more a combination of a glamorous movie queen of the past fused with a royal princess of the future. The event raised $600,000 to buy prostheses and finance rehabilitative programmes for land mine victims.

Although Diana was visiting Washington in a private capacity, not as an official representative of the British nation, she nevertheless reaped the rewards of her many recent charitable enterprises in the United States, as well as her harmonious relations with Buckingham and St. James's palaces. The result was that she was treated seriously enough to warrant a breakfast meeting with Hillary Clinton at the White House and a visit to Bethesda Naval Hospital, to meet a Brazilian land mine victim whose foot had been blown off on a cleaning-up exercise on the border of Nicaragua and Honduras. She had every reason to hope that she might one day take the leap and become an official representative of Britain again.

Diana returned to London for a few days to see William and Harry and ran right into another squall. She took the boys to the Odeon Kensington, her neighbourhood cinema, to see *The Devil's Own*, a pro-IRA movie from which children under fifteen were prohibited. When word got out, Diana was roundly criticized in the British media. Pleading that she did not know the subject matter of the film, she was then lambasted for using her rank to talk the cinema authorities into letting her in with her underage younger son.

Glad to leave that squabble behind, Diana boarded a Concorde for New York to honour a commitment to Mother Teresa, who greeted her at her Bronx AIDS hospice and took her on a tour, after which they posed outside for photographers.

In the peculiar juxtaposition of deprivation and privilege that Diana had woven into the unique fabric of her life, she left Mother Teresa's hospice to join the British editors Anna Wintour, of *Vogue*, and Tina Brown, of *The New Yorker*, for lunch at New York's chic Four Seasons restaurant. That evening, as if the polarities needed any more highlighting, Diana attended an exclusive preview party hosted by Lord Hindlip of Christie's. This was to stimulate interest in the sale of her dresses, which were due to be auctioned the following day. In a display of the good taste for which she was rightly known, Diana departed for London the following day, while the auction was underway. The seventy-nine dresses raised $3.26 million.

Diana returned to London for her thirty-sixth, and last, birthday. She celebrated it as the guest of honour at a ball at the Tate Gallery with 550 guests, who were not her personal guests, but had paid to attend yet another of the fund-raisers which had become such a feature of her life. Touchingly, her brother, Charles, whom she had flown to see a few months earlier at his new home in South Africa, was there, their differences papered over. This was the last time he would see the sister who had "mothered" him when they were children, left "motherless" in the wake of their parents' acrimonious divorce, and who had frozen him out when he reneged on his offer of a house on the Althorp Estate.

In recognition of the progress the Princess of Wales had made, both within herself and in the more public spaces of her life, Tony Blair asked her and William and Harry down to Chequers, the Prime Minister's official rural residence, left by Sir Winston Churchill to the nation, for a private Sunday lunch *en famille*. Although the Prime Minister made no official approaches, nor gave any hints, Diana did say that she believed Blair would know how to use her. "He's told me he wants me to go on some missions," she confided to Tina Brown, a sentiment he confirmed the following month when he stated that Diana had unique talents and that they should be utilized.

Diana, however, was not pinning everything on hope. Not only had she now established the basis for an international forum which required minimal involvement with and approval from the British authorities, but she was also seeking to extend her interests, to diversify her activities. Although specifically banned from any activity which enriched her commercially, she could nevertheless engage in fund-raising. Resourceful and inventive as ever, she put her imagination to good use and came up with many irons to keep her fire warm. The first was her autobiography, which she planned to write for Random House. Irony of ironies, she intended to write the exact book that I had originally suggested to her that we do as a fund-raiser. Banned as she was from revealing in print anything private about the Royal Family, she intended to focus on her charity work, slipping in sufficient personal details to make the book salesworthy. Contracts had already been drawn up and an advance (allegedly $500,000) was on the table. The editor was supposed to have been Paul Sidey, Random House's gifted senior editor, and an old friend of mine, who confirmed to me, "Yes, I was going to work with her and edit the book." Sadly, the events of 31 August intervened, scuppering that plan.

There were other, previously unreported fund-raising ideas which Diana also had on the boil. Riccardo Mazzuchelli, Ivana Trump's ex-husband who had helped her make a success of the House of Ivana, and whose first wife Stella used to sit with me on Pida Ripley's United Nations Association's fundraising committees in the 1970s, told me, "I had lunch with Diana at Mossiman's (a chic dining club in Belgravia) a few weeks before she died. We discussed the possibility of setting up a House of Diana to sell clothes and jewellery, mostly on television to raise funds for her charities. We arranged to meet at the end of summer to progress the idea."

There was yet another innovative idea the Princess of Wales was toying with. For a year she had been in negotiations by telephone with Kevin Costner to play herself in a sequel to *The Bodyguard,* the movie which originally starred Whitney Houston and himself. A special thirty pages of script for her character had been sent to her for her consideration, and she had even dined with studio bosses at Warner Brothers. When she died, she was still considering whether to go ahead with the film.

If the prospect of Diana appearing on the screen seems shocking, it should not be. There are ample precedents of princesses who sought acting careers. Princess Soraya, the ex-Queen of Iran; Lee, Princess Stanislaus Radziwill, Jackie Kennedy Onassis's sister; and Princess Ira von Furstenburg, had all attempted the leap from reality to fantasy, albeit without success. While it is pleasant to think Diana might have been more successful, there was no prospect of her actually pursuing a career as an actress. Such forays as there would have been would have had to be strictly limited to fund-raising endeavours under the terms of her divorce.

After her death, when word of the film negotiations leaked out, Kevin Costner was unfairly suspected of fancifulness. This is neither true nor fair. Not only is Costner's connection to Diana traceable – he is a friend of David Tang, who is a friend of the Duke and Duchess of York and a friend of Diana – but Sarah York herself has said, "It's all true."

In summer 1997, it seemed as if Diana, Princess of Wales had the world at her feet. She even had the prospect of a memorable summer holiday with William and Harry. This was important to her. Since the separation, Diana, like many former spouses of richer and more powerful partners, had found it increasingly hard going to provide her sons with the opportunities Charles had at hand. Not only did he have the royal estates, with the myriad country activities which William and Harry loved, but he also had an army of royal relations and billionaire friends, such as John Latsis, to provide their own palaces or yachts and private planes.

At the beginning of June, in her capacity as patron of the English National Ballet, Diana had attended the première of that company's production of *Swan Lake* at the Royal Albert Hall. Afterwards, there was a dinner at the Churchill Hotel in Portman Square. Diana was seated beside Mohamed Al Fayed, the flagship of whose business interests, Harrods, was sponsoring the season. He was an old friend of her late father and stepmother, Raine, who worked for Harrods. When he asked Diana what she was doing for the summer, and she replied nothing, he suggested that she and the boys join his wife and children at their property near St. Tropez. They would have their own guest cottage and would be free to come and go as they pleased. If they wished to spend time with the Fayed family, they could do so. If they chose to be on their own, they would have the freedom to do that. Moreover, there would be amusing toys for the boys. Fayed had recently taken delivery of the 140-foot powerboat *Jonikal*. Not only would they have that at their disposal, but they would also have the motorboats, jet-skis and other paraphernalia that are the ordinary accessories of such craft. Diana thanked Fayed for his invitation and said she would get back to him.

Diana had good reason to be captivated by Fayed's invitation. Not only had she known him through her father for years, but her stepmother was an admirer of the Egyptian-born businessman. Raine and Diana, who had once been sworn enemies, were now fast friends. This was largely owing to two disparate factors. Diana had long been aware that Prince Philip and Prince Charles were both of the opinion that, as the Duke of Edinburgh put it, "Raine is a woman who knows how to get things done." Moreover, as her divorce battle with her husband had intensified, Diana had become alienated from various members of her family, including her middle sister Jane, her brother, Charles, and her mother. She had also become friendlier with Mohamed Al Fayed, identifying with this man who considered himself a victim of an uncaring establishment. Fayed, in turn, had appointed Raine a nonexecutive director of Harrods, and was instrumental in fostering relations between his grand employee and her even-grander stepdaughter. Appreciating for the first time in her life just how difficult her family had been towards Raine, and understanding how much she could benefit from the guidance of someone with Raine's worldliness and sophistication, Diana waved the olive branch at her stepmother and suggested getting together for lunch. To her credit, Raine decided to let bygones be bygones, and the two women changed the structure of their old relationship beyond recognition.

"She was closer to Raine at the end than she was to her mother," Joseph Sanders said. Gone were the previous two decades of bitterness, wiped clean by a forgiving Raine, who, it must be said, had much to forgive. Aside from the innumerable petty humiliations and hostilities foisted upon her by her four stepchildren, there had been some major ones, such as Charles and Diana crushing Raine's belongings into black plastic bin liners and hurling them out the upstairs windows at Althorp House right after their father died. Or Diana pushing Raine down a flight of stairs just before her sixtieth birthday party at Althorp and retorting, when told that she could have killed her, "Who's going to charge the Princess of Wales with murder?" Nevertheless, Raine and Diana had become close in the final couple of years. "Raine's wise," Diana said. "She gets results." Diana appreciated this, especially as she finalized her divorce and launched herself as a single woman. They often talked and met, and Diana used Raine as a sounding board for ideas as well as for advice.

"It was Raine who talked up what a good time Diana would have" if she accepted Mohamed Fayed's invitation, Joseph Sanders said Diana told him. "She was all for it. She told Diana she'd have the time of her life." Of course, Raine had no idea at the time what the eventual consequences of this invitation would be. "It's something of a sore point with her. She feels responsible for what happened."

Encouraged by Raine, Diana telephoned Mohamed Al Fayed to accept his invitation. They made plans for her to fly out to Nice Airport on 11 July with Prince William and Prince Harry, to stay with the Fayed family at their eight-acre property near St. Tropez on the Cote d'Azur. While Mohamed, his wife, Heini, and their four children would stay in the main house, Diana and her sons would have the guest cottage. Unknown to Diana, she was making more than plans for a summer holiday. She was reaching out from one world to another, in the literal as well as the figurative senses.

Diana was about to meet her destiny.

Nineteen

Diana's choice of host was not as earth-shattering as it has been made out to be. While it is true that Mohamed Al Fayed was even then a controversial figure upon the British commercial stage, he was not, at the time Diana accepted his invitation, the pariah certain segments of the press – and Fayed himself since Diana's death – have made him out to be. For years Harrods had sponsored the Windsor Horse Show, with Mohamed Al Fayed *in situ* beside the Queen playing "host" to the monarch. This is not a privilege he would have been allowed had he been deemed beyond the pale. No one, of course, was nominating him for sainthood, but then, he was neither an imam nor a priest.

Although Fayed's application for British citizenship had been denied by the Tory Government, this refusal had been linked to the Department of Trade and Industry's report on his takeover of the House of Fraser, Harrods' parent company. In it, he had been roundly criticized for having fabricated a grand background although his antecedents in Egypt were simple; for having stated that he came from a family of means when they were not; and for claiming that he was rich, when the money to buy Harrods had reputedly come from the Sultan of Brunei. The Sultan, incidentally, denied having provided Fayed with the backing. In the world of high finance, the fact that someone tells a few fibs about his background hardly constitutes an offence so serious that he will thereafter be deprived of the opportunity to become the British citizen he has long yearned to be. As the Conservative Government refused application after application, always failing to provide a reason why he was denied citizenship, he actually began to acquire sympathizers. Was the British

Establishment so hypocritical, or was there some more sinister motive afoot? If it was sinister, was it prejudice against Fayed because of his racial origins, as he seemed to believe and started to say, or did the Home Office know something that the general public did not?

Whether pro- or anti-Fayed, everyone was agreed that the Pharaoh, as he is known in certain quarters, was a colourful character. From the time he took over Harrods, he had been involved in a public feud with Tiny Rowland, the Lonrho tycoon and former business associate of the Hon. Sir Angus Ogilvy, Princess Alexandra's husband and the brother of the then Lord Chamberlain, the Earl of Airlie. According to Rowland, the largest shareholder in Harrods at the time of the takeover – he also wished to acquire the world-famous store for himself – he and Fayed struck a deal over ownership. Fayed then reneged. Rowland had since pursued Fayed relentlessly. Through the *Observer*, which he controlled, he kept the British nation informed about the activities, antecedents and antics of the man he dubbed The Hero From Zero in a tome he had distributed free of charge with his newspaper. Then, in 1993, Tiny and the Pharaoh ostensibly made up, shaking hands in Harrods in front of a stuffed shark named Tiny. This, however, was only the entr'acte. Rowland then alleged that Fayed had discovered that he kept a safe-deposit box at Harrods and arranged for it to be broken into. He sued Fayed for the return of emeralds allegedly missing and also sought an injunction preventing the Pharaoh from using or showing private papers he supposedly photocopied. This led to the police arresting Fayed on 2 March 1998. Quite what the outcome would be at the time of Diana's death remained to be seen. The only certainty was that the Battle for Harrods had had as many twists and turns, and as much acrimony, as the War of the Waleses did. In the end, however, the police did not charge Mohamed Al Fayed with any offence though, after his death, his widow pursued his legal action for the recovery of damages against the owner of Harrods for the loss of the emeralds. Mohamed Al Fayed was made to pay a substantial sum in compensation.

Had Fayed been hounded by anyone but Tiny Rowland, his reputation would have suffered more than it did. Rowland, however, had been criticized in the early 1970s as the "unacceptable face of capitalism," a rebuke which brought about Angus Ogilvy's fall from the mercantile heights and ensured that the press would thereafter view Rowland with suspicion.

What Rowland failed to achieve, Fayed did himself, wiping out much of his respectability with dubious political activities. For years he had been cultivating Conservative politicians. Some he treated to large hampers from Harrods. Others he put up gratis at the Ritz Hotel in Paris, which he also owned. Some he sent on guided tours to the Windsor residence in the Bois de Boulogne, whose lease he took over from the City of Paris after the death of the Duchess of Windsor. According to him, he even gave bribes to various Members of Parliament in brown envelopes stuffed full of cash. In Fayed's scheme of things, such patrimony should have translated into major influence. He therefore decided that the Conservatives had cheated him. Although the MPs whom he compromised thought he was buying limited influence, such as the odd question here or there to be asked in Parliament, he believed he was paying for more. When his latest application for citizenship was refused, shortly before the last general election, he went public with allegations of sleaze. Not only did he bring about the downfall of a handful of MPs, but he also helped to bring down the Government.

It was Fayed's polluting of the political system with allegations of bribery, more than anything else, which lost him support within Establishment circles. However, he was not exactly suffering from a dearth of companionship. He was sufficiently established to have a wide circle of acquaintances, and to mix regularly with the *crème de la crème*, including the Princess of Wales and Raine, Countess Spencer. Certainly, he was then respectable enough, and Diana was now sufficiently "in" with the Royal Family, for the Palace to accede to her request to take William and Harry with her to stay with his family at St. Tropez.

On 11 July Diana and the boys flew out from London to Nice Airport. There they joined the *Jonikal* for the journey to Castel Ste. Hélène, the Fayed residence near St. Tropez, with its main villa, guest house and private beach.

Diana and the boys did have the time of their lives, as Raine had promised they would. Mohamed was a host in the finest Middle Eastern tradition, where hospitality has been raised from social convention into an art form. They were made to feel welcome whether they joined the Fayed family or stayed on their own. One evening they did go into St. Tropez on their own, but Diana so enjoyed the warmth of Mediterranean family life that she happily spent most of her time with the Fayeds. Lunch was usually taken on the *Jonikal*, where the French chef and the Italian chef outdid themselves with a dazzling array of Near and Middle Eastern dishes. According to Debbie Gribble, the chief stewardess, there would be a variety of pasta dishes, several different vegetables, salads, lobster, fish, various meats and fruit galore. All would be served on silver platters or china.

William, especially, was impressed. Although used to cruising on the *Alexander*, John Latsis's yacht, which is an ocean liner compared to the *Jonikal*, William had never seen such lavish hospitality before. His exposure had not really gone beyond the thriftiness of royal life, where food is calculated to within an ounce of your life and even the blank sides of typescript get used as notepaper. He was therefore taken aback when a whole fish was sent back to the kitchen untouched. Diana told Debbie Gribble, "I don't think he's ever seen so much food."

According to Trevor Rees-Jones, Dodi's bodyguard, who was the sole survivor of the crash which killed his boss, Diana and their driver, Henri Paul, William and Harry were relaxed, easy-to-talk-to young men. William had inherited Diana's diving ability, and frequently treated onlookers to his elegant and graceful dives from the deck of the *Jonikal* into the Mediterranean; while Harry enjoyed jet-skiing.

Dinner was taken on the deck of the *Jonikal* or on land. There would be yet another display of traditional Middle Eastern hospitality, with yet another multitude of platters being borne in by yet another plethora of staff. After Diana, the boys and the Fayeds had taken what they wanted, the food, much of which had not even been touched, would be whisked away, never to be seen again. For the Fayeds, "leftovers" were never on the menu.

For the first couple of days, the house party consisted of Diana, Prince William, Prince Harry, Mohamed Al Fayed, his Finnish-born wife, Heini, and their four children. They were then joined by Fayed's eldest son, Dodi. Born Emad Fayed, Dodi, who never used the particular Al in his name, despite what such authorities as Paul Burrell seem to think, was the product of Fayed's first marriage, to the Saudi Arabian tycoon Adnan Khashoggi's sister, Samira. He had made his name as a film producer, having invested money in films including the Oscar-winning *Chariots of Fire*. He was not taken as a serious player in the film world, however. "He used to hang out with Bernie (Cornfeld, the late financier and for much of the second half of the twentieth century one of the world's richest men). He was always at Greyhall (Cornfeld's Beverly Hills residence, which Douglas

Fairbanks and Mary Pickford built before subdividing the estate and moving across the road to Pickfair). He was very sweet, but he was not terribly substantial," Lorraine Dillon Vidal, Bernie Cornfeld's wife, who knew Dodi Fayed well, told me. This opinion was substantiated by Alan Frame, the former deputy editor of the *Daily Express* who left that newspaper and went to work for Mohamed Al Fayed. "Dodi was a nice guy, but he was rather childlike. He certainly didn't work hard. Although Dodi had his own office, in all the time I worked with Mohamed, I never once saw him in that office. He was terrified of his father, though. Always trying to please him."

According to the many friends we had in common, Dodi was the greatest people-pleaser they had ever known. He was the very soul of kindness and generosity. He never asked for anything in return, except that the object of his largesse like him. All our mutual friends agree that he had had a big cocaine problem "some years back." However, he shook it off. Even then, he was so keen that everyone like him that he used to buy $20,000 worth of coke a week. This would be left around the place for his friends, many of whom were well known within the film world, to help themselves to.

Possibly because so much of Dodi's money was going for cocaine, he could be careless about settling his bills and repaying his debts. He wrote bad cheques to American Airlines for $5,657 and to the Hotel Bel Air for $5,000. American Express sued him for $116,890. On one occasion, Marlene Dietrich's grandson Peter Riva was having difficulty collecting $15,000 from Dodi, who had been with him at the exclusive Swiss boarding school Le Rosey. The debt had been incurred when Dodi had asked him to stay as his guest at the Ritz Hotel in Paris (owned by Mohamed Al Fayed since 1979). When Riva was checking out, however, the management presented him with a bill. Dodi promised to make good the debt, but kept on giving his old school friend the runaround. "The way he got it from Dodi was to accost him in the lobby of the Pierre Hotel in New York and tell him he wasn't letting him leave until he gave him the money," a mutual friend, who wishes to mreain anonymous, told me. "He said, Dodi, you and your friends stick more than what you owe me up your noses every week. Give me the money.' When Dodi saw he meant business, he gave him the money. Naturally, the friendship wasn't ever the same again."

Dodi was careless only with debts and with women he no longer wanted. With everyone and everything else, he was thoughtfulness personified. The Australian socialite Pauline Ryan, who worked for the Khashoggis for decades and remembered Dodi from childhood, told me, "He was truly one of the nicest, gentlest men. He was very quiet. Very self-effacing. If he knew you well, he could be very amusing. He was a real delight."

Six months before Diana went to the South of France as Fayed's house guest, she had told the Greek multimillionaire shipowner and journalist Taki Theodorocopulous over lunch that Mohamed Al Fayed was always suggesting that she "get together with Dodi." It was therefore inevitable that his father ensured that the son whom women found so attractive be around when the Princess of Wales was his house guest. Dodi flew in once Diana had arrived. He did not stay with the family, but on his father's schooner, the *Sakara*. This was because Dodi was not alone. With him was the former *Vogue* model who had been the lady in his life since they had met the previous July in Paris. Tellingly, whenever Dodi visited his family, he left his fiancée Kelly Fisher on board the *Sakara*. The reason is clear. Just as the Prince of Wales was the ultimate catch for Lady Diana Spencer, the Princess of Wales was the ultimate catch for Dodi Fayed. In other words, if flint and fuel ignited a fire, so much the better. If not, Dodi could fall back on Kelly, who was then blissfully oblivious to the reason for her fiancé's absences.

On Bastille Day, 14 July, the flame was struck. Fortress Diana, which had already started the process of crumbling under the might of the Fayed charm, lowered her symbolic drawbridge in characteristic fashion. According to the chief stewardess of the *Jonikal*, the boat had moored to give the guests a good view of the fireworks display which would celebrate France's national day. Dodi was eating fruit and dropped some. Diana picked it up and kittenishly threw it at him. He threw it right back. Diana retaliated with a mango in the face and another in the back. A full-fledged food fight of the sort eight-year-olds normally have ensued. "They were chasing each other and laughing and giggling like a couple of kids. Then they wrestled a bit and stopped – just staring at each other." Physical contact had been established, with all the implications inherent.

Electrifying as that encounter was, it was no more so than Diana's other confrontation that very day. She set out from the *Jonikal*, taking care to jump from the yacht into the dinghy, which would take her to the media representatives stationed some way away, in such a way that she provided the photographers with graceful and elegant pictures as she sailed through the air with her arms spread-eagled dramatically. When her dinghy pulled up beside them, she stopped long enough to pose before launching into a tirade: "My sons are always urging me to live abroad and to be less in the public eye. Maybe that is what I should do, given the fact that you won't leave me alone. I understand I have a role to play, but I have to be protective of my boys. William gets very distressed, and he can get freaked out with all the attention. But you are all going to get a big surprise with the next thing I do . . ." she said, cutting herself short and returning to the *Jonikal*.

This confounded the press. Up to that point, Diana and Mohamed Al Fayed had given every indication of enjoying the attention they were getting. They were obviously posing for pictures from a distance, providing photo opportunities even when none were being requested. The more seasoned among their number were convinced that Diana had grasped the nettle to outshine Camilla Parker Bowles, whose fiftieth-birthday party was being hosted by the Prince of Wales on the 18th. This was duly reported in the press, and Diana, hypersensitive as ever to criticism, realized she had better curtail her competitiveness and withdraw from public view if she wished to maintain her image within the media and the well-being she had been generating with her ex-husband and his family.

Also reported was a statement Diana had issued from Kensington Palace denying the comments she had made to the media. This did little to enhance her credibility, and, taken in conjunction with the denials she also issued when her interview with the French publication *Le Monde* was published – she had made remarks she regretted – Diana was building up trouble for herself for the future.

The following day, Diana learned of Gianni Versace's murder. Proving that it was indeed possible to limit the paparazzi's access if she wished to, she kept out of view as she continued pursuing her budding relationship with Dodi, made arrangements to attend the designer's funeral the following week, and sensibly let the spotlight shine upon Camilla and her milestone birthday.

Once Camilla's party was safely out of the way, Diana, who was indeed the "media junkie" Sir David English described her as being, was back on parade for her fix. By now, she was so experienced at creating photo opportunities that she came up with poses no one else would have thought of. She got a young girl to hose her down on the deck of the *Jonikal* on one occasion, and on another, like Jane from Tarzan, swung from a rope on the *Jonikal* into the sea. Both photographs, needless to say, circled the world, as did the delightful shots of mother and son together on the jet-ski when she and Harry took to the water, playing games with and without Dodi.

On 20 July, Diana and the boys flew back to London on the Harrods private jet. That evening she kissed William and Harry goodbye, promising to see them on Sunday, 31 August, when they returned from Balmoral. A measure of the serenity she was developing was the fact that she did not balk at her sons' spending more than twice the time with their father than they did with her that summer. She knew this was what they wanted. They loved Balmoral and all the sporting activities it had to offer. The choice was theirs, and she respected it. "Divorce is awful. I don't see as much of my boys as I'd like," she said to me and to many other people. She was learning that happiness is not about getting everything you want, but being able to enjoy what you have, even when circumstances force you to accept things you would prefer not to.

Twenty-four hours after arriving in London, Diana flew to Milan on Elton John's private jet, the bitterness of the *Rock & Royalty* débâcle forgotten in the wake of Versace's murder. The following day she consoled the rock star as they sat in the family pew with the Versaces.

After Milan, Diana and Dodi had a discreet weekend at the Ritz Hotel in Paris. He took her to see the Windsor residence in the Bois de Boulogne, and they returned to London before boarding the Harrods jet yet again. Once more she was headed for Nice, to board the *Jonikal* for another cruise, this time for six days, with Dodi and herself as the sole guests. The boat had been moored at St. Laurent du Var, and the budding lovers happily went aboard for a cruise to Corsica and Sardinia.

Dodi occupied the master stateroom, a large wood-paneled cabin with an adjoining marble bathroom. Diana was quartered in the primary guest suite.

For the first two nights, Diana slept in her quarters and Dodi in his, according to Debbie Gribble, who noted that "you see these things as a stewardess." Meanwhile, they were building up to a crescendo. To set the mood, as the *Jonikal* motored towards Sardinia on a sea that was as still as a pond, with a huge moon and the stars out in their thousands, Dodi and Diana ate a dinner consisting of caviar, pâté de foie gras and champagne. Background music consisted of the odd classical CD, the occasional Frank Sinatra song, but mostly the sound track from *The English Patient* or George Michael's album *Older*. The Anglo-Greek singer was not only a friend of Diana's, but also the songwriter of her absolute favourite song, "You Have Been Loved," which she and Dodi played over and over again.

That third evening, the caviar, champagne, still sea, moon, stars and "You Have Been Loved" did the trick. Debbie Gribble caught Diana and Dodi necking on the sofa in the saloon after dinner. But it was the state of their beds the following morning which told her that they were now openly a couple. Although Diana's bed had been purposely trussed up, it had not been slept in, while Dodi's looked as if a tidal wave had swept through it.

Thereafter, Diana and Dodi threw appearances to the wind and made no pretence about being lovers. They slept together, Diana not bothering to truss up her bed. Whenever Debbie Gribble or one of the stewards took them Perrier on deck, they saw the gentle Egyptian and his sensual English rose intertwined, feet, hands, arms, legs interlocking in a jigsaw of desire.

At the end of the cruise, Diana and Dodi flew back to London. In many ways, he was perfect for her. Emotionally, they were compatible. He liked nothing better than pleasing those he admired. Diana liked nothing better than being pleased by those she wanted to admire her. He had long been looking for someone whom he could adore. Diana had long been looking for someone who would adore her, and whom she in turn would adore. Both were impulsive. Dodi dabbled at working; he was "marginal," according to Bill Condon, the scriptwriter on the sequel to *F/X*, to films Dodi coproduced after *Chariots of Fire*. That gave him all the time in the world to dedicate to Diana, who wanted someone with time for her. She was tired of men like the Prince of Wales and Hasnat Khan, who put their duty before the serious business of romance. "I am a romantic," Diana said. So, too, was Dodi, according to Jack Weiner, his producer partner for seven years, who judged him to be "the victim of his . . . romantic dreams." Weiner thought that Dodi was "a character in a movie," whereas Diana's brother-in-law Robert Fellowes told another courtier, "She doesn't understand that life isn't the cinema."

On the profound as well as the practical levels, Diana and Dodi were well suited. Not only did he genuinely admire her humanitarianism, as he said to friends including his best friend, the actor Christopher Lambert, but he was from a world where matrimony is not a sacrament. It is a contract. This makes a big difference in attitude between Christians and Muslims. While Dodi wanted love, he also required all the benefits of the best deal he could strike. In other words, he required a trophy – and Diana was the ultimate trophy, one who would raise him in the eyes of the world as nothing else had done before. Moreover, it would gain him the everlasting respect and gratitude of his father, whom he adored and whom he telephoned every day, or every other day, when they were apart.

Even on the profound level, Diana's and Dodi's flaws were complementary. Both had had childhoods which left them with feelings of deprivation, despite the backdrops of great wealth. Both were from broken homes. Both felt ignored as children. They were therefore both emotionally needy, with the same tendency to rely upon outsiders to provide for them what they should have been generating within themselves. These gaps within them left them both yearning for approval, admiration and respect from others. It made them status-conscious and yearning for the limelight. Both of them loved publicity and enjoyed the adulation that went along with public life. Both deplored the downside of celebrity, vociferously complaining about the irritations, while giving the impression that they thrived upon its drama and the resulting rush of adrenaline. Both of them loved the panoply of celebrity: Diana, the staff to execute her wishes, comb her hair daily, apply her make-up, cook for and clean up after her, iron her clothes and sheets, and execute the myriad chores that her princely state required; Dodi, who lived like a medieval prince, never anywhere without a retinue, an excess of staff to cater to his needs and desires. Although both of them were informal and did not stand on ceremony, they also needed the respect due to their rank, and made sure they got it, Diana by being every inch the royal princess even when she no longer was, and Dodi by surrounding himself with retainers and security guards, as if he were a president or someone of equal merit. Both of them had been pampered and petted since childhood, which was part of their charm as well as part of their problem. They had both entered adult life ill-prepared for the pressures and hard knocks that are an inevitable part of growing up, whether you live in a slum or a palace. In early adulthood, neither, therefore, had the resources of character to cope when pain became interwoven with privilege. In Dodi's case, it was the early deaths of his maternal grandmother, Samiha Khashoggi (after a face-lift which went wrong) and his mother, Samira, from cancer; while Diana was only recently recovered from the illnesses that had dogged her once she married into the Royal Family and found that she had responsibilities as well as privileges for the first time in her life. Both were "naïve" and "childlike," according to many of their friends, among them Marie Helvin, Rosa Monckton and Lorraine Dillon Vidal, yet both of them were also nice people.

On a more mundane level, Diana and Dodi were also compatible. Neither was an intellectual. Both of them loved movies but would screw up their noses if you mentioned plays or the theatre. Each of them had a heightened awareness of the importance of appearances, and of their own appearance, and spent more time and money on grooming than most people will ever see in a lifetime. They shared a fascination with Hollywood and the world of modelling. Both of them relished their friendships with movie stars, seeming to place a higher value upon the celebrity of a Tom Cruise or a Nicole Kidman than upon the accomplishments of a John Kenneth Galbraith or a Henry Kissinger. The same was true of their associations within the world of modelling, Dodi with model girlfriends and a model ex-wife, Suzanne Gregard, and Diana with her cultivation of the fashion editors who plastered her on the front pages of their magazines. "I wish I could've been a model," Diana said to me, and, once separated, she set about emulating the visage of her friend Cindy Crawford as she posed for Patrick Demarchelier and Mario Testino. Already a fashion icon, she was now becoming a modelling paradigm as she lost her coyness, gained confidence and understood the meaning of the fashion mantra "Less is more."

Even the Fayed wealth made Dodi ideal for Diana. Although Dodi was not personally wealthy, he had an income of $100,000 per month from his father and unrestricted access to Mohamed's worldly goods. These included residences in London, New York, Paris, Dubai and Italy; exclusive use of "his own" flats at 60 Park Lane in London and near the Champs-Elysees in Paris, as well as Julie Andrews's former five-acre compound on Paradise Cove in Malibu, which Highcrest Investments Ltd. bought for $7.3 million on 20 June 1997; a Scottish castle surrounded by a 40,000-acre estate; the *Sakara* and *Jonikal*; the Harrods' Sikorsky helicopter and Gulf stream IV jet; and various cars, including Ferraris, Mercedes-Benzes and Rolls-Royces.

Although Diana had fantasized about marrying Hasnat Khan, and had even told her hairdresser that she would "have to support him" because his doctor's salary made him so poor, she was used to a splendid lifestyle, to the best of everything. What she spent on make-up alone in a year, most secretaries had to live off for the duration. And that was before she had treated herself to the constant stream of couture clothes, which filled several rooms; the hundreds of pairs of shoes, filling other rooms; the innumerable hats; the countless cashmere sweaters; T-shirts, jeans, bathing suits, all filed away in their own drawers and labeled systematically – just like Dodi's. They even shared a fetish for tidiness, which was yet another area of compatibility.

Diana was materialistic, as her own brother, Charles, confirmed in Andrew Morton's biography, attributing it to their parents' practice of presenting them with the Hamley's catalogue at Christmas and giving them the freedom to choose anything they liked. Her whole life had been lived amid ever-increasing degrees of wealth. Dodi, on the other hand, liked giving gifts. When she admired a cashmere sweater in the south of France, he bought her one of that style in every colour. The same thing happened when she wanted a pair of shoes. He gave her more expensive presents too, including a diamond bracelet on their second cruise together. Although Rosa Monckton has Diana saying to her, "It (Dodi's gift-giving) makes me uneasy. I don't want to be bought. . . I just want someone to be there for me, to make me feel safe and secure," the fact is, Diana was being disingenuous. She loved being given presents and had no problem accepting them, as can be seen from the alacrity with which she accepted King Juan Carlos's Bijan watch. Moreover, she also gave presents, although on a more modest scale. She bought Dodi a silver cigar cutter from Asprey, the fashionable London jeweller, and had the words, "With love from Diana" engraved on it. Even more tellingly, she presented the man she "adored," to quote her friend Lady Bowker, with a pair of cuff links which had belonged to her father, and which had sentimental value beyond the price of rubies. It is true that she valued being loved above being showered with presents, but when she was in a romantic relationship, she expected a man to show his feelings in kind and in emotion, as she did. One person who would have no doubt of that was Sarah-Jane Gaselee, the daughter of Prince Charles's horse trainer at the time of their marriage. "I remember clearly when I first met Lady Diana, as she then was. She gave me a little Indian bracelet and made me go up to Prince Charles and say, Look what Lady Diana has given me.' It was to make him feel guilty about presents," which Charles did not give.

Whether Diana would subsequently have married Dodi or merely remained his paramour, she would have been moving up a peg or two in terms of lifestyle. Harrods "toys" would have been far more readily available for her to play with than royal ones had been, with the threat of official sanction if they were over-or misused, and the newspapers policing every use of the Queen's Flight or the royal yacht *Britannia*. And there was no question but that Mohamed Al Fayed would have opened the chequebook as never before, to ensure the happiness of Diana, had she become a member of his family circle.

On 8 August, the day after Dodi and Diana returned from the cruise, she flew to Bosnia as the guest of the Land Mine Survivors Network. While her American hosts, Jerry White and Ken Rutherford, both of whom had lost limbs in the Golan Heights and Somalia respectively, toured with her throughout the war-ravaged former Yugoslav state, Diana and her inimitable capacity for garnering the world's attention ensured the anti-land mine campaign worldwide news coverage.

Diana returned to London on 11 August, and she and Dodi flew in the Harrods helicopter to meet with Rita Rogers, her psychic, on 12 August. There followed a few days of love in London, with Diana spending each evening at Dodi's flat on Park Lane before returning home to Kensington Palace early the following morning.

For nearly two weeks, the tabloids had been full of stories of the romance between the Harrods heir and the Heir to the Throne's ex-wife. Unbeknownst to either Dodi or Diana, Kelly Fisher, in Los Angeles, had swung into action, hiring Gloria Allred as her advocate. On 14 August 1997, she sued Dodi, claiming he had dumped her for Diana after insisting that she give up her career for him. Her evidence included a cheque which Dodi had written out to her for $200,000 on a bank account that was closed.

While Kelly Fisher was in Los Angeles with Gloria Allred, at a press conference, Diana was in London being resolute about remaining unaffected by the fracas. As she packed to go on a cruise of the Greek islands with her friend Rosa Monckton in a boat lent to her by a longstanding chum of mine, the Greek socialite and accomplished charity fundraiser Chrisanthy Lemos and her shipowner husband, Panagiotis, she was not about to allow tabloid hell to encroach upon and sully her own romantic heaven. Diana had waited too long to have the sort of relationship she was having with Dodi to have any outsider mess it up.

Diana and Rosa Monckton flew from London to Athens aboard the Harrods jet. After Diana's death, Monckton wrote a piece about their trip together for the *Sunday Telegraph*, the right-wing establishment organ edited by her husband, Dominic Lawson. In it, Monckton rather ungraciously stated that she and Diana mocked the taste of their host, with Diana describing the jet's decor as tacky, with "green pile carpet covered in pharaoh's heads." While there is little doubt that she was quoting accurately – Diana was renowned for the waspishness of her observations about taste – Monckton omitted two salient points, which would have put their conduct into context. Diana, who rightly considered her taste to be of the finest quality, was always mocking the carpets at Kensington Palace as well, in particular the ones with the Prince of Wales motif. The second point omitted was that Monckton was a dyed-in-the-wool British establishment figure, the daughter of Viscount Monckton of Brenchley, and the pro-Zionist wife of a Jew, while Mohamed Al Fayed was an anti-establishment Arab. Rosa Monckton had made just enough anti-Dodi and anti-Fayed comments to Diana for her to be on her guard about her, as Diana made clear to Joseph Sanders. There is little doubt that, had she lived, and had her relationship with Dodi continued on the path it was heading down, Diana would have once more relegated Rosa Monckton to Siberia, this time with more justice than on the first occasion.

While Diana and Monckton were enjoying five sybaritic days free of publicity and public attention, Dodi was in Los Angeles, dealing with the new Malibu house and the Kelly Fisher lawsuit. He flew back to London to greet Diana upon her return on 20 August.

The following day, the lovers took the Harrods Gulfstream yet again to go on another cruise in the Mediterranean.

Time was running out.

Twenty

The last ten days of Diana's romance with Dodi, and of the lovers' lives, were the most important. It was then that the relationship went into an even more intensive and joyous stage. "Joyous" is the right word, too. When her brother, Charles, spoke during his funeral oration about the "joy" Dodi had brought into Diana's personal life, he was merely speaking the unvarnished truth. Although few people saw them together during the last days of their lives, everyone who did speaks in glowing terms of the happiness they shared. The chief stewardess of the *Jonikal* said, "They were so in love. It was wonderful to see." Even Trevor Rees-Jones, the bodyguard who flew down with the couple to Nice and survived the fatal crash, said in the reserved way typical of bodyguards, "The Princess seemed happy and so did Dodi."

Diana herself attested to her happiness. She made her friend Rosa Monckton listen to "his wonderful voice" on the answering machine. She told another good friend, Lady Bowker, "Elsa, I adore him. I've never been so happy." The journalist Richard Kay, whom she telephoned the evening before her death, concurred that "she was in love with him, and perhaps more important, she believed that he was in love with her and that he believed in her." He also told me that Diana herself told him, "I'm so happy."

Similarly, two days before his death Dodi told his friend Christopher Lambert, "This is it. This is the girl I've been waiting for all my life. She's the most wonderful person. I'm in love with her in a way I've never been in love before. There will be no more women for me."

So in love were the couple that they were already laying plans which involved Diana's work. According to Kay, Diana said that Dodi's father had agreed to "help finance a charity for the victims of mines." Dodi also encouraged her to sketch out "the framework of a plan to open hospices for the dying all over the world."

The very existence of those plans gives credence to the theory that Diana and Dodi were talking about the possibility of ending up together, whatever form the final relationship took. "Her work was charity," said Joseph Sanders. "She took a practical approach to what had become a vocation, helping the infirm and suffering."

There were other, more nebulous plans under discussion. According to her butler, Paul Burrell, during the last two weeks of her life Diana asked him if he would be prepared to move to America with her. In his memoir, *A Royal Duty*, he even says that she showed him plans of the former Julie Andrews house, which she intended to live in, and allocated rooms for William and Harry.

Quite mindless of the ramifications of his statement, Burrell also states that Dodi was nothing but a holiday romance, and that the relationship would have fizzled out had the couple lived. He enlarges upon his theme, stating that he regarded Dodi Fayed as unsuitable and sought Rosa Monckton's intervention to put the skids under the relationship. His stance is that he was far more than a mere butler or even a close friend, but a vastly influential friend who could influence her decisions about which men she was or was not in love with. According to him, he knew "all" Diana's secrets and friends like Rosa Monckton also knew "everything." To those of us who know that the former Julie Andrews house had been bought by and was registered in the name of a Fayed company, his assertion does not show his knowledge, nor does it enhance his authority, for why would Diana have been planning to live in a house owned by Dodi Fayed unless she was going to live there with him?.

Regrettably, what Burrell's assertion does show is that he was a lot less in the loop, and a lot more ignorant, than he realizes. He does not even know Dodi's correct name, or that Dodi never styled himself Dodi Al Fayed. What he does show, however, is that Darren McGrady, her chef (who worked alongside Burrell for years and was equally knowledgeable, albeit commendably discreet and loyal) was absolutely right when he said, "His is fond of saying he was so close to Diana that she called him her 'rock'. Nothing could be further from the truth. In fact, Diana wanted to sack him because she couldn't stand his endless snooping."

Mistakenly, Diana thought she had time on her side, and that Burrell, whose ambition it was to work with a Hollywood film star, would make the leap to someone like Tom Cruise and Nicole Kidman, who had been sent his CV. That way she could be safely rid of him without having to worry that he would betray any of the secrets servants inevitably acquire as they proceed about their daily chores, for any indiscretion about her on his part would ultimately have made him unemployable with one of the other celebrities he hankered after working for.

Of course, death would change that scenario, and with it, Burrell's prospects, occupation and profile.

In the meantime, however, Diana was intent on keeping her inquisitive butler in the dark about the depth of her new romance, while lining him up so that he would make the leap with her to a new life and a new world, before he catapulted himself out of her life into a Hollywood star's.

Meanwhile Diana also had to deal with the outcry her recent interview in *Le Monde*, the French publication, had generated. Diana was quoted making remarks favourable to the Labour Government and disparaging to the former Conservative Government.

While contending with her latest media controversy, Diana was optimistically planning the golden future she thought she had, as she and Dodi cruised on the *Jonikal* for the last ten days of their lives. They had set off from St. Tropez. From there, they headed towards Monaco, where the lovers dropped in to Repossi, the jewellers. Dodi ordered a $205,000 diamond ring for Diana to add to her already considerable collection of jewels. From there, they headed towards Portofino, where they dropped anchor for the night.

Cruising on a private yacht, which is invariably referred to as a "boat" in smart circles, was one of Diana's favourite pleasures. Quintessentially luxurious, it is also one of the favourite pastimes of the superrich. There can be few greater delights than spending a week or two on a well-appointed craft, with a full complement of crew, who feed you delicious meals, fetch and carry for you to such an extent that you do not even have to interrupt the serious business of swimming, snorkeling, water-skiing, reading, tanning and chatting to get yourself even a glass of water, much less a stronger drink. The seductiveness of the sea, the relaxation of the air, the healthiness of maritime activity, the beatific sense of oneness with nature and the welcome distance from the cares of dry land are so sybaritic they are transcendental. In other words, the ideal venue for a romance.

After the *Jonikal* left Portofino, Diana and Dodi headed for the Bay of Poets, where they dropped anchor the following day. From there, the captain turned the boat towards Sardinia and the exotic Costa Smeralda, which the Aga Khan developed and turned into one of the most chic summer spots on earth.

While Diana and Dodi were basking in the warmth of their love and the sun, Trevor Rees-Jones, Dodi's bodyguard, kept out of the way, spending his time on the bridge of the boat or reconnoitring for suitable restaurants where the lovers might wish to dine. "Sometimes we'd be bothered by photographers. Other times we wouldn't be."

Until Sardinia, Diana and Dodi had had a relatively paparazzi-free time. The easiest place on earth to avoid the press is upon the seas, especially if you have a powerboat and are being chased by photographers in motorboats or dinghies. The fact that they now dropped anchor on the Costa Smeralda indicates that the lovers wished to share the progress their romance was making with the world. This was a natural-enough sentiment for them to have. Diana often spoke about her special relationship with her public, and of her love for a group of people she did not know, but nevertheless had feeling for. And Dodi was known to be at home in the company of the famous and to bask in the spotlight whenever it was turned upon him.

Nevertheless, after a few days of this, Diana and Dodi experienced the mixed feelings that most public figures have when the full glare of media attention both warms and scorches. Even though publicity has its appealing element, its attentiveness reaffirming one's desirability and importance, it is never entirely free of pain. This resulted in Diana worrying about the way the tabloids were portraying Dodi. She even asked Richard Kay whether the media was "anti-Dodi" because he was rich. Kay believed that Mohamed Al Fayed's controversial reputation was the real reason for the adverse response the romance was receiving, to which she responded with a thoughtful and noncommittal "Hmmmm."

Having discovered that there is more than one way of getting scorched when you disport yourself in the public glare of a fashionable place like Sardinia, Diana and Dodi settled down to enjoying themselves despite the intrusion. By this time, the Jonikal was moored in the bay of Cala di Volpe. This is the bay which adjoins Porto Cervo, where, at any one time, there are several billion dollars' worth of private boats in the harbour. This is also where the Aga Khan has his summer residence.

Although Cala di Volpe is smaller than Porto Cervo, it is also more select. It is taken up exclusively by the Cala di Volpe Hotel, which was built by the Aga Khan and is surely the most elegant summer hotel in the world.

That last evening in Italy, Dodi and Diana did what "everyone" who has a boat moored in the bay of Cala di Volpe does: They had drinks at the hotel, where guests and visitors sit on the terrace looking at the picturesque scenery, the magnificent boats and each other.

The following morning, the last of her life, Diana awoke happy and fulfilled. Beside her in the master stateroom was the man she loved, a man who fulfilled her, who made her feel "covered in love," to use the words she employed when describing him to Lady Bowker. This morning, however, was not going to be dedicated to love, with breakfast at 11 a.m., the way many of her mornings had been on this and the other cruises with Dodi. She and Dodi had made plans to return home via Paris. They were diverting there to pick up the $205,000 ring which Diana had chosen from the Monaco showroom of the jeweller Alberto Repossi, and which Dodi had arranged to pick up in Paris once it had been sized for Diana's finger. Even though the paparazzi had them in their sights, picking up the ring was the true reason for leaving when they did.

Contrary to what the tabloids said, their plan had always been to end the holiday on Sunday, 31 August, when Diana had to be in London to meet her sons.

For the last time, Diana and Dodi left the Jonikal for the pier of the Cala di Volpe Hotel. With them as they stepped ashore was twenty-nine-year-old Trevor Rees-Jones, Dodi's regular bodyguard and a former paratrooper. They cut through to the front of the hotel, where Tomas Muzzu, a sixty-nine-year-old local taxi driver, was waiting with his white Mercedes. While Muzzu loaded the trunk with their luggage, Rees-Jones slipped into the front passenger seat, after Diana and Dodi had taken their seats in the back. Then they set off for Olbia Airport, a forty-minute drive with views of the dramatic mountains of Sardinia and the magnificent Mediterranean shoreline.

When the Mercedes reached Olbia Airport, two freelance Sardinian journalists were waiting to snatch photographs of Diana and Dodi. They had been tipped off by someone who knew their travel plans.

Although no one but Diana, Dodi and their entourage knew their destination, when the Harrods Gulfstream IV touched down at Le Bourget Airport outside Paris at 3:20 p.m., nearly thirty photographers were waiting for them. Dodi was irritated, Diana serene.

Amid scenes reminiscent of a stag hunt, Dodi and Diana entered a black Mercedes-Benz, driven by Dodi's regular driver, Philippe Dourneau, which had been sent by the Ritz Hotel to meet them. Henri Paul, the hotel's deputy director of security, drove the second vehicle, a bottle-green Range Rover carrying the luggage destined for Dodi's apartment near the Arc de Triomphe. They set off in convoy, pursued by the paparazzi. Paul engaged in some skilful driving, blocking the road with his vehicle and enabling Dourneau to spirit his charges away to the former residence of the Duke and Duchess of Windsor.

At the Bois de Boulogne residence, Dodi showed Diana around again. This time Diana took a deep interest in everything, giving Gregorio Martin, the caretaker who had been the Windsors' chauffeur, the impression that she was looking over a potential future home. According to Martin, "They looked at everything in the house: the boiler, every cupboard. The Princess even opened the fridge door to look inside. She had a detailed interest in everything, including the garden. The Princess was asking about rooms for the staff and security."

Having feasted their eyes upon the restored but empty house, whose contents had been dispatched for sale in New York, Dodi and Diana left for the Ritz Hotel, owned by his father since 1979. They were shown straight up to the Imperial Suite, for which the charges were $10,000 a night.

Dodi and Diana, both telephone addicts, promptly availed themselves of the convenience, Dodi calling California about Julie Andrews's former house at Malibu, which he had recently purchased, while Diana spoke to her good friend, Associated Newspapers' journalist Richard Kay. He thereafter said that Diana told him she was going to retire from public life in November, although she did stress that she intended to continue her charity work. Although Kay did not know about her and the Fayeds' plans to set up an international string of hospices, his comments support the contention that she and Dodi were indeed discussing a life together. He said, "All was well in her world. She was as happy as I ever heard her."

Dodi was informed that his stepfather's brother, Hassan Yassin, was in the hotel. Telephoning him in his suite, Dodi told him, "It's serious. We're going to get married." They then made arrangements to meet for a drink later, after dinner. In the event, Dodi and Diana left early because of the presence of the paparazzi.

After Dodi's and Diana's deaths, Hassan Yassin's credibility was questioned, due to the misunderstanding that he is akin to, and a kin of, Mohamed Al Fayed, who "puts a spin on everything," to quote the former deputy editor of the *Daily Express*, Alan Frame, latterly a Fayed employee. In fact, the Yassins and the Fayeds were not related, nor did Hassan Yassin put spins on anything. His brother married Samira Khashoggi Fayed when she and Mohamed were divorced. To say that there was no love lost between the Yassins and Mohamed Fayed would be the grossest understatement. "They can't stand the man Fayed," Soraya Khashoggi told me. Yassin, moreover, was a distinguished diplomat. The idea of him lying to advance Mohamed Al Fayed's social aspirations was so ludicrous it would be laughable, were the slur upon his credibility not so insulting.

After speaking to his stepuncle, Dodi, accompanied by his bodyguard, Trevor Rees-Jones, was driven the few yards down the street from the Ritz to the Paris showroom of Alberto Repossi. His purpose was to collect the ring. According to Alice Valentin, niece of Albert Repossi, "The ring was from our collection of engagement rings called Tell Me Yes. It was in the window of their main showroom on Place Beaumarchais in Monte Carlo and they both came in to have a look. It was from the top of the range. The Princess said, 'That's the one I want.' Unfortunately it didn't fit and we had to send it away for alteration. At around 6:30 on the Saturday night of 30 August Mr Dodi Fayed's private secretary and bodyguard came in and checked over the shop to make sure everything was secure and make sure there were no photographers. Then Mr Fayed came over himself. He was only here for a few minutes, but it was clear he was extremely happy. He was obviously very much in love and the ring meant an awful lot."

The diamond ring safely in his pocket, Dodi returned to the Ritz, collected Diana, and they set off for his apartment on the second floor of 1 Rue Arsene-Houssaye, near the Arc de Triomphe and the Champs-Elysées.

Dodi had booked a table for 8:45 p.m. at Chez Benoit, the chic bistro near the Pompidou Centre. However, when the lovers were ready to leave, they noticed that paparazzi had gathered outside the entrance to the apartment building. Supposing that they would never be left to dine in peace, they cancelled the reservation and headed for the Ritz, where they arrived at 9:50 p.m., to be greeted by nearly sixty photographers.

As the biographer Donald Spoto observes in *Diana: The Last Year*, "For people who ostensibly wished to avoid the media, they spent an inordinate amount of time going out." Of course, neither Diana nor Dodi knew how their lives would end, and the thrill of the chase, with the paparazzi on the scent, doubtless added excitement to an already electrifying atmosphere. If they were indeed contemplating marriage, as the indications are, or were merely considering the alternative of committing themselves to being together without the benefit of matrimony for the present, as the anti-Fayed camp prefer to believe, they would have been in highly charged moods. In such a state, their desire, to see and be seen, would be explicable, indeed natural.

It was as the eye of the hurricane that Diana and Dodi entered Espadon, the Ritz's excellent restaurant. Their presence was enough to unleash a hush of open-mouthed stares. Although Diana was well-used to such conditions, and usually ignored them with equanimity, Dodi was not, so they went upstairs to dine in the Imperial Suite.

While waiting for their dinner, Dodi asked the management to get in touch with Henri Paul, the deputy director of security, whom he trusted. He then decided that he wanted Paul to drive Diana, Trevor Rees-Jones and himself back to Rue Arsene-Houssaye from the back of the hotel, taking the Rue Cambon exit. His own driver, Philippe Dourneau, would leave as a decoy from the front of the hotel in his Mercedes with the Range Rover following.

Although Paul was already off duty, he was called back to the hotel. While Diana and Dodi dined upstairs, he sat downstairs in the bar with Trevor Rees-Jones and Kes Wingfield, another Fayed bodyguard. Significantly, in the light of subsequent events, both bodyguards confirm that there was absolutely no indication that Paul was anything but cold sober. The visual confirmation of this is contained on the video footing taken minutes before Henri Paul departed on that fateful journey. He is seen getting down on his haunches to tie his shoe laces in as eloquent a refutation of drunken uncontrolledness as it is possible to display. Having accomplished that feat with all the dexterity of the sober, he then bounces back onto his feet with the balance of a gymnast. Bearing in mind that the American police use toeing-the-line as the acid test for drunkenness, someone who could perform such a balancing act could hardly be regarded as having had his faculties impaired by drink or drugs, whatever his alcohol and drug levels.

At 12:15 a.m., the Imperial Suite put security downstairs on standby. Diana and Dodi were on their way down. They exited through the back, Diana taking a seat behind Trevor Rees-Jones, who occupied the front passenger seat of the black Mercedes S-280, while Dodi sat behind Paul on the left side of the car. None of the occupants had on their seat belts, though Rees-Jones did put his on sometime before the crash.

At 12:20, the car pulled out onto the Rue Cambon, followed by paparazzi on motorbikes. As the car headed towards the Rue de Rivoli, it gathered speed. At the Place de la Concorde, Paul jumped a red light in a successful attempt to put distance between him and the photographers giving chase. He hurtled at speed (estimates range from 62 – 121 mph, but the fact is, no one knows for sure, as Mercedes-Benz speedometers are designed to return to 0 upon impact, and this one performed accordingly) towards the Pont de l'Alma, and an underground tunnel with a slight ski-jump effect at its barely curving entrance, and a speed limit of 30 miles per hour. Within seconds, the car hit a pillar in the tunnel.

It was 12:24 a.m., Sunday, 31 August 1997.

Twenty-one

Whether there will ever be a precise or accurate reconstruction of the events leading up to the deaths of the Princess of Wales, Dodi Fayed and Henri Paul, remains to be seen. At the time of writing, the only certainties are the pieces of the puzzle that indicate what happened.

The security cameras at the Ritz give the time of the car's departure. It was 12:20 a.m. Four minutes later the Mercedes carrying the passengers was a crumpled heap, its front buckled against the thirteenth column in the Pont de l'Alma tunnel. What happened in those four minutes has been hotly disputed, and seems set to remain a matter of contention for some time to come – if not forever.

One point that is worth noting at this juncture is the state of the car immediately after the accident. It was *not* crumpled front and back, as many people, who have seen the photograph of it being hoisted onto a lorry for removal after its occupants had been cut out of it, seem to think. There was absolutely no damage to the back of the vehicle, as photographs which I have seen prove. All damage sustained was to the front, where the engine was situated.

Chloe Papazahariakis and Vlad Borovac, winners from Australia of a fashion contest, were outside the Ritz taking a souvenir video when, according to Chloe, "It all happened so quickly. Two guys came running out of the hotel, jumped into a Mercedes and Range Rover and took off." These were the decoy vehicles, driving the wrong way up the street. Intent on capturing the drama, she trained her camera on them, noticing that they were being followed by a white Citroën AX, similar in size and design to the Fiat Uno which later became the subject of an intensive search. Having captured that vignette on film, Chloe and Vlad continued on their trip, thinking no more about what they had seen until they returned to Australia. Four months later, a friend told them about the nationwide search for the white car, and, appreciating the possible significance of the car captured on their video, they got in touch with the Australian police. The video was handed over to the judge in charge of the investigation, Hervé Stephan.

Whatever the role of the Citroën AX may have been, it seems unlikely that it played a fundamental part in the tragedy, for the vehicle which, according to one theory, is meant to have been the catalyst, was a white Fiat Uno. This has been determined by the relics found on the Mercedes or on the Place de l'Alma itself – the remnants of a wing mirror, shards of plastic and glass, paint used on Fiat Uno models between 1983 and 1989.

To date, several independent witnesses have stated that there was a motorcycle approaching or in the tunnel at the time of the crash. This bike seems to have belonged to a twenty-eight-year-old chef named Eric Petel. He was riding his motorcycle near the entrance to the underpass when he saw a car in his rearview mirror flashing its lights "several times," as a warning to keep clear. It roared past. "I heard a deafening crash. At first I thought it was my bike, so I looked down at the engine and there was nothing wrong. But when I looked up again I saw the accident – the car which had overtaken me was facing the wrong way. The front was completely smashed in and there was smoke coming out of the engine. I stopped and parked my bike by the car's boot.

"It was dark in the tunnel and I couldn't see much. I saw a woman who had slid down off the back seat. Her head was between the two front seats and her back was to me. I could only see her hair."

According to Petel, he wanted to get the only female in the car out before it caught on fire. He wiped the hair from her face, laid her head on the back armrest, and her eyes flickered, though she did not open them. "It was then that I realized it was Diana, and from that moment I did not touch her again." Pushing the door closed, he ran to his bike and set off to get help. Within a minute he had reached a telephone box. He dialled the emergency services but they refused to believe him when he said that "Lady Diana" had been involved in a car crash. So he rode to the Avenue Mozart police station, where he was once more derided before being handcuffed for half an hour. Then he was questioned for two hours before signing a statement. "They wanted me to admit I hadn't phoned," he said.

Petel later contacted Antoine Deguines, a lawyer who confirmed that he "gave me lots of details about the accident which only appeared in the press much later." Both Petel and Deguines assumed that the dossier detailing Petel's comments had been passed to Judge Hervé Stephan. By chance, however, Deguines discovered that this was not so when he met up with Stephan during a trial in Paris. "When I spoke about Petel, it was clear he was surprised and didn't know what I was talking about."

Although Petel does not remember any other cars being in the tunnel when he reached Diana and Dodi's car, other witnesses have different recollections. It is possible that the vehicle could have left the tunnel by the time Petel reached the scene of the accident, or that its back lights were not functioning.

Gary Hunter, a London solicitor in Paris for the weekend with his wife, told Scotland Yard that he had seen a small car, possibly a Fiat Uno, roaring off from the tunnel exit just seconds after the crash. Georges and Sabine D, a Parisian couple who wish to remain protected, were on the slip road, into which the tunnel exits, when they saw a battered white Fiat Uno bobbing and weaving its way out of the tunnel. It was backfiring furiously and the driver, who had a large dog in the back seat, "didn't see us at all, he was so busy watching what was going on in his rearview mirror." The driver was about forty, had short brown hair, and was wearing a bomber jacket; the car was "about ten years old, with body work in bad shape. It had little dents everywhere." It also had a Paris license number, and while they could not be sure, they believed it was 92, denoting the densely populated suburb of Hauts-de-Seine. The time was approximately 12:25 a.m.

Martine Monteil, the chic and attractive chief superintendent of the Paris Criminal Brigade, headed the elite force that investigated the accident and deaths. In her possession are several other statements from witnesses who saw a second car coming from the tunnel after the crash. One is from a man who was walking above the entrance and happened to notice a small car about to enter the tunnel in the slow, righthand lane, and the Mercedes bearing up at a high speed in the fast, lefthand lane. Within moments, there was the crash.

Despite the best endeavours of Monteil and her team, who concentrated their search on Hauts-de-Seine, quizzing many of the 1,800

Fiat Uno owners and garage mechanic after mechanic, they were unable to find any Fiat Uno that matched the description supplied to them until they had a stroke of luck. A man came to settle a minor traffic infraction at a police station in Clichy, a suburb three miles from the Pont de l'Alma. He was driving his brother's Fiat Uno, which was freshly sprayed despite being twelve years old. The Clichy police passed their suspicions on to Monteil's team, who sent six officers at 6 a.m. one morning in November to raid the owner's council-owned apartment. There they found Le Van Thanh, a second generation Vietnamese immigrant, with short dark hair and two rottweilers, Max and Nen.

According to Thanh, when he bought the jalopy last summer, it was white, but his brother, who works in a Citroën garage, offered to respray it red. This he did hours after Diana's death.

Monteil's men duly arrested Thanh, questioned him, tested the paint on his car and released him. "Once they realized the paint did not match, they were very nice to me. They didn't even telephone work to check my story. They eventually released me about 12:30 p.m. the same day."

Monteil claimed she ruled him out of her investigation, which she then closed within months of the accident, but other sources said they were keeping an open mind on Thanh and a few other Fiat Uno owners.

One such owner was James Andanson, a paparazzo who had often photographed Diana and other celebrities, and who was reputed to have connections with the secret services in France. He drove a white Fiat Uno of a similar age and identical colour. One of the conspiracy theories which evolved had him using his vehicle to obstruct the path of the Mercedes, thereby forcing it to brake suddenly and hit the pillar. The fact that he died two years later in his locked car, engulfed in flames, has been employed to feed the suspicion that he might have been eliminated to silence him before he could go public about his part in Diana and Dodi's assassination.

There is not, nor has there ever been, one scrap of proof that Andanson's car was the white Fiat Uno involved in the crash. It would have been a simple enough matter to compare the paintwork of his car with the scrapings found in the Pont d'Alma tunnel after the crash. The fact that not even Mohamed Al Fayed's team did so, nor made the request that the officials do so, despite his belief that his son and Diana had been murdered, pours a healthy dose of cold water on this theory. Nor is there any proof that Andanson was a member of the secret services. Even if he had been, it is highly unlikely that the French (or the British, for that matter) sercret services would have been using a part-time informer as a hitman, when they would have had professional operatives whose services they could call upon in preference.

Had James Andanson gone on record claiming to have had a hand in the death of Diana (he did not), in the absence of any corroborating evidence (there was none), there might have been some room for doubt, but the fact is that he made no such claims.

As if that dearth of evidence and adequate claims, even from the supposed perpetrator, were not enough to shed light on this impenetrable conspiracy theory, its espousers point to James Andanson's death two years later to support their theory that he was the hitman. He was found dead, locked in his burnt-out car. The conspiracy theorists point to that as proof that he was eliminated by the secret services to keep him quiet before he had a chance to go public with his part in the assassination. They completely ignore the fact that he had two years in which to go public but did not do so, and two years is a very long time in which to make a financial killing if you are as prone to do so as they would have us believe Mr Andanson was. They also ignore the fact that his death, while being horrendous and grotesque, could have been self-inflicted, and, even if it was not, there were sufficient other suspects with whom he had been involved (by their own account, not mine) who had as much motive, if not more, as the supposed secret services in eliminating him.

Yet another conspiracy, equally implausible, is that Henri Paul was an MI6 operative who undertook the task of eliminating Diana. The fact that he had £102,000 in thirteen different bank accounts is used as substantiation of that theory. While it is no part of my brief as a biographer to propound alternative theories, it seems to me, as it surely must to anyone of reason and sophistication, that the deputy head of security at the Ritz Hotel in Paris could have had a variety of alternative means of validly acquiring such a sum. Without intending to slur Mr Paul's memory in any way, he could easily have been having nice little earners on the side, from assisting Saudi Princes with their pleasureable activities (they would tip between £1,000 and £10,000 per trip for such facilitation), to other equally innocent activities that form the part and parcel of elite living. The fact that such an explanation has never been furthered before, indicates to me that it is not Mr Paul's malignant conspiratorial activities that has been responsible for base accusations being levelled against a dead man, but the commentators' ignorance of how life is lived at a certain level. It strikes me that it does stretch the imagination to expect reasonable people to accept that Henri Paul would commit suicide, or run the risk of doing so, to assassinate Diana. Surely the whole purpose of being a murderer is that you live to enjoy the benefits of your crime? Or are rational people now to accept as reasonable the theory that an MI6 operative was so dedicated to his task that he was prepared to endanger his own life?

According to the conspiracy theorists, Henri Paul's blood samples were switched. They point to the high level of carbon monoxide in his blood as substantiation. While those of us who like to keep an open mind do so, the fact remains that, even if his blood samples were switched (which seems unlikely, for four days after the accident, on 4 September 1997, the investigating judge, Hervé Stéphan, went back to the morgue and had additional samples of Paul's blood, hair and tissues taken in the presence of police inspectors – and took the additional precaution of photographing the whole procedure, as a result of Mohamed Al Fayed having disputed the findings of the original samples), that does not prove anything but sloppiness or cover-up on the part of the investigating authorities. Certainly it does not prove murder, and I say this as someone who does keep an open mind regarding those samples, for every doctor I have spoken to has pointed out that, had Henri Paul had such a high level of carbon monoxide in his blood while driving, he would not have been able to do so. Indeed, he wouldn't have been able to stand, much less drive. Moreover, like all reasonable people, I have used my eyes and my brain and have come to the inescapable conclusion that, even if he had been three times over the drink-drive limit, as we have been led to believe by those blood samples that he was, he patently cannot have had his faculties impaired to the extent that he was incapable of co-ordinated function, because the video footage shows him, minutes before he stepped behind the wheel of the death car, getting down onto his haunches and tying his shoes laces with the grace of a ballet dancer. There is an explanation which covers some of these anomalies, but I shall provide it later.

Another conspiracy theory is that James Andanson or a photographer or a secret service agent (the identity of the perpetrator depends on the conspiracy thoeorist) stunned Henri Paul with a bright light, thereby blinding him and causing the crash. Of all the conspiracy theories, that is the one which holds up most strongly to examination, and moreover offers a motive for switching Henri Paul's blood samples, but I shall not deal with it here, but later. What I will say at this juncture, however, is that it is the only theory that has an outside chance of being proven to have any validity, and it is, moreover, the scenario which provides a possible rational explanation for an element of the conduct of the French authorities.

According to Martine Monteil, "We believe this was an accident. The conspiracy theories are rubbish. We have done our utmost and our conclusion is tragic but simple: Diana, Dodi and Henri Paul's deaths are nothing more than a terrible, unfortunate accident."

In France, investigations are confidential until their conclusion. The police are therefore not supposed to speak about ongoing matters, but one source told me in the months following Diana's death, "We're pretty confident whoever owns the car (the Fiat Uno) was just in the wrong place at the wrong time. The circumstances speak for themselves. A car going 120 kilometres per hour approaches a tunnel with a ski-lift curve. In front of it is another car going 30 miles per hour. Maybe the slow car is too far into the road or maybe the driver of the fast car is just having difficulty controlling his vehicle. For whatever reason, he collides with the slow car. His front bumper grazes the back light of the Fiat. They brush aside one another as the Mercedes flies past. Skid marks indicate the driver is wrestling for control. He can't control the vehicle. It's now out of control. It slams into one of the pillars in the centre of the tunnel. The driver of the other car, he might have had a bit too much to drink. He might have no insurance. He might be worried about his insurance rising if he's involved in an accident, and he can't afford to pay a higher premium. He might be some poor guy or an immigrant who's afraid of the police, of authority, who's terrified he's going to get into trouble and be blamed for the crash. So what does he do? He drives off and disappears into the night. The following day, he discovers he's been involved in the crash that killed the Princess of Wales. Given the facts we know, that is the only theory that stands up to all the evidence.

"As for the conspiracy theories, *merde*. No one knew the route Diana and Dodi were taking. How can you stage a crash in front of a car you didn't know was going to be there, especially a powerful car like a Mercedes going at 121 kilometres per hour?! The proposition is preposterous. If Diana and Dodi had been wearing seat belts, they might well have lived – especially Diana. Who's going to stage a hit where the victims will survive and where there are so many variables? If anyone had been going to kill Diana and Dodi, they'd have done it the week before, while they were swimming. Send in a frogman or two, grab the intended victim's foot, pull them underwater long enough to drown them, then release them. A good, clean hit, with all the hallmarks of an accidental death due to cramp.

"People always want to be fanciful. The fact is, there was no hit. The crash was an accident between a high-powered car going four times over the speed limit and a battered old car going within the speed limit. That's all it was, a tragic accident.

"It's an accident that might well have happened whether the Fiat Uno was in the tunnel or not. Henri Paul was nearly three times over the drink limit. He was going four times over the speed limit. And he started having difficulties as soon as he entered the tunnel, as the evidence proves. That should not be surprising to people. There's the ski-lift aspect to the tunnel, which also curves quite sharply as it descends. And there's the change in the quality of the light. No one mentions the light, but it's important. All of a sudden, you have someone who's not totally in control of himself driving too fast and wrestling for control as the light changes and temporarily stuns him. All these factors coming together. He's wrestling to control the car that's taking off like a skier, as the tunnel turns and he's momentarily blinded. Maybe it was too much for him to cope with. Maybe it would've been too much for anyone to cope with, drunk or sober, whether the Fiat Uno had been there or not. As you English say, it could well have been the straw that broke the pony's (sic) back."

The police point of view has validity and raises the question: Who has ultimate responsibility for the accident? While there can be no doubt that Henri Paul must share responsibility, if indeed he was inebriated or doped (the jury must still remain out on that one until all doubts are removed), he was nevertheless so capable a driver that he had Dodi's trust. And Dodi's trust was not easily gained, as Barbara Broccoli, his close friend, indicated, stating that "Dodi was nervous of speed." Moreover, Paul had been specially trained in avoidance techniques and was a "better driver drunk than most drivers when sober," to quote what Mohamed Al Fayed told a friend. The likelihood, therefore, is that Paul would most likely have safely delivered Diana and Dodi to his apartment on the Rue Arsene-Houssaye, had they not been travelling at the speed they were, or had there not been a catastrophic intervention, which cannot yet be ruled out.

That raises the question of how Paul came to be driving at the speed he was. Whether it was 60 or 90 miles per hour (or indeed at an even greater speed) is a moot point, but what is not, is that he was driving way above the speed limit, as eyewitnesses, whose comments I recount later, stated to the French investigators. No one who has ever been an employer or an employee can seriously believe that any driver would travel at two or threee times the speed limit on a city street, except at the behest and with the approval of his superiors. While it might never be possible to determine whether Dodi or Diana gave the order to lose the paparazzi, it seems likely that he did so, for it was his staff driving. But it is ludicrous to imagine that any man, desperately in love with what he considers to be the most desirable woman in the world, would instruct his staff to carry out orders he did not expect to please the object of his adoration. Whether Dodi had given the order or not, Diana also had the power to make Paul slow down. One word from her and Dodi, ever eager to please, would have transmitted her desire, or supported her order, in an instant. The very fact that Diana and Dodi both sat in that car, laughing as it entered the tunnel strongly suggests that they condoned the speed at which he was travelling. And for those sceptics who do not wish to accept their shared responsibility, I will point out that there is a photograph, which I have seen, taken *after* the car entered the tunnel, showing Diana and Dodi laughing uproariously in the back seat a second or two before the crash. Henri Paul and Trevor Rees-Jones are staring straight ahead, the former concentrating fixedly on his driving, the latter just staring intently. Neither man is smiling, which suggests that they were serious while Diana and Dodi were not.

Wherever the fault lies, the fact is, the Mercedes slammed into the thirteenth pillar of the underpass of the Pont de l'Alma at 12:24 a.m. at speed. The mighty car buckled, the radiator pushed to where Henri Paul was sitting. He died instantly, as did Dodi, who was seated behind him. Diana was hurled between the front seats, semiconscious but alive, while Trevor Rees-Jones, who had put on his seat belt some time before the point of impact, was horribly injured. There has been the supposition that his injuries were caused not by the first point of impact, when the car hit the pillar, and the airbag inflated, but by the second impact, when the car spun around and slammed against the wall. By this time the airbag was deflating, which would have left his face vulnerable to blows.

If Eric Petel's account is accurate, a second and third good Samaritan happened upon the scene of the accident by chance soon after he went off to seek help. While an off-duty fireman tended to Trevor Rees-Jones, Frederic Mailliez, a doctor who works for the French emergency service SOS Médecins, and who subsequently lectured with me at Goldsmith's College at a symposium on Diana, attended to her, after blocking the road with his car and telephoning the emergency services on his mobile telephone. "There was the smell of fuel and burning," Mailliez said. "The driver was obviously dead and so was the male passenger in the back. I began examining the young woman in the back. I could see she was beautiful but at that stage I had no idea who she was." The doctor and Eric Petel both agree upon her position. "She was semiconscious, muttering, but never saying anything precise." The doctor "tried to comfort her as best I could and ask where the pain was. I said that the ambulance would soon be there and that everything would be OK. All the things you say to soothe someone who is suffering." He "altered her position to clear her airways" and "gently put a resuscitation mask over her mouth." Then the ambulance arrived and Dr Mailliez, who still had no idea whom he had been treating, departed.

Seven months later, when Rees-Jones's memory, which had been affected during the crash, started to return, he stated that he heard a woman "who must have been Diana, calling out Dodi's name." This recollection is not incompatible with what Dr Mailliez said, but does not entirely rule out his recollection, for Rees-Jones might have heard her calling to the man she "adored" immediately after the crash, or at some point before Dr Mailliez arrived.

It is fairly certain, however, that Diana never spoke after the doctor left and the emergency services took over. By then she was slipping deeper and deeper into unconsciousness as she bled internally. According to Bernard Kouchner, France's Health Minister, her injuries were catastrophic, "the blood vessels in her heart so badly ruptured that she could not have survived." A simple tear of the pulmonary artery was not the only injury, which foils the claim that Diana might have survived had she been taken to the hospital quickly enough.

While Diana lay dying, the paparazzi who had been giving her chase caught up with the car. Others soon heard of the accident and arrived as well. "They did not impede my efforts," Dr Mailliez said, putting paid to the claim that they stopped the doctors from doing their work.

Laurent Sola, a photographer who has won awards for photography in war-torn areas and is well known for the standard of his work, told me, "I was there. It is unfair to say that they (the paparazzi) caused the crash or were getting in the way of the doctors. Of course we took pictures of the scene. We're photographers and it was a valid news story. But neither I nor anyone at my agency will ever sell a photograph of Diana as she was dying. Yes, I have photographs of her. Yes, she did look lovely. No damage to her face. But I will never sell one. We're not animals. It's unfair that we were made out to be in the aftermath of the crash."

Subsequently, the French emergency services were also lambasted. A doctor at La Pitié-Salpêtrière said, "Criticism of the French emergency services could not be less justified. They moved heaven and earth to keep Lady Diana alive. Had they moved her suddenly, she would have died *en route* to the hospital. The public has no idea how tenuously she was clinging to life. She'd have died twenty minutes after the accident if it hadn't been for the medical team on the scene. What they were trying to do was keep her alive in the vain hope that when they got her to the hospital something could be done to save her. But it was obvious from early on that she'd need a miracle to survive. That doesn't mean they didn't do their job well. They kept her alive for nearly an hour and a half past the time she should've been dead. It's not their fault the miracle didn't come."

Dr Mailliez agreed with that assessment. "Nothing could have saved her. She didn't stand a chance."

Despite the best efforts of the emergency services, Diana, Princess of Wales, suffered cardiac arrest around the time she arrived at Pitie-Salpetriere. The medical team at the hospital went to superhuman lengths to attempt to save her. For two hours they kept pumping her heart, trying to revive the beautiful young woman who lay dead on the operating table. Finally, they had to accept the unavoidable, Diana was indeed dead.

This was not the first of Diana's heart attacks. Twenty minutes after the crash, she suffered her first attack, as she was being tended to by the recovery services and cut out of the car. They did not know it at the time, but Diana's superior left pulmonary artery was ripped and her pericardium ruptured. In other words, one of the main arteries that draws blood from the lungs back to her heart had been torn off, and was pouring blood into her internal cavity instead of into her heart, while the membrane enclosing her heart had ripped, allowing it to spill out into the right side of her chest cavity. Dr Kenneth Azan, an eminent American cardiologist, told me, "She could not possibly have survived an injury like that." In lay terms, Diana's heart had been torn from its mooring at the moment of impact, disconnected and come to rest in the wrong place in her chest cavity, the right side of it oozing out of its ruptured protective membrane. She also had a fractured right arm, two large gashes to her right thigh, wounds to her forehead and left ankle, as well as bruising to her body and hands. The fact that she did not die after her first heart attack is in itself a testament to the expertise of the French recovery services.

Throughout the ordeal, the Prince of Wales and the Queen were kept closely informed. Once the police in Paris realized that Diana, Princess of Wales had been injured, they contacted the Interior Minister, Jean-Pierre Chevenement, who sped to the hospital in time to be there for her arrival at 2 a.m. Before doing so, he contacted Sir Michael Jay, the British Ambassador to Paris, who telephoned Robin Janvrin, the Queen's Assistant Private Secretary, at Balmoral. He woke up the Prince of Wales to give him the news. Charles woke up his mother, and together they decided not to disturb the children but to let them sleep in peace. Mohamed Al Fayed, meanwhile, had also been contacted. He flew to Paris immediately.

That Sunday morning of 31 August 1997, William and Harry awoke expectantly. They would be flying south today to see their mother before returning to school early in September. The sad task of telling them they would never see her again fell to their father. Stunned, they elected to adhere to the routine of their day, and set off for church with their father and grandparents. Later, the Royal Family would be roundly criticized for taking the boys to church, but Princess Margaret said, "Can you think of a more appropriate place for children to go at a terrible time like this?" Meaning, with their beloved grandparents, who respected their request for a continuance – and through it, reassurance – of the expected.

After church, William and Harry returned to Balmoral with their grandparents while Charles went to Aberdeen for a flight to Paris. There he linked up with Diana's sisters, Sarah and Jane, the former grief-stricken because they had died close, the other disconsolate because they had never patched up their differences.

Diana's mother was also disconsolate, and for the same reason as her middle daughter. According to Joseph Sanders, "Diana herself told me she wasn't speaking to her mother. Anything you hear to the contrary is untrue. She hadn't been speaking to her for the last year, ever since Frances had given that interview to *Hello!*"

In May 1997, Diana's mother, a devout Roman Catholic, had sold an interview to the social magazine to raise funds for her church in Scotland. Not only was Diana incensed that her mother was "making money out of me," but she was apoplectic when she read Frances saying, "I thought it was absolutely wonderful that Diana was stripped of her HRH title." This, to Diana, was tantamount to treason. She had taken the loss of her royal rank badly, and was "bemused" that her mother could exult in something which had caused her such distress. "She must have been drunk," Diana said to Joseph bitterly, going on to recount that she believed her mother had a drinking problem and she was sick of it.

According to Alan Frame, there was merit in Diana's comments. "When I was at the *Daily Express*, Mrs Shand Kydd would often phone up and have a go at us about something we'd written about her daughter. She'd rail on, slurring her words and giving the impression of being under the influence. Sometimes, this would be before ten o'clock in the morning. We used to laugh about it. It came as no shock to any of us when she lost her driver's licence through drunk driving."

Death, of course, is a great leveller and can also be a great healer. Charles, Sarah and Jane arrived at the hospital, to be greeted by twelve members of the Guarde Républicain in their red, blue and gold uniforms. As they stepped inside, they were greeted by President Jacques Chirac and two of the doctors who had tried to save Diana, the cardiac surgeon, Professor Alain Pavil, and the anesthetist, Professor Bruno Riou. After a few words, the shocked and grief-stricken trio set off to see the woman who had played such an important part in their lives. Although both the Prince of Wales and Lady Jane Fellowes had had troubled relationships with Diana, they had both loved her as well. The conflict and grief they must have felt can only be imagined as they prepared to view her body, which had been prepared by Paul Burrell, her capable butler. He had flown over from London with her make-up and had made her up so that she would once more be the beautiful Diana that everyone knew.

Because Diana had died a private citizen and no longer royal, she was not actually entitled to special treatment. Technically, her body should have been taken to the Fulham mortuary, which caters for Kensington, the district where the palace is located. Charles, however, insisted that the woman he had once loved, the mother of his children, be accorded all dignity, a decision with which the Queen was in accordance. "He's the one who wanted her treated as a full royal and said where she was to be taken," Princess Margaret said.

Twenty-five minutes after Charles, Sarah and Jane had arrived at La Pitié-Salpêtrière, they left. The coffin, draped in the Royal Standard brought by the Prince of Wales, was borne to the hearse by French pallbearers walking behind the Reverend Martin Draper of the Anglican St. George's Cathedral in Paris.

At the airport, Charles and Diana's sisters fought back tears as the Princess was loaded into the hold of the BAe 146 aircraft for the flight back to RAF Northolt. There to meet it, with eight RAF pallbearers to unload the coffin, was the Prime Minister, Tony Blair, who had talked, only weeks before of the "useful contribution" someone of Diana's special gifts could make to the national life; the then Lord Chamberlain, Lord Airlie, whose sister-in-law is Princess Alexandra; the Defence Secretary George Robertson, and the Queen's representative, the Lord Lieutenant of London, Field Marshal Lord Bramall. Twelve minutes later, the coffin was on its way to the mortuary for the family's own medical examination. Charles promptly returned to the plane, to fly back to Aberdeen and Balmoral, where the boys were waiting for his return with their grandparents.

At the same time, Dodi Fayed's coffin, draped in a black cloth with gold lettering, was being flown back to Britain on the Harrods Gulfstream IV, which had been the scene of so much happiness for Diana and himself. In accordance with the Muslim religion, which requires people to be buried within twenty-four hours, he was taken straight to the Regent's Park Mosque, where six hundred mourners gathered for the funeral service. From there, the coffin was taken to Brookwood Cemetery in Surrey, where it was interred.

Diana's body, meanwhile, was taken from the mortuary to the Chapel Royal at St. James's Palace, where she lay in state. Also at St. James's Palace was the book of condolence, which attracted such queues that some people had to wait four hours to sign it.

The six days between Diana's death and her funeral were a fraught time for the media. On the day of her death her brother, Charles, resident in South Africa, accused the media of having "blood on its hands," laying the blame for her death squarely at their feet. This, of course, was not particularly fair. Although the paparazzi had been chasing Diana and Dodi, they had not ordered the driver to travel at a deadly speed, nor had they tipped themselves off as to Diana and Dodi's destination after Sardinia. They were not sitting in a car going at high speed on an urban road without seat belts buckled. While they were a contributory factor, in that they were chasing the car for a photograph, it was ludicrous to suppose that the paparazzi were attempting to snatch images through tinted car windows. Such images would be unusable. They were merely doing their job, seeking to capture Diana and Dodi as they entered his apartment building. If they got a sensational picture, so much the better. But, at that precise moment, when news of the Diana and Dodi romance was the world's leading story, even a boring snap would have satisfied public curiosity – a curiosity which Diana herself had helped to stimulate in the previous weeks, and which she and Dodi could easily have appeased by walking out of the Ritz in the normal fashion, instead of skulking off like modern movie stars.

The fact is, the lovers and the paparazzi were all participants in a game. This game of publicity was one which Diana herself had been playing for years, not always happily but always vigorously and voluntarily, avid for the attention even though she was sometimes upset by the downside.

Nor was Diana the only member of the Spencer family who had been playing this game. Her brother had also been doing so for years, claiming to be a journalist and public figure when it suited him, and a private citizen when it did not. Like Diana, he had quite forgotten that public interest had come as a result of his connection with the Royal Family, and not because he was a Spencer – a family that had been of no general interest to the public in two hundred years, save as fodder for the intermittent scandals to which they treated the public, and the occasional mention in the gossip columns.

Charles Spencer, of course, was adept at manipulating the media, at providing the one photograph, the one sound bite, the one comment which would zing its way around the world, assuring him of the front page. In the circumstances immediately following his sister's death, however, his behaviour was not only inappropriate, but it was also unwise. Of course the media reported his comments about them having "blood on their hands," for such remarks were newsworthy. But they also remembered with rancour that he used the occasion to take an unwarranted swipe at them. Moreover, they were not blind to his hidden agenda, shoring up his complaint of invasion of privacy against certain British tabloids at the European Court, in an attempt to force a British privacy law through the back door.

During that week between Diana's death and her funeral, while the media reeled from the public perception that it did indeed have "blood on its hands," the Royal Family found themselves dragged into the loop. Always vulnerable to criticism of being out of touch, due to the privileged existence they lead, the Prince of Wales, Prince William, Prince Harry, the Queen and the Duke of Edinburgh were nevertheless behaving as any family would in similar circumstances. They had retreated from public view to come to terms with the tragedy in private, and to help Diana's children adjust to what was, in any terms, one of life's greatest traumas. Despite this perfectly normal conduct, and doubtless because the media needed to shift some of the condemnation from themselves, the Royal Family were dragged into the bloody arena and condemned for callousness.

Nor is this fanciful reasoning on my part. I was there, as a participant, speaking on CNN, NBC, ABC, CBS, the BBC and countless foreign TV and radio stations, being interviewed by newspaper after newspaper, magazine after magazine. There was no doubt in my mind what the tabloids, who kicked off the anti-Royal Family sentiment, were doing, and why.

In this world of instant communication, where one segment of the media leads, the others follow suit, rather like ducks trailing the leader on a migratory flight path to new feeding grounds. The upshot was that the Royal Family was immersed in controversy and had to react politically. Prince William and Prince Harry flew down from Balmoral with their father to go on a royal walkabout outside Kensington Palace, inspecting the hundreds of thousands of floral tributes left outside the palace gates, shaking hands with the public mourners and thanking them for their interest. The Queen and the Duke of Edinburgh also arrived at Buckingham Palace the day before the funeral to inspect the floral tributes outside those palace gates, and to meet the public. Afterwards, the Queen gave her first live television broadcast, paying tribute to Diana's "kindness" and saying that "there are lessons to be learned" from the public reaction, which she intended to take on board. To those cynics who doubted the sincerity of Her Majesty's words, her subsequent conduct, and the changes in style of the Royal Famiy, show that those words were not merely idle chatter.

The public reaction was indeed extraordinary. Not only in Britain, but in the United States as well, television stations cleared their decks and focused on Diana's life and death. Said Dr Basil Panzer, "She never interested me at all until she died. What makes her death so interesting is the public response. It was enormously fascinating. It was deep, extraordinarily rare. If you look for similar responses in the twentieth century in the whole Western world, there may be a dozen responses of this magnitude – Kennedy, Monroe, to name two.

"So how do I, as a psychologist, account for this nonrational response, this enormous response, of people who had no contact with her? The reason is that a person died whom we thought we knew well. Because we saw her picture every day, year in year out. A familiar person left our lives. Another reason is that this is a person whom we could identify with in our fantasies on many levels, because she stood for many things for us. Things we would like to identify with: youth, beauty, wealth, travelling in high circles and the jet set.

"She also stood for some psychologically deeper things. She was the fairy-tale princess and we all, men and women, have a fairy-tale princess in our mind. Let me explain. Every woman fantasizes about a fairy-tale princess within herself, and every man has a fairy-tale princess within himself he can rescue, etc. So she stood for the outside materialization of both men and women. She touched people with this. In addition, there were all the good works she dabbled in, allowing us to rationalize what a good person she was, dealing with the sick and poor. Most of us feel guilty about those people. She loved them in an open display, which made her very attractive to us, as it's something we don't want to touch. By touching them for us, she allowed us to touch them.

"She also stood for something else on another attractive unconscious level: the adolescent rebelliousness that all of us have. She rebelled against the establishment. In-laws. What was expected of her. Against dullness and duty. And she was the mother of two lovely boys, so everyone could watch and identify with her.

"It is conceivable that her life and tragic death has contributed to an upheaval in the Western world of a coming-into-legitimacy of pop culture against fuddy-duddy messy emotion and family values. There is also some glamorizing of the good instinct to help sick people, because we all have strong instincts but do nothing about them. So it was wonderful to have someone to act out these things that we have within us.

"And she died young. You have to die young for your death to have maximum impact."

Diana's royal title of Princess of Wales also undoubtedly added to the impact of her death. Had she died as Lady Diana Fayed, the reaction would doubtless have been considerably more muted. The panoply of royalty, with all its attendant splendour, was a dimension that should not be ignored. It also created the platform and focus for an outpouring of grief that helped bind the nation together, and reinforce the bonds of monarchy at the very moment that they were being tested. The mere fact that Kensington, Buckingham, and St. James's palaces existed meant that they became focal points for mourning. Once the Royal Family went on their walkabouts and the Queen had given her televised speech, the media and public seemed satisfied. Their grief – the people's, not the royals' – had been acknowledged. Their anger was assuaged and it abated. They now hugged themselves to the bosom of monarchy, one nation united in grief under the Crown, ready for the final outpouring: the funeral.

Royal funerals, as the world learned on 6 September 1997, are stirring, heart-wrenching, magnificent affairs. Diana's, like her wedding, was the most watched event of its kind in the history of the world. Diana, of course, was no longer royal. Although Diana was not entitled to a state funeral, she was given as close to one as someone who is not a sovereign or consort can have. "The funeral was mostly the doing of the Prince of Wales, who talked the Queen into it with the help of Tony Blair. The role of the Prime Minister is to advise. Even if Diana had still been married to Prince Charles," a royal, who did not wish to be identified, said, "she was not entitled to anything more than a semi-public funeral at St. George's Chapel, Windsor, followed by interment at Frogmore. That's the full extent of it. She had no right to a public funeral, a funeral at Westminster Abbey, or a semi-state occasion. It's to the Prince of Wales's credit that he understood how important it was for his sons and for the nation that she get a good send-off, so to speak. And it's to the Queen's credit that she was flexible enough to agree." Death had sped up Diana's rehabilitation, which had begun after the divorce, dramatically, proving her claim to Joseph Sanders that "I have a good relationship with the Queen. I have no problems with her."

The funeral was more than just a semi-state occasion. It was also intensely personal, reflecting Diana's tastes and interests. Of course, it was organized with all the flair and experience that the Earl Marshal's office has at its disposal. Some touches were brilliant, like Diana's two beloved boys walking behind the coffin from Buckingham Palace, with their father, their grandfather the Duke of Edinburgh, and their uncle Charles Spencer, to Westminster Abbey. Another poignant touch was the members of the many charities she had supported before her divorce, walking behind the family members in a testament to the work she had done, and the lives she had touched.

As the guests filed into the Abbey, they, too, typified the particular blend that was uniquely Diana. The charity workers, the aristocrats, doctors like Hasnat Khan; movie personalities Tom Cruise and Nicole Kidman, Steven Spielberg, Tom Hanks, the Arnold Schwarzeneggers; pop stars like George Michael and Sting; fashion editors like Liz Tilberis of *Harper's Bazaar;* fashion personalities like Sandro and Donatella Versace, Karl Lagerfeld, Christian Lacroix; photographers like Patrick Demarchelier. Although all the Royal Family was present, including the Duchess of York *en famille* for the first time since 1992, other royals were thin on the ground. In ordinary circumstances, this would have been a slap in the face, but considering the anomalies of her position, it was appropriate. Tony Blair had called her the People's Princess, causing the Tory Party to accuse him of playing politics by tying her to his cause, but they were as wrong as he was. She was really a "pop" Princess, the embodiment of the values and mores of her age. She belonged to all people who were in tune with contemporary life.

In his funeral oration, Earl Spencer made the point that Diana was no "saint." The Cardinal-Archbishop of Westminster, Basil Hume, who knew her well and with whom she did a lot of her homeless work, also felt compelled to point out that Mother Teresa, who died within days of Diana, was the saint, not the Princess he had known and liked. Diana herself was frequently at pains to state that she and sainthood were incompatible. Two of the many people to whom she said this were Liz Tilberis and Roberto Devorik, the Argentine fashion entrepreneur, who was a friend of hers. That, of course, was the secret of Diana's success. She had a compulsion to be recognized as a feeling and flawed human being, which is, of course, what we all are. Hence the readiness for people to identify with her.

Regrettably, Spencer's eulogy, which was brilliant and moving, was besmirched by the bitter swipes he made upon the Royal Family and his own mother. "Was it really necessary to allude to the lonely train journeys he and Diana had made between their divorced parents, in Frances's presence?" Lady Sarah Spencer-Churchill said. "What did he hope to accomplish by accusing the Royal Family of treating Diana badly? And what rubbish was he jabbering on about when he said Diana needed no royal title to wield her particular brand of magic. Did he think anyone would have heard or cared about her if she'd remained Lady Diana Spencer? Is the title Princess of Wales not a royal title? His speech, for speech is what it was, was more suited to the political hustings than a sister's funeral." Nevertheless, like most cheap shots that are well aimed and dramatically delivered, it hit its mark to public acclaim.

In the immediate aftermath, Spencer was hailed a hero. He had staked his claim to the moral high ground. He and the remainder of the Spencer family would be the guardians of William's and Harry's spirits. They would see that these could "sing free" with "joy" instead of being ossified by "duty and tradition," the way royal souls are. As if duty were a failing instead of a virtue.

Empty vessels, of course, are known to make the most noise. Within months, the acclaim that had rung in Charles Spencer's ear had turned to a drumroll of condemnation. His application to have his divorce heard in South Africa instead of London was bitterly contested by his wife, the former model Victoria Lockwood, on the grounds that she could expect to receive a substantially lower settlement in the former British dominion. It emerged that this multimillionaire, worth some £100 million, had offered his wife a mere $500,000 after eight years of marriage and four children. Moreover, he turned out to have mind-boggling double standards. Where his sister Diana's eating disorders were concerned, she was entitled to sympathy and the Royal Family deserved condemnation when the royals were involved, but not when he, Charles Spencer, was. Then, Diana was devious, manipulative, callous, a fickle friend, mentally ill and self-centred, and should clean up her act and grow up. Where his wife's eating disorders were concerned, however, there was no commensurate split: He was entitled to all the sympathy and she to none, because she was, as his mother put it, devious and cunning and a liar, like all other people sharing her disorder! The family seems not to have cared about the inconsistencies in their attitude, but then, victory, not consistency, was the object of the exercise. Of course, Charles Spencer had not expected to have his dirty linen washed in public. He did not understand that in South Africa, unlike in Britain, divorce applications are open to the public.

The media had been waiting for the moment to ambush Charles Spencer ever since he had attacked them for having his sister's blood on their hands. They were happy to expose him as a cruel, arrogant, bully who admitted in writing to his mistress that he had been all of those things to his wife; who had dismissed her out of his life as soon as she came out of the hospital, after being treated for anorexia and alcoholism, calling her into the bathroom where he was bathing to inform her that he no longer loved her and that the marriage was over; who then coldly informed her that he had had twelve mistresses in the time that she was being treated in the hospital; who made a speech when she was sick with anorexia alluding to how "thick" she was mentally and how "thin" she was physically; who prevented her from attending Diana's funeral, taking, instead, his girlfriend, the former Calvin Klein model Josie Borain.

By the time the media were through with Charles Spencer, never again would he be able to seize the moral high ground and proclaim himself as fitter than their own father to guide the destinies of Prince William and Prince Harry.

Since then, Spencer has reaped the rewards of what he sowed. Having buried Diana on an island, The Oval, Spencer implemented plans to convert outbuildings into a permanent museum to his sister. Each of six rooms has a theme, chronicling Diana's childhood, marriage, and charity work, and it was at first hailed an outstanding success and a money spinner when it opened in 1998. It was commonly regarded as being in good taste and interesting, as good a museum to Diana as it would be possible to create, even if the whole enterprise was laden with irony, for the man who could not give her a house in life had given her a grave as well as a museum in death. The publicity and attention which he had sought to avoid in her life, he tolerated in her death, accompanied as it was by the sweet sound of cash registers ringing up the takings of visitors who had to pay a healthy stipend to visit the Diana museum and look at the burial site from a respectful distance. They were not allowed to view the grave itself, or even step foot on the island, upon which the grave was sited, but part of the entrance price allowed them to view a pavilion with Diana's name carved into it. For two months each year, from Diana's birthday on 1 July to the anniversary of her death, of 31 August, the Princess of Wales attracted visitors to Althorp House in a way nothing else did before, although at the time of writing the word is that the museum will close its doors permanently at the end of the 2004 season owing to declining attendance numbers.

The intractable problem, of finding an attraction which would entice sufficient visitors to ameliorate significantly Althorp House's running costs, seemed to have been solved by Diana. The problem of running the house at a deficit of £400,000 per annum no longer existed. Diana in death had accomplished what even Diana could not in life, when the house had never made it into the top league of stately homes, despite the royal connection. There simply hadn't been enough to see or do, and, no matter what Raine and Johnnie or Charles did, nothing brought in the viewers, not even Diana's eminence.

"How she must be spinning in her grave," Joseph Sanders said to me. "Charles couldn't give her a house on the estate when she was alive. He couldn't cope with the inconvenience of the added security. Now he makes the sacrifice."

And the Royal Family, with whom she had such patchy relations for so many years, are also perceived as having benefited from her death. They have been able to come out of the long and dark shadows which her illness privately and her popularity publicly caused them. They have re-examined the role of the monarchy in the wake of the public reaction to her death, have become more open in style, and far more informal and approachable than they used to be.

Death is completing the healing process that Diana had already started in life.

Twenty-two

The inevitable consequence of the death of a loved one is grief. Since the tragic events of 31 August 1997, Diana's boys, family and friends slowly then surely came to terms with her death. "The boys have been fantastic," a royal cousin, who does not wish to be identified, told me in the months following her death. "Harry elected to go back to school when he could've stayed with the Prince of Wales beyond the start of term. William is Diana's son, more complex and highly strung than Harry. But he, too, seems to have accepted her death and got on with his life."

Of course, the loss of a parent is traumatic when children are fifteen and nearly thirteen, as William and Harry were. Although life has to go on, coming to terms with the reality takes years, and it did. Indeed, many psychologists are of the opinion that the death of a parent while a child or teenager is something that those children or teenagers have to deal with for the rest of their lives. In a way, therefore, they never entirely get over the trauma, even if they resolve it effectively.

"The Prince of Wales wiped whole blocks of time clear to be with the boys," the royal cousin said. "His office (had) specific instructions to avoid the boys' exeats (breaks from boarding school) and holidays wherever possible." When that was not possible, such as Charles's trip to South Africa during Harry's half-term break in the winter term of 1997, he had his son accompany him. On that occasion, "Harry met the Spice Girls. It was a big treat for him."

Since then, both boys have gone from strength to strength, graduating from Eton and, in the case of William, attending St Andrews'

University in Scotland. At the time of writing, Harry has been on a gap year and there is talk of him going into the Army rather than taking a second year off.

One difficulty in achieving closure for the family is the unresolved state of the inquiry in Britain into the deaths of the Princess and Dodi Fayed, now that the French authorities have concluded their inquiries into their deaths and Henri Paul's. Some six years after Diana's death, their findings were, unsurprisingly, that the deaths were accidental, caused by Henri Paul's high speed and the effects of the drink and drugs in his system.

With the French investigation concluded, the British authorities announced that the Royal Coroner, Michael Burgess, would be overseeing the inquests, which are due to take place some time next year, of both Diana and Dodi. As part of his inquiries, Mr Burgess invited the Metropolitan Police Commissioner, Sir John Stevens, to institute his own inquiries, and even accompanied him to Paris in April 2004, when they visited the Pont d'Alma tunnel with Martine Monteil of the Paris Criminal Brigade. Sir John stated publicly, "The whole credibility of my investigation would be jeopardized if I did not visit the accident scene and assess the evidence for myself. We have got to do everything we can so that when it comes to the inquest a line is drawn one way or another on this particular inquiry."

No one yet knows all the facts about the events leading to the deaths, and there remains a question mark as to whether Trevor Rees-Jones, the bodyguard who survived, will ever recover his memory sufficiently to fill in all the blanks. One thing we do know, is that Diana would have survived the crash had she been wearing her seat belt.

Another difficulty in achieving closure has been the rumours that arise whenever a famous person dies in a tragic accident. The two most painful areas of speculation for the family have been whether Diana was pregnant and whether she was murdered. The first story is easily dealt with. According to Dr Lily Hua Yu and Rosa Monckton, she was not. Dr Hua Yu treated Diana for premenstrual tension just before she left for her Greek trip. Rosa Monckton was on that cruise and confirms that pregnancy was a "biological impossibility." In other words, Diana was having her period two and a half weeks before her death.

Yet the pregnancy rumour has been persistent. I first heard it the day after her death, when a journalist asked if it was true. I next heard it, repeated as fact, from one of the former private secretaries. Another well-placed Palace source then asserted Diana was forty-five-days pregnant, which meant that Dodi had impregnated her the night before her departure from the South of France on that first trip with the boys. A surgeon at St. Thomas's Hospital, Dr Laura Jackson, then informed me that a counterpart at La Pitié Salpêtrière who had seen Diana's blood workup said, "She was definitely pregnant. For the first three days after the accident, her papers were in free circulation around the hospital. One of the doctors there told me that he saw them and they stated that she was pregnant. Then, three days after the accident, the papers were pulled. Since then, they've disappeared. Plainly word came from on high to remove the papers from circulation."

When dealing with stories about the famous, responsible writers have to use strict criteria for accepting statements as fact. Although there is no doubt that Dr Jackson is a credible witness and her words deserve the respect her status brings to them, the fact that she personally did not see the papers means that one has to be sceptical about accepting the word of her Parisian opposite number. This is not to cast aspersions upon his character, but simply to apply the strictest criteria to accepting as fact evidence that remains questionable in the light of being second hand. Moreover, the fact that the story took hold so soon after Diana's death in itself presents a warning against accepting it. While it is possible that Rosa Monckton was trying to protect her friend, it is less likely that Dr Hua Yu would lie. In the absence of a copy of the blood test or the post mortem report contradicting Dr Hua Yu, good sense and high standards of authentication indicate that her word ought to be final.

The conspiracy theories also sprang up within twenty-four hours of Diana's death. Libya was the first country to put forth the idea that Diana and Dodi had been killed because the British Establishment did not want a Muslim stepfather for the future King William V. Of course, it suited Libya to attribute anti-Muslim feeling to the British. There was then an ongoing dispute between the two countries over where the two Libyans wanted for the bombing of Pan Am 103 over Lockerbie should be tried. Britain has a large Muslim population, and Colonel Gaddafi has always had pretensions to being accepted as one of the leaders of the Muslim world. It was therefore in his political interest to present the British establishment as anti-Muslim and anti-Arab. If he could undermine

Muslims' faith in the attitude of the British establishment, and maybe even stir up some anti-British feeling among Muslims resident in Britain, so much the better. Under the circumstances, all reasonable people ought to have adopted a healthy scepticism toward anything the Libyans said about the British establishment, and I say this as someone who in 1977 was the Private Secretary of the Libyan Ambassador in London, and therefore had a degree of personal experience of the workings of the Libyan regime.

It would appear, however, that many people are only too ready to believe any conspiracy theory, no matter its source. Within forty-eight hours of Diana's death, the Libyan conspiracy theory was being touted all over the world as fact. One can only assume that the people who were so ready to believe it did not even know the source, much less stop to consider the reasons for its furtherance.

In the months following Diana's and Dodi's deaths, Mohamed Al Fayed began supporting the Libyan theory, since when he has accused everyone from Prince Philip to MI5 and MI6 of killing her and his son. Of course, it is never easy to lose a loved one, but to lose one's eldest son and, according to him, a prospective daughter-in-law of such eminence, under such tragic circumstances, must be hard indeed. One can sympathize with a parent's loss and understand how his grief has propelled Fayed's espousal of extravagant surmises.

Mohamed Al Fayed, however, is no ordinary parent. As Alan Frame, the former deputy editor of the *Daily Express* who worked for him pointed out to me, "Mohamed puts a spin on everything." The conclusion one reluctantly comes to is that Fayed has his own agenda. He is consumed with bitterness because he has not been granted British citizenship, despite his many contributions to British life in the form of taxes, commercial success and support for charities. When he claims that he is "99.9 percent sure" that Diana and Dodi were "killed" because "the establishment" viewed his son as a "nigger," and "didn't want them to be together," you have to stop and ask: What does Mohamed Al Fayed stand to gain? The obvious answer is that he discredits the very establishment which he blames for preventing him from becoming a proper Englishman.

Spin doctors do not let facts stand in the way of their theories, and in that, Mohamed Al Fayed has been true to his kind. He has ignored the fact that Henri Paul had been drinking and was on prescription drugs, which he had been on for some time beforehand, as the doctor who prescribed them has confirmed. Irrespective of whether they incapacitated him, he should therefore not have been taking the chance of driving at speed. He ignores the fact that Diana and Dodi's route was known to no one except to the four individuals in the car. He ignores the conditions prevailing at the time: the ski-jump effect of the tunnel entrance, the effect of the change of light upon a driver's eyesight, the possible existence of another car travelling into, or being in, the tunnel lawfully.

While conspiracy theories doubtless have their appeal to a public which has rightly become cynical over the years at the hypocrisy and self-interestedness with which the establishment, judiciary, police, bureaucracy and government go about their business, facts cannot be flicked off like flies pitching inconveniently upon one's shoulder.

Indeed, the Libyan/Mohamed Al Fayed theory is dubious and he ought to know it. He has spent more than three decades cultivating the British establishment in the hope of being assimilated into it. After all that time, he should have some understanding of how the system works. It is ironic that an Arab would accuse the British establishment of being anti-Arab, when it is a well-known fact, frequently deplored by the Zionists, that the British establishment is among the most pro-Arab in the world.

Moreover, the idea of the security forces receiving permission to "hit" a member of the Royal Family, even a semidetached one, does not stand up to examination. If the security forces functioned like that, they would surely have removed Diana years before, when she was doing damage to the monarchy by colluding with the media. While it is true that Diana had lost much of her credibility within the British establishment in the years preceding her death, not only had she started to regain some ground, but those segments of the establishment which wished she'd disappear – and there were many – were about to have their dream come a step closer to realization. Had Diana married Dodi Fayed, her popularity would have plummeted, not only in Britain, where the general public is significantly less pro-Arab than the establishment, but also in the US, where neither the establishment nor the populace is generally pro-Arab.

People only need to cast their minds back to 1968, when Jackie Kennedy married Aristotle Onassis, to have an indication of the effect a marriage with Dodi Fayed would have had upon Diana's standing. If Jackie's popularity had disappeared overnight when she married the older man, who was at least a man of substance and accomplishment whatever his reputation, how much more would Diana's have declined when she married the sweet but insubstantial son of a father of even more controversial reputation than Onassis? While Mohamed Al Fayed's sense of his own frustration leads him to speculate that the establishment wished to prevent a marriage so that he could be frozen out yet again (the government's refusal to grant him citizenship always being to the forefront of every Fayed pronouncement or theory), he quite fails to appreciate the true impact that any marriage between Diana and his son would have had. Not only would she have ceased to be a Princess of Wales, becoming instead Lady Diana Fayed, but she would also have had to spend years clawing back the respect which her public had lost when Dodi had slipped the ring on her finger. In other words, the establishment would not have needed to kill someone who was, according to Fayed, planning to commit populist suicide via matrimony.

And I say all of the above from the vantage point of one who believes that Mohamed Al Fayed has indeed made an outstanding contribution to British life. In my view, he should have been awarded British citizenship many years ago. He has breathed fresh life into Harrods, which was on the decline when he took it over from Sir Hugh Fraser, a charming man but no businessman. I know, through friends, of some of the quite wonderful charity work he has undertaken quietly and privately. If Tiny Rowland and Robert Maxwell could have been granted British citizenship, then there is every reason why Mohamed Al Fayed should have been as well. He is right to be bitter. Successive governments' refusal to grant him citizenship has been an injustice, when you stop to think of the flotsam and jetsam who are granted it.

His vociferous denunciation of the authorities, his vituperative bitterness, may be justified in terms of the frustration he feels as a result of seeing many less worthy characters than himself being granted the citizenship he so craved, but such sentiments do not add up to a plausible conspiracy theory. The facts do not support a hit, at least not the way Mohamed Al Fayed presents it.

Since the establishment did not have a motive for killing Diana, if there was a conspiracy, and if she, Dodi and Henri Paul were murdered, who might have done it? And why? There has been a theory that Diana's anti-land mine crusade might have triggered the armaments industry into wiping her out to prevent damage to their business. This theory does not hold water for two reasons. First, cleaning up the mines was always going to bring as much business to the manufacturers as making them did. Second, Diana's role was not as crucial as the press has made out. Neil Thorns of the Red Cross told me, "It is difficult to evaluate how much her participation helped. The Ottawa Treaty banning land mines was already scheduled to be signed before she got in touch with Mike Whitlam and volunteered to help. The timing of the treaty was already in place, so her involvement did not help there. What it might have influenced was the number of countries which signed up." Just as John F. Kennedy's death proved to be a potent help in securing passage of his political programmes for President Lyndon Johnson, so, too, would Diana's death prove to be invaluable in applying pressure upon countries to sign up. In other words, the armaments manufacturers had no motive to kill Diana, and every reason to keep her alive.

The only conspiracy theory that has a plausible motive is the one that connects Libya and Mohamed Al Fayed. The Department of Trade and Industry investigation into the Fayed takeover of Harrods and the House of Fraser group concluded that the Fayed brothers did not have the funding to buy such a large group of companies, and that they were acting as front men for another party. The Sultan of Brunei has often been identified as that individual, but he has consistently denied the claim. There is, however, another party which is whispered about in the corridors of power. Libya is meant to have been the source of the funding, hence the British government's reluctance to endow Fayed with British citizenship.

According to this conspiracy theory, Fayed and his backers fell out, and he has been riding high on their proceeds ever since. Dodi was murdered as a warning to Fayed that he must make up with them. While I no more accept this theory as being factual than I do any of the others, it does have the merit of explaining away Mohamed's and Dodi Fayed's obsession with security. Neither father nor son was ever known to go anywhere without security. George Martin once asked Dodi who he thought would want to kidnap him, and Dodi replied, "I'm very valuable." Mohamed Al Fayed does not cross the street from his offices on the Brompton Road to walk into Harrods without a posse of security men encircling him as if he is the President of the United States, as Alan Frame confirmed to me. While onlookers have always thought both father and son were indulging in harmless displays of self-importance, if the Libyans had been the source of the funding, and there had been a falling out, this would put a different complexion on the need for such stringent security.

According to this theory, Diana was not the target of the assassination. Her presence, however, was a bonus for the anti-British Libyans. Not only did they hurt the Royal Family personally, but they also embarrassed the establishment and their spooks, MI5 and MI6, who have been held responsible for her murder.

A rather more plausible explanation for how the crash came about is one which was whispered to me by 'someone in the know' who cannot be identified for legal reasons. The existence of the photograph of Henri Paul intently driving the Mercedes into the tunnel while Trevor Rees-Jones sits stern-faced beside him, with Diana and Dodi laughing uproariously in the backseat, lends credence to this explanation, which is as follows: Henri Paul was breaking the speed limit. The traffic camera at the entrance of the tunnel flashed and photographed him as he entered the tunnel. Unfortunately, the flash stunned and temporarily blinded him He jammed his foot on the brakes to give himself time to regain sight of where he was going. The difficulties of making this adjustment were compounded by the differences in the degree of light inside and outside the tunnel. However, he made the adjustment and was therefore took his foot off the brakes as the car reached the fifth column.

It is useful at this juncture to remind British readers that the French drive on the right hand side of the road. It is imperative to make them understand that driving practices in France are radically different from those in England. The French, as a matter of course, respect the road traffic rule of adhering to the right lane on a dual carriageway in a way the British do not with their equivalent lanes. (The tunnel is a dual carriageway.) I say this as someone who has driven tens of thousands of miles in both countries and has driven under that tunnel on several occasions. Although in Britain we all think of and refer to the "slow lane" and the "fast lane", the French do not. To them, the right lane is for driving in, the left lane for overtaking. It is virtually unknown in France to see a vehicle with French registration plates hogging the left lane the way drivers customarily do with overtaking lanes (erroneously called fast lanes, to the frustration of the AA, RAC and police) in the UK. This detail is important, for it accounts for what happened next.

Significantly, Henri Paul entered the tunnel in the right lane or, in English terms, the slow lane. This shows that he was driving in the 'correct' lane, the left lane being used in France only for overtaking. Unfortunately for him and the other occupants of the car he was driving, no sooner did he regain his sight at the fifth column than he saw a vehicle driving significantly slower than himself in front of him. He therefore slammed his foot on the brakes again as the car was parallel to the seventh column, and pointed the braking vehicle towards the right, or overtaking lane, in an attempt to avoid ploughing into the back of the grey Citroën B.x. The brake marks left on the road confirmed that the car skidded from the 7th to the 13th columns, impacting with the latter one in the devastating manner we all now know.

The French authorities have known since the day after Diana's death, that a grey Citroën BX was being driven by Mohamed Medjahdi, for his girlfriend and passenger, Soaud Moufakkir, contacted the Gendarmerie at that time and they both gave witness statements.

According to Medjahdi, twenty-three years old at the time of the accident, "I was in front of the Mercedes. I heard the terrible noise of screeching brakes and screaming tyres and saw a big car slewing out of control across the carriageway behind me and hurtling towards my car." So loud was the sound of the screeching brakes that they drowned out the sound of the radio being played in his car.

As Henri Paul desperately tried to slow down to avoid hitting Medjahdi's Citroën, the Algerian accelerated with the same objective in mind. A second or two later he heard a tremendous explosion, the sound magnified by the echo of the tunnel, as the Mercedes hit the 13th pillar. According to Medjahdi in an account borne out by other witnesses who heard the crash, "It was a dreadful sound. Like a bomb exploding."

Medjahdi and Mouffakir are the only eyewitnesses to the crash who have a recollection of it (Trevor Rees-Jones being the other eyewitness, but without any memory of it). He stated, "I got a complete picture from my side and rear-view mirrors of what was happening behind me."

"This car, which I recognized as a big Mercedes, was travelling far faster than me and it just seemed inevitable it was going to hit me.

"But as I accelerated away, it hit the pillar. I heard a huge noise just like a bomb going off.

"The front of the car exploded. It disintegrated, with pieces flying off in every direction. It seemed to be happening in slow motion but it was over in a couple seconds.

"I saw no other vehicles in my field of vision. There were no cars with the Mercedes. No photographers on motorbikes around the car. There was no one else there."

Souad Moufakkir, twenty-seven years old when she saw the accident, said, "I saw the vehicle spin around and smash into the wall on the other side of the road. I could very clearly see the driver's body crunching into the steering wheel."

As Medjahdi exited the underpass, Moufakir kept on saying ,"They're dead. They're dead." Medjahdi, thinking she might be right, stopped to console her and they were intending to telephone the rescue services (in France it is against the law to fail to go to the assistance of someone whose life is in danger) when they heard the sound of sirens. So they drove home.

The following morning , Sunday 31 August 1997, Medjahdi went as usual to the market at 10 o'clock. There, a friend asked him if he had heard how 'Lady Di', as the French frequently referred to Diana (and still do), had been killed in a car crash in the Pont d'Alma underpass the night before. Realizing that he and Moufakkir had witnessed Diana's death, he rushed back home, only to learn that, while he was out, "Souad's brother had called with the news and she had already contacted the Gendarmerie. They told us to come into headquarters and give statements, which we did."

Both eyewitnesses provided statements for some two hours, after which the gendarmes examined his car so thoroughly that, "I felt as if I were almost a suspect."

At that point in time, the French authorities, having arrested a clutch of paparazzi who were photographing the death car as it lay in the underpass, were progressing their enquiry under the erroneous premise that those men had somehow been responsible for the crash. Medjahdi said, "They asked me whether I saw any camera flashes, motorbikes or photojournalists that could have distracted the Mercedes driver or got in the way. I said I saw nothing like that."

Three times in the following week Medjahdi was interviewed. Time and again they asked him the same questions. Each time he gave them the same answers. "I read in the papers that some people were saying there had been a plot and Diana had been murdered. The gendarmes kept on asking me if I'd seen anything suspicious. I had to say no. It was obviously an accident, given the speed of the car."

Moufakkir was also categoric, "It was an accident. There was no one else in the tunnel with us. There were no photographers or motorbike riders in front of or behind the car."

Medjahdi's car also answers the description of the vehicle Gary Hunter, the London solicitor, saw leaving the underpass "just seconds" after he heard the crash.

Tellingly, Medjahdi was also asked by the investigating authorities if they had seen any flashing lights or stun-guns operating when they became aware of the Mercedes behind them. He said, "I didn't see any blinding light."

Of course, Medjahdi and Moufakkir would not necessarily have seen the speed camera flash the Mercedes as it entered the underpass because by then they would have been well inside it by then. They were travelling in keeping with the speed limit of 90 kilometres per hour at around 50 miles per hour and there is no question that the Mercedes was doing well in excess of that as it tore up behind them. Therefore, a flash that might have been blinding to Henri Paul could easily have been unremarkable and therefore undetectable to Medjahdi.

At the time of the crash, the authorities provided the media with the information that the Mercedes had been travelling at 121 kilometres per hour as it entered the tunnel. If, as they now maintain, the traffic camera was not working, how did they know the speed at which the car was moving? Mercedes has confirmed that its speedometers revert to zero upon impact, and this one did so, so the canard that the French authorities obtained that information from the death car is unfounded.

Moreover, the existence of the photograph, which I have seen and which has also been widely circulated on the continent and in America, begs the question: If there was no one in front of the Mercedes (and, seven years down the line, there is still not one shred of evidence that anyone was at any time in front of the Mercedes, except for Medjahdi's Citroën B.x.), who took that photograph if the traffic camera above the underpass did not?

Of course, it is not a part of a biographer's brief to provide conclusions while an inquest is ongoing into the deaths of two individuals, but these are certainly questions which Michael Burgess ought to be addressing.

Diana's children and her many admirers deserve an answer. Moreover, both the British and the French authorities have an absolute duty to everyone who drives on their roads to provide us with a truthful answer as to whether the traffic camera was the catalyst which set in train a disastrous series of events, resulting in the deaths of three healthy and able-bodied people, two young and one about to enter middle age. If indeed that flash blinded Henri Paul, there is much more than the embarrassment of the French authorities at stake here. The whole question of the safety of traffic cameras is raised, and unless it is addressed meaningfully and responsibly, there could well be a repetition of the disaster, with the loss of other lives in the future, as yet more traffic cameras stun yet more drivers. It is frankly unacceptable for governments potentially to suppress the truth of a death crash and continue ratcheting up revenue, despite the dangers of the manner in which they obtain such income, and until such time as the French and the British authorities publicly confirm the circumstances surrounding the taking of that photograph of the four occupants of the Mercedes shortly before it crashed, those two governments deserve to be questioned until we, the driving public, are given acceptable and believable answers.

Not surprisingly, this theory has never been aired in public before, involving as it does confidential information, a cover-up by the French authorities, and the rather unglamorous issue of revenue-raising and traffic cameras, instead of the more glamorous and newsworthy (not to mention unendingly sustainable) conspiracy theories involving secret services and royal families. The possibility that the French themselves were inadvertently responsible for the crash does, however, have some credence, though it is not the only plausible interpretation of the crash.

Another plausible explanation involves the white Fiat Uno, which has never been found, but whose paintwork on the Mercedes, and fragments on the road at the entrance of the underpass, confirmed that there was a collision between the two cars. The precise site of the impact is important, for the Mercedes entered the underpass in the right-hand, i.e. correct, lane for a vehicle that was not overtaking another one. It is a fact that airbags can be activated by lowgrade impacts. A vehicle can be travelling at no more than twenty or thirty miles per hour and graze one another, resulting in the airbags immobilizing the driver and front passenger, while the cars themselves sustain only minor damage as a result of their impact.

There is every possibility that the airbags in the Mercedes activated when it clipped the Fiat Unto as it was entering the underpass. The effect would be to incapacitate Henri Paul, preventing him from seeing in front of him or controlling the vehicle. If such an eventuality occurred, it would explain why Henri Paul began braking with the force he did. It would also explain why he lost control of the vehicle. It also ties up a lot of other loose ends, such as Trevor Rees-Jones's facial injuries, which are consistent with his airbag having deflated by the time of impact with the 13th column, and the fact that Souad Moufakkir was able to see the steering wheel of the Mercedes crushing Henri Paul. The reasoning is simple: Had the airbags activated when the Mercedes hit the 13th column, as they would have had they not activated beforehand owing to another, more minor collision, she would not have been able to see Henri Paul, only the airbag. Moreover, this interpretation explains the apparent anomaly regarding the high levels of carbon monoxide in Henri Paul's blood which was 20.7% in the blood sample drawn from his heart and 12.8% in the sample from his femoral vein in the upper thigh. According to Dr Gilbert Pépin, one of the toxicologists, and Dominique Lecomte, the medical examiner who conducted Henri Paul's autopsy, he breathed in the carbon monoxide when the airbags detonated. As they have also confirmed that Henri Paul died on impact, by a ruptured aorta and severed spine, the only reasonable conclusion is that he had to have inhaled the fumes prior to the impact, for his death was instantaneous, simultaneous with the car's collision with the 13th column – and dead men can't breathe.

Once more, this is an interpretation of the crash which militates for the driving public to be provided with accurate information so that they can protect themselves, should they ever have the misfortune of finding themselves in a situation akin to that which killed Diana, Dodi and Henri Paul. There is a popular misconception that airbags activate only when there are high-velocity collisions. As they do not, and do sometimes cause accidents by activating when there are low velocity collisions which would not otherwise result in driver incapacitation or serious injury, car manufacturers and driving organizations ought to allow the public to benefit from the tragedy of three deaths that were caused, not by Henri Paul's incapacity owing to an excess of drink and drugs, but by the fact that the airbags activated prematurely with devastating and deadly results.

It remains to be seen what the findings of the Royal Coroner will be. Hopefully they will be incisive, will clear up the anomalies that exist, will provide a cogent and cohesive interpretation of the accident, and will thereby provide closure. If only for the sake of William and Harry, Diana's ghost needs to be laid to rest along with the wilder theories about her death.

Pregnancy, conspiracy theories and plausible explanations for the accident aside, Diana's death has left her loved ones with two legacies. The first is the pain of loss, the second pride in the affection in which she was held. Even her sons have said that the outpouring of love for their mother at the time of her death helped them. There is also the Diana Princess of Wales Memorial Fund, founded to perpetuate the good works for which she was known and respected. Money has flooded into it in Britain and the United States, where it has also been registered as a charity. Originally headed by Diana's divorce lawyer Anthony Julius, her sister Lady Sarah McCorquodale and her last Private Secretary, Michael Gibbins, also sat on its Committee with a friend, Vivienne Parry, and her butler, Paul Burrell. Subsequently, Anthony Julius stood down and the Fund's chief executive became Dr Andrew Purkis, formerly the Archbishop of Cantebury's private secretary. While in the American edition of this book I expressed the hope that it would be managed well, its practice has proven to be otherwise. It has been involved in ruinous legal disputes in the United States, trying to lay claim to exclusive use of every aspect of Diana's image and reputation. In the process, it has frittered away millions of pounds of donors' money on litigation with such companies as Franklin Mint, whose only offence was to honour Diana in death as they had in life, by bringing out tasteful and decorative limited edition dolls in her likeness. It is difficult to see what its objectives have been, short of an aggressive vaingloriousness tainted with greed, for it sought to deprive Franklin Mint of the right to produce dolls of a kind they had been producing while Diana was alive, despite the fact that she had never made any objection in her lifetime. The result was that the fund was roundly and justifiably trounced in the American courts. The lawyers, of course, got rich, while the fund's grants to worthwhile causes has been disproportionate to the amount it has spent on litigation and legal fees. The future does not bode well for the fund unless it has a change of heart and direction, which is sad. That memorial fund ought to be the living embodiment of Diana's legacy. Through it, others ought to be able to continue her work from beyond the grave, but, unless they behave differently and stop wasting donations in futile and vain legal endeavours which only enrich the lawyers, they will ultimately dissipate the fund's funds, its goodwill, and the value it could have had.

Another regrettable effect of Diana's death, for which she was not responsible, has been that her executrices, her mother Frances Shand Kydd, who died in June 2004 of Parkinson's Disease, and her sister Lady Sarah McCorquodale, have not carried out her wishes that a quarter of her £21.7 million estate should be distributed amongst her seventeen godchildren. These include George Frost, the sixteen-year-old son of Sir David and Lady Carina Frost, and fourteen-year-old Jack Bartholomew, the son of her old flatmate Carolyn Pride and William Bartholomew. Several of the godchildren are now over eighteen and all ought to have received goods or chattels or cash to the value of £319,000, instead of which they have received such ignominious trinkets as a tacky picture from Argos and a porcelain rabbit, none of which is worth even £100.

It seems that a distance of seven years from Diana's death begins to cast light upon her legacy. Although she did much good, and touched the lives of many in a positive way, putting her children aside, the further people were away from her the more they respected her and valued her contribution to their lives. Many of those closest to her had more mixed feelings and mixed motives, and have either let her down or feel that they were let down by her.

Whatever her complications and failings, Diana basically wanted only to be loved and to love, to be liked and to like, to relieve suffering and help those in need. She was a flawed person, but, to her credit, she made no pretence of being a saint. Admittedly, she was not all sweetness and light. If she was crossed or felt threatened, she could be an awesome and formidable opponent who did not play by the Queensberry Rules. Occasionally, she was vengeful and destructive. Otherwise, that strength, that power, that inventiveness, that determination were used to enhance life, including the lives of people she did not know and never would.

If Diana is examined dispassionately, there can be few people who would deny that she was a unique individual. Hers was not always the easiest road to travel. Despite the privileges, the wealth, the status and the beauty, she had to battle against physical and mental illness for years. The fact that she did so, accomplishing as much as she did while ill, and afterwards, when she was on the road to health and fruition, says much about her love of life and of people. She was an ordinary human being who turned herself into an extraordinary woman trying to live up to and conquer the circumstances of an unbelievable life. She did not need perfection. She had humanity. The world was a richer and more interesting place for her having been a part of it.